AN EARTHED FAITH:
Telling the Story amid the "Anthropocene"
Volume 1

TAKING A DEEP BREATH FOR THE STORY TO BEGIN . . .

TAKING A DEEP BREATH FOR THE STORY TO BEGIN
An Earthed Faith: Telling the Story amid the Anthropocene, volume 1

Copyright © 2022 Ernst M. Conradie. All rights reserved. Except for brief quotations in critical publications or reviews, no part of this book may be reproduced in any manner without prior written permission from the publisher. Write: Permissions, Wipf and Stock Publishers, 199 W. 8th Ave., Suite 3, Eugene, OR 97401.

Pickwick Publications
An Imprint of Wipf and Stock Publishers
199 W. 8th Ave., Suite 3
Eugene, OR 97401

www.wipfandstock.com

PAPERBACK ISBN: 978-1-7252-8331-2
HARDCOVER ISBN: 978-1-7252-8332-9
EBOOK ISBN: 978-1-7252-8333-6

Cataloguing-in-Publication data:

Names: Conradie, Ernst M. | Pan-chiu, Lai

Title: Taking a deep breath for the story to begin: An earthed faith: telling the story amid the anthropocene, volume 1 / Ernst M. Conradie and Lai Pan-chiu.

Description: Eugene, OR: Pickwick Publications, 2022. | An Earthed Faith: Telling the Story amid the Anthropocene. | Includes bibliographical references and index.

Identifiers: ISBN 978-1-7252-8331-2 (paperback). | ISBN 978-1-7252-8332-9 (hardcover). | ISBN 978-1-7252-8333-6 (ebook).

Subjects: LCSH: Theology. | Human ecology. | Ecotheology. | Trinity. | Storytelling.

Classification: BR115 T10 2022 (print). | BR115 (ebook).

AN EARTHED FAITH:
Telling the Story amid the "Anthropocene"
Volume 1

Taking a Deep Breath for the Story to Begin . . .

Editors
Ernst M. Conradie
Pan-Chiu Lai

☙PICKWICK *Publications* • Eugene, Oregon

Religious studies domain editorial board at AOSIS

Commissioning Editor: Scholarly Books
Andries G. van Aarde, MA, DD, PhD, D Litt, South Africa

Board Members
Warren Carter, Professor of New Testament, Brite Divinity School, Fort Worth, TX, United States of America
Christian Danz, Dekan der Evangelisch-Theologischen Fakultät der Universität Wien and Ordentlicher Universität professor für Systematische Theologie und Religionswissenschaft, University of Vienna, Vienna, Austria
Pieter G.R. de Villiers, Associate Editor, Extraordinary Professor in Biblical Spirituality, Faculty of Theology, University of the Free State, Bloemfontein, South Africa
Musa W. Dube, Department of Theology & Religious Studies, Faculty of Humanities, University of Botswana, Gaborone, Botswana
David D. Grafton, Professor of Islamic Studies and Christian-Muslim Relations, Duncan Black Macdonald Center for the Study of Islam and Christian-Muslim Relations, Hartford Seminary, Hartford, CT, United States of America
Jens Herzer, Theologische Fakultät der Universität Leipzig, Leipzig, Germany
Jeanne Hoeft, Dean of Students and Associate Professor of Pastoral Theology and Pastoral Care, Saint Paul School of Theology, Leawood, KS, United States of America
Dirk J. Human, Associate Editor, Deputy Dean and Professor of Old Testament Studies, Faculty of Theology, University of Pretoria, Pretoria, South Africa
D. Andrew Kille, Former Chair of the SBL Psychology and Bible Section, and Editor of the Bible Workbench, San Jose, CA, United States of America
William R.G. Loader, Emeritus Professor, Murdoch University, Perth, Western Australia
Isabel A. Phiri, Associate General Secretary for Public Witness and Diakonia, World Council of Churches, Geneva, Switzerland
Marcel Sarot, Emeritus, Professor of Fundamental Theology, Tilburg School of Catholic Theology, Tilburg University, Tilburg, the Netherlands
Corneliu C. Simut, Professor of Historical and Dogmatic Theology, Emanuel University, Oradea, Bihor, Romania
Rothney S. Tshaka, Professor and Head of Department of Philosophy, Practical and Systematic Theology, University of South Africa, Pretoria, South Africa
Elaine M. Wainwright, Emeritus Professor, School of Theology, The University of Auckland, Auckland, New Zealand; Executive Leader, Mission and Ministry, McAuley Centre, Australia
Gerald West, Associate Editor, School of Religion, Philosophy and Classics in the College of Humanities, University of KwaZulu-Natal, Durban, South Africa

Peer review declaration
The publisher (AOSIS) endorses the South African "National Scholarly Book Publishers Forum Best Practice for Peer Review of Scholarly Books." The manuscript was subjected to rigorous two-step peer review prior to publication, with the identities of the reviewers not revealed to the author(s). The reviewers were independent of the publisher and/or authors in question. The reviewers commented positively on the scholarly merits of the manuscript and recommended that the manuscript be published. Where the reviewers recommended revision and/or improvements to the manuscript, the authors responded adequately to such recommendations.

Research Justification

This volume is embedded in an envisaged series entitled "An Earthed Faith: Telling the Story amid the 'Anthropocene'." The series as such builds upon an international collaborative project (2007–2014) on "Christian Faith and the Earth" that involved more than one hundred leading scholars in the field of Christian ecotheology. Since Christianity is widely regarded as complicit in ecological destruction, a crucial part of any response to the impact of the "Anthropocene" has to include a critique and constructive reinterpretation of the Christian faith. The envisaged series addresses this challenge through ecumenical collaboration between the leading scholars in the field, together with some emerging voices. The ambitious aim is to capture the state of the current debate on twelve core themes and then take the debate forward through a set of constructive contributions that optimize diversity in terms of geographical contexts; confessional traditions; theological schools; and issues of gender, race, and age. The contributors for each volume are hand-picked accordingly. Each volume includes an introductory essay that seeks to capture the current state of the debate (through a literature survey) and then outlines a core, unresolved question that has to be addressed in order to take the debate forward. The rest of the volume is then structured in the form of ten constructive responses to this question engaging with each other through cross-references. Such engagement is made possible through a series of meetings between contributors to discuss and critique each other's work. For the first volume, this question is formulated as follows: "How does the story of who the Triune God is and what this God does relate to the story of life on Earth?" In other words, is the Christian story part of the earth's story or is the earth's story part of God's story, from creation to consummation? The contributors come literally from around the globe, namely, Sigurd Bergmann (Norway/Sweden), Sharon Bong (Malaysia), Ernst Conradie (South Africa), Celia Deane-Drummond (UK), Heather Eaton (Canada), Marcial Maçaneiro and Rudolf von Sinner (Brazil), Pan-Chiu Lai (Hong Kong), Teddy Chalwe Sakupapa (Zambia/South Africa), Upolu Lumā Vaai (Fiji), and Mark Wallace (USA). Each of them has a remarkable record of publications and builds on that by offering a constructive attempt to address a crucial question. It would be arrogant to claim that this volume could resolve the question that is addressed here (a question spanning 2000 years), but any future scholarly contributions in ecotheology on this theme would need to be on the basis of and with reference to this volume. In this way, its ambitious aim is to shape the future of the debate by identifying "current paths" and suggesting "emerging horizons" in the field. Although each contributor necessarily builds upon previous work in the field and is invited accordingly, each contribution is original. Self-plagiarism is avoided through careful referencing to such previous work. The volume is written by leading scholars and aimed at other scholars, primarily in the fields of Christian ecotheology and systematic theology.

Ernst M. Conradie, Department of Religion and Theology, University of the Western Cape, Cape Town, South Africa.

Pan-Chiu Lai, Department of Cultural and Religious Studies, The Chinese University of Hong Kong, Hong Kong, China.

Artist statement

Garth Erasmus is a South African artist born in Uitenhage and currently based in Cape Town. At a recent exhibition of his art at the Gallery University Stellenbosch (GUS) he explains his Xnau Drawings in the following way:

"Decolonisation is firmly foregrounded across the multiple mediums in which I work. In my work it means unsettling the hegemonic, exclusionary constructions of African and "coloured" identity in the South African context."

"The works that I have produced during my GUS residency forms part of a larger continuous series called The Xnau Drawings. Xnau is a Khoi-Nama word and means initiation. XNAU is pronounced "now" but with a click-sound at the beginning. This initiation, however, is not the same as the classic universal understanding of rite of passage i.e. it does not involve, for example, ritualistic circumcision etc. Rather, it is a sacred process of self-initiation [usually undertaken as an adult already] that entails a process of isolation and sensitization in a traditional and sacred setting. The need for the Xnau arises out of the fact that one has been cut off from one's culture through the processes of colonization, urbanization, westernization. It is an example of tradition that has evolved naturally with the necessities of prevailing conditions and reshaped itself through time. The Xnau is simply a process of realignment with the values of one's lost heritage in the context of a post-Apartheid South Africa" (see https://www.gus-gallery.co.za/xnau).

Xnau Drawing #199

"The physical body and parts of the physical body are constant themes in my work. The condition of the physical body becomes a metaphor for the condition of the soul. As in most of my work I explore the nature of my personal deep-rooted trauma as well as examining the phenomenon of inherited trauma and how it manifests in visual format as in this work where symbols of dismemberment and separation of forms becomes the primary narrative."

Contents

Abbreviations, Figures and Tables Appearing in the Text and Notes	xv
List of Abbreviations	xv
Notes on Contributors	xvii

The Story Behind the Series — 1
Ernst M. Conradie

The Christian Faith and the Earth Project	1
A New Series	3
The Structure of the Envisaged Series	7
Taking a Deep Breath for the Story to Begin . . . An Earthed Faith 1	7
How Would We Know What God Is Up To? An Earthed Faith 2	8
The Place of Story and the Story of Place? An Earthed Faith 3	8
Making Room for the Story to Continue? An Earthed Faith 4	9
The Saving Grace of the Story? An Earthed Faith 5	9
The Keepers of the Story? An Earthed Faith 6	9
Where the Story Ends and Its Ends . . . An Earthed Faith 7	10
Being Blessed as the Inner Logic of the Story? An Earthed Faith 8	10
The Spirit of the Story? An Earthed Faith 9	11
The Letter of the Story? An Earthed Faith 10	11
In Communion with the Story Teller(s)? An Earthed Faith 11	11
What, then, Is the Moral of the Story? An Earthed Faith 12	12
The Publication of the Series	12
Bibliography	13

On Setting the Scene for the Story to Begin — 15
Ernst M. Conradie & Pan-Chiu Lai

Grand Narratives, Metanarratives, and Meganarratives in the "Anthropocene"	15
The Many Strands of Narrative Theology	21
A Few Cairns for the Journey of Engaging in Narrative Theology	30
On Telling the Christian Story in the "Anthropocene"	33
Where Does One Begin to Reconstruct the Story?	35
A Core Question	37
A Fivefold Typology	39

The Christian Story Encompasses the Universe Story	40
The Universe Story Encompasses the Christian Story	40
The Christian Story and the Universe Story Remain Apart from Each Other	41
The Universe Story May be Interpreted through the Christian Story	41
The Christian Story May Transform the Universe Story	42
To Conclude	43
Bibliography	43

Faith in Weather Lands: Toward an Ecocene Perspective — 49
Sigurd Bergmann

Trinitarian Cosmology—Compassion, Justice, Beauty, and Health	49
Weather Wisdom	52
Atmospheres of Synergy—In Geoscience, Arts, Philosophy, and Theology	56
Toward a Contextual Theopolitics of the Earth as Ecocene	61
Bibliography	68

Telling the Story: An Asian Feminist Perspective — 73
Sharon A. Bong

The Christian Story in *Laudato Si'*	74
Other Stories	84
Conclusion: The Christian Story Revisited	91
Bibliography	92

On the Hope That the Christian Story May Transform the Universe Story: A South African Reformed Perspective — 95
Ernst M. Conradie

The Christian Story and the Universe Story	95
A Very Brief Account of How the Christian Story Came into Being	97
Reflections on God's Revelation in the Reformed Tradition, Especially in South Africa	103
Six Theses on General and Special Revelation	105
On the Hope that the Christian Story of God's Work Will Transform the Universe Story	115
Bibliography	117

The Trinitarian Spirit of Wisdom: A Catholic Exploration of Nature and Grace   119
Celia Deane-Drummond

A Hybrid Story   119
The Story as Theo-ontology or Onto-theology?   122
Philosophical Approaches to the Transcendent   124
Nature and Grace   127
Trinitarian Spirit of Wisdom in Sergius Bulgakov: A Critical Engagement   129
Preliminary Conclusions   137
Bibliography   138

In the Beginning . . . The Universe was Dreaming   141
Heather Eaton

Introduction   142
Stories   143
    Cultural Narratives, Worldviews, Metanarratives   143
    Symbolic Consciousness: Structures, Attributes, and Narratives   145
    Attributes of Symbolic Consciousness   147
    The Storytelling Animal   148
The Universe, Earth and Christian Stories in the "Anthropocene"   149
    Cosmology, Earth Sciences, and Planetary Thinking   150
    Debates on a Universe Story(ies)   154
    The Universe Story: A Meganarrative   156
    The Christian and Universe Stories: Connections and Conflicts   157
    How Does God Relate to the Story of Life on Earth?   158
    Religious Experiences and Spiritualities   159
    Revelations and Hope   159
Conclusion   161
    Bibliography   161

Taking a Deep Breath for the Story to Begin in the Public Sphere: A Chinese Christian Perspective   163
Pan-Chiu Lai

Introduction   163
Ecological Discourses in Chinese Context   164
Chinese Christian Ecological Discourses   167
Analysis and Evaluation   173
Reconsidering the Breath   175
Bibliography   179

Hearing and Telling Old and New Stories from Latin America: Challenges and Inspirations for an Earthed Faith — 183
Marcial Maçaneiro & Rudolf von Sinner

Introduction	183
Indigenous Insights: Notions of buen vivir in Bolivia, Ecuador, and Beyond	186
African Brazilian Insights	189
Gods of Creation and Their Powers	193
The Orixás and Nature	196
Concluding Remarks	199
Bibliography	201

The Decolonial Imperative in African Ecotheology: A Zambian Perspective — 205
Teddy C. Sakupapa

Introduction	205
Christianity and Ecology in Zambia	206
An Ecumenical Paradigm of Advocacy	208
The Decolonial Imperative in African Ecotheology	210
African Ecotheology: African Reinterpretations of the Interconnectedness of Reality	213
A Retrieval of African Communality	214
A Pneumatological Understanding of African Communality	215
African Eco-Narratives and Narratives of the "Anthropocene"	216
Humanity as a Geological Force: Engaging Narratives of the "Anthropocene"	217
The Anthropos of the "Anthropocene"	219
Conclusion	220
Bibliography	221

The Ecorelational Story of the Cosmic Aiga: A Pasifika Perspective — 225
Upolu Lumā Vaai

Introduction: "Born of a Cosmic Womb"	225
"Stories Are Liquid Versions of Life"	226
"Everything is Flesh, Bones, and Blood"	227
"We are, Therefore We Live"	231
"We Don't Have the Ocean . . . We Are the Ocean"	235
Conclusion: "Eat a Little and Leave a Little"	238
Bibliography	239

Even Rocks Are Alive: Christian Animist Disruptions of the Species Divide   **241**
Mark I. Wallace

Carnal Subscendence   241
New Materialism   246
Decolonizing Theology   249
Feral Rock Religion   251
Two Problems   255
Bibliography   256

Index   **259**

Abbreviations, Figures and Tables Appearing in the Text and Notes

List of Abbreviations

ATR	African Traditional Religion
CCZ	Council of Churches in Zambia
LS	*Laudato Si'*
RH Act	*Responsible Parenthood and Reproductive Health Act*
RNA	Ribonucleic Acid
SRH	Sexual and Reproductive Health
SRHR	Sexual and Reproductive Health and Rights
UN	United Nations
WCC	World Council of Churches
ZCCB	Zambia Conference of Catholic Bishops

Notes on Contributors

Sigurd Bergmann is an emeritus professor in Religious Studies at the Norwegian University of Science and Technology in Trondheim, Norway. He is affiliated to Uppsala University and Lund University, and a fellow at the Rachel Carson Center on Environment and Society at Munich University. He has initiated the European Forum for the Study of Religion and the Environment, and his previous studies explored God and nature in late antiquity, contextual theology, indigenous arts, architecture, and religion in climate change, and ethics, culture, and science in the SARS-CoV-2 pandemic. He is the author of *Weather, Religion, and Climate Change* (Routledge, 2020), the editor of *Eschatology as Imagining the End: Faith between Hope and Despair* (2018), and the coeditor with Mika Vähäkangas of *Contextual Theology: Skills and Practices of Liberating Faith* (2021). Recently, a Festschrift was published in his honor entitled *Eco-Theology: Essays in Honor of Sigurd Bergmann*, edited by Hans Günter Heimbrock and Jörg Persch (Ferdinand Schöningh, 2021). He is registered as a co-researcher at UWC for the project "An Earthed Faith: Telling the Story amid the 'Anthropocene'."
ORCID: https://orcid.org/0000-0001-7729-7189
Email: sigurd.bergmann@ntnu.no

Sharon A. Bong is an associate professor of Gender Studies at the School of Arts and Social Sciences, Monash University, Bandar Sunway, Malaysia. She works in the intersection of feminist theology, feminist ecotheologies, and sexual ethics. She is an author of *Becoming Queer and Religious in Malaysia and Singapore* (2020) and *The Tension between Women's Rights and Religions: The Case of Malaysia* (2006), coedited *Gender and Sexuality Justice in Asia* (2020), and edited *Trauma, Memory and Transformation in Southeast Asia* (2014). She is a forum writer for the Catholic Theological Ethics in the World Church and former coordinator and consultant of the Ecclesia of Women in Asia. She is registered as a co-researcher at UWC for the project "An Earthed Faith: Telling the Story amid the 'Anthropocene'."
ORCID: https://orcid.org/0000-0003-2021-4586
Email: sharon.bong@monash.edu

Ernst M. Conradie is a senior professor in the Department of Religion and Theology at the University of the Western Cape in South Africa. He works in the intersection between Christian ecotheology, systematic theology and ecumenical theology and comes from the Reformed tradition. He is the author of *The Earth in God's Economy: Creation, Salvation and Consummation in Ecological Perspective* (2015), *Redeeming Sin? Social Diagnostics amid Ecological Destruction* (2017), and *Secular Discourse on Sin in the*

Anthropocene: What's Wrong with the World? (2020). He was the international convener of the Christian Faith and the Earth project (2007–2014), the leading editor (with Sigurd Bergmann, Celia Deane-Drummond, and Denis Edwards) of *Christian Faith and the Earth: Current Paths and Emerging Horizons in Ecotheology* (2014), and coeditor with Hilda Koster of *The T&T Clark Handbook on Christian Theology and Climate Change* (2019). He is responsible for registering the project "An Earthed Faith: Telling the Story amid the 'Anthropocene'" at UWC.

ORCID: https://orcid.org/0000-0002-0020-6952
Email: econradie@uwc.ac.za

Celia Deane-Drummond is the director of the Laudato Si' Research Institute and Senior Research Fellow in Theology at Campion Hall, University of Oxford. She is also an honorary visiting professor in Theology and Science at the University of Durham, UK, and until 2019, she is a professor of Theology at the University of Notre Dame. Her recent publications include *The Wisdom of the Liminal: Human Nature, Evolution and Other Animals* (2014); Technofutures, Nature and the Sacred, edited with Sigurd Bergmann and Bronislaw Szerszynski (2015); *Ecology in Jürgen Moltmann's Theology* (2016; 2nd edition); *Religion in the Anthropocene*, edited with Sigurd Bergmann and Markus Vogt (2017); *Theology and Ecology Across the Disciplines: On Care for Our Common Home*, edited with Rebecca Artinian Kaiser (2018); *Theological Ethics through a Multispecies Lens: The Evolution of Wisdom, Volume 1* (2019); and *Shadow Sophia: The Evolution of Wisdom, Volume II* (2021). She is registered as a co-researcher at UWC for the project "An Earthed Faith: Telling the Story amid the 'Anthropocene'."

ORCID: https://orcid.org/0000-0002-8033-9930
Email: celia.deane-drummond@campion.ox.ac.uk

Heather Eaton is a professor of Conflict Studies at Saint Paul University in Ottawa, Canada. Her current research includes ecological, gender/feminist, and religious dimensions of peace and conflict studies; and theories of conflict, social justice, nonviolence, and animal rights. Her publications include *Advancing Nonviolence and Social Transformation with Lauren Levesque* (2016); *The Intellectual Journey of Thomas Berry* (2014); *Ecological Awareness: Exploring Religion, Ethics and Aesthetics*, with Sigurd Bergmann (2011); *Introducing Ecofeminist Theologies* (2005); and *Ecofeminism and Globalization*, with Lois Lorentzen (2003). She is registered as a co-researcher at UWC for the project "An Earthed Faith: Telling the Story amid the 'Anthropocene'."

ORCID: https://orcid.org/0000-0002-1722-0769
Email: heaton@ustpaul.ca

Pan-Chiu Lai is a professor in the Department of Cultural and Religious Studies, The Chinese University of Hong Kong. His research interests include inter-religious dialogue, Christianity and Chinese culture, modern Christian thought, and environmental ethics. He is a coauthor with Lin Hongxing of *Confucian-Christian Dialogue and Ecological Concern* (2006, in Chinese), a coeditor with Jason Lam of *Sino-Christian Theology: A Theological Qua Cultural Movement in Contemporary China* (2010), and an author of Towards a *Trinitarian Theology of Religions: A Study of Paul Tillich's Thought* (1994), *Mahayana Christian Theology* (2011, in Chinese), and *Sino-Christian Theology* in the Public Square (2014, in Chinese). He is registered as a co-researcher at UWC for the project "An Earthed Faith: Telling the Story amid the 'Anthropocene'."

ORCID: https://orcid.org/0000-0003-1695-651X
Email: pclai@cuhk.edu.hk

Marcial Maçaneiro is a professor of Systematic Theology in the postgraduate program in Theology at the Pontifical Catholic University of Paraná (PUCPR), Curitiba, Brazil. He is also a visiting professor of Catholic-Pentecostal Dialogue at the Centro de Estudios Bíblicos, Teológicos y Pastorales de América Latina, Bogotá, Colombia, and a collaborative researcher at the Research Center for Theology and Religious Studies, Portuguese Catholic University, Lisbon, Portugal. As a Catholic presbyter of the Congregation of the Sacred Heart of Jesus (also known as Dehonians), his main work is on ecotheology, pneumatology, ecumenical, and inter-religious dialogue. Among his published works are *Religiões e ecologia. Cosmovisão—valores—tarefas* (2nd edn. São Paulo: Paulinas, 2011); *O labirinto sagrado: ensaio sobre religião, psique e cultura* (São Paulo: Paulus, 2011) and *As janelas do Vaticano II* (Aparecida: Ed. Santuário, 2013), with R. Manzini e J. C. Almeida. He is registered as a co-researcher at UWC for the project "An Earthed Faith: Telling the Story amid the 'Anthropocene'."

ORCID: https://orcid.org/0000-0003-3085-8588
Email: marcial.macaneiro@pucpr.br

Teddy Chalwe Sakupapa is a senior lecturer in the Department of Religion and Theology at the University of the Western Cape in South Africa where he teaches ecumenical studies and social ethics. Originally from Zambia, his research traverses the fields of ecumenical studies, systematic theology and social ethics, decoloniality, African theology, and the history of Christianity in Africa on which he has published several articles and book chapters. He is an ordained minister in the Presbyterian tradition. His PhD thesis (2017) is entitled "Ecclesiology and Ethics: An Analysis of the History of the All Africa Conference of Churches."

ORCID: https://orcid.org/0000-0002-6837-0310
Email: tsakupapa@uwc.ac.za

Rudolf von Sinner is professor of Systematic Theology and head of postgraduate program in Theology at the Pontifical Catholic University of

Paraná in Curitiba, Brazil, and professor extraordinary at the University of Stellenbosch, South Africa. A Lutheran theologian with Reformed roots, his main work is in Public Theology with its implications in Systematic Theology, Political Ethics, Religious Pluralism, and the Secular State. Beyond using it as a transversal perspective, he has also been working on Ecumenical and Inter-religious Hermeneutics and Theology. He is the author of *The Churches and Democracy in Brazil: Towards a Public Theology Focused on Citizenship* (2012) and the main editor of *Teologia pública no Brasil e na África do Sul: um diálogo teológico-político* (2020, forthcoming in English) and has a forthcoming book entitled *Public Theology in the Secular State: A Perspective from the Global South* (2021).

ORCID: https://orcid.org/0000-0002-0487-4237
Email: rudolf.sinner@pucpr.br

Upolu Lumā Vaai is a professor of Theology & Ethics and principal of the Pacific Theological College in Suva, Fiji. He works in the intersection between Pasifika contextual ecorelational theology and Trinitarian systematic theology within the frame of relationality and how this could be used as a decolonial tool to liberate communities from dominant imperial developments. His publications include *Relational Hermeneutics: Decolonising the Mindset and the Pacific Itulagi* (2017) and *The Relational Self: Decolonising Personhood in the Pacific* (2017). He is registered as a co-researcher at UWC for the project "An Earthed Faith: Telling the Story amid the 'Anthropocene'."

ORCID: https://orcid.org/0000-0003-1243-0852
Email: ulvaai@ptc.ac.fj

Mark I. Wallace is a professor of Religion, Environmental Studies, and Interpretation Theory at Swarthmore College near Philadelphia, USA. At Swarthmore, he directs the Chester Semester program in which college students work alongside Chester PA city partners in high-value internships focused on social and environmental justice. He has been a visiting professor at The University of Pennsylvania, Princeton Theological Seminary, and Japan International Christian University, and he is the core faculty for the US State Department's Institutes on Religious Pluralism at Temple University. Recent books include *When God Was a Bird: Christianity, Animism, and the Re-Enchantment of the World* (2019), awarded the 2019 Nautilus Gold Award for best book in Western religious thought; *Green Christianity: Five Ways to a Sustainable Future* (2010); and *Finding God in the Singing River: Christianity, Spirit, Nature* (2005). He is registered as a co-researcher at the University of the Western Cape for the project "An Earthed Faith: Telling the Story amid the 'Anthropocene'."

ORCID: https://orcid.org/0000-0003-0662-7878
Email: mwallac1@swarthmore.edu

The Story Behind the Series
Ernst M. Conradie[1]

■ The Christian Faith and the Earth Project

In August 2012, the culminating conference of the Christian Faith and the Earth project took place at the Sustainability Institute near Stellenbosch, South Africa. This was a seven-year project in which more than one hundred scholars from six continents participated to explore the content and significance of the various aspects of the Christian faith from the perspective of ecotheology.

While it covered most aspects of the Christian faith, much of the energy of this project focused on issues of methodology,[2] especially on the relationship between God's work of creation and of salvation. The intuition was that the message of salvation must be understood as salvation for the whole earth and not from the earth. However, it soon became clear that it is not so easy to hold together the first and the second articles of the Christian creed. The underlying problem is best expressed by Mercy Amba Oduyoye, the mother of African women's theology in a profound question: "Is the God of our redemption the

---

1. Ernst M. Conradie is senior professor in the Department of Religion and Theology at the University of the Western Cape in South Africa.

How to cite: Conradie, E.M., 2021, 'The Story Behind the Series', in E.M. Conradie & P.-C. Lai (eds.), *Taking a deep breath for the story to begin*... (An Earthed Faith: Telling the Story amid the "Anthropocene" Volume 1), pp. 1-14, AOSIS, Cape Town. https://doi.org/10.4102/aosis.2021.BK264.01

same God of our creation?"³ As I have often noted before, this question is born out of the African quest for continuity between a pre-Christian African notion of the Supreme Being as Creator and the Christian message of redemption that took root in Africa following the work of Western missionaries. Since the earliest Bible translators used the same word and name for the God of our ancestors and for the God of Christian proclamation, there appears to be some continuity but, given the legacy of colonialism, certainly also deep tensions in this regard. The theme of creation and salvation was subsequently explored in a double issue of *Worldviews*⁴ and in two edited volumes published by LIT Verlag.⁵

The outcomes of the Christian Faith and the Earth project were published in a volume entitled *Christian Faith and the Earth: Current Paths and Emerging Horizons in Ecotheology*⁶ and in an issue of the journal *Scriptura*.⁷ The project itself came to an end but was continued as three subsequent projects, namely, on pneumatology and ecology,⁸ on ecclesiology and ecology,⁹ and on "Redeeming Sin?"

Through a series of colloquiums, the project on "Redeeming Sin?" explored the prospects of retrieving the category of sin in the public sphere by suggesting the notion of "social diagnostics."¹⁰ The assumption is that Christian sin-talk could be regarded, at least from the outside, as a form of diagnostics. Christian theology, alongside many other disciplines, may offer perspectives on what has gone wrong with the world.¹¹ Following the medical analogy, if ecological destruction may be regarded as symptoms at the surface level, what are the deepest underlying causes of the "disease"?¹²

Toward the end of this project, the focus shifted to controversies around naming this underlying problem the "Anthropocene."¹³ At least this brought

---

3. See Oduyoye, *Hearing and Knowing*, 75.

4. See Conradie and Jenkins, "Ecology and Christian Soteriology."

5. See Conradie, *Creation and Salvation, Volume 1* and *Creation and Salvation, Volume 2*. See also the constructive proposal in Conradie, *The Earth in God's Economy*.

6. Edited by Ernst Conradie, Sigurd Bergmann, Celia Deane-Drummond, and Denis Edwards.

7. See Conradie, "Christian Faith and the Earth: Respice et Prospice."

8. See Conradie, "Pneumatology and Ecology."

9. See Ayre and Conradie, *The Church in God's Household*.

10. See Conradie, *Redeeming Sin?*

11. On this question, see Conradie, *Secular Discourse*.

12. For an overview of this project, building on a series of colloquiums, see Conradie, "Project and Prospects."

13. One influential volume that shaped such discourse is by Deane-Drummond, Bergmann, and Vogt, *Religion in the Anthropocene*.

the recognition that (some) humans have become "a geological force of nature" and that the "disease" is not only affecting ecosystems or bioregions but the integrated earth system. This recognition is carried forward into the subtitle of the new series, namely, "Telling the Story amid the 'Anthropocene'" where the "amid" signals both the disturbances in the earth system and the power relations at play in the root causes of the "Anthropocene."

However, naming the "Anthropocene" as such is highly contested given generalizations on the presumed "anthropos," hiding its affluent Caucasian male identity. Naming the present is certainly elusive. Nevertheless, each of the many proposed alternatives acknowledges that (some) humans have come from a geological force of nature. To tell the story of who God is and what God is doing "amid" the "Anthropocene" is therefore not merely to acknowledge a geological marker but also to symbolize that discourse on that geological marker is dominated by those who speak on behalf of this presumed *anthropos*. For Christians, to tell this story "amid the 'Anthropocene'" is therefore not to legitimize the destructive impact or indeed naming the marker as such, but an act of resistance against multiple layers of domination that include academic discourse on what is named by some "the Anthropocene," even a "good Anthropocene." It is, therefore, best to indicate the "Anthropocene" with quotation marks. Theological reflection is necessarily situated "amid" such multiple layers of domination.

■ A New Series

One of the main outcomes of the Christian Faith and the Earth project was that it brought together scholars with common interests from around the world, from diverse confessional traditions and theological schools. It helped to foster links between existing networks through the Forum on Religion and Ecology, the European Forum for the Study of Religion and the Environment, the Canadian Forum on Religion and Ecology, the Earth Bible project, the Theological Society of South Africa, and many others. Often, the annual meetings of the American Academy of Religion served the purpose of providing a meeting place. A collaborative spirit was also fostered through working together on several large edited volumes involving the same scholars with others joining the conversation.[14]

The new series on "An Earthed Faith" grew from ongoing consultations within these networks. The aim of this series is to offer collaborative, constructive contributions to understanding the content and significance of twelve important themes of the Christian faith from the perspective of

---

14. In addition to the volumes already cited, see Kim, *Making Peace*; Kim and Koster, *Planetary Solidarity*; Conradie and Koster, *Christian Theology and Climate Change*; and Andrianos et al., *Kairos for Creation*. Further references can easily be multiplied.

Christian ecotheology. Inversely, it approaches ecotheology from the perspective of systematic theology, while recognizing the role of other theological subdisciplines (e.g., biblical hermeneutics, history, ethics, practical theology, missiology, and religious studies), resisting the fragmentation of such subdisciplines, and addressing the deep underlying methodological tensions. The series therefore stands in the tradition of reflecting on faith (*fides quaerens intellectum*) in a systematic and disciplined way, typically yielding what is always inadequately termed a "summa," "institutes," a "dogmatics," or a "systematics." Since searching for systems and an abstract logic always has the danger of rigidity and self-sterilization, doing theology is better understood as searching for directions during the course of a journey, a *theologia viatorum* situated among a people of the way, with some companions on the way.[15]

Compared to such work, produced by famous theologians of the past, there are some obvious differences in the way this series is conceptualized:

First, the approach is deeply contextual given the prophetic recognition of the need to discern the signs of the time.[16] These reflections are offered "amid the 'Anthropocene'" with the recognition that a "business as usual" way of doing theology is no longer appropriate. We live in a time where the balance between earth systems has become disturbed and where (western) Christianity stands accused by many to be one of the deepest causes of the underlying problem. The shifting center of gravity in global Christianity cannot undo its historical association with the western "Anthropos" reflected in the name "Anthropocene." An apologetic approach cannot suffice.

Second, in recognizing the significance of context, it is vital that ecclesiology (Faith and Order) and ethics (Life and Work) not be separated from each other although the one also cannot be reduced to the other.[17] Ethical concerns prompt critical reflection on the content of faith, while the indicative of grace cannot but yield the imperative of good work. The significance of the faith (*fides qua creditur*) cannot be separated from its content (*fides quae creditur*). The emphasis on such content implies that the focus is not on a study of faith itself (empirical studies on what Christians actually believe) but on the identity and character of the God in whom trust is placed (what Christians ought to believe).

---

15. See again Bauman, Conradie and Eaton, "The Journey of Doing Ecotheology"; also Moltmann, *Experiences in Theology*, xvii.

16. For a discussion, see Conradie, "What is God really up to?"

17. The relationship between ecclesiology and ethics was explored through a four-year project registered at the University of the Western Cape. This continued a World Council of Churches project leading to a volume edited by Best and Robra, *Ecclesiology and Ethics*. See also Sakupapa, "Ecclesiology and Ethics: An Analysis of the History of the All Africa Conference of Churches (1963–2013)" and a volume of articles from the culminating conference of this project, edited by Conradie, Engdahl, and Phiri, "Ecclesiology and Ethics: The State of Ecumenical Theology in Africa."

Put differently, the focus of contextual theology is not on the context but on understanding the context in the light of (the Word of) God, that is, in the light of the Light of the World.

Third, this series reflects on the content and significance of the Christian faith from the perspective of contemporary Christian ecotheology. This has become a rather amorphous field of study located in different geographical contexts, confessional traditions, and theological schools of thought. It covers all the traditional theological subdisciplines and engages in conversation with a wide variety of other disciplines, philosophies, and religious traditions. It is plagued by all the old methodological disputes. Despite these differences, one may argue that ecotheology has retained both a two-fold critique and a two-fold constructive task, that is, "an ecological critique of Christianity and a Christian critique of ecological destruction,"[18] and a constructive contribution to Christian authenticity and, on that basis, to multidisciplinary discourse on ecological concerns in the public sphere.[19] The genius of ecotheology depends on its ability to hold these four tasks together. Arguably, the three Greek roots in the term ecotheology (*oikos* + *theos* + *logos*) could be understood in a Trinitarian way: there is an interplay between the inhabitation of the Spirit, the transcendence of God, and the mediating role of the Logos. All the disputes on the identity and character of God (the "Theos" in ecotheology) come into play when juxtaposed with the terms *oikos* and *logos*. From this perspective, the perichoresis between these terms should prevent the one from dominating the other. Yet, multiple distortions remain possible, including the danger that Logos would come to dominate Theos. This is the modernist logic that underplays the brokenness of the cross, embodies hubris through knowledge, science and technology, and tends to displace God as the focus of theology.

Fourth, theological reflection can best be done collaboratively and not individually by "lone ranger" researchers. It has to be done ecumenically for two contrasting reasons, namely, the recognition of the earth as a common home and for the sake of the integrity of Christian witness. This ecumenical spirit comes to fruition in a series of edited volumes where editors and contributors are hand-picked to reflect a variety of geographical locations, a diversity of confessional traditions, issues of gender and race (and perhaps class), and where a proper mix of senior scholars and emerging voices is encouraged. In this way, any dangerously tidy system suggested by a biblical twelve volumes becomes fragmented by an irreducible plurality of dissenting voices from around the world.

Fifth, this series draws on various strands of narrative theology from around the world (see the introductory essay on "Setting the scene" discussed further).

---

18. See Conradie, "The Four Tasks," 2–3.

19. See Conradie, "The Four Tasks."

The assumption is that the Christian faith has a narrative shape and structure. It tells a story of who God is and what God has done, is doing, and is expected to do within our world. By implication, the Christian faith is not primarily (or at least not merely) to be understood as a set of propositional truths, a system of laws, a cluster of values, a range of (religious) experiences, or even a community of divine and human persons (only). Christians tell a story and then seek to capture the meaning and moral of that story through witnesses, confessions, creeds, and moral injunctions. This invites an interplay between narrative, confession and narrative expositions of such a confession. This focus on narrative theology is explored in greater depth in the first volume of this series.

Sixth, the scale of this story is certainly "grand" even where some incredulity toward grand narratives is maintained. It tells a story from creation to consummation, including themes such as the emergence of humanity and human sin, providence, election, salvation (whether understood as liberation, reconciliation, or reconstruction), Israel, the church, and God's mission. On the basis of this story of what God has done (the so-called economic Trinity), it becomes possible to reflect on God's identity and character (the so-called immanent Trinity). The structure of the series follows this logic (discussed further). Holding these two aspects together, this series speaks of "telling the story" where "the" refers to the multiple versions of the story of who God is and what God has done found in Christian witness. The assumption is that this is a story about one and the same Triune God, despite an irreducible complexity of perspectives, typically clustered together around the three symbols of God as Father, Son, and Spirit, or, to use John Calvin's more gender-sensitive analogies, God as Source, Wisdom, and Power (see his *Institutes* I.13.18). Either way, the use of the definite article "the" suggests the need to relate the three symbols to each other, to clarify that the Christian faith is not about a notion of God in general but expresses God's identity and character in particular. What is remarkable about this storyline is not (only) that Jesus is like God but that God is like Jesus of Nazareth.

Seventh, there is clearly not only one way of telling the story. There are indeed many such ways—and even more ways of messing up the story.[20] It is a story that has to be told over many Arabian nights. It is a story that can only be told in fragments, but then with the assumption better: the hope that these fragments somehow do belong to the same clay pot even if this cannot readily be reconstructed. There is no correct place to start telling the story. One may start from the middle, the climax, the end, from the perspective of any of the characters—and even from the beginning, although none of us were there "in the beginning." In this series, the creative tension between the one story and

---

20. See Conradie, "How Are They Telling the Story?"

the many contested versions of the story will be kept alive by the various contributors that are selected in order to radicalize and hopefully optimize such diversity without imposing hegemony in any way other than producing a set of twelve volumes. Likewise, each of the twelve themes selected here is clearly core to the Christian faith but is by no means comprehensive—as a "systematic" theology would suggest.

Finally, the term "earthed" is a reference to the way in which electricity needs to be earthed as a precautionary measure. In a more figurative way, the generation of such electricity needs to be earthed as well, namely, to ensure, also as a precautionary measure, that this is done in a sustainable way given the global threat of climate change and its "equally evil twin" of ocean acidification.

In a theological sense, the Christian faith needs to be properly "earthed" too. Or, to use another metaphor, it needs to become deeply rooted in local soil in order to grow and flourish. By implication, there is a need to overcome the prevailing interlocking dualisms of heaven and earth, soul and body, spirit and matter, culture and nature, human and animal, public and private—and their devastating impact through domination in the name of differences of gender and sexual orientation, race and class, caste and culture. Both reductionism ("pulling things down") and Gnostic escapism ("pulling things up") need to be avoided in order to ensure that the Christian faith can indeed be earthed, can become earthen, and can be of some earthly significance. In order to address this task, many former binary distinctions need to be revisited—including the book of nature and the book of Scripture, general revelation and special revelation, revelation and experience, faith and reason, God and world, nature and grace, church and society, and religion and theology.

■ The Structure of the Envisaged Series

With a point of departure in various strands of narrative theology, the following structure for the twelve volumes is proposed. In each volume, a single question will be raised and addressed by each of the ten contributing authors. The series is, therefore, held together by a set of questions related to a story and not by any system. Here is the provisional layout that will remain flexible and will be constantly revised as work on the series proceeds:

Taking a Deep Breath for the Story to Begin . . . An Earthed Faith 1

This volume will address the following question: "How does the story of who the Triune God is and what this God does, relate to the story of life on Earth?" In other words, is the Christian story part of the earth's story or is the earth's story part of God's story, from creation to consummation? This raises many issues on the relatedness of religion and theology, the place of theology in multidisciplinary collaboration, the notion of revelation, the possibility of knowledge of God, hermeneutics, the difference between natural theology and a theology of nature, etc. The word "breath" in the title suggests the Spirit of God as the source of inspiration for the story, already present in any further deliberations. It hints at an air of anticipation, indicated by the three dots in the title.

How Would We Know What God Is Up To? An Earthed Faith 2

This volume will address the following question: "Given what we know about the Anthropocene, how does one even begin to answer the question: What is this God up to and how ought humans respond?" This is a question of theological method, including the sources and interlocutors of Christian theology, its aims and starting points, social theories shaping it, and presuppositions grounding it. Addressing this question is the classic task of doing contextual theology, namely, to describe and analyze a particular context and to consider how this context may best be addressed theologically and practically. The question highlights the need for prophetic theology to discern the "signs of the time," to recognize a "moment of truth" (Kairos), and to discern counter-movements of the Spirit. The question of method opens the door to a constructive critique of how theology has been done and to a creative and faithful reimaging of how the human creature ought to know and respond to God in each new time and place. In terms of the narrative theory and rhetorical theory, method and context account for the compelling plot upon which the narrative hinges; the sense of crisis that will draw together the characters; and the exigencies that invite passion, reflection, and persuasion. Theological method is inherently a theological question, about sin and salvation, creation and redemption, God and God's world—and shapes where the story may lead and how it may be told. Often, clarity on method (= meta + hodos) emerges only in hindsight (reflecting on the road that was traveled) and not only as foresight (planning for the road ahead).

The Place of Story and the Story of Place? An Earthed Faith 3

This volume will address the following question: "What difference does it make to the story of cosmic, planetary, human and cultural evolution to re-describe this as the creative work of God's love?" Inversely, what difference does it make to the story of God's love to describe it in evolutionary terms? Addressing this question will require theological reflection on creation and cosmic, biological, hominid, and human evolution (the story of place). Such reflection on the beginning is of course not situated "in the beginning" but entails a narrative reconstruction of the story where current interests, positions of power, and fears are necessarily at stake (the place where the story is being told). This is a contested space, indeed a "site of struggle," often dominated by issues of race rather than by grace. How, then, is this story to be told given a sense of place? It will not be possible to avoid questions around suffering, sin, evil, and the tragic (the theme of the next volume), but the focus will be on why on earth a loving God would deem this story to be "very good"—despite the prevalence of suffering, injustice, and oppression?

Making Room for the Story to Continue? An Earthed Faith 4

This volume will address the following question: "How could the suffering of God's creatures in the Anthropocene be reconciled with trust in God's loving care?" Addressing this question will require theological reflection on the classic themes related to the doctrine of providence, including *creatio continua*, *conservatio*, *gubernatio*, and *concursus*. For some, God's providence (common grace) is a necessary requirement to allow (to make room for) the history of salvation to proceed. For others, the suffering embedded in God's "good" creation requires responses to the theodicy problem: Why would a loving God allow creatures to suffer so much? What is the relationship between so-called natural evil and social evil? Is the underlying problem human sin, or is it the inadequacies, the tragic dimension, indeed the violence embedded in God's world? Again, this last question is hinted at in the question mark after the title.

The Saving Grace of the Story? An Earthed Faith 5

This volume will address the following question: "How is the Christian message of salvation to be interpreted given current ecological destruction and apocalyptic fears associated with the Anthropocene?" Is this message at all plausible given the failure of Christianity to address so many other urgent problems over twenty centuries? This will require theological reflection on Christological symbols such as atonement and Pneumatological symbols such as liberation, healing, reconciliation, regeneration, moral guidance, justification, and sanctification—insofar as these may be pertinent in the Age of the "Anthropocene.". The title is ambiguous and ironic to indicate that the story is highly contested but is at best to be understood as good news for the whole Earth.

The Keepers of the Story? An Earthed Faith 6

This volume will address the following question: "What is the place and significance of the church in God's 'household', now situated in the destabilizing context of the Anthropocene?" Addressing this question will require theological reflection on the formation, up-building, and very nature of the church, on its many ministries and missions. Presumably, the question is no longer whether there is salvation outside of the church, but indeed whether there is salvation to be found within the church. Can it still be said that the church is God's main (even only) instrument (sign, sacrament, icon) to bring salvation, given the challenges posed by the "Anthropocene?" Or is the task of the church the monastic one of "keeping" the story with authenticity, that is, to maintain the inner secret to the mystery of history, amid dark clouds looming. Or, when few outsiders take any notice, should the church aim, instead, at contextual relevance, ensuring that it does not answer questions that no one any longer asks? Does this not sound too much as if it is the church that needs to come to God's rescue, or is the inverse true?

Where the Story Ends and Its Ends . . . An Earthed Faith 7

This volume will address the following question: "How should the content and significance of Christian hope be understood in the context of the Anthropocene?" Addressing this question will require theological reflection on the eschatological symbols of the final judgment as a sign of hope, on the resurrection of the dead, on the coming reign of God, and on eternal life. It will also have to assess whether such hope is to be understood as the restoration (neo-Calvinism), elevation (Roman Catholicism), replacement (Anabaptism), recycling (liberalism/secularism), or divinification/theosis (Eastern Orthodoxy) of this world. Does the meaning of the story lie in its end or in the journey/pilgrimage toward that end? Any answer to such questions will remain provisional because the story has not ended yet, one may say because God is not finished with us yet. This is hinted at through the three dots in the title.

Being Blessed as the Inner Logic of the Story? An Earthed Faith 8

This volume will address the following question: "Can the notion of being God's chosen people or instrument be retained in a religiously plural world under the threat of the Anthropocene?" Addressing this question will require theological reflection on the themes of divine election and vocation. Can "being blessed" by God be understood as the inner logic of the story? Is such blessing, and the implied calling, not often experienced as a curse? What about divine reprobation, punishment, and justice for the victims and perpetrators of history? How is a theology of religions to be understood in a context characterized by common threats, the need for tolerance, and compassion across religious divides? How can Christians move beyond the options of exclusivism and relativism in the context of the "Anthropocene?" What does it mean to be blessed, for the whole of creation to receive God's blessing?

The Spirit of the Story? An Earthed Faith 9

This volume will address questions around the identity and character of God's Spirit. It will require theological reflection on how the very notion of spirit should be understood in relation to person, matter, ideas, force, energy, and related concepts. What does it mean that this Spirit is "holy" and makes things "holy"? Is this Spirit able to overcome what is "demonic" in the "Anthropocene?" Is it money or love that makes the world go round? Or is this Spirit the spirit that makes matter move, even if this movement is not all that obvious and requires discernment?

The Letter of the Story? An Earthed Faith 10

This volume will address questions around the identity and character of Jesus of Nazareth, proclaimed to be the Christ, anointed by God's Spirit, the One who would inaugurate God's coming reign. It will require theological reflection on the significance of all six Christological symbols, namely (deep) Incarnation, Cross, Resurrection, Ascension, Session, and Parousia as these may relate to the coming of the "Anthropocene." What is the ecological significance that the Word (the letter) literally became flesh? If the cross is a concrete symbol of the history of imperialism and oppression, can the (bodily?) resurrection still function as an equally concrete symbol of hope in the "Anthropocene?" How is the interplay between the letter and the spirit of the story to be understood given long-standing ecumenical divides on the *filioque* controversy—that still divides the East and the West, the North and the South—over whether the Spirit works (only/primarily) on the basis of the Letter (as most so-called mainline churches assume)? Or should the relative independence of God's Spirit be emphasized (as many others presume)?

In Communion with the Story Teller(s)? An Earthed Faith 11

This volume will address questions around the doctrine of the Trinity as the inner secret/apophatic mystery/doxological culmination of the Christian faith. It will offer theological reflection on how the economic Trinity and the immanent Trinity are related by exploring God's identity and character. The question is which of God's characteristics need to be foregrounded in the Age of the "Anthropocene." In particular, how is God's mercy related to God's justice given the interactions between God as Father, Son and Spirit? Can these (patriarchal) symbols be maintained in the "Anthropocene?" Should one favor the social analogy (emphasizing communion) or the psychological analogy (perhaps allowing for a more generic notion of God) for understanding the Trinity? What difference does faith in such a God make (if any) in the Age of the "Anthropocene?" Moreover, who is telling the story? Are we (Christians?) the ones responsible to tell the story or are we characters in a story ultimately told by Godself? Given these reflections, what does it mean to believe in "God" (a God, any God) in the world in which we now live? Note that this (philosophical) question is not addressed upfront but penultimately. For Christians, the question remains whether this Triune God can be regarded as an apt expression of the ultimate mystery of the world?

What, then, Is the Moral of the Story? An Earthed Faith 12

This volume will address questions around the relationship between Christian doctrine, Christian ethics, Christian spirituality, and Christian praxis—between the ultimate and the penultimate, and between the indicative of God's grace and the imperative of ecological gratitude. Such relatedness has been implicitly there in all the other volumes but needs to be made explicit here. In dealing with climate change (for example), there is a need to find common moral ground with those standing in other religious traditions and with organizations in civil society. This has implications for all the relevant ethical categories—such as moral vision, virtues, duties, rights, responsibilities, values, middle axioms, action steps, et cetera. For Christians, the question will be whether and, if so, how such common moral ground is deeply rooted in the story of who God is and what God has done, is doing, and will be doing toward the coming of God's reign, "in every square inch of society."

To make the logic of this structure explicit, the first two volumes will be introductory, dealing with issues of epistemology and methodology; volumes three to eight will reflect on the story of God's work (the economic Trinity), with the last of these (on election) focusing on the inner logic of that story. Volumes nine to eleven will focus on the person of God in an inverse order starting with the Spirit, then the Christ of the Spirit, and then the Triune communion as doxological conclusion. The last volume will return to the narrative structure explored in the first volume by exploring the dynamic between doctrine and ethics.

■ The Publication of the Series

A long-term project like this faces many challenges, not least in finding some continuity over many volumes. To address this challenge, a core team of senior scholars, building on participants in the Christian Faith and the Earth project, have been invited who will each contribute to more than one volume. Coeditors are invited to ensure topical focus but also sufficient diversity, not least in recognizing emerging voices from around the world.

There is no guarantee that those who started with the project will be able to see it through to the end. Some who served as sources of inspiration, including James Cone, Denis Edwards, Sallie McFague, and Vítor Westhelle, already belong to the communion of the saints. Such a project can only proceed in good faith, the faith that the story that is being told here is not in our hands, that the God about whom this story is told, is not done with us yet, that telling the story is not ultimately our responsibility because this story is being told about us. If so, God may be the "Grand Recounter," the storyteller who weaves us, creatures, as characters into a storyline?[21]

The series is being published through a cooperation agreement between AOSIS, a publisher based in South Africa, and Wipf and Stock, a publisher based in Oregon, United States of America. This allows for a foothold in the global South and in the global North, for open access after an embargo period, and for continuous availability of hard copies through print on demand on a relatively affordable basis. In a market already saturated with volumes on ecotheology, such a series is always in danger of producing "more consumer goods for an increasingly empty time and an ecologically devastated space."[22] Let this remain a challenge for the authors and editors of each volume!

A final word is necessary on the envisaged readers of the series. The volumes are scholarly in nature and therefore primarily aimed at other scholars and postgraduate students. The series is primarily situated in the field of Christian ecotheology, which by definition is found in multiple geographical regions, confessional traditions, and theological schools around the world. In that sense, the series is indeed ecumenical in vision and scope. In widening circles, the series should also be relevant to other forms of constructive theology reflecting on the content and significance of the Christian faith, other theological subdisciplines, multireligious dialogue on ecological concerns, and for discerning the signs of the time in discourse on what is named and contested as the "Anthropocene."

■ Bibliography

Andrianos, Lukas, et al., eds. *Kairos for Creation: Confessing Hope for the Earth*. Solingen: Foedus, 2019.

Ayre, Clive W. and Ernst M. Conradie, eds. *The Church in God's Household: Protestant Perspectives on Ecclesiology and Ecology*. Pietermaritzburg: Cluster, 2016.

Bauman, Whitney, Ernst M. Conradie and Heather Eaton, eds. "The Journey of Doing Ecotheology." *Theology* 116 (2013), 1-3, 4-44. https://doi.org/10.1177/0040571X12459318

---

21. See Serres, *The Incandescent*, 20.

22. Tracy, *On Naming the Present*, 6.

Best, Thomas F. and Martin Robra, eds. *Ecclesiology and Ethics: Ecumenical Ethical Engagement, Moral Formation and the Nature of the Church.* Geneva: World Council of Churches, 1997.

Conradie, Ernst M., ed. "Christian Faith and the Earth: Respice et Prospice." *Scriptura* 111 (2012), 309–432. https://doi.org/10.7833/111-0-11

———. *Creation and Salvation, Volume 1: A Mosaic of Essays on Selected Classic Christian Theologians.* Berlin: LIT, 2011.

———. *Creation and Salvation, Volume 2: A Companion on Recent Theological Movements.* Berlin: LIT, 2012.

———. "How Are They Telling the Story?" *Scriptura* 97 (2008), 1–136 and *Scriptura* 98 (2008), 137–243.

———. "Pneumatology and Ecology." *Journal of Reformed Theology* 6 (2012), 189–305. https://doi.org/10.1163/15697312-12341269

———. *The Earth in God's Economy: Creation, Salvation and Consummation in Ecological Perspective.* Berlin: LIT, 2015.

———. "The Four Tasks of Christian Ecotheology: Revisiting the Current Debate." *Scriptura* 119 (2020), 1–13. https://doi.org/10.7833/119-1-1566

———. "The Project and Prospects of 'Redeeming Sin?': Some Core Insights and Several Unresolved Problems." *Scriptura* 119 (2020), 1–21. https://doi.org/10.7833/119-2-1689

———. *Redeeming Sin? Social Diagnostics amid Ecological Destruction.* Lanham: Lexington, 2017.

———. *Secular Discourse on Sin in the Anthropocene: What's Wrong with the World?* Lanham: Lexington, 2020.

———. "What is God really up to in a Time like this? Discerning the Spirit's Movements as Core Task of Christian Eco-Theology." In *Kairos for Creation: Confessing Hope for the Earth*, edited by Lukas Andrianos, et al., 31–44. Solingen: Foedus-Verlag, 2019.

Conradie, Ernst M., Hans S.A. Engdahl and Isabel Apawo Phiri, eds. "Ecclesiology and Ethics: The State of Ecumenical Theology in Africa." *The Ecumenical Review* 67:4 (2015), 495–97, 498–663. https://doi.org/10.1111/erev.12187

Conradie, Ernst M., Sigurd Bergmann, Celia E. Deane-Drummond and Denis Edwards, eds. *Christian Faith and the Earth: Current Paths and Emerging Horizons in Ecotheology.* London: T. & T. Clark, 2014.

Conradie, Ernst M. and Willis Jenkins, eds. "Special Issue: Ecology and Christian Soteriology." *Worldviews: Global Religions, Culture, Ecology* 14:2&3 (2010), 107–265. https://doi.org/10.1163/156853510X507248

Conradie, Ernst M. and Hilda P. Koster, eds. *The T&T Clark Handbook on Christian Theology and Climate Change.* London: T. & T. Clark, 2019.

Deane-Drummond, Celia E., Sigurd Bergmann and Markus Vogt, eds. *Religion in the Anthropocene.* Eugene: Cascade, 2017.

Kim, Grace Ji-Sun, ed. *Making Peace with the Earth: Action and Advocacy for Climate Justice.* Geneva: WCC, 2016.

Kim, Grace Ji-Sun and Hilda P. Koster, eds. *Planetary Solidarity: Global Women's Voices on Christian Doctrine and Climate Justice.* Minneapolis: Fortress, 2017.

Moltmann, Jürgen. *Experiences in Theology: Ways and Forms of Christian Theology.* Minneapolis: Fortress, 2000.

Oduyoye, Mercy Amba. *Hearing and Knowing: Theological Reflections on Christianity in Africa.* Nairobi: Acton, 2000.

Sakupapa, Teddy Chalwe. "Ecclesiology and Ethics: An Analysis of the History of the All Africa Conference of Churches," PhD diss., University of the Western Cape, 2017.

Serres, Michel. *The Incandescent.* London: Bloomsbury, 2018.

Tracy, David. *On Naming the Present: God, Hermeneutics, and Church.* Maryknoll: Orbis, 1994.

On Setting the Scene for the Story to Begin

Ernst M. Conradie[1] & Pan-Chiu Lai[2]

"There is no possibility in our period for a single, all-embracing 'scientific' cosmological narrative. There is also no possibility, on the theological side, for a complete system of final understanding of God-self-world. What there is, however, is an envisionment of reality informed by the hope afforded by the Christian construal of all reality from the perspective of Jesus Christ"—David Tracy.[3]

■ Grand Narratives, Metanarratives, and Meganarratives in the "Anthropocene"

What has gone wrong with the world? The symptoms of the underlying problem are evident given economic inequality, the many faces of violence, global pandemics, and ecological destruction. In the "Anthropocene," these

---

1. Ernst M. Conradie is a Senior Professor in the Department of Religion and Theology at the University of the Western Cape in South Africa.

2. Pan-Chiu Lai is a Professor, Department of Cultural and Religious Studies, The Chinese University of Hong Kong. He is registered as a co-researcher at the University of the Western Cape, South Africa, for the project on "An Earthed Faith: Telling the Story amid the 'Anthropocene'."

3. Tracy, *On Naming the Present*, 79.

How to cite: Conradie, E.M. & Lai, P.-C., 2021, 'On Setting the Scene for the Story to Begin', in E.M. Conradie & P.-C. Lai (eds.), *Taking a deep breath for the story to begin . . .* (An Earthed Faith: Telling the Story amid the "Anthropocene" Volume 1), pp. 15–47, AOSIS, Cape Town. https://doi.org/10.4102/aosis.2021.BK264.02

intertwined symptoms have become related to the interaction between the four main earth systems, namely, the geosphere, the hydrosphere, the atmosphere, and the biosphere, together with their subsystems. Since the balance between these systems (the earth system in the singular) has become disturbed, the Holocene stability that allowed human civilizations to flourish is being undermined.

What are the root causes of such symptoms? In an age that cannot name itself, to name the "Anthropocene" as such suggests that one species in the biosphere is the agent that drives such (anthropogenic) changes through the noosphere (i.e., the technosphere, the econosphere, and so forth). But is the human species as such the problem or a particular phase in human history—so that the "Anthropocene" can be dated more precisely? Or does the implied anthropos refer to a particular group of humans and not to the species as such? The debate on naming the "Anthropocene" as such cannot be resolved here. It suffices to say that this naming is best used critically and not as a recognition of some "good Anthropocene." Put differently, the name "Anthropocene" is already a form of domination, imputing guilt on those who are the victims of forces well beyond their locus of control. Perhaps more than one name, a few nicknames, may be needed. The "amid" in the series title ("amid the 'Anthropocene'") cannot be a legitimation of such impact or of naming the "Anthropocene" as such. At best, it serves as a reminder of the multiple layers of domination involved, including Christian complicity in such domination.

Analyses and critiques of the root causes of such destruction abound: the culprit is said to be imperial and colonial conquest, industrialization, capitalism, economic growth, globalization, consumerism, modernity, patriarchy, white hegemony, and also the Jewish-Christian tradition. Consider, for example, the frankfurter Schule's notion of the dialectic of the Enlightenment, the critique of modernity in (French) postmodernism, ecofeminist analyses of interlocking dualisms, and postcolonial (especially subaltern) or decolonial critiques of western imperialism. Such critiques are extended to the very notion of an "Anthropocene:" is the pedigree of the "anthropos" named here not all too white, male, western, and situated in the consumer class?[4]

One symbol of such critiques is the "incredulity toward metanarratives" first articulated by Jean-François Lyotard in *The Postmodern Condition: A Report on Knowledge* (1979). The argument is that such metanarratives, often described as "grand narratives," are totalizing stories about the direction that human history is taking. Such metanarratives ground knowledge and legitimize

---

4. References can be multiplied readily. See, for example, Malm and Hornborg, "The Geology of Mankind?"; Yussof, *A Billion Black Anthropocenes or None*; Haraway, *Staying with the Trouble*. For the need to nevertheless recognize a common humanity amidst the predicament posed by the "Anthropocene," see Chakrabarty, *The Climate of History*; also Hamilton, *Defiant Earth*.

economic modes of production and cultural modes of consumption. As Lyotard rightly observes, "The nineteenth and twentieth centuries have given us as much terror as we can take. We have paid a high enough price for the nostalgia of the whole and the one . . ."[5] Philosopher Richard Kearney adds that:

> Post-modern thinking refuses to reduce the complex multiplicity of our cultural signs and images to a systematic synthesis [. . .] (it) renounces the modern temptation—from Descartes and Spinoza to Hegel and Marx—to totalize the plurality of our human discourse in a single system or foundation.[6]

With the advent of the "Anthropocene," western stories of unification—the idea of progress, Enlightenment universalism, Hegel's reign of the mind, Marx's classless society, Comte's march toward positivism, Nietzsche's will to power—have become successfully extended to affect the whole earth system.

Lyotard's critique focuses on the self-congratulatory self-legitimation of modernity. At its best, postmodernism offers resistance against complacent humanist self-understandings, against claims to presence not mediated through history and language, and against totalizing systems that reduce everything to more of the same (Foucault). Such ideological legitimation is readily extended toward religious legitimation, with Constantinian Christiandom playing a crucial role. Although the plausibility of the Christian story is supposedly undermined by modern science and secularization, the Christian story retains some cultural force to legitimize human dominion as "masters of the planet."[7]

In a discourse on the "Anthropocene," there is a renewed interest in such totalizing grand narratives given their impact not only on ecosystems but also on the earth system.[8] However, there is also a recognition that such narratives cannot be readily avoided. All disciplines reflecting on the "Anthropocene" ultimately need to reflect not only on its heavily debated starting point to be marked by a "golden spike" and its subsequent history (often dubbed the "great acceleration") but also on its end(s). What kind of geological epoch or era will follow the "Anthropocene?" Will some new balance return where humans are no longer the main agents of geological change? Will there still be humans present? Not surprisingly, the return of what may be called meganarratives in a discourse on the "Anthropocene" has been recognized by astute observers such as Michel Serres and Peter Sloterdijk. Serres acknowledges that grand narratives cannot be avoided and observes that

---

5. Lyotard, "The Postmodern Condition," 74.

6. Kearney, *Poetics of Imagining*, 182.

7. This critique was famously expressed by the American historian Lynn White in his thesis on "The Historical Roots of Our Ecologic Crisis," building on Max Weber's even more famous and equally controversial thesis on "The Protestant Ethic and the Spirit of Capitalism."

8. The next three paragraphs draw from Conradie, *Secular Discourse*.

Enlightenment universalism has been broadened four times with the cosmic big bang, the cooling of our planet, and the appearance of Ribonucleic acid (RNA) and of *homo sapiens*.[9] Sloterdijk describes the history of globalization from the circumnavigation of the globe onward as the grand narrative within which its critics ineluctably also live.[10] Arguably, to speak of "a shift from the Holocene to the Anthropocene" constitutes such a meganarrative (in just eight words).

There is a need to explain how we reached this point in planetary history and also a need to guard against distortive versions of such a story. One example is the triumph of consumerism (and boredom), as the end goal of capitalism so that communism is best understood as "a stage on the way to consumerism,"[11] declaring that the "end of history" has arrived since the last alternatives to liberalism have been eliminated.[12] Another example is the narrative that allows policy-makers to continue with business as usual with a few added environmental cautions. Indeed, "The delay-climate-action-and-make-nature-pay-later story is not a wise one to tell ourselves."[13] How, then, is a new grand narrative of history in stages that merely perpetuate the possibility of domination to be avoided?[14]

In a particularly helpful analysis, Christophe Bonneuil observes that such narratives attribute a certain value to the state of things at the beginning and at the end of the story; select a focus and a framing that highlights some actors while leaving others in the shadow; put time into sequences, pinpointing certain turning points while downplaying others; and constitute a dramaturgy with implicit or explicit moral lessons.[15] He outlines four grand narratives of the "Anthropocene."

The dominant grand narrative is the modernist one popular in scientific cultures where "Man" moves from environmental obliviousness to environmental consciousness, from "Man" equaling nature's power to "Man" repairing nature through the role of science. The second, utopian (or ecomodernist) grand narrative celebrates the end of nature and welcomes the advent of the "good Anthropocene" and thus radicalizes the modernist version of progress and enlightenment. The third, eco-catastrophist narrative warns of the collapse of industrial civilization by depicting limits, tipping points,

---

9. Serres, *The Incandescent*, 103, 195.

10. Sloterdijk, *In the World Interior of Capital*.

11. Sloterdijk, *In the World Interior of Capital*, 176.

12. See the famous essay by Fukuyama, "The End of History?"

13. See Lewis and Maslin, *The Human Planet*, 399.

14. See Bonneuil and Fressoz, *The Shock of the Anthropocene*, 47-64.

15. Bonneuil, "The Geological Turn," 17-18.

collapse, violence, and wars. This narrative rejects the faith that greener technologies can save the planet:

> It argues for the urgent need to radically change the dominant ways of living, consuming and producing, and rejects the belief in technological fixes that would save the planet within the frame of an unchanged socio-economic system.[16]

Science and technology alone cannot save the planet; only social innovations emerging from a dynamic civil society could. The fourth, eco-Marxist narrative focuses on capitalism's inability to ensure sustainability due to the processes of dispossession and commodification associated with capitalist expansion and imperial domination. This narrative privileges the term Capitalocene rather than "Anthropocene." Bonneuil notes that one may add similar ecofeminist and subaltern narratives that relate domination in the name of differences of gender and caste to the degrading of the Earth.[17]

Indeed, how is the story of the advent of the "Anthropocene" to be told? Can such a story be told, if the "Anthropocene" is indeed unprecedented in human history? How does one weave the linear, if exponential "great acceleration" into any narrative plot?[18] What about the postmodern claim that "history" does not exist, that there is no grand all-encompassing narrative guaranteeing a sense of history in terms of meaning or direction?[19] If so, not only the "end of history" is to be announced but that there never has been any history—or for that matter any her-story. But even if there is no history, perhaps there can at least be a story, or stories? Or should such stories be censured, perhaps on the basis that the accidental truths of history cannot provide proofs for the necessary truths of reason? Or perhaps on the basis of the opposite suspicion that any search for "truth" implies hegemony? Are we humans not at heart storytelling and story-dwelling animals—who make stories and are made by our stories?[20] Of course, there is more to it than telling stories, but such stories seem to be integral to all human cultures throughout human history. If so, the oral, typically indigenous versions of such stories have a primacy over written versions (novels) or academic reflections on such stories.

One may therefore say that the question is not whether or not such a grand narrative is constructed and legitimized, but which story is being told of what went wrong in the world. There may be one thing that is worse than totalizing grand narratives and that is the naive assumption that these can be totally avoided—and the failure to tell an alternative, subaltern story. Telling the story

---

16. Bonneuil, "The Geological Turn," 27.

17. See Bonneuil, "The Geological Turn," 29.

18. See Ten Bos, *Dwalen in het Antropoceen*, 124, following insights from Maurice Blanchot.

19. See Žižek, *Living in the End Times*, 184.

20. See McGrath, *Narrative Apologetics*, 107, 109.

of where we are now in human history, how we came to be where we are, and what the future may hold is a multicentered task that has to be addressed in many different geographical and cultural locations and from within a wide spectrum of academic and other disciplines. We need a compelling story to guide our collective human actions around mitigation and adaptation in a changing climate. That does not mean that only one big overarching story is needed—one that would subdue all others. As Donna Haraway observes, "We relate, know, think, world, and tell stories through and with other stories, worlds, knowledges, thinkings, yearnings."[21] It does mean that the encompassing scope of such narratives has to be recognized. What is needed are "big enough stories" that are open-ended, keeping the edges open, able to gather up the complexities accounting for a lot but not everything.[22] Such encompassing cosmological narratives may best be called *mega*narratives and not *meta*narratives although reflection about the meaning (doctrine) and moral (ethics) of such meganarratives cannot be avoided either. Is the problem then not with metanarratives or meganarratives per se but with a specific kind of metanarrative (i.e., modernist *master* narratives of domination)?[23]

This is quite tricky: while stories and cosmological narratives (and ethical codes) are always in the plural,[24] metanarratives (also in the plural) seek a metaperspective beyond such destabilizing plurality. Even the recognition of such plurality is already a metaperspective. Umbrella terms (such as "religion") cannot be avoided even though they carry the dangers of hegemony. Religious pluralism can easily and paradoxically become "the only way" where exclusivist claims cannot be tolerated—precisely in the name of religious tolerance.

What seems to be needed is a way of intertwining such stories without falling in the modernist trap of totalizing and imperialist ways of thinking. As Nicholas Lash observes:

> The discernible oneness of the world, the interconnectedness of everything, not only makes the telling of some story of the world, some story of the whole world, a possibility; it makes it a necessity.[25]

He adds that "No story says everything, not even a story of everything."[26]

Where can such stories be found? This is a triple question: Does the integration of earth subsystems also require an integrated version of the

---

21. Haraway, *Staying with the Trouble*, 97.

22. Haraway, *Staying with the Trouble*, 50, 101, 185.

23. See the assessment by Alister McGrath and his suggestion (following Tolkien) of "a story of a larger kind" in *Narrative Apologetics*, 43.

24. See Lai, "Inter-religious Dialogue."

25. Lash, *Holiness, Speech, and Silence*, 28–29.

26. Lash, *Holiness, Speech, and Silence*, 31.

story? Can such a story be found? Is there a proper place where such a story can be told? In the "Anthropocene," the category of place itself has become contested: whose place is it anyway?[27] Added to this is the problem that a holistic perspective is not only impossible but also arrogant. As Bruno Latour rightly observes, "One is never as provincial as when one claims to have a 'global' view."[28] He adds that "he who looks at the earth as a Globe always sees himself as a God."[29] If we tell a story from somewhere, we cannot tell the whole story, not least because the story is still ongoing. At the same time, any one place is connected to all others given the way earth subsystems have an impact on each other.

As noted above, this task of telling relatively more adequate stories is one among many tasks and is addressed in different aspects of human culture, including the academy. In the academy, this is necessarily a multidisciplinary endeavor, crossing long-established divides between the so-called natural sciences and the humanities. Can Christian theology, alongside religious studies, philosophy, and ethics, offer a contribution to such multidisciplinary discourse? Given the quite devastating ecological critique of (western) Christianity, can ecumenical Christian discourse (covering the "whole inhabited world") contribute anything with any credibility? More specifically: What can Christian theology contribute that is not already offered from within other disciplines with more expertise? Does it have anything to say? A silent, compassionate presence may be dignified but any multidisciplinary collaboration requires at some point clarity on the specific contribution of each discipline. Moreover, is the Christian story of who God is, what God has done and is expected to be doing at all plausible in such a multidisciplinary context, even for those within the Christian fold?

This is the daunting challenge taken up in the series on "An Earthed Faith: Telling the Story amid the 'Anthropocene'."

■ The Many Strands of Narrative Theology

The Christian confession of faith in the Triune God is arguably structured in the form of a narrative. This suggests that God is not a cosmic principle or an abstracted philosophy, but a not less than personal God who acts in cosmic and especially human history. Yahweh is the God of Israel's history and indeed of world history, the God who acts[30] and who is self-identified by contingent temporal events. In the Old Testament, God is identified as the One who

---

27. For a decolonial critique of an anthropocentric notion of space and place, see Morton, *Dark Ecology*, 10.

28. Latour, *Facing Gaia*, 135.

29. Latour, *Facing Gaia*, 73.

30. The implied reference here is to G. Ernest Wright's book *God Who Acts* (1952).

liberated Israel from the house of slavery in Egypt. In the New Testament, God is identified as the One who raised Jesus from the dead. The word God is as much a verb as it may be a noun, a way of doing rather than a form of being or even being itself.[31] The vision expressed in the Christian liturgy is of God as the one who was, is, and will come. Christ has died, Christ has risen, and Christ is coming again. The Spirit hovered over the waters, is dwelling in us, and will come to renew the whole creation. God does not have stories; God creates history, and God is history. The Christian message of redemption assumes a narrative from a state of corruption to salvation (whether understood as liberation or reconciliation) and toward consummation.[32] The coming reign of God promises a renewed creation that cannot be captured in cyclical or indeed linear notions of time, but only through story, drama, or opera, with some sense of direction.

Likewise, Christian theology assumes an underlying narrative: It tells a story of who the Triune God is and what this God has done, is doing, and is expected to do. For Christian theology, this story is the story of God's "economy," which is expressed in the awkward term "economic Trinity." The inner secret of this story, the understanding of God's identity and character, may then be described as the so-called immanent Trinity. Naming the Triune God as such is therefore a highly compressed version of the story.[33] The task of telling the story of what God has done cannot be addressed without assuming the task of identifying who this God is and vice versa. What is at stake here is an understanding of the character of the Triune God if compared with other divinities, confessed to be a loving God, with the implications of mercy and therefore of justice, instead of a powerful but fickle Lord (Ba'al), a dispenser of goods and services whose favor has to be secured through bribes and sacrifices.

The emphasis on the category of narrative suggests that Christianity, especially the Christian faith, is best understood not (only) as a set of propositional truths, a cluster of symbols or values, a system of laws and moral injunctions, a form of transcendental inquiry, a range of (religious) experiences, a set of convictions, emotional attachments, a range of passions, a wisdom

---

31. The Hebrew phrase "אֶהְיֶה אֲשֶׁר אֶהְיֶה" (Exod 3:14) could be translated in either the present or the future tense or both. This suggests some temporality in Israel's understanding of God. If God may be said to be "eternal" this does not imply a timeless eternity or the antithesis of change, but assumes some contingency in order to act within history. In his early work, Wolfhart Pannenberg suggested on this basis that futurity (the power of potentiality over actuality and hence the ontological priority of the future) forms part of God's very being. In a restricted sense, God does not yet exist: "God's being is still in the process of coming to be." See Pannenberg, *Theology and the Kingdom of God*, 56. This stimulated a debate in Germany between Pannenberg, Eberhard Jüngel, and Jürgen Moltmann who each stressed the role of the future but in diverging ways; God's being is in becoming or in coming, not just in process. See also Jüngel, *The Doctrine of the Trinity; God as Mystery*, 380.

32. See Root, "The Narrative Structure of Soteriology."

33. Jenson, *Systematic Theology 1*, 46.

tradition, an emancipatory praxis (discipleship), or even a community of divine and human persons. It tells a story and then seeks to capture the meaning and moral of that story through witnesses, confessions, creeds, moral injunctions, ecclesial structures and practices, and lives lived. This invites an interplay between narrative, confession, and narrative expositions of such a confession. Doctrines then offer a regulative interpretation of the biblical roots and subsequent history of the Christian tradition. If separated from the underlying drama, doctrine becomes abstract, speculative, and arid.

This does not imply that narrative is the only appropriate or even the primary genre for the Christian faith or for theological reflection on such faith. Obviously, that would be an overstatement. "Story" is one category alongside many others and "telling the story" may serve as one metaphor alongside others to understand the tasks of Christian theology as a whole. There is no need to choose between the God of Abraham, Isaac, and Jacob (God as a proper name) and the God of the philosophers (God as a metaphysical concept), between narrative theology and metaphysics.[34] The use of the colloquial "story" does not suggest that the Christian faith is based on myths and is itself best understood as a form of fiction that therefore obfuscates questions about truth.[35] It does mean that recognizing the underlying narrative is a necessary condition (*sine qua non*) to make sense of Christian witness.

This is recognized, intuitively or explicitly, in many diverging strands of narrative theology. The following schools of thought may merely be listed here to capture something of the conflicting plurality of approaches:

- Many would associate narrative theology with the emergence of the so-called Yale School of Theology where H. Richard Niebuhr is recognized as a "founding father" and where the influence of Hans Frei, George Lindbeck, and several others is typically mentioned.[36] There is a Barthian retrieval of the category of revelation and also the recognition of an experiential dimension (to avoid the category of revelation being turned into authoritarian dogmatism), expressed by Niebuhr as the difference between history and "the story of our lives."[37] The assumption is that the biblical stories construct, as it were, a habitable world, a frame of reference that enables people to orient themselves and to cope with life and

---

34. Lash, "Ideology, Metaphor and Analogy," 135.

35. This fear about the popularity of the term story in theology is expressed by Pannenberg, among others. See his *Introduction to Systematic Theology*, 5; also *Systematic Theology 1*, 231-32. In this series "story" does not imply fiction, nor does it render that which the story is about of secondary significance.

36. See Niebuhr, *The Meaning of Revelation*; Frei, *The Eclipse of Biblical Narrative*; and Lindbeck, *The Nature of Doctrine*; also Thiemann, *Revelation and Theology*.

37. Niebuhr, *The Meaning of Revelation*, 23-48.

its many demands.[38] It is not as if we need to relate the text with a context outside of the text; the contemporary context is itself part of the encompassing Christian story. The adequacy of Christian doctrines and practices should therefore not be assessed in terms of external criteria. To explain the Christian faith in terms of philosophical categories such as the infinite, authentic existence, "ultimate concern" or emancipatory praxis is reductionist; it is to turn it into something that it is not.[39] The plot of the Christian story cannot be subsumed under something else. According to some critics, this leads to the danger of self-isolation, rendering little more than a sophisticated form of fideism.

- A quite different mode of narrative theology[40] is associated with the University of Chicago given the influence of Paul Ricoeur and his work on *Time and Narrative*. Ricoeur's "long route to ontology"[41] suggests that we do not have direct access to the world around us except through metaphor and symbol; neither do we have direct scientific or phenomenological access to understanding time but through the indirect mode of narrative.[42] Influenced by Ricoeur (and behind him Hans-Georg Gadamer's retrieval of the notion of tradition), David Tracy adopts such insights to describe the "analogical imagination" at work in the Christian tradition.[43] One may also mention the work of Sallie McFague here. She comments that ours is a dynamic, unfinished, "story-shaped universe."[44]

- Scholars in the field of virtue ethics have recognized that the formation of virtue requires the construction of a narrative identity embedded in long-standing traditions. We are storytelling animals. In order to know what we need to do, we need to know of which stories we find our lives to be a part.[45] Here the influence of Alasdair MacIntyre, Stanley Hauerwas,[46] James

---

38. See Lindbeck, "Scripture, Consensus and Community."

39. Comstock, "Two Types of Narrative Theology," 693.

40. See the comparison by Comstock in terms of description, explanation, and justification in his essay "Two Types of Narrative Theology."

41. For a remarkably insightful discussion of Ricoeur's hermeneutics, see Tracy, *Fragments*, 211–38, especially 215.

42. This is the conclusion that Ricoeur reaches at the end of the third volume of his *Time and Narrative*, 241.

43. See Tracy, *The Analogical Imagination*. Already in *Blessed Rage for Order* he comments: "human beings need story, symbol, image, myth, and fiction to disclose to their imaginations some genuinely new possibilities for existence, possibilities which conceptual analysis, committed as it is to understanding present actualities, cannot adequately provide" (207). In his later work, Tracy maintains the emphasis on narrative but with more attention to the interruption of counter-narratives, including the memory of suffering of poor and oppressed people. This elicits a dialectic between fragmentation and gathering such fragments.

44. See McFague, *The Body of God*, 105.

45. MacIntyre, *After Virtue*, 216.

46. An emphasis on the role of narrative (in Ethics) is found in essays scattered throughout Hauerwas's oeuvre. See especially Hauerwas and Jones, *Why Narrative?*

McClendon, and Nancey Murphy may be mentioned. Many, including the most recent work of Steven Bouma-Prediger,[47] have adopted such a virtue-based approach to ecotheology.

- A more radical strand of postmodern narrative theology holds that the symbol God is created through human storytelling as a form of mythic make-belief. There is no escape from language where meaning can be self-present; meaning is constantly being deferred. God is inside language as the play of signifiers upon the void.[48] One example of this strand, namely that of Don Cupitt, may suffice. Such a position may be born from consumerist ennui but clearly expresses the incredulity toward metanarratives from within Christian theology. The danger here is that God is then reduced to a (human) story, that God *is* a story, so that the adopted method in effect replaces the subject matter of theology.[49]
- There is a widespread recognition of the role of biography in religious reflection. The early roots may be found in Niebuhr's essay on "The Story of our Life"[50] and James McClendon's *Biography as Theology* (1974).[51] Since then it has been picked up by many others, including the feminist scholar Carol Christ, the retrieval of slave narratives by James Cone, the doyen of black theology,[52] liberation theologian Robert McAfee Brown,[53] and the political theology of Johann Baptist Metz.[54] They each claim in one way or another that the deeply held convictions that are at the heart of theological reflection depend on some form of narrative for their intelligibility and significance.[55] There is always a story behind such convictions. Such stories matter and become paradigmatic—as becomes evident in the retrieval of women's her-stories and the retrieval of the Exodus narratives in many liberation theologies. The life experiences of oppressed peoples offer a lens to understand the biblical stories and therefore a means of discerning God's redemptive work today.

---

47. See Bouma-Prediger, *Earthkeeping and Character*.

48. See the discussion by Loughlin in *Telling God's Story*, 10–17.

49. See Murphy, *God is Not a Story*, 1.

50. See again Niebuhr, *The Meaning of Revelation*, 23–48.

51. See also McClendon, "Narrative Ethics and Christian Ethics."

52. David Tracy sees in Cone's retrieval of narrative a fragmentation of the totalizing narratives of settler colonialism. See Tracy, "Form and Fragment," 74.

53. Brown eloquently overstates the theological significance of story-telling: "Our faith, after all, did not initially come to us as 'theology,' and particularly not as 'systematic theology.' It came as story [. . .] Out of such stories the systems begin to grow, with results we know only too well: stories about a garden become cosmological arguments; stories about Jesus become treatises on the two natures; stories about salvation become substitutionary doctrines of atonement; stories about the church become by-laws of male-dominated hierarchies. Who could care less?" Quoted in Comstock, "Two Types of Narrative Theology," 548.

54. See also Metz, *Faith in History and Society*, 205–18.

55. See Goldberg, *Theology and Narrative*, 12.

- A striking apology for narrative theology is found in the work of Johann Baptist Metz. For Metz, narrative, keeping alive the dangerous, subversive memory of the passion of Jesus Christ, is the medium through which salvation takes place. It elicits hope for those who are without hope, doomed to fail. Dangerous stories have the power to break through the spell of a modern, rationalist consciousness that tends to deny the history of suffering. Instead, every rebellion against suffering is incited by the subversive power of remembered suffering[56]—which necessarily has a narrative structure. Such a narrative has a performative and practical dimension that does not exclude the need for argumentation but indicates its relative value.[57]
- Metz's emphasis on theology as biography is affirmed in the political theology of Jürgen Moltmann. The Jewish-Christian tradition assumes an emphasis on time born from experiences of exile that yields a disequilibrium of a past remembered and a future anticipated—and not so much an equilibrium of mutually harmonizing forces or a modern linear notion of time. Theological reflection is therefore situated between remembrance and hope by discerning the current movements of God's Spirit in history.[58] Telling the story of *God's* history with us has to focus on who God is and what God has done, but cannot be separated from God's history *with us*.[59] To paraphrase Calvin's opening of the *Institutes*: we cannot tell God's story without telling our own story, but without telling God's story we cannot tell our own story.
- In *God as the Mystery of the World,* Eberhard Jüngel also partly draws on Metz to suggest that it is the humanity of God that requires a story to be told and to be passed on to others in the form of kerygma.[60] The material task of dogmatics is "to narrate the being of God as history and this history as the mystery of the world."[61] In *The Logic of Theology,* Dietrich Ritschl offers a distinctly different account. He recognizes the role of multiple stories and the need for "complete stories" or metastories (as in a biography) where individual stories are juxtaposed and linked with each other. Whereas individual stories can be repeated in full, a metastory can only be told in fragments.[62]
- A rather different version of the story is offered in Teilhard de Chardin's account of evolutionary history as a movement from cosmogenesis to

---

56. Metz, *Faith in History and Society*, 110.

57. See Metz, *Faith in History and Society*, 205-28.

58. See Moltmann, *Experiences in Theology*, 28-42.

59. Moltmann, *Experiences in Theology*, xix.

60. Jüngel, *God as Mystery*, 299-314.

61. Jüngel, *God as Mystery*, 390.

62. Ritschl, *Logic of Theology,* 20-21.

noogenesis to Christogenesis. Thomas Berry took such insights further in celebrating the scientific ability to reconstruct the story of the universe as a new revelatory event that will challenge our Ptolemaic understanding of the cosmos and the place of humanity in the cosmos.[63] In fact, for Berry, the expanding universe itself is the primary revelation of the divine.[64] There is, then, a clear ecological moral to the universe story. Their followers such as Brian Swimme and Mary Even Tucker took that further in their account of the "journey of the universe."[65] Here insights from postmodern science are employed to confirm but perhaps also to supersede the ecological wisdom embedded in Axial religions.[66]

- In the wake of Alfred North Whitehead's process ontology, many philosophers and theologians have been drawn to narrative accounts of this process, understood as cosmic and biological evolution. One may mention here the otherwise diverse contributions of scholars such as John Haught and Catherine Keller. Holmes Rolston, for example, speaks of three big bangs: the evolution of the cosmos, of life, and of consciousness.[67]

- Some Asian theologians make use of narratives (usually myths from traditional Asian cultures) to articulate their Asian theologies, but their interpretations of these narratives usually focus on political, social, and economic issues. In engaging with the universe story, most Asian Christian theologians would follow a cosmological or even metaphysical approach focusing on the concept of Chi – which is comparable to the concept of Pneuma and may be translated as energy or material force.[68]

- The role of storytelling is recognized probably in all forms of indigenous theology all around the world. This certainly applies to the main exponents of African Christian theology, especially African women's theology, including John Mbiti, John Pobee, and Mercy Amba Oduyoye. They draw on a rich array of traditional African narrative forms including legends, myths, fables, folk tales, wise sayings, idioms, proverbs, riddles, oral histories, and of course songs, in addressing the need for what is variously

---

63. See especially Berry, *The Dream of the Earth; The Christian Future*; Swimme and Berry, *The Universe Story*.

64. See Berry, *The Christian Future*, 25.

65. Swimme and Tucker, *Journey of the Universe*.

66. Swimme and Tucker, *Journey of the Universe*, 4–5. They regard the universe story as "a story of the story," speak of the need to "integrate the universe story into our diverse human cultures," recognize that the universe story is not intended to "override or ignore these other stories," but nevertheless believe that the universe story has "the power to awake us more deeply to who we are" and to "bring into focus the challenge of creating a shared future." See also Heather Eaton's essay in this volume.

67. See Rolston, *Three Big Bangs*.

68. Some examples may be found in Chung et al., *Asian Contextual Theology*.

called inculturation, indigenization, or contextualization.[69] Likewise, the role of personal biographies, especially the stories of women living under conditions of patriarchy, is widely recognized. Indeed, as Ellen Kuzwayo once said, "Africa is a place of story-telling."[70]

- In addition to all these strands of narrative theology, one also finds those who would suggest that narrating the story of God's work forms part of something else, often called a drama (a melodrama or theo-drama), perhaps an opera (as in *opera Trinitatis*) or a liturgy. This helps to stress the performative role of the storytelling embedded in such a drama or opera. Scholars who adopt such a notion of theology range from Roman Catholics such as Hans Urs von Balthasar and Celia Deane-Drummond to evangelicals such as Kevin Vanhoozer and Michael Horton.[71]

There is indeed a conflicting plurality of narrative theologies. One may well ask what, exactly, is narrative about narrative theology? Surely not the prescribed genre for doing theology! The human imagination seems capable of expressing narrative experiences in secondary, nonnarrative forms.[72] Perhaps then the narrative backbone in the biblical roots of the Christian faith that serves as the frame around which the canonical texts are constructed and that includes reflection on such narratives?[73] Although story provides the "raw material," the task is not merely to retell the story but also to make comparisons and critical judgments across different narratives so that theology has not merely a narrative but also a regulative function.[74] Or should the focus be on the narrative quality and structure of consciousness, of personal experience, of confession, and of personal or communal identity, given the temporal modalities of past (memory), present (sensory awareness, attention), and

---

69. Since references may be easily multiplied, for example to publications emerging from the Circle of Concerned African Women Theologians, it may suffice to mention the early account by Healy and Sybertz, *Towards an African Narrative Theology*.

70. This was said in the context of the proceeding of the South African Truth and Reconciliation Commission. To quote this in full: "If you cannot understand my story, you do not accept me as your neighbour. I am an African woman. I try to share my soul, my way of seeing things, the way I understand life. I hope you understand. Africa is a place of storytelling. We need more stories, never mind how painful the exercise might be. This is how we will learn to love one another. Stories help us to understand, to forgive and to see things through someone else's eyes." Quoted by Charles Villa-Vicencio, "Telling One Another Stories," 115.

71. See Von Balthasar, *Theodrama*; Deane-Drummond, "Hans Urs von Balthasar"; Vanhoozer, *The Drama of Doctrine*; Horton, *The Christian Faith*, 13–33; also Conradie, *The Earth in God's Economy*.

72. See Crites, "Narrative Quality," 308.

73. See Stroup, *Promise of Narrative Theology*, 86.

74. This is the argument of Ritschl and Jones in *"Story" as Rohmaterial der Theologie*. See also Ritschl, *The Logic of Theology*, 25.

future (anticipation)?[75] Or a set of deeply held convictions that are rooted in some narrative?[76] Or the personal biographies of those who engage in theological reflection? Or perhaps the narrative that is at stake here is indeed human history, even the history of the universe, so that the task of theology becomes that of understanding the meaning, the purpose, the direction of history (Pannenberg)? Or should one maybe focus on the only slightly less preposterous task, namely, to understand the significance of this moment in history and one's place in it? Does such a focus on narrative, following the modern turn to the subject (with Schleiermacher), not displace "God" as the subject matter of theology (reduced to "telling the story of God")? Is the story not God's story—the story of who God is and what this God is doing in history? But if the reference is to the Triune God, then it would still be a story told by Christians! Or should one reject such a narrative approach altogether, perhaps given the postmodern view that any such narrative structure is imposed on life's fragmented experiences in order to make sense of that or, if need be, enforce some sense upon it?

One may conclude from this list of narrative theologies that Christian theology cannot avoid a reference to narrative, especially paradigmatic narratives,[77] even meganarratives and metanarratives, if perhaps not grand narratives. This recognition should lead to some trepidation given the dangers associated with the theological legitimation of such grand narratives and the postmodern incredulity toward metanarratives. Nevertheless, a *tu quoque* argument may be appropriate here. This tendency to construct meganarratives is also found in postapocalyptic films, in science fiction, in ancient myths, in indigenous religions, and in children's stories alike. Indeed, as Larry Rasmussen observes, storytellers of all cultures seem to refuse to stop short of telling the cosmic story itself, however pretentious that may seem.[78] They seem unwilling to adhere to postmodern repudiations of the search for ultimate origins and destinies. With an astonishing sense of that which is ultimate, they tell stories, sometimes even quite brief stories, about the cosmos as a whole and about the origins and the destiny of the entire universe. Again, the question is not whether we tell such a story, but which stories we tell and how these stories are being told or messed up.

---

75. See especially Crites, "Narrative Quality." On "the story of our lives" as the necessary form to articulate personal identity, see also Stroup, *Promise of Narrative Theology*, 101.

76. See Goldberg, *Theology and Narrative*, 36, following insights from James McClendon.

77. See Goldberg, *Theology and Narrative*, 37. Goldberg explains the term in this way: "they claim not only to be true accounts of what has happened in the past, but they also claim the capacity to ring true to common aspects of human experience, thus being paradigms of our existence which can sustain and transform that existence now and in the future" (37–38).

78. Rasmussen, "Cosmology and Ethics," 176.

■ A Few Cairns for the Journey of Engaging in Narrative Theology

At the very least, one needs to heed a few cairns that may be derived from these strands of narrative theology for how the Christian story may be told amid the "Anthropocene".

First, there is a need to reflect on the narrative plot. The genre of narrative helps us to understand events by placing them within meaningful patterns. Any narrative is selective in that it identifies and groups together a sequence of actions and experiences while excluding others. It imposes a certain structure on events that can facilitate but also distort understanding. The plot configures a series of events into a particular narrated sequence that confers upon distinct images a certain coherence and meaning.[79] As Paul Ricoeur notes, the plot grasps together and integrates multiple and scattered events into one whole story.[80] He draws on Aristotle's notion of emplotment [*muthos*] as the mimesis of action but develops a dialectical understanding of three aspects of mimesis, namely, the familiar notion of the sequence of actions (prefiguration), poetic composition (grasping together) through a new configuration, and leading to a poetic refiguration of temporal experience through emplotment.[81] In this way, the wholeness and concordance introduced or imposed by *poiesis* allow for and encompass a tragic discordance.[82]

Second, unlike a novel and perhaps more like a sequel (or soap opera!), the Christian story is open-ended. We are telling the story as we are participating in it, with a sense of what has happened in the past, in order to make sense of the present and in anticipation of what the future may hold. Christians have no privileged revealed information about how the story will end, if it is even meaningful to speak about such an "end of the world." The whole story does not exist yet, and the plot is therefore necessarily provisional. This allows the faithful to write their own stories into this unfinished story.[83] The truthfulness of the story cannot be established yet, since the story remains incomplete and

---

79. See Stoker, *Is Geloof Redelik?*, 153.

80. Ricoeur, *Time and Narrative II*, x.

81. Ricoeur, *Time and Narrative II*, xi, 52-87.

82. See Ricoeur, *Time and Narrative II*, 38-39. Ricoeur notes that the notions of the beginning, middle, and end (or origin, life and destiny) are not taken from experience but are functions of narrated time. The whole (*holos*) is a necessary dimension of *poiesis* and is imposed on the selected data through a "synthesis of the heterogeneous" 66.

83. In the words of Edmund Arens, "Storytelling is fundamental for faith because it is only through this act of telling that our story can be connected with that of God and Jesus; because this story must be told; and so that it can be told as an unfinished story into which the faithful write their own stories and, in doing so, move the story forward. Thus at its basic level, the Christian faith has a deep narrative structure." Quoted and translated by Alister McGrath in *Narrative Apologetics*, 9-10.

subject to future verification.[84] The biblical canon ends on an unsettling apocalyptic cry: "Come Lord Jesus, come!"

Third, any story is socially constructed, situated, historically conditioned, and therefore relative.[85] We can only tell the larger Christian story in fragments, from a local and parochial perspective.[86] As creatures, we have to live with and from such fragments without some nostalgia for the lost whole. For David Tracy, a fragment is not a broken-off bit of a lost but nostalgically longed for the whole but an event that shatters any totality system, any false whole with imperialist ambitions.[87] There is always a temptation to tell the story with a clearer apprehension of the plot than what the available evidence warrants.[88] This is in any case not a story that can be told in one session but only over many Arabian nights and then with the awareness that a focus on any one episode may distort the others. This kind of story includes nothing less than the very beginning and the very end, but reconstructions of the shape of the p(l)ot on the basis of some collected fragments have to remain provisional and local as well. While the subject matter of the story may be all-encompassing and ultimate, the language is always particular, historically and socially situated.[89] Since storytellers do not know how the story will end, their stories remain finite, provisional, subject to correction. There is greater continuity and flow in a storyline than what may be warranted. The need for proleptic anticipation of the eschaton implies an apophatic (and doxological) dimension in any theological reflection on the story. That our knowledge of the infinite is necessarily finite is an assumption of all God-talk and not merely the product of the hermeneutic, linguistic, social, gendered, and spatial "turns."[90]

Fourth, in order to avoid a rudderless relativism where any story would do and each justifies itself (including stories legitimizing oppression), it is

---

84. This is a core theme in Wolfhart Pannenberg's theology. See his *Systematic Theology 1*, 257.

85. Richard Niebuhr already recognized the situatedness of any "point of view" in *The Meaning of Revelation*, 1-22.

86. See the reflections by David Tracy on classic "fragmenting forms" such as apocalyptic theology and apophatic theology and the postmodern retrieval of such fragmenting forms in order to resist modernist attempts at totalizing systems or closure. He contrasts the category of "fragment" with that of "symbol" where the hope is maintained to grasp something of the whole. By contrast, fragments fragment, shatter all totalities and oppressive closed systems, opening them for difference and otherness, to "liminal Infinity," to being bearers of infinity. See Tracy, "Form and Fragment" and, more recently, his *Fragments*, also Conradie, "David Tracy on Fragments."

87. See Tracy, *Fragments*, 1, 5, 21.

88. Lash, "Ideology, Metaphor, and Analogy," 121.

89. See Niebuhr, *The Meaning of Revelation*, 45: "The standpoint of the Christian community is limited, being in history, faith and sin. But what is seen from this standpoint is unlimited."

90. See Pannenberg, *Systematic Theology 1*, 55. See also Tracy, *Fragments*, 209: "Theology is a finite interpretation of God the Incomprehensible Infinite One through a quantitative infinite number of interpretations and interpreters."

necessary to allow for debate across storylines.[91] One important step is to acknowledge different types of narratives, including fables, myths, histories, biographies, and autobiographies, each possibly embodying a specific kind of truth.[92] The particular form of narrative is hermeneutically dependent upon what is narrated.[93] If the question regarding which story is being told cannot be separated from whose story that is, there is a need to critique dominant narratives and to invite subaltern narratives.

The formation of the biblical canon suggests that it is important to see stories as intertwined with each other so that one story corrects another, merely by being juxtaposed. This implies a need for gathering together some of the available fragments. The story may be highly particular in origin but has to be rendered public (now with a planetary, if not "universal" scope). This task has theological implications where a distinction between the local situatedness of a story and its encompassing subject matter has to be recognized. The particularity of the incarnation (in Jesus of Nazareth) does not detract from it but is the very condition for its universal significance (as the Christ).[94] Christian theology is a language dealing with nothing less than God.[95] The question that therefore arises is whether the fragments belong to the same clay pot? Are the stories that are gathered together about one and the same God or about different gods altogether or no god whatsoever? This task can only be approached upon the shattering of the triumphant totality systems imposed by Christendom and modernism alike, by recognizing in God language an Other that cannot be assimilated, domesticated, reduced to more of the same.[96] This has important implications for inter-religious dialogue given the many attempts to name the infinite (to use one category), including the too self-assured assumption that there is indeed some communality between religious traditions.

Fifth, it is perhaps not all that important where one begins the story itself. Good storytellers know that one may begin with the climax, with this present moment, with the expected end, and even with the beginning! It is not even

---

91. This is the main agenda of Michael Goldberg's *Theology and Narrative.* On the need for justifying narrative truth claims, see also Comstock, "Two Types of Narrative Theology."

92. As Goldberg observes, this avoids the danger of fundamentalists treating all biblical narratives as histories and secularists treating all of them as myths. See *Theology and Narrative*, 204.

93. Jüngel, *God as Mystery*, 313.

94. See Tracy, *Fragments*, 14.

95. Niebuhr recognized the danger, from Schleiermacher onwards, that the "feeling of absolute dependence" becomes the subject matter of theology (or "faithology"), thus "directing the attention of faith toward itself rather than to God." He adds that this anthropocentric shift is based upon confidence in "man's" superiority over nature. See *The Meaning of Revelation*, 14, 16.

96. See Tracy, *Fragments*, 20.

"the end of the world" if the story is messed up since that is almost inevitable in a fallen world. It is also not an option not to tell some or other story. The question is not whether we tell a story but which one. What is more important is that the distorted stories be put right, that is, that they become justified and sanctified.[97]

Finally, telling the story is a challenge that requires something like "bold humility,"[98] a sense of being sojourners, companions, witnesses, or in Martin Luther's terminology, beggars who have found some bread and are willing to share that. This challenge requires taking a deep breath . . . ! Christians may ultimately ascribe such fresh air to the Breath of Life. They have to live from the conviction that God's story ultimately can only be told by Godself. Knowledge of God is inconceivable unless it is enabled by God. Christians do not possess the story as if it is theirs to tell. At best, they are possessed not by the story but by belonging to that story's God. This insight is crucial for protecting storytellers from the totalizing and oppressive strategies that are evident in so many cosmological narratives. Christians may be witnesses to the One who is the Truth, the Life and the Way, but they do not possess the truth and cannot serve as self-appointed judges of the truth (e.g., by adding that Jesus is indeed "the *only* way"). Christians are witnesses, not bulldozers! For Christians witnessing to the cross of Jesus Christ—claimed to be the hinge upon which history turns—this is indeed quite a *crucial* insight.

■ On Telling the Christian Story in the "Anthropocene"

One may therefore say that Christians tell a story of God's economy, that is, the narrative of God's work in the world. To remember what God has done in the past is to bring its redemptive power to bear on the present situation.[99] This story can be told in rather different ways. It can be messed up in even more ways. In the context of the "Anthropocene," it would amount to a failure of nerve not to address the underlying question that those listening to Christian accounts of such a narrative will have: What is God actually doing?[100] What is this God up to, for example, given what we already know about climate change? Where can signs of God's presence and creative engagement with

---

97. See Stroup, *Promise of Narrative Theology*, 227.

98. This notion of "bold humility" is derived from the missiology of David Bosch, from whose work this paragraph draws broadly speaking.

99. See Stroup, *Promise of Narrative Theology*, 167, 258.

100. The next three paragraphs again draw on Conradie, *Secular Discourse on Sin*. The question how we could know what God is up to will be explored in more depth in the second volume of the series on *An Earthed Faith*.

the world be found (*vestigia Dei*)?[101] How should we understand divine providence and governance in history (*gubernatio*)? Which counter-movements of the Spirit can be discerned?[102] How can theology trace God's own thoughts?[103] There may be one thing that is worse than telling the story, given such dangers, and that is failing to dare to even begin telling the story.

How, then, should the story of what God is doing be told? Where is God at work and at play in this world? In the "Anthropocene" with its uncertainties over what the future may hold, this question is one filled with anxiety—if the extremes of fatalism and fanaticism can be avoided. But can the plotline of creation, sin, reconciliation, and consummation still be maintained?[104] How dare one speak of any "promised land" or final consummation amid the "great acceleration"? Is a Jewish-Christian philosophy of history and its secularized form in the nineteenth-century notion of progress not precisely the root of the problem? Should one then instead follow Dante's *Divine Comedy* and abandon hope? For Christians, this is only an option if we begin to believe that God has indeed abandoned us (and the covenant with Noah) and is making other ominous long-term plans, or if we concur that the divine parent has actually passed away, perhaps for our sake, that our Father is dead, that is, "in heaven" only. Indeed, is God doing anything at all? Is the absence of evidence not evidence of absence? Do we have to admit, if we are honest, that we no longer expect anything at all?[105] How should divine action in the world be understood?[106] Is such a claim at all plausible? But even if "God" is nothing more than an imaginative human construct, an idea (whether good or bad or ugly), a vision for the future, a way of talking about human agendas, then this question still has to be addressed: How should we understand this moment in history, the advent of the Age of the "Anthropocene?"

Christians would want to be alert to what South African theologians typically speak of as a kairos moment, a moment of truth, a moment when the gospel is at stake, when decisions about life and death, salvation or destruction,

---

101. On the hermeneutics of nature, see Moltmann, *Sun of Righteousness*, 189–208.

102. See Conradie, "What is God Really Up to?"

103. This is one way of construing theos-logos. See Bavinck, *Reformed Dogmatics* 1, 44.

104. This is the traditional storyline, also evident in the biblical canon. It is, for example, adopted by Gabriel Fackre in his *The Christian Story* (1984). However, such a step-wise storyline (for Fackre creation-fall-covenant-salvation-consummation) is widely disputed given the terms employed, their proper sequence, and their plausibility. Some opt to start in the middle (Christ), others at the end, some with current ecclesial praxis, or forms of religious experience, others with the ecclesial tradition (Nicaea). Further options may be multiplied.

105. Teilhard, *The Divine Milieu*, 152.

106. See the twenty-year research project initiated by the Center for Theology and the Natural Sciences, culminating in *Scientific Perspectives on Divine Action* (2008). This question will be addressed especially in volumes 3, 4, and 5 of the envisaged series.

orthodoxy or heresy, are at stake.[107] The prophetic urge is not to predict the end times, but to speak truth to power in present, penultimate times, to recover the liberating, redeeming message of truth, reconciliation, justice, and peace. However, views on God's involvement in history have typically been extremely dangerous, as is well recognized by the South African theologian Jaap Durand in an essay on "the finger of God" in history, with reference to apartheid theology.[108] Often, narrow group interests are expressed in answering this question, thus serving as a theological legitimation of such interests. Moreover, alternative responses can be as distortive as the ones they replace. If there is a need for narrative theology, it may well be to resist dangerously distorted versions of the story. As David Tracy observes, there is a real danger that modern historical consciousness is driven by an unconscious desire to replace the disruptive and disturbing biblical narratives of a God who acts in history with a progressive, evolutionary narrative from the perspective of the victors, leaving little room for the victims of such history.[109]

How, then could one proceed to tell the Christian story?

■ Where Does One Begin to Reconstruct the Story?

What to say first is the subject matter of any traditional prolegomena to a dogmatics. Consider the following options and issues where much is at stake:

- Even if Scripture, tradition, reason, and experience (as consciousness, conscience, or feeling) are all recognized as sources for doing theology (the Methodist quadrilateral), what relative weight is assigned to each? Can confessional differences in this regard—arguably between Protestantism, Catholicism, liberalism, and pietism or Pentecostalism—be overcome?
- What role does Scripture play in theological reflection, given ongoing debates on its authority, necessity, sufficiency, and clarity, if not its "infallibility" or "inerrancy"? What about the inspiration of Scripture and the conviction that it *is*, or better at times *becomes* the Word of God, speaking anew in changing circumstances?
- Does one take as a point of departure pre-Israelite religions, Israel's history, the historical Jesus, Pentecost, the canonized biblical witnesses, Nicaea, or contemporary religious experience? Each of these has its supporters!
- Does one first need to explain categories such as faith, worldviews, spirituality, the holy, or religion and then proceed to situate Christianity in that context? How, for example, is the Christian faith related to faith, belief,

---

107. On the "Anthropocene" as *Chronos* and as *Kairos* see Northcott, "Eschatology in the Anthropocene."

108. See Durand, "God in History."

109. Tracy, *On Naming the Present*, 50–51.

and trust (also convictions and commitments) among humans in general? Is this rooted more deeply in animal trust (or perhaps distrust) between species?
- Since the biblical witnesses are professed to be about God's revelation in Israel, in Jesus Christ and the early church, is it not necessary to first offer an exposition of the concept of revelation?
- Does one need to focus on faith in a divine being and then proceed to explain the category of God in order to situate the particular Christian notion of the Triune God against that background? Or should one start, like Karl Barth does, with an exposition of the doctrine of the Trinity in order to avoid the content of the Christian faith being determined by foreign concepts? Such foreign concepts may help to explain this faith but more often than not turn this faith into something that it is not. But where do words such as revelation, the divine, God, or faith come from in the first place?
- Does one privilege the so-called cultural despizers of religion (Schleiermacher) or does one assign an "epistemological privilege" to the poor and oppressed because God is situated among them (liberation theology)? Whose story is it anyway given the history of imperialism and colonialism legitimized by Christianity?
- Does one start with the questions people have about their faith (to avoid answering questions that arguably no one raises) or with an exposition of that faith (to recognize that people do not always know what questions they have)?
- Does one privilege the lived but often pre-critical faith of the laity or the abstract reflections of learned theologians? How, then, does one overcome the traps of civil religion?
- Does one first need to engage in social analysis in order to determine human needs, or does the Christian faith help people to understand what their deepest needs are? Is the risk of irrelevance worse than the risk of losing authenticity (adapting the message to fit the prevailing mood)?
- Finally, in reconstructing the story the question remains what the place of such a story may be in understanding the Christian faith. If Christianity is allegedly the most materialist of world religions, how is word (therefore consciousness, ideas, noetic content, stories, symbols) related to that which is material, bodily, and earthly (and therefore sacramental)? How is the role of Scripture to be understood in the *media salutis*? Does salvation come via the ear only?[110] Or is salvation induced by changing material (economic) contexts or by infusing grace like a medicine? In other words, what are the limitations of the category of narrative?

---

110. See Conradie, "Is the Ear More Spiritual than the Eye?"

These issues cannot be explored here in any detail and are therefore merely noted. Some of these questions will also feed into subsequent volumes of the series on *An Earthed Faith* (e.g., on method), but need to be recognized here as well. Two further cairns may suffice:

One may again suggest that it does not matter all that much where one begins to reconstruct the Christian story. It is not as if a sound point of departure will provide a guarantee against subsequent distortions. It is far more important to keep a rigorous and critical interplay going between these aspects. Like a juggler, it does not matter which cone is tossed up first; the task is to keep juggling the cones. To focus on one will lead to dropping the others.

If so, one perhaps simply needs to take a deep breath for the story to begin. It also situates theological work Pneumatologically. This allows for proleptic anticipation. This is appropriate because the story may blow you away. This is an awe-inspiring story, partly because it is so awesome but also because many aspects are so awful. Either way, it is necessary to take a deep breath. The word "breath" in the title of this volume suggests the Spirit of God as a source of inspiration for the story, already present in any further deliberations. It hints at an air of anticipation, indicated by the three dots in the title.

■ A Core Question

As indicated above, an emphasis on narrative cannot suffice. There is a need to relate one story to another in order to test its truthfulness. The core question that will be explored in this volume does exactly that: *How does the story (as told by Christians) of who the Triune God is and what this God does relate to the story of life on Earth?* Is the Christian story part of the earth's story or is the earth's story part of God's story, from creation to consummation? This raises many classic theological questions on the relatedness of religion and theology, the place of theology in multidisciplinary collaboration, the notion of revelation, the possibility of knowledge of God, faith and reason, the secular and the sacred, hermeneutics, the difference between natural theology and a theology of nature, the role of worldviews,[111] and so forth. The various essays included in this volume will touch on these themes but they will not be explored systematically.

One may observe that while the underlying narrative structure of the Christian faith has at times been underplayed, a new awareness of the dynamic, ever-changing history of the universe is emerging from contemporary science. The realization that nature (and not only humanity) is inherently historical is

---

111. For a discussion of the reigning confusion in this regard, see Conradie, "Views on Worldviews."

perhaps *the* most significant discovery of modern science.[112] For Thomas Berry, the:

> [*E*]ntire scientific venture of the past few centuries culminates in a capacity to tell this story with amazing insight into the sequence of events and their interdependence from the beginning until the present.[113]

Brian Swimme states that the universe, at its most basic level, is not so much a matter or energy but a *story*. The laws that govern the universe are not immutable but are the result of developments in time.[114] Nature itself has the character of a narrative and scientists have, despite some initial resistance, become storytellers.[115] This signals a shift from a metaphysics of substance to recognize the significance of the event—in mathematics, cosmology, philosophy, and theology alike. Reality is best described by verbs, not nouns.[116] Given a historical understanding of physics, metaphysics may now be named more appropriately as metahistory.[117]

The reconstruction of this story into an integrated whole is a relatively recent scientific achievement in which the insights emerging from astrophysical, geological, and biological sciences have been weaved together with those of paleoanthropology, the social sciences, and history. It is crucial to recognize that the four phases—the galactic story, the Earth story, the story of life, and the human story—are all one single story. The story can be told in diverse ways but the continuity between the nonhuman and the emergence of the human is indispensable.[118] As Thomas Berry insists, "There is ultimately only one story, the Great Story."[119] At the same time, it is necessary to add that any such integration readily becomes contested as any storyline reflects power relations.

With the advent of the "Anthropocene," this has become crucial because of the diverging ways in which the story is told, especially the story of what went wrong, when, and where. It is therefore not surprising that the category of narrative is employed in discussions of the "Anthropocene,"

The story of the universe is clearly a story of many stories. There are multiple layers of the story and also conflicting versions of the story. The

---

112. For this insight, see Von Weizsäcker, *Geschichte der Natur.*

113. See Berry, *The Christian Future*, 29.

114. Swimme, "Cosmic Creation Story," 50.

115. See Haught, *The Promise of Nature*, 62, 122.

116. See Tracy, *Fragments*, 2.

117. See Tracy, *Fragments*, 114.

118. See Berry, *The Christian Future*, 41.

119. See Berry, *The Christian Future*, 53.

question addressed in this volume focuses on two encompassing versions of the story, namely, the "universe story" and the Christian story (more specifically: God's story, not the story of Christianity). The "universe story" here refers to many contemporary attempts to integrate scientific insights within a narrative structure. The "Christian story" refers to the stories that Christians tell about who the Triune God is (the immanent Trinity) and what this God does (the economic Trinity). Of course, these are only two versions of such an encompassing meganarrative, alongside many others in other academic disciplines, in forms of cultural expression and in various religious traditions alike. Again, the various contributions to this volume will recognize that these two stories (which will be the focus of this volume) cannot be isolated from such other stories.

■ A Fivefold Typology

How, then, is the universe story related to the Christian story? The authors contributing to this volume have been asked to address this question constructively, from within their own geographical context, social location, and confessional tradition. These will not be summarized here as each author may speak for himself or herself. A provisional typology may nevertheless be helpful.

In a recent paper prepared for the eighteenth European Conference on "Science and Theology on Creative Pluralism? Images and Models in Science and Religion," to be held in Madrid, from April 29 to May 02, 2020 (but postponed due to the COVID-19 pandemic), Ernst Conradie offered a typology of the available logical options to address this question.

The typology builds on two famous typologies, namely, the one developed by H. Richard Niebuhr in *Christ and Culture* and the other developed by Ian Barbour in *Religion and Science*.[120] It may be noted again that Niebuhr is the intellectual father of at least one school of narrative theology, while, remarkably, Barbour was a student of Niebuhr at Yale Divinity School in the early 1950s. Any typology is shaped by the terms adopted so that replacing the categories adopted by Niebuhr and Barbour by "universe story" and "Christian story" requires significant adaptations.

Here is the abbreviated typology.

---

120. See Niebuhr, *Christ and Culture*; Barbour, *Religion and Science*, 77–136. As Craig Carter argues, Niebuhr's typology assumes Christendom, while Barbour's assumes the marginalization of religion by a culture epitomized by science. See Carter, *Rethinking Christ and Culture*. Moreover, Niebuhr employed "culture" as a shorthand for "civilization" (the "artificial secondary environment imposed by humans on nature"—32) in order to address the "enduring problem" of the rejection of Christ in the name of civilization. This raises further questions on contested notions of "civilization" given inter-religious dialogue and postcolonial and decolonial critiques of "Empire."

The Christian Story Encompasses the Universe Story

Most Christian theologians traditionally assumed that the story of life on earth forms part of the Christian story of God's work from creation to consummation. How the universe came to be, its subsequent history, and how it may come to an end are situated within a larger framework given the faith in God as the Triune Creator.[121] The history of the universe is nothing but God's story. The task is not to interpret the Christian story in terms of the universe story but to interpret the universe story in terms of the Christian story. Accordingly, the disastrous error of modern liberal theology has been to fit God's story into whatever has been the prevailing story of the world (evolution, progress, Marxist dialectics, consumer capitalism), thereby exchanging one story for another.[122] However, wherever such a priority for the Christian story is affirmed, there is a sectarian temptation to tell the Christian story in ecclesial communities, in isolation from the universe story (see the model of separation discussed further), avoiding the critique of religion and more specifically an ecological critique of Christianity. Then, the world of faith becomes something separate from the world of everyday experience (see type 3).

The Universe Story Encompasses the Christian Story

As a contrast, many contemporary scholars assume that the story of Christianity (which includes Christian versions of the story) forms part of the history of humanity and that this is embedded in evolutionary history. In other words, Christianity is one religion alongside others, religion is an aspect of culture, and culture pertains to the history of one species, alongside many others in the evolution of life on earth.[123] This is perhaps the default position in secular circles but also in liberal forms of Christianity.[124] This allows for a critique of culture but more often than not the Christian story is domesticated to legitimize the prevailing contemporary culture, illustrated by Christian legitimations of Nazism, other nationalisms, and consumerism.

---

121. Hans Frei comments on the "great reversal" that has taken place in modern theology: "interpretation was a matter of fitting the biblical story into another world with another story rather than incorporating that world into the biblical story." See Frei, *Eclipse*, 130.

122. See Loughlin, *Telling God's Story*, 34.

123. For one example of such an approach see Matthews, Tucker and Hefner, *When Worlds Converge*.

124. Thomas Berry captures this view: "For the first time we can tell the universe, the Earth story, the human story, the religion story, the Christian story and the Church story as a single comprehensive narrative." Elsewhere he sees the universe story as the fulfillment of the biblical narrative, given a basic compatibility between them. See Berry, *The Christian Future*, 25, 32.

The Christian Story and the Universe Story Remain Apart from Each Other

This option is widely recognized in typologies on science and religion. One may observe that this is an understandable theological response to the default secular position sketched earlier where the universe story encompasses the Christian story. It would be maintained by scientists who are Christians and find it unnecessary to reconcile their scientific work with their Christian beliefs in the same way that one could distinguish between what is public and what is private. This position is also adopted by secular scientists who wish to allow a separate domain for religious beliefs (e.g., Stephen Jay Gould's notion of non-overlapping *magisteria*). A variation of this model allows for collaboration between science and the humanities to address complex social problems, for a moral vision, and for sustainable forms of praxis. To enable such "consilience" (E.O. Wilson), the ultimate truth claims embedded in the Christian story have to be bracketed, typically leading to reductionist notions of religion and reverting to the previous type. Like relativism, separation is an option that may be entertained but not one that can be sustained since this continues to raise questions about the relation between these stories.[125]

The Universe Story May be Interpreted through the Christian Story

This approach may be regarded as a variation of the first approach but one that recognizes the need for a longer route to return to the conviction that the Christian story encompasses the universe story. It recognizes the fact that the Christian story (and the creeds) are products of a long process (coming toward the truth) and that retelling the story requires a similar process (not merely defending already established truths). While a position of faith is therefore maintained, the methodology adopted is inductive (drawing from experience) more than deductive (making logical deductions from the creeds). The data derived from the various sciences have to be taken seriously. With scientists and analysts, this approach recognizes the fact that nature/the world around us is open to interpretation. Against many Christian apologists, it does not seek support for Christian truth claims in nature (e.g., proofs of God's existence) or human history. Instead, it addresses, together with other disciplines, the penultimate questions that emerge in trying to make sense of the world around us with conceptual tools derived from the Christian tradition—and in the process test the adequacy of such tools. The Christian story with its Trinitarian logic thus offers a framework through which one can

---

125. Likewise, Niebuhr's "Christ against culture" type (and Barbour's "conflict" type) is hard to sustain since that depends on which forms of culture are focused upon. Bavinck may be correct that the assertion that modern culture is in conflict with Christianity is a meaningless phrase. See *The Philosophy of Revelation*, 253.

help to make sense of other stories, including the universe story.[126] Whether it does help to make such sense cannot be taken for granted but has to be demonstrated with reference to the available data and in conversation with other disciplines on an ongoing basis.[127] Put cryptically in terms of the category of worldviews, the emphasis here is not on *viewing* the world (looking at the viewing) but on viewing the *world*—as it is, could be, and should be. It seeks to see the world through God's eyes, with compassion and therefore justice.[128]

The Christian Story May Transform the Universe Story

The word "transform" suggests some continuity with the fifth type in Niebuhr analysis on "Christ and culture." One may say that this type also constitutes a return to the agenda of the first type but only after the long route as circumscribed by the fourth type has been followed. As a result, there is no longer an attempt to defend Christian truth claims in conversation with contemporary science or to set parameters for scientific endeavors. The task is also not merely the revisionist one of reinterpreting the content and significance of the Christian faith in the light of the results of contemporary science (which may be prone toward the second type). There is indeed room for a dual critique, namely, a Christian critique of the scientific enterprise (if not the actual results) and a self-critique of the plausibility of particular interpretations of aspects of the Christian story. However, the task here is not only of a critical nature, but also of a constructive nature.

If so, the task is to tell the Christian story anew (having gathered insights from contemporary science and other disciplines) and then in such a way that this will ultimately lead to a transformation of the direction in which the universe story, especially the story of life on earth, is heading toward. One may say, following Marx, that the task is not only to interpret the universe story but also the bolder one of changing it. Or in the words of Donna Haraway, "we must change the story; the story must change" (must induce change).[129] The term "transform" by itself only indicates a change in form but does not indicate the direction of such change. Transformation can also be destructive

---

126. See McGrath, *Narrative Apologetics*, 104.

127. For one early example, see Bavinck, *Philosophy of Revelation*, engaging in erudite discussions on the limits of philosophy, natural science, history, and religious studies to make sense of the data explored in these disciplines. If his conclusions and conversation partners are now outdated, the scope of his vision is to be lauded.

128. In *The Earth in God's Economy*, (51–59); Ernst Conradie explained this in terms an emerging liturgical vision. This builds on aphorisms attributed to Desmond Tutu, namely, to see the plight of a prostitute but to see her as a sister, the beggar as a brother, and the rapist as an uncle.

129. Haraway, *Staying with the Trouble*, 40.

so that such direction, the actual content of the storyline, remains crucial. There is always the possibility that the attempt to transform culture can revert into being transformed by culture, not least in a consumer society. This has been a constant challenge for the Christian tradition—the Hellenization of Christianity or the Christianization of Hellenism(?)[130]—that has also played itself out in modernity and again in the geographic spread of Christianity in the Americas, Africa, Asia, and Oceania.

■ To Conclude

As indicated above, the ten essays included in this volume will each address the core question, namely, how the story told by Christians as to who the Triune God is and what this God does, is related to scientific reconstructions of the universe story. Each contributor will address that from within a particular geographical region, social location, theological school, and confessional tradition. Such a variety of contexts allows for a critical engagement with the core question. This is to be welcomed. Each contribution will speak for itself and cannot be constrained in any summary form. Since the diversity embedded in the volume has multiple dimensions, there is no obvious logic as to how the essays are to be ordered. It was therefore decided to simply include them in alphabetical order. They are juxtaposed to allow for creative tensions that will stimulate further reflection.

A volume such as this can set an agenda and can channel some energies but cannot be conclusive. The story of who God is and what God is doing needs to continue. As editors, we hope that this volume will stimulate further reflection, in widening circles, in Christian ecotheology, in constructive discourse on the content and significance of the Christian faith, in other theological subdisciplines, in multireligious dialogue, and for discerning the signs of the time in discourse on what is named and contested as the "Anthropocene."

■ Bibliography

Barbour, Ian G. *Religion and Science: Historical and Contemporary Issues.* San Francisco: Harper & Row, 1997.

Bavinck, Herman. *The Philosophy of Revelation.* London: Longmans, Green & Co., 1909.

———. *Reformed Dogmatics, Volume 1: Prolegomena.* Grand Rapids: Baker Academic, 2003.

Berry, Thomas. *Befriending the Earth: A Theology of Reconciliation between Humans and the Earth.* Mystic: Twentythird, 1991.

———. *The Christian Future and the Fate of the Earth*, edited by Mary Evelyn Tucker and John Grim. Maryknoll: Orbis, 2009.

———. *The Dream of the Earth.* San Francisco: Sierra Club, 1988.

---

130. See Tracy, *Fragments*, 106.

Bonneuil, Christophe and Jean-Baptiste Fressoz. *The Shock of the Anthropocene: The Earth, History and Us.* London: Verso, 2017.

Bonneuil, Christophe. "The Geological Turn: Narratives of the Anthropocene." In *The Anthropocene and the Global Environmental Crisis*, edited by Clive Hamilton, Christophe Bonneuil and François Gemene, 17–31. London and New York: Routledge, 2015.

Bouma-Prediger, Steven. *Earthkeeping and Character: Exploring a Christian Ecological Virtue Ethic.* Grand Rapids: Baker Academic, 2020.

Carter, Craig. *Rethinking Christ and Culture: A Post-Christendom Perspective.* Grand Rapids: Brazos, 2006.

Chakrabarty, Dipesh. "The Climate of History: Four Theses". *Critical Inquiry* 35:2 (2009), 197–222. https://doi.org/10.1086/596640

Chung, Paul S., et al., eds. *Asian Contextual Theology for the Third Millennium.* Eugene: Pickwick, 2007.

Comstock, Gary. "Two Types of Narrative Theology." *Journal of the American Academy of Religion* 55:4 (1987), 687–717. https://doi.org/10.1093/jaarel/LV.4.687

Conradie, Ernst M. "Views on Worldviews: An Overview of the Use of the Term Worldview in Selected Theological Discourses." *Scriptura* 113 (2014), 1–12. https://doi.org/10.7833/113-0-918

———. *The Earth in God's Economy: Creation, Salvation and Consummation in Ecological Perspective.* Berlin: LIT, 2015.

———. "Is the Ear More Spiritual Than the Eye? Theological Reflection on the Human Senses." In *Issues in Science and Theology: Do Emotions Shape the World?*, edited by Dirk Evers, et al., 177–88. Heidelberg: Springer, 2016.

———. "David Tracy on Fragments, Fragmentation and Frag-events." *Stellenbosch Theological Journal* 7:1 (2021), 1–9. https://doi.org/10.17570/stj.2021.v7n1.a1

———. *Secular Discourse on Sin in the Anthropocene: What's Wrong with the World?* Lanham: Lexington, 2020.

———. "What is God really up to in a Time like this? Discerning the Spirit's Movements as Core Task of Christian Eco-Theology." In *Kairos for Creation: Confessing Hope for the Earth*, edited by Lukas Andrianos et al., 31–44. Solingen: Foedus, 2019.

Crites, Steven. "The Narrative Quality of Experience." *Journal of the American Academy of Religion* 39:3 (1973), 291–311. https://doi.org/10.1093/jaarel/XXXIX.3.291

Deane-Drummond, Celia. "Hans Urs von Balthasar (1905–1988)—A Theo-Drama." In *Creation and Salvation, Volume 2: A Companion on Recent Theological Movements*, edited by Ernst M. Conradie, 71–76. Berlin: LIT, 2012.

Durand, Jaap. "God in History: An Unresolved Problem." In *The Meaning of History*, edited by Adrio König and Marie Henri Keane, 171–8. Pretoria: Unisa, 1980.

Fackre, Gabriel. *The Christian Story: A Narrative Interpretation of Basic Christian Doctrine.* Grand Rapids: Eerdmans.

Frei, Hans. *The Eclipse of Biblical Narrative.* New Haven: Yale University Press, 1974.

Fukuyama, Francis. "The End of History?" *The National Interest* 16 (1989), 3–18.

Goldberg, Michael. *Theology and Narrative: A Critical Introduction.* Eugene: Wipf & Stock, 2001.

Hamilton, Clive. *Defiant Earth: The Fate of Humans in the Anthropocene.* Cambridge: Polity, 2017.

Haraway, Donna. *Staying with the Trouble: Making Kin in the Chthulucene.* Durham: Duke University Press, 2016.

Hauerwas, Stanley and L. Gregory Jones, eds. *Why Narrative? Readings in Narrative Theology.* Eugene: Wipf & Stock, 1997.

Haught, John F. *The Promise of Nature: Ecology and Cosmic Purpose.* Mahwah: Paulist, 1993.

Healy, Joseph and Donald Sybertz. *Towards an African Narrative Theology.* Maryknoll: Orbis, 1996.

Horton, Michael. *The Christian Faith: A Systematic Theology for Pilgrims on the Way.* Grand Rapids: Zondervan, 2011.

Jenson, Robert W. *Systematic Theology Volume 1: The Triune God*. Oxford: Oxford University Press, 1997.

Jüngel, Eberhard. *The Doctrine of the Trinity: God's Being is in Becoming*. Translated by Horton Harris. Edinburgh: Scottish Academic Press, 1976.

——. *God as the Mystery of the World.* London: Bloomsbury, 2014.

Kearney, Richard. *Poetics of Imagining: From Husserl to Lyotard*. London: Harper Collins Academic, 1991.

Lai, Pan-Chiu. "Inter-religious Dialogue on Environmental Ethics." *Studies in Interreligious Dialogue* 21:1 (2011), 5–19.

Lash, Nicholas. "Ideology, Metaphor and Analogy." In *Why Narrative? Readings in Narrative Theology*, edited by Stanley Hauerwas and L. Gregory Jones, 113–37. Eugene: Wipf & Stock, 1997.

——. *Holiness, Speech, and Silence: Reflections on the Question of God*. Aldershot: Ashgate, 2004.

Latour, Bruno. *Facing Gaia: Eight Lectures on the New Climate Regime.* Cambridge: Polity, 2017.

Lewis, Simon L. and Mark A. Maslin. *The Human Planet: How We Created the Anthropocene.* London: Penguin, 2018.

Lindbeck, George A. *The Nature of Doctrine: Religion and Theology in a Postliberal Age*, Philadelphia: Westminster, 1984.

——. "Scripture, Consensus and Community." In *Biblical Interpretation in a Crisis,* edited by Richard J. Neuhaus, 74–101. Grand Rapids: Eerdmans, 1989.

Loughlin, Gerard. *Telling God's Story: Bible, Church and Narrative Theology.* Cambridge: Cambridge University Press, 1999.

Lyotard, Jean-François. "The Postmodern Condition". In *After Philosophy: End or Transformation?*, edited by Kenneth Baynes, James Bohman and Thomas McCarthy, 67–94. Cambridge: MIT, 1987.

MacIntyre, Alasdair. *After Virtue: A Study in Moral Theory.* 2nd ed. Notre Dame: University of Notre Dame Press, 1984.

Malm, Andreas and Alf Hornborg. "The Geology of Mankind? A Critique of the Anthropocene Narrative." *The Anthropocene Review* 1:1 (2014), 62–69. https://doi.org/10.1177/2053019613516291

Matthews, Clifford N., Mary Evelyn Tucker, and Philip Hefner, eds. *When Worlds Converge: What Science and Religion Tell Us about the Story of the Universe and Our Place in it.* Chicago & La Salle: Open Court, 2002.

Metz, Johann Baptist, *Faith in History and Society: Toward a Practical Fundamental Theology.* London: Burns & Oates, 1980.

McClendon, James W. "Narrative Ethics and Christian Ethics." *Faith and Philosophy* 3:4 (1986), 383–96. https://doi.org/10.5840/faithphil19863430

——. *Biography as Theology: How Life Stories Can Remake Today's Theology*. Nashville: Abingdon, 1974. Second edition published by Trinity Press, 1991, reprinted by Wipf & Stock, 2002.

McFague, Sallie. *The Body of God: An Ecological Theology.* Philadelphia: Fortress, 1993.

McGrath, Alister E. *Narrative Apologetics: Sharing the Relevance, Joy, and Wonder of the Christian Faith.* Grand Rapids: Baker, 2019.

Moltmann, Jürgen. *Experiences in Theology: Ways and Forms of Christian Theology.* Minneapolis: Fortress, 2000.

——. *Sun of Righteousness, Arise: God's Future for Humanity and the Earth*. Minneapolis: Fortress, 2010.

Morton, Timothy. *Dark Ecology: For a Logic of Future Coexistence.* New York: Columbia University Press, 2016.

Murphy, Francesca Aran. *God Is Not a Story: Realism Revisited.* Oxford: Oxford University Press, 2007.

Niebuhr, H. Richard. *The Meaning of Revelation.* New York: MacMillan, 1941.

———. *Christ and Culture*. New York: Harper Torch Books, 1951.

Northcott, Michael. "Eschatology in the Anthropocene." In *The Anthropocene and the Global Environmental Crisis,* edited by Clive Hamilton, Christophe Bonneuil and François Gemene, 100–11. London and New York: Routledge, 2015.

Pannenberg, Wolfhart. *Theology and the Kingdom of God.* Philadelphia: Westminster, 1969.

———. *Introduction to Systematic Theology.* Grand Rapids: Eerdmans, 1991.

———. *Systematic Theology Volume 1.* Grand Rapids: Eerdmans, 1991.

Rasmussen, Larry L. "Cosmology and Ethics." In *Worldviews and Ecology: Religion, Philosophy and the Environment*, edited by Mary Evelyn Tucker and John M. Grim, 173–80. Maryknoll: Orbis, 1994.

Ricoeur, Paul. *Time and Narrative, Volume 2.* Chicago: University of Chicago Press, 1985.

———. *Time and Narrative, Volume 3.* Chicago: University of Chicago Press, 1988.

Ritschl, Dietrich. *The Logic of Theology.* Philadelphia: Fortress, 1987.

Ritschl, Dietrich and Hugh O. Jones. *"Story" as Rohmaterial der Theologie.* Munich: Kaiser, 1976.

Rolston, Holmes (III). *Three Big Bangs: Matter-Energy, Life, Mind.* New York: Columbia University Press, 2010.

Root, Michael. "The Narrative Structure of Soteriology." In *Why Narrative? Readings in Narrative Theology*, edited by Stanley Hauerwas and L. Gregory Jones, 263–78. Eugene: Wipf & Stock, 1997.

Russell, Robert John, Nancey Murphy, and William R. Stoeger, eds. *Scientific Perspectives on Divine Action: Twenty Years of Challenge and Progress.* Berkeley: Center for Theology and the Natural Sciences/Vatican City: Vatican Observatory, 2008.

Serres, Michel. *The Incandescent.* London: Bloomsbury, 2018.

Sloterdijk, Peter. *In the World Interior of Capital: For a Philosophical Theory of Globalization.* Cambridge: Polity, 2014.

Stoker, Wessel. *Is Geloof Redelik? Een Geloofsverantwoording.* Zoetermeer: Meinema, 2004.

Stroup, George W. *The Promise of Narrative Theology: Recovering the Gospel in the Church.* Eugene: Wipf & Stock, 1997.

Swimme, Brian. "The Cosmic Creation Story." In *The Reenchantment of Science: Postmodern Proposals*, edited by David Ray Griffin, 47–56. Albany: State University of New York Press, 1988.

Swimme, Brian and Thomas Berry. *The Universe Story: From the Primordial Flashing Forth to the Ecozoic Era*. New York: Penguin, 1992.

Swimme, Brian and Mary Evelyn Tucker. *Journey of the Universe.* New Haven: Yale University, 2011.

Teilhard de Chardin, Pierre 1960. *The Divine Milieu.* New York: Harper & Row, 1960.

Ten Bos, René. *Dwalen in het Antropoceen.* Amsterdam: Boom, 2017.

Thiemann, Ronald F. *Revelation and Theology: The Gospel as Narrated Promise.* Notre Dame: University of Notre Dame Press, 1985.

Tracy, David. *Blessed Rage for Order: The New Pluralism in Theology*. New York: Seabury, 1975.

———. *The Analogical Imagination: Christian Theology and the Culture of Pluralism*. London: SCM, 1981.

———. *On Naming the Present: God, Hermeneutics, and Church.* Maryknoll: Orbis, 1994.

———. "Form and Fragment: The Recovery of the Hidden and Incomprehensible God." *Reflections* 3 (2000), 62–88.

———. *Fragments: The Existential Situation of Our Time: Selected Essays, Volume 1.* Chicago and London: The University of Chicago Press, 2020.

Vanhoozer, Kevin J. *The Drama of Doctrine: A Canonical Linguistic Approach to Christian Doctrine.* Louisville: Westminster John Knox, 2005.

Villa-Vicencio, Charles. "Telling One Another Stories: Towards a Theology of Reconciliation." In *Many Cultures, One Nation: Festschrift for Beyers Naudé*, edited by Charles Villa-Vicencio and Carl Niehaus, 105–21. Cape Town: Human & Rousseau, 1995.

Von Balthasar, Hans Urs. *Theodrama: Theological Dramatic Theory, Volume 4: The Action.* Translated by Graham Harrison. San Francisco: Ignatius, 1994.

Von Weizsäcker, Carl Friedrich F. *Geschichte der Natur.* Göttingen: Vandenhoeck & Ruprecht, 1948.

Wright, G. Ernest. *God Who Acts, Biblical Theology as Recital.* London: SCM, 1952.

White, Lynn. "The Historical Roots of our Ecological Crisis." *Science* 155 (1967), 1203–7. https://doi.org/10.1126/science.155.3767.1203

Yusoff, Kathryn. *A Billion Black Anthropocenes or None.* Minneapolis, Minnesota: University of Minnesota Press, 2018.

Žižek, Slavoj. *Living in the End Times.* London and New York: Verso, 2011.

Faith in Weather Lands: Toward an Ecocene Perspective

Sigurd Bergmann[1]

■ Trinitarian Cosmology—Compassion, Justice, Beauty, and Health

Remembering our theological ancestors in the patristic times we can learn how intimately interconnected faith in the Triune God and the awareness of being bodily alive has been in late antiquity. Might also we, at home in late modernity, have a share in such a wisdom about the deep connection between the Creator's being and acting and our earthly life? What can we learn from our theological ancestors and their way of telling the Christian story about how God acts with us here and now, and in the universe?

According to Gregory of Nazianzus (329–390), the Triune's inner life is characterized by a relationality of peace, beauty, nonviolence, and communality,

---

1. Sigurd Bergmann is Emeritus Professor in Religious Studies at the Norwegian University of Science and Technology in Trondheim, Norway. He is registered as a co-researcher at the University of the Western Cape, South Africa, for the project on "An Earthed Faith: Telling the Story amid the 'Anthropocene.'"

How to cite: Bergmann, S., 2021, 'Faith in Weather Lands: Toward an Ecocene Perspective', in E.M. Conradie & P.-C. Lai (eds.), *Taking a deep breath for the story to begin . . .* (An Earthed Faith: Telling the Story amid the "Anthropocene" Volume 1), pp. 49–71, AOSIS, Cape Town. https://doi.org/10.4102/aosis.2021.BK264.03

and the Creator shares these qualities with the spiritual and physical world as creation:

> These blessings originate with the Holy Trinity, whose unity of nature and internal peace are its most salient characteristic, are received by the angelic and divine powers who are peaceably disposed toward God as well as one another, extend to the whole of creation, whose glory is its absence of conflict, and regulate our own life: in our soul, on the one hand, through the reciprocal and cooperative allegiance of its virtues; in our body, on the other, through the happy marriage of form and function in its constituent members. Of these, the former both is and is called beauty; the latter, health.[2]

The Cappadocian theologian and rhetor—honored as one of the three most acknowledged in the Eastern Orthodox tradition (with the title "the Theologian")—identifies the inner life of the three persons in the Trinity with the relational life of the Earth.[3] The Triune's inner life, the so-called immanent Trinity, coincides with God's external acting, the so-called economic Trinity. The Creator "extends" his/her being to the world. No conflicts are taking place in its harmony, and form and function are happily married in our bodies. Spiritual beauty and bodily health are intertwined and characterizing the quality of both God and the Earth.

One can summarize the church father's worldview with the help of notions such as "Trinitarian cosmology"[4] and "Trinitarian ecology,"[5] and one should not simply displace such Eastern patristic theology as Platonism in the museum of historical theology. For Gregory and the believers in the Empire of late antiquity, the analogy of God's and the world's being was not just "ontology."[6] They were, in the same way as the believers of whom the biblical sources told about, able to perceive and recognize the Triune Creator within and amid their own social and ecological life. The Creator appeared and acted with, for and in Creation, within[7] the environment and peaceful harmony of the believers' material and spiritual life world.

---

2. Gregory of Nazianzus, *Homily 22.14*.

3. Cf. Bergmann, "The Legacy of Trinitarian Cosmology in the Anthropocene."

4. The term "cosmology" was unknown in antiquity as a technical term; it derives from Christian Wolff, who distinguished between rational and empirical cosmology. The term "Trinitarian cosmology" simply expresses that Gregory unfolds an (in the old sense) empirical and rational cosmology that is ontologically dependent on the Triune. See Bergmann, *Creation Set Free*, 10.

5. "Ecology" is not a term known in the Antiquity either. There is no real concept of "ecology" before 1866, when Haeckel invented it, because modernity itself generated the need for such a concept. See Bergmann, *Creation Set Free*, 27–30. "Trinitarian ecology" is certainly a part of cosmology, but as a term it connotes more specifically the "relational patterns between the nature and work of the triune God and the environments of his creation." Bergmann, *Creation Set Free*, 284.

6. Interpreted in the lens of Celia Deane-Drummond's essay in this volume, Gregory might join her thinkers of theo-ontology.

7. On the significance of God's "within," see Bergmann, "With-In: Towards an aesth/ethics of prepositions."

What counted was that one could perceive, encounter, and experience the Triune at work on Earth. Lived religion took place in the lived space, where God appeared as a Life-giving Lover and Liberator of the Earth. In order to express this faith in a formula, I depicted the Cappadocian's theology as "cosmology as soteriology."[8] The world was perceived as a dynamic universe where everything was striving for the salvation of the whole. God's history of salvation did not simply take place in the world as theater but all created life was regarded as a dynamic coworker in synergy with the liberating Creator. In this way, the daily experience of a liberating God in one's own life world was the central driving force of Christian Trinitarian cosmology. Hereby creation theology at that time was not simply a philosophical system (even if it also developed as such in close dialogue with Stoicism and Platonism) but it was God-talk and lived faith that included the whole of the Earth's being in the Triune's history of salvation.

One central presupposition for this theology was that God is even able to suffer (in the body of the Incarnated Son): if one can see God suffering, one can also see the entirety of creation partaking in suffering and redemption.[9] God is a God of empathy in direct opposition to antiquity's belief in divine *apatheia*. God is, in Gregory's view, community, movement, and suffering, and this is why he or she can liberate the Earth from violence, conflict, and injustice.

Trinitarian cosmology and Trinitarian ecology, therefore, imply not just a theoretical postulate about belief in God as the world's Creator but also a lived practice of acting in synergy with the life-giving and liberating driving force of what characterizes life on earth at its depth. Through the Christian faith, this force is experienced as compassion, peacebuilding, justice, and reciprocal being-in-love with each other and the other/stranger. God is aesthetically/ethically experienceable. Love for the poor and love for the stranger are, according to Gregory,[10] consequently the clearest expressions of love for God, for oneself, and for one's neighbor. Where such love is manifest, the Spirit of the Triune is at work, and the story of the Earth takes a new turn.

On the basis of such a theological understanding of the Triune and the Earth, I will not talk in generalizing terms about the Earth but move a bit closer to its bodily perceived reality by emphasizing *weather*. I will regard weather as a complex path to reflect on how life can evolve and what this means for Christian lived faith. What might weather wisdom mean for God taking place on Earth? How does the "Anthropocene" story emerge if we approach it both from our bodily-being-alive-in-weather-lands and from the

---

8. The life of the cosmos takes in this sense place as a part of the Triune's history of salvation. Mark Wallace explains in his essay in this volume how "Cosmic benefaction makes possible human salvation."

9. See Bergmann, *Creation Set Free*, 133–37.

10. Gregory of Nazianzus, *Homily 14: On Love for the Poor*.

science of meteorology? How can the scientific theory about the atmosphere enter in dialogue with philosophical and theological understandings of the atmosphere in the "Anthropocene?" Finally, I will lift my eye beyond the "Anthropocene," a concept that in my view should by no means have the final word about the whole of our common future and the evolution of life at Earth, and depict a vision of the *Ecocene* beyond the "Anthropocene," potentially already growing gently amid the "Anthropocene."

■ Weather Wisdom

Weather belongs to the essential conditions of all life on Earth including our human bodily life. Weather is within and all around. Being alive is a process that takes place in the open, inhabiting a world of becoming. As created beings in ecological synergy with each other, we live in "weather lands," within a larger surrounding "weather world."[11]

Nevertheless, even though weather impacts us all, in every place and at every moment, it seems difficult to embed and locate it properly in our worldview and self-understanding. Certainly, weather forecasts are given so much importance that they are located directly after the political news in media reports. Many listen carefully to the meteorologists' prognosis about what awaits us tomorrow. Again and again it fascinates anew: to see and listen to someone who intends to predict the future, my future, our common future, and the future of mother "Earth, our home."[12]

Without doubt, both weather and the climate are:

> [*T*]he theatre where human existence, humanity's history, is taking place. This is indeed most significant, as it in the broadest sense sets the scene, delimits potentials, and sets boundaries for what can happen on Earth, however not for what in fact happens or will happen.[13]

In spite of a growing awareness of anthropogenic climate change, related changes of weather, and especially extreme weather patterns in the public discourse, weather still appears as an underrepresented sphere if one looks at both science and the humanities. Meteorology represents weather in the scientific community, although in a narrow and instrumentalist way. Meteorological data and models are certainly used in other disciplines such as

---

11. Coining the term "weather lands" is inspired by Tim Ingold's coinage of the term "weather-world." According to Ingold, fundamental to life "is the process of respiration, by which organisms continually disrupt any boundary between earth and sky, binding substance and medium together in forging their own growth and movement. Thus to inhabit the open is not to be stranded on the outer surface of the earth but to be caught up in the transformations of the weather-world." Ingold, "Earth, Sky, Wind, and Weather," 19. See Bergmann, *Weather, Religion, and Climate Change*, 1–5.

12. See http://www.earthcharter.org/.

13. Lauer, *Klimawandel*, 5 (my translation).

biology, geosciences, and physics, which treat weather empirically simply as a range of data that can be classed with other data and arranged according to systems with particular theoretical interests, where the overarching epistemological question determines the answers found in nature. The complexity and ubiquity of weather seem to have quite a weak representation in the sciences, even if meteorologists often express their respect and wonder with regard to the atmosphere's enormous capacity for alteration. While weather does not cease to fascinate in ordinary life, science, nevertheless, encounters it as mere data in a metric system. The humanities have little more to offer. Certainly, weather appears in history as a part of different narratives about human ecology through the ages. Weather was registered as an important "fact" that was able to impact on warfare and power negotiation as well as on people's potential to cultivate and survive.

My own disciplines, theology and religious studies, follow the mainstream and have not much to offer either, even if we can observe an intense activity of reflecting about the challenges of climatic change.[14] Naturally, religious belief systems of all traditions imply an interpretation of how the environment and weather within it reveals God, gods, and the spirits, and how believers should respond to these. But even if the last 30 years have brought an impressive development of the study of religion and the environment, weather still does not receive much emphasis in itself.[15]

In the same way as all life is dependent on light, weather also surrounds and embraces us. According to Tim Ingold, the flux of wind and weather reminds us that we are alive in an open world:

> In this mingling, as we live and breathe, the wind, light and moisture of the sky bind with the substances of the earth in the continual forging of a way through the tangle of lifelines that comprise the land.[16]

Weather is, according to such a perspective, not just a surrounding physical element but is fundamental for every living being who breathes in air. Living in a weather world, every being is destined to combine the elements of weather in the continuation of existence.

To be alive in such a sense means to exist within the weather, to be exposed to the sun that shines, to the rain that falls, and to the wind that blows. My mother tongue, German, offers a wonderful adjective for this deep anchoring-in-weather also with regard to one's health: "Being exposed to the weather and being unwell of it" is expressed as *wetterfühlig*, to be emotionally

---

14. Bergmann and Gerten, *Religion and Dangerous Environmental Change*; Gerten and Bergmann, *Religion in Environmental and Climate Change*; and Conradie and Koster, *T&T Clark Handbook*.

15. For some exceptions, see Wiggins, *Weathering the Psalms*; Young, "Religion and Weather"; and Kittsteiner, *Gewissen und Geschichte*.

16. Ingold, *Being Alive*, 115.

connected to the weather.[17] In this context, one can allude to Johann Wolfgang von Goethe, who has aptly depicted how nature and the human mirror each other, and ask: do we only know ourselves as well as we know the weather, which we only become aware of in ourselves, and is it only in the weather that we become aware of ourselves?[18] Is weather something that takes place as much within every created being as around it?

As weather reveals one of the most open, unpredictable, and uncontrollable dimensions of life, its uncertainty has been interpreted in the Jewish-Christian tradition as an elementary screen for the interaction between creation and the Creator. As such, weather certainly does not do anything other than weathering, but has nevertheless served as a screen for the projection of God's presence and the moral relation to his/her created beings. The Hebrew Bible, and especially the book of Psalms,[19] is extremely clear that weather has to be understood as the most just and equal gift of God to all on Earth. Sunshine, rain, and wind are given equally to all, and weather does not make any distinction with regard to those that it nurtures:

> He [*your Father in heaven*] causes his sun to rise on the evil and the good, and sends rain on the righteous and the unrighteous.[20]

Weather is in such a view a deep expression of God's love to creation and his/her practice of sharing equally both the gifts and challenges of life without any consideration of the individual. Also environmental and climatic justice anchors at depth in such a belief. As everyone can equally be struck by weather, everyone is equally valued and loved by the Creator. In practice, however, weather impacts mirror social, environmental, and spatial injustices, where the poor are exposed to much higher risks and suffer to a greater extent from extreme weather.

According to such an ancient religious code, weather on the one hand demands respect for the life and dignity of every creature. Disasters and catastrophes in extreme weather on the other hand represent a punishment for humans within this code. Where humans did not fulfill their tasks as images of God, and where the relation between God and man/woman was broken, the Creator uses weather as an educational tool. Sinning through injustice, lack of solidarity and compassion, oppression of the poor, and violence against

---

17. Interestingly, German offers a technical term in the adjective "wetterfühlig," while English lacks such a term and circumscribes the state of being. The phrase "being under the weather" certainly draws on weather as a metaphor but aims at being unwell in general.

18. See Goethe, "Bedeutende Fördernis durch ein einziges geistreiches Wort," 306–309: "The human being only knows herself as far as she knows the world, which she only becomes aware of in herself, and only in the world she becomes aware of herself."

19. Wiggins, *Weathering the Psalms*, interprets the Psalms in the lens of what he calls "Meteorotheology."

20. Matthew 5:45, NIV.

one another result in God's pedagogically intended reaction, which is revealed by dramatic weather change. The meteorological screen allows reading and interpreting the signs about the state of relation between Creator and creation. Both love and anger are made visible to us in the sky. Through the uncertainty of weather, God stays in touch with his/her created world. Weather serves as a natural stage and screen for reading the Creator's relation and interaction with creation.[21] It offers a kind of moral barometer.

The relationship between morality and weather was sometimes violently intimate, such that specific weather witches were blamed for catastrophes such as rain and floods, thunderstorms, and bad harvest. From classical antiquity, through the medieval period, and at least up to the early Enlightenment, women have been (and sometimes still are) blamed for causing dangerous weather.[22]

From both meteorology and poetry, including the Songs, we can learn that weather shifts are never ever simply displacements from one frozen state to another but take place as ongoing complex polyvalent movements that follow musical principles of harmony, consonance, and dissonance. Weather can sound, metaphorically as well as physically. Weather also paints in colors. Wind blows whistling in the leaves and rain patters on the roof. God "makes the clouds his chariot and rides on the wings of the wind. He makes winds his messengers" (Ps 104:3-4, NIV). Weather appears as humidity on our skin but it also sounds in our ears and manifests in colors in our eyes. It continuously captures our awareness, perception, thinking, and acting. Therefore, only a synesthetic[23] approach to weather, and its religious imagination, seems reasonable.

I hope that the reader so far has mobilized his/her own emotional membrane, remembrance, and productive imagination to open for weather as a rich, complex, and dynamic sphere of encounter between God and the Earth. Weather alteration appears herein not just as a part of the story of God and the Earth but also as writing itself the story of life. Does God still act through, with, and in weather? What wisdom can we learn from weather? Can weather teach about our common future and atmosphere on Earth, our home? Can weather wisdom nurture hope and establish practices to manifest this hope

---

21. See volume 4 of this series, that explores the belief in common grace, and the question how the suffering of God's creatures in the "Anthropocene" be reconciled with trust in God's loving care.

22. On the bad impacts of weather shocks on violence against women in Africa and their economic dependence, see also Konte and Tirivayi, *Women and Sustainable Human Development*, 42-43.

23. *Synaesthetics* derives from "synaesthesia" (Greek "together" and *aisthesis*, "sensation" or "perception"). In arts and aesthetics, it means that the senses cannot be separated from each other but are interacting. A color can, for example, be experienced as sound and a number as a spatial position. Sounds can evoke colors. It is also a medical term to define a neurological condition where a fusing of sensations occurs when one sense is stimulated which automatically and simultaneously causes a stimulation in another of the senses.

for "the world to come"?[24] How do we cope with a more and more politicized weather (where its impacts produce new injustices and challenges, and sharpen existing ones)?[25] How do we make ourselves at home with weather, and how do believers encounter the Triune's Holy Spirit as a Giver of Life and Weather? "A change in the weather is sufficient to recreate the world and ourselves,"[26] it once dawned upon Marcel Proust. Might weather wisdom then also recreate the world and us?

■ Atmospheres of Synergy—In Geoscience, Arts, Philosophy, and Theology

Meteorology is defined as "the study of the atmosphere and its phenomena,"[27] and weather is defined as "the condition of the atmosphere at any particular time and place."[28] "Atmosphere" offers the central term in science for the investigation of weather, while it, at the same time, also offers a broad range of denotations in ordinary language and an exciting concept in phenomenology. Accordingly, one can explore the term as a highly promising field of encounter between science, philosophy and ordinary life. And even if theologians have not yet discovered the depth of the concept, it is without doubt exciting to develop, for example, Pneumatology as a reflection about the Holy Spirit's work in "atmospheres of synergy."[29]

The atmosphere and its weather and climate are in addition intimately interconnected with our human bodily and emotional life. Especially, artists and thinkers in the Romantic times have explored this relation at its depth. Painters have intensely studied the method of "skying" or "clouding" at the same time when scientific meteorology made its progress. Especially, Joseph Mallord William Turner and Caspar David Friedrich have driven this exploration to its extreme with outstanding results in paintings that never cease to enchant. Goethe lauded Luke Howard for his studies on the systematics of clouds and emphasized the intertwinement of the human self and its weathering surrounding. Alexander von Humboldt wrote about climate in his *Cosmos* as "all changes of the atmosphere that affect our organs distinctly" and underlined especially the complexity of the atmosphere in his overarching view of nature as a painting, as *Naturgemälde*. Our modern image and concept

---

24. "καὶ ζωὴν τοῦ μέλλοντος αἰῶνος" (. . . and the life of the world to come), First Council of Constantinople (381).

25. See Schmitt's poignant remark that "it never has been so political as now to talk about weather" in "Politische Energie," 1.

26. Proust, *Le Côté de Guermantes*, 1014.

27. Ahrens, *Meteorology Today*, 16.

28. Ahrens, *Meteorology Today*, 15.

29. Bergmann, "Atmospheres of Synergy."

of weather were invented at this time both in science and arts of the nineteenth century. Continuing on the path of this tradition, rethinking weather today needs to approach the atmosphere not only as a geophysical entity but also as a multilayered sociocultural, spiritual, aesthetic, ethical, and historical agency.

While not only the romantics but also many earlier times and cultures had a rich imagination of the natural phenomena wherein weather arose, modern science pulls together these manifold images into one single entity. Where the sky, clouds, heaven, air, wind, breath, meteors, and blowing weather constituted the flux in our surroundings, the scientific notion of the atmosphere absorbs all these domains and "'kills the air, stripping it of animacy and meaning.'"[30] According to Bron Szerszynski:

> [W]eather was in effect turned into a laboratory artefact, was "brought indoors," in an attempt to tame its material and semiotic unruliness.[31]

A fruitful way to overcome the reductionism of science in this regard is to contrast the scientific to the phenomenological understanding as it has been elaborated in environmental aesthetics. "Weather" is not only a natural phenomenon; it is "a rhetoric."[32] Therefore, one must also be aware of how language creates weather, and how talking about weather is deeply connected to the history of sincerity, as Lisa Robertson shows. For her, "the history of the description of weather parallels the history of sincerity as a rhetorical value,"[33] an insight well in harmony with the Jewish-Christian biblical tradition's image of weather.

Weather as "the condition of the atmosphere at any particular time and place"[34] takes place in the atmosphere that science understands as a thermodynamic system that unfolds in constant change and variation and that takes place on such a large scale that humans have to accept and respect its unpredictability. Environmental aesthetics can allow us to take atmospheric thinking further and also open for a deeper spiritual awareness.

Atmosphere in aesthetics is understood in a different sense than in geoscience. Together with related notions such as "aura," "ambience," and "mood" (German *Stimmung*), it makes it possible to entangle the outer with the inner human life. Such an understanding of the atmosphere can[35] overcome

---

30. Szerszynski, "Life in the Open Air," 33.
31. Szerszynski, "Reading and Writing the Weather," 21.
32. Robertson, "The Weather."
33. Robertson, "The Weather."
34. See Ahrens, *Meteorology Today*, 15; and Kraus, *Die Atmosphäre der Erde*, 11.
35. Bergmann, "Atmospheres of Synergy."

the split between the subjective and the objective and allow us to become aware of all that is taking place in between the inner and the outer. According to Gernot Böhme, aesthetics is a self-aware human reflection on one's living-in-particular-surroundings.[36] An "ecological aesthetics of nature is as much a subjective self-reflection on human identity as it is a reflection on that which surrounds us"[37] and, in addition, on the distinction between humanity and its enveloping environment. The notion of atmosphere achieves in this view a central function that allows us to interpret the qualities of the environment and the human being's *sich-befinden*, that is, how one is emotionally and bodily situated.[38]

Experiencing atmospheres, in fact, dissolves the distinction between subject and object. It should be obvious that such dissolution offers ecotheology a significant path to overcome dichotomies and to locate environmental God-talk straightaway in the midst of the atmosphere openly including both objective and subjective dimensions. It is the interaction between them that becomes the focus for our meditation then. Atmospheres emerge in natural surroundings as well as in built environments. Not only names but also building materials are able to create atmospheres; they can "evoke history, enhance the habitability of a city."[39]

While geoscientists and meteorologists depart from a clear spatiality and objectivity of what they regard as atmosphere, philosophers operate with a much more differentiated concept of spatiality, which is regarded as surfaceless and frameless:

> Atmosphere in this sense is a frameless, indivisibly extended occupation of a surfaceless space.[40]

Mónika Dánél strikingly summarizes the richness of such an understanding of atmosphere where the aesthetic, social, and geocultural potentials are simultaneously present. On this understanding, atmosphere can be seen as an aesthetic category, as a multisensorial bodily experience, as *passibilité* (Mădălina Diaconu) calling forth reception, as energy with a powerful effect on the senses of olfaction and touch, as the in-betweenness of emanation and perception that can be grabbed as an affective power.[41]

---

36. Böhme, *Für eine ökologische Naturästhetik*, 8. See Porteous, *Environmental Aesthetics*, 5–41.

37. Bergmann, Hoff and Sager, *Spaces of Mobility*, 15.

38. Böhme, *Atmosphäre*, 23.

39. Diaconu, "City Walks and Tactile Experience," 10.

40. See Schmitz, "Von der Scham zum Neid," 20.

41. Dánél, "Atmospheric Adaptation as Cultural Translation."

Bringing together the atmosphere of geoscience and aesthetics makes it necessary to interconnect the physical and the embodied spiritual. While science usually excludes, or rather operates with a reductionist view of the human dimension, aesthetics, as we can see, keeps the scientific perspective at a distance. Geoscience in this sense needs to learn on the one hand how weather, in the lens of atmospheric analysis, impacts on human bodies and souls as well as on the whole of human sociocultural being and history. The so-called affective atmosphere[42] offers, from this perspective, a distinct part of the planet's atmosphere. Environmental humanities and aesthetics, on the other hand, need to learn more about the givenness of an atmosphere in constant change.

Reflecting on what weather does to us, and what we do to the Earth's climate, can, as we can see here, lead us to an integrated thinking where both scientific structures and processes of the atmosphere and human, sociocultural, historical, and spiritual dimensions of being impacted and embraced by weather are interacting. What weather does to us and how we perceive weather can by no means be explained by an aesthetic of natural beauty, as Diaconu aptly shows. Nature, weather, and the atmosphere serve as screens for our imagination (*Einbildungskraft*), and weather is seldom enjoyed for itself but as a part of landscapes, waterscapes, or cityscapes. Diaconu notes how the ideal of fine weather has obviously evolved over a long cultural history; in late antiquity church Fathers, such as Saint Ephrem the Syrian, were already describing paradise in a fictitious meteorological vision where the atmosphere is temperate, shaping ideal conditions for the fertility of the soil, and "where the months' tempests are overcome" so that they cannot "pollute the glorious air."[43] Our vision of a good creation also includes fine weather, far away from its extreme threats.

Reflecting on the atmosphere in aesthetic contexts is closely connected to aesthetic modes of experiencing the quality of life. What I am wondering about is whether weather also can enhance human compassion and empathy in a kind of synergy between our inner and outer surroundings. Can one develop aesthetic atmospheric thinking anchored in the practiced sensibility and quality of the encounter with the other, or *the strange/r*?[44] Compassion would then be able to serve as a central quality for atmospheric feeling, perceiving, thinking, and acting.[45] By breathing, therefore, we are staying alive together and for each other as created beings within the atmosphere. Being

---

42. On the psychology of affective atmosphere, see Anderson, "Affective Atmospheres."

43. Saint Ephrem, *Hymns on Paradise*, 149, quoted according to Diaconu, "Longing for Clouds," 5.

44. On the strange(r), see Bergmann, "The Strange and the Self."

45. On this topic, see also the remarkably inspiring work of environmental artists Reiko Goto and Timothy Collins on empathy with nature. Goto and Collins, "The Black Wood."

God's image means to be a weathered image, being alive in weather lands. Might synthetic atmospheric thinking then provide a method of "reading insights through one another,"[46] where the meteorologically regarded atmosphere of course represents some kind of megamaterial and all-embracing structure that can be "read" by us at the same time as it can also "read" us? Maybe similar to Dorothee Sölle's thought-provoking belief about "the Bible reading me"? Might we then approach both books, the book of nature/weather and the book of the Bible (*liber naturae* and *biblica*) as "books reading us"?[47] Are the two stories embedded in each other, the story of the "Anthropocene" and faith in the Earth as Creation, not only narrations that are told by us human beings, but are these stories also reporting us, similar to the process of "weather reporting on us."[48] Might storytelling then in such a deeper sense represent what Georg Picht intriguingly circumscribed as "thinking as a process within nature."[49] In such a view, weather reporting on us might play a central role in "the model of reality as an animate communion of sacred beings."[50]

Striving for weather wisdom, we can also learn from the experience of how weather is embracing us how to feel, perceive, think, and act with and through each other in a true process of what Catherine Keller has depicted as *inter-carnation*.[51] The flux of weather would then make and keep our bodies/souls/communities alive from above, below, within, and throughout. Wind and wisdom will blow and breathe life into Earth and/in/at/for the Earth's inhabitants on an atmosphere-nurtured Earth, our home. The incarnation of the Son would then continue in the Spirit's inhabitation of Earth, and by breathing embraced by the weather we live with, for, and in the Triune's mystery.

---

46. The term "new materialism" was coined by Manuel DeLanda and Rosi Braidotti in the second half of the 1990s. It opposes dichotomist thinking and searches for new ways out of these traditions. Nature and culture are always understood as *naturecultures* (Donna Haraway) and the human mind is always regarded as material. In Karen Barad's view, for example, quantum physics inspires a new way of entangling matter and meaning, in a way that she has circumscribed as "diffractive methodology, a method of diffractively reading insights through one another, building new insights, and attentively and carefully reading for differences that matter in their fine details, together with the recognition that there intrinsic to this analysis is an ethics that is not predicated on externality but rather entanglement". See https://quod.lib.umich.edu/o/ohp/11515701.0001.001/1:4.3/--new-materialism-interviews-cartographies?rgn=div2;view=fulltext, accessed 29 November 2019.

For a survey see the EU-supported project "New Materialism: Networking European Scholarship on 'How Matter Comes to Matter'": https://newmaterialism.eu/, accessed 29 November 2019.

47. As Sölle once said, quoting an African woman, in *Das Fenster der Verwundbarkeit*, 295. On the metaphor of nature as book, *liber naturae*, see Bergmann, *Religion, Space, and the Environment*, 284.

48. Horn, *Weather Reports You*.

49. Picht, *Der Begriff der Natur und seine Geschichte*, 137.

50. See Mark Wallace's essay in this volume.

51. Catherine Keller invented the notion of "inter-carnation" as being-members-of-each-other. See Keller, "Members of Each Other"; *Intercarnations*.

Such an approach might lead us from our consciousness about being alive as God's images in weather lands to an alternative self-understanding and understanding of what is circumscribed as "the Anthropocene." My final section will explore how one might approach discourse on the "Anthropocene" theologically and how one might overcome it with tools from contextual theology, atmospheric thinking, and Trinitarian cosmology. "Anthropocene" discourse should in my view by no means have the final word about our common future and the evolution of life on Earth. I will therefore depict a vision of the Ecocene amid and beyond the "Anthropocene."

■ Toward a Contextual Theopolitics of the Earth as Ecocene

Ever since the Stratigraphy Commission of the Geological Society of London made a case in 2008 for incorporating the "Anthropocene" into the geological time scale, the debate about the understanding of the "Anthropocene" has made massive waves.[52] The term "Anthropocene" implies a shift from the Holocene to a new epoch in the Earth's history, where human impacts since the so-called Industrial Revolution in the eighteenth century have increased to such a scale that the human imprint "rivals some of the great forces of Nature."[53] Among many other types of evidence, such as accelerating rates of species invasion and extinction, water mismanagement, rising sea levels, and human-caused disturbance of the climate system, the traces of human activities (such as nuclear waste, plastic waste, and soot) on planet Earth have increased on a significant scale.

Karl Polanyi analyzed already in 1944 itself an unprecedented change that occurred with what he in his book title described as "the great transformation" of the English society into a technological market society. It was a transformation of "the natural and human substance of society into commodities" that are unlimited and which "must disjoint man's relationships and threaten his natural habitat with annihilation."[54] Scientists later coined the notion of the "great acceleration" to summarize the radical shift that took place when CO_2 emissions increased and the process of global warming accelerated. Later again, climate scientists adapted the term anew and declared, in a widespread memorandum from the Nobel Cause symposium in Potsdam 2007, "the need for a great transformation."[55] It is important to remember that what is described

---

52. For the state of the debate and the understanding of "the Anthropocene," see Waters et al., "The Anthropocene."

53. Steffen et al., "The Anthropocene," 842.

54. Polanyi, *The Great Transformation*, 44.

55. Schellnhuber, "Global Sustainability."

here as great transformation is not simply about natural processes, "but first and foremost, a question of economy, society, and culture," as aptly pointed out by Claus Leggewie and Harald Welzer, and explored and presented in vivid details by Uwe Schneidewind, who also includes arts and faith communities as significant actors in the process.[56]

How is religion in general, and Christian theology in particular, affected by this discourse? Religion and theology cannot simply start to relate to the "Anthropocene" and its discourse, but are already affected by it as faith unfolds as a practical and ideological human activity that in itself, for good and bad, impacts on the environment and the history of the Earth. Theology, and religion,[57] necessarily takes place today *within* the "Anthropocene." Faith and its rational reflective systems, therefore, need to reinvent themselves as critical driving forces *amid* and in my vision also *beyond* the "Anthropocene." One of the most central and significant contexts for practicing faith today is the ongoing anthropogenic change of the planet's atmosphere and lifeworlds. As weather and climate change, this also changes faith. How can faith then bring a change to our ongoing negotiation about that change?[58]

In the following, I will discuss some critical arguments against the triumphalist interpretation of the "Anthropocene" and its depoliticizing function. Herein I will try to formulate some central challenges within the discourse—for faith communities as well as other agents. Finally, theological skills will be explored in order to widen our vision from the past and present to a future beyond the "Anthropocene." A move toward a contextual theopolitics of the Earth experienced as the Ecocene will conclude the argument.

Should we, as many scientists, embrace the narrative about the age of the humans fully or rather keep a critical distance? Personally, I have, due to the narrative's ambiguity, moved more and more away from supporting what now seems to function as a homogenizing concept and a problematically generalizing screen for projection.[59] The normative ambitions of the "Anthropocene" narrative, as a "grand narrative about reality,"[60] remain at best ambivalent,[61] with a Janus-faced character, and at worst these ambitions

---

56. Leggewie and Welzer, "Another 'Great Transformation'?" On the need for an extensive social transformation, see Schneidewind, *Die Große Transformation*.

57. As we have shown in Deane-Drummond, Bergmann and Vogt, *Religion in the Anthropocene*.

58. See Bergmann, "Climate Change Changes Religion."

59. For a more detailed discussion of the criticism, see Bergmann, "Is there a Future in the Age of Humans?" This section builds upon the argument of that essay.

60. Hoiß, "Das Anthropozän," 19.

61. Deane-Drummond, Bergmann, and Vogt, "The Future of Religion in the Anthropocene Era," 14.

encourage a depoliticizing attitude, where the "Anthropocene" turns into an "Anthropo-(Obs)cene."[62]

Three critical points should in my view be emphasized. First, will the insight into the all-embracing impact of humans lead us to a new humility toward both human and other life forms, or will it fertilize a new triumphalist self-understanding of humankind[63] and a utilitarian agenda with regard to human technocratic and economic management? At present, it is hard for me to see how the narrative about the "Anthropocene" can produce any antidotes against anthropocentric superiority and absolutism. Instead, the opposite seems to be the case, as the concept of the "Anthropocene" is deeply depoliticizing, as Erik Swyngedouw has shown. Its central postulates about humanity causing the great acceleration are misleading, as the majority of the planet's inhabitants have not partaken at all in the process of damaging the environment. What is depicted as "humanity" in the discourse instead concerns a small minority of nations that have enriched themselves at the expense of others. As this was true decades ago, one must, however, today differentiate the situation in a more complex way, when countries like China, India, and Russia with large populations fuel climate change with high carbon emissions.

By contrast, religions typically reflect on nature as a source of gifts and commons of life,[64] regard the human as an integral part of nature, while Earth system analysis often, even if not in general,[65] operates with a poor reductionist understanding of the human and social, which stands in sharp contrast to its highly sophisticated model of complexity with regard to natural processes. While religions compress the narrative into the language of "respect toward," "wisdom about," and "compassion and wonder within" nature, science continues to take an external, somehow metaphysical position from which to describe nature.

A second criticism regards the lack of power analysis in the narrative. Andreas Malm and Alf Hornborg rightly accuse the narrative of neglecting the uneven distribution of wealth as a condition for the very existence of modern, fossil-fuel technology and of ignoring the fact that humans have caused global

---

62. Swyngedouw, "Interrupting the Anthropo(Obs)cene."

63. See Bergmann, *Weather, Religion and Climate Change*.

64. For a detailed theological discussion of the "commons," see Keller, Ortega-Aponte, and Johnson-DeBaufreeds. *Common Goods*.

65. An increasing number of earth scientists, however, seem to have become aware of this, and some are engaging in more holistic approaches; see for example the LOOPS activity: www.pik-potsdam.de/research/projects/activities/copan/loops, and its Special Issue: www.earth-syst-dynam.net/special_issue18.html, accessed 27 November 2019. For a reflection on "deeper human dimensions," including religious ones, see the thought-provoking and forward-looking argument in Gerten, Schönfeld, and Schauberger, "On Deeper Human Dimensions."

warming over the course of their long history.⁶⁶ Is "Anthropocene" thinking simply extending the natural scientists' worldviews to society?

Obviously, there is a risk in talking about climatic change in the "Anthropocene" nurturing an illusion that we can adapt to change by establishing technological, political, and economic instruments that make sure that we—in our values, ideologies, lifestyles, and ordinary consumerist behaviors—do *not* (really) need to change. Is it enough to talk about "policy change" and will this also change the human deep down, or is Rilke's persuasive demand still valid: *Du mußt Dein Leben ändern* (you must change your life)⁶⁷— which undoubtedly also leads to the unavoidable *Du mußt Dich selbst ändern* (you must change yourself)? How should theologians interpret the Jewish and Christian plea for "daily conversion" environmentally in the age of humans? In my view, this would best take place in a new political theology where one does not avoid conversion and transformation in a new grand scientific narrative but, instead, encourage interruptive political action. A theological criticism of the modernist "Anthropocene" narrative⁶⁸ would then aim at retelling the story in a process of re-politicization.

My third critical point focuses on the somewhat apocalyptic tone of the (eco-catastrophist) "Anthropocene" narrative.⁶⁹ Have we really reached the end? Is the whole of the planet's future from modernity onward at the mercy of humans now and hereafter? Might there come a new-*cene* [Greek *cene* = recent, new] after the "Anthropocene," and might there be other forces that impact on our common future and our common earth? Humans are, as we have seen, generalized in a misleading way, and essential conflicts and injustices are obscured. "Anthropocene-talk" might in its worst form serve as a fetishizing instrument that precludes striving for change. Theologically, we must, therefore, state that it breaks with an essential understanding of eschatology.⁷⁰ From the believer's perspective, the future of creation must always remain open, for the Creator and for creation's own power of evolution. Time, as well as space and place, cannot simply be confined by humans in the

---

66. Malm and Hornborg, "The Geology of Mankind?," 64.

67. Rainer Maria Rilke, in his poem *Archaïscher Torso Apollos* from 1908. See Peter Sloterdijk's essay from 2009 with the same title *Du mußt dein Leben ändern*, but subtitled *Anthropotechnik*, wherein he fatally transfers Rilke's tremendously life-giving struggle to deepen the human's interaction and entanglement with his/her surroundings into abyssal solipsistic egomania in line with the philosopher's other self-absorbed work.

68. See Christophe Bonneuil who identifies four grand narratives of the "Anthropocene" (modernist, eco-modernist, eco-catastrophist and eco-Marxist), as discussed in the introduction to this volume.

69. On fantasies of apocalypse as both a product and a producer of the "Anthropocene," see Ginn, "When Horses Won't Eat." On how previous concepts of human extinction, including religious apocalyptics, change in the context of climate change, see Colebrook, "The Future in the Anthropocene."

70. More on the eschatological dimension of the "Anthropocene" in Volume 7 of this series. For a thought provoking perspective see Grau, "The Revelations of Climate Change: A Petro-Eschatology."

cage of technical models. However much computer monitoring is done in empirical scenarios, it is the bodily awareness and perception of our environment that remains significant for what we feed into the computers.[71]

Life as a gift cannot simply be turned into a scientific scenario, and it can definitely not be turned into a commodity to be managed and exchanged along the well-known paths of fetishizing capitalism. The modernist narrative of the "Anthropocene," and especially its depoliticizing function, therefore leads to a radically new re-politicization of the human condition of being alive. And it also demands a new understanding of visuality, as the production of images now moves into the center of our understanding of the world and us within it.[72]

From the perspective of the Abrahamic religions, with their belief in the world as a creation of the One, the challenge is deeply painful. How can one believe in a good Creator while his/her own creatures threaten the Earth as a habitable place? How can one continue to believe in a good creation, and envision a *creatio continua* and *creatio futura* in such a situation?[73] How is the image of God connected to the (scientifically designed) images of the world? Delineating the spiritual pain so sharply should sufficiently convince us not simply to regard the anthropogenic impact on the Earth as a question of environmental ethics, but to become aware that being alive in the "Anthropocene" implies a radically new challenge to reconstruct one's identity, worldview, and image of God. This demands re-politicizing interruptions that are able to make visible the divisions and injustices in interhuman and human-nonhuman relations. No more, no less.

My strongest objection to the "Anthropocene" narrative[74] lies in the question of how we imagine what we might meet *beyond* the "Anthropocene." Is there any space to imagine a new geological era beyond the "Anthropocene?" Or should we abandon the method of periodization in general? For me, the vision of an "Ecocene," where humans and other life forms overcome their divisions and conflict and cohabit on Earth in fully just and peaceful entanglements, offers a more appropriate path to the future.[75] This would in my view also

---

71. See Sobecka, "The Atmospheric Turn."

72. Emmelhainz, "Images Do Not Show."

73. On this and related questions, see volume 3 of this series.

74. See, for example, Sharp, "Not all Humans."

75. Thomas Berry coined already in 1991 the notion of *the Ecozoic Era*, a term that was not received in a deeper way and discussed further by others. Berry intended to replace the ecological with the ecozoic and described "this new mode of being of the planet" as "the Ecozoic Era, the fourth in the succession of life eras thus far identified as the Paleozoic, the Mesozoic, and the Cenozoic." It remains open to what degree Berry's rather categorical depiction of a radically new age of human-nature relations and the Earth can inspire our discourse on the Ecocene amid and beyond the "Anthropocene." See Berry, *The Ecozoic Era*.

appear partly as a "post-technocene" where the fetishization of money and machines has been overcome and technical spaces have turned into lived spaces.[76]

Seeds of the Ecocene are already growing amid the "Anthropocene," and our forthcoming discourse would need to monitor the process of what we might call ecocenic flourishing already here and now before we can move toward a shift from the one age to the other. The ecorelationality at the core of Pacifica cultures (analyzed by Upolu Lumā Vaai in his essay), local practices and ideologies that deconstruct systems of centralized power, approaches, and experiences of lived post-growth economies as well as indigenous communities characterized by nature-anchored and not profit-accumulating value systems, and much more, would need to come into view in such a perspective. Ecotheology would then in the long run need to explore carefully how the Ecocene is taking shape. Shamanic theologies of sacred sustainability, depicted by Sharon Bong in her essay, and animist beliefs in places, things, and elements around us as living beings with relational capacities, expounded by Mark Wallace in his essay, offer just some of these spiritual ecocenic seeds. Returning to Trinitarian cosmology one can again ask where and how the suffering and liberating Triune's Spirit is taking place in the growth of the Ecocenc amid and beyond the "Anthropocene?"

The term "Ecocene" is in the air and has most recently entered the discourse not so much in science but in other spheres such as architecture, design theory, and theology. It refers to a geological period beyond the "Anthropocene," or rather a slow transformation from the one into the other, where the whole of the ecological sphere embraces and integrates the human. Design theorist Rachel Armstrong states that:

> [*T*]here is no advantage to us to bring the Anthropocene into the future [. . .] The myth of the Anthropocene does not help us [. . .] we must re-imagine our world and enable the Ecocene.[77]

It is probably the lack of a qualified reflection on potential sustainable and unsustainable futures that accelerates the triumphalist and depoliticizing danger of celebrating this new period in the ecomodernist narrative as a new period of human geo-management. One can also wonder if this lack is part of a wider cultural shift where our ways of imaging of the future (and the past) are undergoing a radical shift in the modern time regime.[78]

---

76. For the notion of "technocene" see Hornborg, "The Political Ecology of the Technocene." For the notion of "technical space" see Bergmann and Sager, *The Ethics of Mobilities*. Keller does not tumble into this abyss, but offers quite a homemade—mixed up with Pope Francis's concept of an "integral ecology" (in his *Laudato Si´*)—understanding of the Ecocene as a kind of a subject, an "earthome" (earth+home) that "at once warns and invites" and that "is to be nourished if it is to nourish us." See Keller, *Political Theology of the Earth*, 92.

77. Armstrong, "Architecture for the Ecocene." See Boehnert, *Design, Ecology, Politics*; "Naming the Epoch."

78. Assmann, *Ist die Zeit aus den Fugen?*, 247.

Such an interpretation immediately produces a deep conflict with faith, as the future in the Christian tradition must always remain open for the Creator and Liberator to act upon. According to Jürgen Moltmann, God encounters his/her creation from the future, and I would add also from the past. Time and history, as well as space and place, always remain transparent for the Triune. The Christian creed summarizes this belief in its words about the new world (*aeon*) to come, and this *aeon* can scarcely refer to today's "Anthropocene," a time of human mismanagement and an uninhabitable place for humans to live in as God's images. There is a deep need to hope for what we cannot see (yet): a new world to come beyond the "Anthropocene."

While apocalyptic thinking in its fatalist version imagines the end as a future of chaos and disaster, and manipulates and terrifies its audience, eschatology operates with an integrated present *and* future dimension.[79] It is not simply the interconnection of the now and then but also develops as a spatial theory.[80] The spatial encounter with the God of the *here* and *there* and the God of the *now* and *then* transforms the places in need of liberation. Climatic change represents such a place as it makes it necessary to encounter the life-giving Triune Spirit who takes place both now and then, and both here and there. Faith needs to be reconstructed, faith in the Spirit hovering over the vibrating waters of chaos in the beginning and the Spirit as the Giver of Life and as the source of the new creation to come.[81]

Applying such a spatial and liberative eschatology to the narrative of the Anthropo(Obs)cene, it is impossible to imagine the future as a simple age of humans. "Eschatology as imagining the end" must necessarily stretch beyond the life-threatening anthropogenic impact that the rich nations have executed in the great transformation. Hope needs to flourish so that another age might appear. The reconstructed Christian story and imagery and the story and iconography of the universe can in such a view reemerge in each other when the Ecocene grows amid the "Anthropocene" and gradually transforms this into what is not yet seen and what cannot yet be told.

In my view, such a vision of a re-politicized Ecocene fits perfectly with the biblical vision of a *creatio continua* that flows into a *creatio futura*, that is, the growing creation of the new heavens and new Earth. Biblical imaginaries for such an Ecocene are many: the *seeds* sown is the *reign of God*, the heavenly Jerusalem as a truly eco-urban life-sphere, peaceful pastoral grazing of wild and other animals in the meadows, the pastoral vision of God as good

---

79. Barbara Rossing analyses apocalyptic imagery in the New Testament and makes strikingly evident how it is not necessarily an encouragement to escapism but can also serve as constructive tool to mobilize encountering power in the imperial context. See Rossing, "God's Lament for the Earth."

80. On spatial eschatology, see Westhelle, *Eschatology and Space,* and Bergmann, "Time Turned into Space."

81. On the Holy Spirit, see Volume 9 of this series.

shepherd, and the people and creatures as a herd in a harmonious ecology. Maybe the rainbow could offer us one of the strongest symbols, constantly reminding about the thanksgiving ritual after the flood and climate change disasters when the bow in the sky turns from a symbol of war to a colorful sign of peace between all created beings on Earth, our common home.

■ Bibliography

Ahrens, Donald. *Meteorology Today: An Introduction to Weather, Climate, and the Environment*. 6th ed. Pacific Grove: Brooks/Cole, 2000.

Anderson, Ben. "Affective Atmospheres." *Emotion, Space and Society* 2:2 (2009), 77–81. https://doi.org/10.1016/j.emospa.2009.08.005

Armstrong, Rachel. "Architecture for the Ecocene." https://architectureukraine.org/rachel-armstrong-architecture-for-the-ecocene/ (31 July 2015), accessed 20 November 2017.

Assmann, Aleida. *Ist die Zeit aus den Fugen? Aufstieg und Fall des Zeitregimes der Moderne*. München: Hanser, 2013.

Berry, Thomas. *The Ecozoic Era*. Annual E. F. Schumacher Lecture (October 1991), https://centerforneweconomics.org/publications/the-ecozoic-era, accessed 21 January 2021.

Bergmann, Sigurd. *Creation Set Free: The Spirit as Liberator of Nature* (with a foreword by Jürgen Moltmann), Grand Rapids and Cambridge: Eerdmans, 2005.

———. "The Strange and the Self: Visual Arts and Theology in Aboriginal and Other (Post-) Colonial Spaces." In *Theological Aesthetics After Von Balthasar*, edited by Oleg V. Bychkov and James Fodor, 201–23. Aldershot: Ashgate, 2008.

———. "Atmospheres of Synergy: Towards an Eco-Theological Aesth/Ethics of Space." *Ecotheology: The Journal of Religion, Nature and the Environment* 11:3 (2006), 327–57. https://doi.org/10.1558/ecot.2006.11.3.326

———. "Climate Change Changes Religion: Space, Spirit, Ritual, Technology—through a Theological Lens." *Studia Theologica: Nordic Journal of Theology* 63:2 (2009), 98–118. https://doi.org/10.1080/00393380903345057

———. *Religion, Space, and the Environment*. London and New York: Routledge, 2014.

———. "The Legacy of Trinitarian Cosmology in the Anthropocene." *Studia Theologica: Nordic Journal of Theology* 69:1 (2015), 32–44. https://doi.org/10.1080/0039338X.2015.1027267

———. "Is there a Future in the Age of Humans? A Critical Eye on the Narrative of the Anthropocene." Consortium for the Study of Religion, Ethics, and Society Forum, Spring 2016, Indiana University, https://csres.iu.edu/pages/forum-folder/index.php#Bergmann, accessed 02 February 2021.

———. "Time Turned into Space—At Home on Earth: Wanderings in Eschatological Spatiality." In *Eschatology as Imagining the End: Faith between Hope and Despair*, edited by Sigurd Bergmann, 88–112. London and New York: Routledge, 2018.

———. "With-In: Towards an aesth/ethics of prepositions." In *Arts, Religion and the Environment: Exploring Nature's Texture*, edited by Sigurd Bergmann and Forrest Clingerman, 17–42. Leiden: Brill Rodopi, 2018.

———. *Weather, Religion, and Climate Change*. London and New York: Routledge, 2020.

Bergmann, Sigurd and Dieter Gerten, eds. *Religion and Dangerous Environmental Change: Transdisciplinary Perspectives on the Ethics of Climate and Sustainability*. Berlin: LIT, 2010.

Bergmann, Sigurd, Thomas A. Hoff and Tore Sager, eds. *Spaces of Mobility: Essays on the Planning, Ethics, Engineering and Religion of Human Motion*. New York: Routledge, 2014.

Bergmann, Sigurd, and Tore Sager, eds. *The Ethics of Mobilities: Rethinking Place, Exclusion, Freedom and Environment*. London: Routledge, 2008.

Boehnert, Joanna. *Design, Ecology, Politics: Towards the Ecocene*. London: Bloomsbury, 2018.

———. "Naming the Epoch: Anthropocene, Capitalocene, Ecocene." https://ecolabsblog.com/2016/05/22/naming-the-epoch-Anthropocene-capitalocene-ecocene, accessed 20 November 2017.

Böhme, Gernot. *Für eine ökologische Naturästhetik*. Frankfurt am Main: Suhrkamp, 1989.

———. *Atmosphäre: Essays zur neuen Ästhetik*. Frankfurt am Main: Suhrkamp, 1995.

Colebrook, Claire. "The Future in the Anthropocene: Extinction and the Imagination." In *Climate and Literature*, edited by Adeline Johns-Putra, 263–80. Cambridge: Cambridge University Press, 2019.

Conradie, Ernst M., and Hilda Koster, eds. *T&T Clark Companion on Christian Theology and Climate Change*. London: Bloomsbury, 2019.

Dánél, Mónika. "Atmospheric Adaptation as Cultural Translation (Ádám Bodor—Gábor Ferenczi: The Possibilities of Making Friends, 2007)." *Contact Zones: Studies in Central and Eastern European Film and Literature: A Biannual Online Journal* 2 (2016), 6–23, http://contactzones.elte.hu/atmospheric-adaptation, accessed 03 December 2019.

Deane-Drummond, Celia E., Sigurd Bergmann and Markus Vogt, eds. *Religion in the Anthropocene*, Eugene: Cascade, 2017.

———. "The Future of Religion in the Anthropocene Era." In *Religion in the Anthropocene*, 1–15.

Diaconu, Mădălina. "City Walks and Tactile Experience." *Contemporary Aesthetics* 9 (2011), https://contempaesthetics.org/newvolume/pages/article.php?articleID=607, accessed 03 December 2019.

———. "Longing for Clouds—Does Beautiful Weather Have to Be Fine?" *Contemporary Aesthetics* 13 (2015), http://hdl.handle.net/2027/spo.7523862.0013.016, accessed 14 March 2021.

Emmelhainz, Irmgard. "Images Do Not Show: The Desire to See in the Anthropocene." In *Art in the Anthropocene: Encounters Among Aesthetics, Politics, Environments and Epistemologies*, edited by Heather Davis and Etienne Turpin, 131–42. London: Open Humanities Press, 2015.

Ephrem (Saint). *Hymns on Paradise*. Crestwood: St. Vladimir's Seminary Press, 1990.

Gerten, Dieter and Sigurd Bergmann, eds. *Religion in Environmental and Climate Change: Suffering, Values, Lifestyles*. London and New York: Continuum, 2011.

Gerten, Dieter, Martin Schönfeld and Bernhard Schauberger. "On Deeper Human Dimensions in Earth System Analysis and Modelling." *Earth System Dynamics* 9 (2018), 849–63. https://doi.org/10.5194/esd-9-849-2018

Ginn, Franklin. "When Horses Won't Eat: Apocalypse and the Anthropocene." *Annals of the Association of American Geographers* 105:2 (2015), 351–59. https://doi.org/10.1080/00045608.2014.988100

Goethe, Johann Wolfgang. "Bedeutende Fördernis durch ein einziges geistreiches Wort." In *Zur Naturwissenschaft überhaupt, besonders zur Morphologie: Erfahrung, Betrachtung, Folgerung, durch Lebensereignisse verbunden*. Munich: Chr. Hanser, 1989 (1817–24).

Goto, Reiko and Tim Collins. "The Black Wood: Relations, Empathy and a Feeling of Oneness in Caledonian Pine Forests." In *Arts, Religion and the Environment: Exploring Nature's Texture*, edited by Sigurd Bergmann and Forrest Clingerman, 117–48. Amsterdam: Brill/Rodopi, 2018.

Grau, Marion. "The Revelations of Climate Change: A Petro-Eschatology." In *Eschatology as Imagining the End: Faith between Hope and Despair*, edited by Sigurd Bergman, 45–60. London and New York: Routledge, 2018.

Gregory of Nazianzus. *Homily 14: On Love for the Poor*.

———. *Homily 22.14*.

Hoiß, Christian. "Das Anthropozän: Auf den Spuren einer Narration." In *Crossmediales Erzählen vom Anthropozän: Literarische Spuren in einem neuen Zeitalter,* edited by Sabine Anselm and Christian Hoiß, 13–37. München: Oekom, 2017.

Horn, Roni. *Weather Reports You: A Project of VATNASAFN/Library of Water, Stykkishólmur, Iceland*, London and Göttingen: Artangel/Steidl, 2007, www.artangel.org.uk/project/library-of-water/ (accessed 31 March 2021).

Hornborg, Alf. "The Political Ecology of the Technocene: Uncovering Ecologically Unequal Exchange in the World-System." In *The Anthropocene and the Global Environmental Crisis: Rethinking Modernity in a New Epoch*, edited by Clive Hamilton, Christophe Bonneuil and François Gemenne, 57–69. London: Routledge, 2015.

Ingold, Tim. "Earth, Sky, Wind, and Weather." *Wind, Life, Health: Anthropological and Historical Perspectives, The Journal of the Royal Anthropological Institute* 13 (2007), 19–38. https://doi.org/10.1111/j.1467-9655.2007.00401.x

———. *Being Alive: Essays on Movement, Knowledge and Description*. London and New York: Routledge, 2011.

Keller, Catherine. *Intercarnations: Exercises in Theological Possibility*. New York: Fordham University Press, 2017. https://doi.org/10.1515/9780823276486

———. *Political Theology of the Earth: Our Planetary Emergency and the Struggle*. New York: Columbia University Press, 2018.

———. "Members of Each Other: Intercarnation, Gender and Political Theology." Workshop Presentation at the Faculty of Theology, Lund University, 16 September 2019.

Keller, Catherine, Elias Ortega-Aponte and Melanie Johnson-DeBaufre, eds. *Common Goods: Economy, Ecology, and Political Theology*. Oxford: Oxford University Press, 2015.

Kittsteiner, Heinz-Dieter. *Gewissen und Geschichte: Studien zur Entstehung des Moralischen Bewußtseins*. Heidelberg: Manutius Verlag, 1990.

Konte, Maty and Nyasha Tirivayi, eds. *Women and Sustainable Human Development: Empowering Women in Africa*. Cham: Springer Nature/Palgrave Macmillan, 2020.

Kraus, Helmut. *Die Atmosphäre der Erde*. 4th ed. Berlin, Heidelberg and New York: Springer, 2004.

Lauer, Wilhelm. *Klimawandel und Menschheitsgeschichte auf dem Mexikanischen Hochland*. Mainz, Wiesbaden: Akademie der Wissenschaft und der Literatur, F. Steiner, 1981.

Leggewie, Claus and Harald Welzer. "Another 'Great Transformation'? Social and Cultural Consequences of Climate Change." *Journal of Renewable and Sustainable Energy* 2, 2010. https://doi.org/10.1063/1.3384314.

Malm, Andreas and Alf Hornborg. "The Geology of Mankind? A Critique of the Anthropocene Narrative." *The Anthropocene Review* 1:1 (2014), 62–69. https://doi.org/10.1177/2053019613516291

Picht, Georg. *Der Begriff der Natur und seine Geschichte*. Stuttgart: Klett Cotta, 1989.

Polanyi, Karl. *The Great Transformation*. Boston: Beacon, 2001 (1944).

Porteous, J. Douglas. *Environmental Aesthetics: Ideas, Politics and Planning*. London and New York: Routledge, 1996.

Proust, Marcel. *The Guermantes Way*. *In Search of Lost Time*, Volume 3. London: Vintage Classics, 1996.

Marcel Proust, Le Côté de Guermantes , Paris: Gallimard 1921. Engl. ed., "The Guermantes Way," in: In Search of Lost Time, 6 Volumes, Vol. 3, London: Vintage Classics 1996.

Robertson, Lisa. "The Weather: A Report on Sincerity." DC Poetry (2001), http://www.dcpoetry.com/anthology/242, accessed 17 October 2018.

Rossing, Barbara. "God's Lament for the Earth: Climate Change, Apocalypse and the Urgent Kairos Movement." In *God, Creation and Climate Change: Spiritual and Ethical Perspectives*, edited by Karen L. Bloomquist, 129–43. Geneva: The Lutheran World Federation, 2009.

Schellnhuber, Hans J., ed. "Global Sustainability: A Nobel Cause," Nobel Cause Symposium, Potsdam Memorandum: The Need for a Great Transformation. Potsdam Institute for Climate Impact Research, Potsdam, Germany, 8–10 October 2007.

Schmitt, Stefan. "Politische Energie: Die Hitze Drückt, aber sie Könnte den Ideenwettbewerb der Parteien für den Klimaschutz beflügeln." *Die Zeit* 74:27 (2019).

Schmitz, Hermann. "Von der Scham zum Neid." In *Leib, Ort, Gefühl: Perspektiven der Räumlichen Erfahrung*, edited by Michael Großheim, et al., eds., 19–34. Freiburg and München: Karl Alber, 2015.

Schneidewind, Uwe. *Die Große Transformation: Eine Einführung in die Kunst des Gesellschaftlichen Wandels*. Frankfurt am Main: Fischer, 2018.

Sharp, Hasana. "Not all Humans: Radical Criticism of the Anthropocene Narrative", Environmental Philosophy 17:1 (2020), 143–58. https://doi.org/10.5840/envirophil20202793

Sobecka, Karolina. "The Atmospheric Turn." In *Arts and Religion Responding to the Environment: Exploring Nature's Texture*, edited by Sigurd Bergmann and Forrest Clingerman, 43–58. Leiden: Brill Rodopi, 2018.

Sölle, Dorothee. *Das Fenster der Verwundbarkeit: Theologisch-politische Texte*. Stuttgart: Kreuz Verlag, 1987.

Steffen, Will, et al. "The Anthropocene: Conceptual and Historical Perspectives." *Philosophical Transactions of the Royal Society A* 369 (2011), 842–867. https://doi.org/10.1098/rsta.2010.0327

Swyngedouw, Erik. "Interrupting the Anthropo(Obs)cene." Opening key note, Munich, Deutsches Museum 17 October 2018, at the conference "(Um)Weltschmerz: An Exercise in Humility and Melancholia", arranged by ENHANCE Marie Skłodowska-Curie Innovative Training Network, co-sponsored by the Rachel Carson Center and the Deutsches Museum.

Szerszynski, Bronislaw. "Reading and Writing the Weather: Climate Technics and the Moment of Responsibility." *Theory, Culture & Society* 27 (2010), 9–30. https://doi.org/10.1177/0263276409361915

———. "Life in the Open Air." In *Issues in Science and Theology: What is Life?*, edited by Dirk Evers, et al., 27–41. Cham: Springer, 2016.

Waters, Colin N., et al. "The Anthropocene is Functionally and Stratigraphically Distinct from the Holocene." *Science* 351:6269 (2016), aad2622.

Westhelle, Vítor. *Eschatology and Space: The Lost Dimension in Theology Past and Present*. New York: Palgrave Macmillan, 2012.

Wiggins, Steve A. *Weathering the Psalms: A Meteorotheological Survey*. Eugene: Cascade, 2014.

Young, Serinity. "Religion and Weather." In: *Encyclopedia of Climate and Weather*, edited by Stephen H. Schneider, 639–43. Oxford: Oxford University Press, 1996.

Telling the Story: An Asian Feminist Perspective

Sharon A. Bong[1]

How does the story of who the Triune God is and what this God does relate to the story of life on Earth? Is the Christian story part of the earth's story or is the earth's story part of God's story, from creation to consummation? In response to these overarching, almost overwhelming questions, in drawing from my social-cultural context, I ask what these stories mean from an Asian perspective where the Christian story of creation finds expression in and through the creation stories or more pointedly, ecological responses of other world religions and Asian spiritualities. I also interrogate these questions from a feminist perspective as the Christian story of creation is intrinsically not only an anthropocentric but also an androcentric one; the domination of (hu)man over nature and man over woman, respectively.

I begin with locating the Christian story in Pope Francis's encyclical *Laudato Si'* (henceforth LS) not because it is the first response but that it is arguably the fullest theological response (from the Catholic tradition) to the

---

1. Sharon A. Bong is Associate Professor of Gender Studies at the School of Arts and Social Sciences, Monash University, Bandar Sunway, Malaysia. She is registered as a co-researcher at the University of the Western Cape, South Africa, for the project on "An Earthed Faith: Telling the Story amid the 'Anthropocene'."

How to cite: Bong, S.A., 2021, 'Telling the Story: An Asian Feminist Perspective', in E.M. Conradie & P.-C. Lai (eds.), *Taking a deep breath for the story to begin . . .* (An Earthed Faith: Telling the Story amid the "Anthropocene" Volume 1), pp. 73–93, AOSIS, Cape Town. https://doi.org/10.4102/aosis.2021.BK264.04

ecological crisis.² I take this opportunity to revisit and potentially review an argument that I have made on other occasions—decentering the human in creation—in recognizing, even embracing the end of the "Anthropocene." Is this endeavor that unseats or deprivileges the human in creation, necessarily a post-Christian one? In the second section of this essay, from a Southeast Asian context, I turn to fecund intersections of the materiality of the body vis-à-vis hunger—the Filipino "kumakalam na sikmura" (literally, "gnawing of the stomach")³—is a poignant reminder of the urgency of effecting climate justice and gender justice. Yet, how does one theologize from the bowels of Asia without recolonizing the poor of Asia? Postcolonial liberation ethics point the way in the form of a Shamanic theology of sacred sustainability with church and shamans as interlocutors in dialogue⁴ and the intersection of contemporary ecofeminism with Confucian cosmology.⁵ I offer critical reflections, as an Asian feminist, on what these conversational threads mean for the Christian story of creation.

■ The Christian Story in *Laudato Si'*

The "ground-breaking vision" that permeates Pope Francis's encyclical entirely devoted to climate change in the Age of the "Anthropocene" courageously critiques neoliberal development models that are unjust and unsustainable.⁶ *LS* goes beyond a "purely religious relevance."⁷ The publication of *LS* on 18 June 2015 was strategic as "2015 [was] a critical year for humanity"⁸ which witnessed three landmark assemblies of global experts and policy-makers to address climate change. These high-level and high-impact gatherings include the Addis Ababa Action Agenda that serves as a "global framework for financing development post-2015,"⁹ the UN General Assembly's own 17 Sustainable Development Goals (SDGs), 2015–2030, that build on and extend the largely unrealized eight Millennium Development Goals, 2000–2015,¹⁰ and in particular, COP21, leading to the Paris Agreement on climate change.¹¹

---

2. Pope Francis, "Laudato Si'."

3. Peracullo, "Kumakalam na sikmura."

4. Fung, *Shamanic Theology*.

5. Duncan and Brasovan, "Contemporary Ecofeminism and Confucian Cosmology."

6. Montini and Volpe, "The Need for an 'Integral Ecology'," 65.

7. Montini and Volpe, "The Need for an 'Integral Ecology'," 56.

8. King, "Cardinal hints."

9. United Nations. "Addis Ababa Action Agenda."

10. United Nations, "Sustainable Development Goals."

11. UN News, "COP21."

The "monumental triumph for people and our planet" of COP21 was the pledge of all 195 nations to support the 2030 Agenda, the year of the expiration of the SDGs.[12]

Against this backdrop of UN instruments that are operationalized within human rights, albeit secular frameworks, *LS* holds its own in adding spiritual gravitas that not only holds the Age of the "Anthropocene" accountable for the ecological crisis but more importantly sanctifies the integrity of creation through its Christian story. The encyclical letter comprises six chapters and 246 articles. The preamble[13] starts off with Saint Francis of Assisi's canticle, "Laudato Si'" meaning "Praise be to you." Pope Francis implores us all "to acknowledge the appeal, immensity and urgency of the challenge we face."[14] Thematically, the first three chapters systematically outline the problem and underlying causes which, to some extent, find resonance with the church's anthropocentric "theology of creation." Chapter 1 "What Is Happening to Our Common Home"[15] mirrors the 17 SDGs in its expansive sweep of harm to the ecosystem, from land, sea to sky, and the need for partnership among multilevel and multisectoral stakeholders. The interplay between *LS* and the UN SDGs first lies in the universal turn in exhorting the global community indeed, the "whole of humanity to action."[16] Both documents are also a "sign of the times" in recognizing the urgency of redressing the ecological crisis and the emphasis on "common but differentiated responsibilities" among the developed and developing nations in terms of disparities in consumption and carbon emissions.[17] Chapter 2 "The Gospel of Creation"[18] presents the Christian story of creation. And Chapter 3 "The Human Roots of the Ecological Crisis"[19] articulates the Pope's underlying assumption to his knowledge claim of the near irreversibility of the ecological crisis and humankind's misuse of its gifts in harnessing the gift of creation.

The last three chapters offer solutions and methods in arriving at these solutions, chiefly through dialogue and education. In Chapter 4, "Integral Ecology,"[20] he emphasizes an integrative account of the ecological crisis, in all its multidimensional and intergenerational facets. In Chapter 5, "Lines of

---

12. UN News, "COP21."

13. Pope Francis, *LS*, 1-16.

14. Pope Francis, *LS*, 15.

15. Pope Francis, *LS*, 17-61.

16. Montini and Volpe, "The Need for an 'Integral Ecology'," 62.

17. Montini and Volpe, "The Need for an 'Integral Ecology'," 62-63.

18. Pope Francis, *LS*, 62-100.

19. Pope Francis, *LS*, 101-136.

20. Pope Francis, *LS*, 137-162.

Approach and Action,"[21] he returns to multisectoral, multilevel, and multidisciplinary responses among key stakeholders that are meaningful and coordinated. *LS* culminates in Chapter 6, "Ecological Education and Spirituality," that spiritualizes the call to action where others have politicized it. He exhorts a Christian praxis for all as a call to "ecological conversion."[22] This divine covenant complements UN-sponsored international treatises as humanity's pledge, beyond a pledge of nations, to recognize the sacramental nature of nature premised on the covenant between God and human and nature. This final chapter includes sections on ecological conversion, and the Trinity and the relationship between creatures. The encyclical letter ends, as it starts, with an eulogy to creation vis-à-vis its Creator.

The Triune God as a Creator starts off the Christian story of creation. The main takeaway of the Christian story is order. The first principle of creation is *order from chaos*: "In the beginning was the Word, and the word was with God, and the Word was God" (John 1:1).[23] From a watery womb where "the earth was formless and empty, [and] darkness was over the surface of the deep" (Gen 1:1), God created light to distinguish it from darkness leading to the ordered temporality of day and night, and as "signs to mark sacred times, and days and years" (Gen 1:14). The creation of "the vault" or sky spatially demarcates waters from the sky and land (Gen 1:8–10). The incremental acts of creation from the first day to the sixth day in populating the earth with the great diversity of "living creatures" of the ecosystem (Gen 1:20) culminate in the prime creation; "mankind in his own image, in the image of God he created them; male and female he created them" (Gen 1:27). The mastery of time-space is effectively bequeathed to "mankind" who are fashioned in the likeness of God and this mastery is extended to the rest of creation, that "they may rule over" (Gen 1:26) creatures not fashioned in the likeness of God. The scope of that "rule" bears a similar sequencing of the spatial ordering of sea-sky-land ("ground"): "the fish in the sea and the birds in the sky, over the livestock and all the wild animals, and over all the creatures that move along the ground" (Gen 1:26). It is a complete "rule," the green light to domesticate the wild across sea-sky-land, in the sense that no creature is above "rule" or off-limits to "mankind." This, in turn, confers on "mankind" the Creator's prerogative, indeed power to create order vis-à-vis mastery of that which is not "in his own image."

What is apparent from the logic of creation—the "Word" (*logos*) as God—evidenced through the mastery of time-space, is the creation of mutually exclusive entities. Light is not darkness as day is not night. Land is neither water nor sky, water is neither land nor sky, and sky is neither water nor land.

---

21. Pope Francis, *LS*, 163–201.

22. Pope Francis, *LS*, 202–246.

23. New International Version. Also cited in Pope Francis, *LS*, 99.

Livestock, fish, and birds are differentiated based on their singular habitats (amphibians notwithstanding), for example, livestock cannot live in the sea and sky, fish cannot live on land and in the sky, etc. Male is not female. And "mankind" is not God. This leads us to the concomitant second principle of creation which is *order as hierarchy*. These mutually exclusive entities are not only opposites but ordered hierarchically, for example, light/darkness, male/female (Gen 2:20–24), and God/"mankind" where the first term is dominant and the second term, secondary to and derivative from the first term. "We are not God," as Pope Francis forcefully reminds us.[24] He takes "mankind" to task for following through the original charge to "rule over the fish in the sea and the birds in the sky and over every living creature that moves on the ground" along with "Be fruitful and increase in number; fill the earth and subdue it" (Gen 1:28). On the one hand, Pope Francis alludes to the church's near atonement for "incorrectly [interpreting] the Scriptures" that has inadvertently "encouraged the unbridled exploitation of nature by painting [man] as domineering and destructive by nature."[25] On the other hand, Pope Francis defends "Judaeo-Christian thinking"—the roots of the Christian story—by positing that, "*nowadays* we must forcefully reject the notion that our being created in God's image and given dominion over the earth justifies absolute domination over other creatures" (italics mine).[26] So while nothing that has "the breath of life in it" (Gen 1:30) still remains off-limits, limits are "nowadays"— in the Age of the "Anthropocene"—placed on mankind's "absolute dominion" of not just sentient beings (all that have "the breath of life" in them except humans) but also the ecosystem in its entirety (land, sea, and sky).

To buttress the instrumentality of nature designed to literally feed "mankind" where, as God decrees, "They will be yours for food" (Gen 1:29), those who eat rather than are eaten are "nowadays" exhorted to recognize that "each creature bears in itself a specifically Trinitarian structure."[27] What does this mean for meat eaters, including exotic animal consumers, vegetarians, vegans, those who have too much to eat, those who go hungry of their own volition and those who are hungry because they are poor or those who eat last and the least? What does this mean with regard to consuming genetically modified livestock and birds (e.g., poultry) and fish that choke on our plastic-ridden seas? Pope Francis in citing Bonaventure, that Franciscan saint, explains that "human beings, before sin, were able to see how each creature 'testifies that God is three'."[28]

---

24. Pope Francis, *LS*, 67.

25. Pope Francis, *LS*, 67.

26. Pope Francis, *LS*, 67.

27. Pope Francis, *LS*, 239.

28. Pope Francis, *LS*, 239.

This leads to the third principle of creation which is *order as divine*; the "world was created by the three Persons acting as a single divine principle."[29] "The Father" as the "ultimate source of everything" is the "loving and self-communicating foundation of all that exists." "The Son" born of woman, who reflects "the Father" through the Incarnation, "united himself to this earth." "The Spirit," as the "infinite bond of love, is intimately present at the very heart of the universe."[30] One creates it; the second, once walked the earth; and the third, sustains it. Here is no counterpoint or co-mingling of opposites but rather a fusion of mutually inclusive "three Persons" acting as one, as "a single (albeit masculinized) divine principle" and acting with singularity of purpose. The inter-relationality of the Triune God lays its indelible albeit differentiated mark on creation; "each of them performed this common work in accordance with his own personal property,"[31] far removed from nature's own creative-destructive life forces. The Triune God, as "subsistent relations," is mutually supportive and hence complementary. This "divine model" of creation renders the world, "a web of relationships."[32] The challenge, therefore, "of trying to read reality in a Trinitarian key"[33] is to recognize that as everything is ordered, "Everything is interconnected"[34] but not necessarily equal. It is a call to "go out from [ourselves] to live in communion with God, with others and with all creatures."[35]

Yet is the failure to constantly "live in communion with God, with others and with all creatures," simply a consequence of the "human gaze" that purportedly remains "partial, dark and fragile"?[36] What exactly does it mean to "live in communion" with a world that is already overpopulated, where there has been a faithful adherence to "Be fruitful and increase in number; fill the earth" but not to "subdue it" (Gen 1:28)? Would turning to the "gaze of Jesus" in turn, lift our gaze?[37] The "mystery of Christ" offers a relatable moral compass as Christ embodies the creative tension between transcendence and immanence, as the "divine Word (*Logos*)" that "became flesh."[38] The human condition as "partial, dark and fragile" becomes through the incarnated Christ,

---

29. Pope Francis, *LS*, 238.

30. Pope Francis, *LS*, 238.

31. Pope Francis, *LS*, 238.

32. Pope Francis, *LS*, 240.

33. Pope Francis, *LS*, 239.

34. Pope Francis, *LS*, 240.

35. Pope Francis, *LS*, 240.

36. Pope Francis, *LS*, 239.

37. Pope Francis, *LS*, 96–100.

38. Pope Francis, *LS*, 99.

grounded, messy, and transient. Where the "One Person of the Trinity entered into the created cosmos, throwing in his lot with it, even to the cross,"[39] humankind likewise throws in their lot with the cosmos and have throughout its existence, impinged on the natural world, carbon footprint and all, where Christ "is at work in a hidden manner."[40] In the like manner that Jesus harnessed natural energies, where "even the winds and the sea obey him" (Matt 8:27),[41] humankind has built wind turbines, dams, and solar panels in near "full harmony with creation." As Jesus, son of a carpenter, "worked with his hands," he "sanctified human labour and endowed it with a special significance for our development."[42] What kinds of human-driven technological advances are viewed as humankind's collaboration "with the Son of God for the redemption of humanity"?[43] This Second Person of the Trinity, the human-God who embraced the sensuality of "body, matter and the things of the world" calls to question the second principle of creation which is order as hierarchy where such "unhealthy dualisms (e.g., mind/body, spirit/matter) . . . [have] disfigured the Gospel."[44]

Disfiguring nature, as Pope Benedict instructs, also harms humankind's own nature; "Man does not create himself. He is spirit and will, but also nature."[45] The baser nature of "Man" that perceives and treats nature, both the "natural environment" and "social environment" as "simply [Man's] property" is tantamount to a "misuse of creation"; this alienation with nature is an alienation of the self, and an alienation of the self with its Creator, the Triune God.[46] It is in effect to not recognize the gentle promptings of the Holy Spirit coursing through creation and all in it. Humankind is called upon to collaborate not only "with the Son of God for the redemption of humanity" but also with the Spirit of God which "can be said to possess an infinite creativity, proper to the divine mind."[47] Some semblance of feminization of the Spirit is discernible as "the things we think of as evils, dangers or sources of suffering" which are intrinsically part of the human condition and aspiration for development, are likened to "the pains of childbirth." A gestation and birthing of free will, "the

---

39. Pope Francis, *LS*, 99.

40. Pope Francis, *LS*, 99.

41. Pope Francis, *LS*, 98.

42. Pope Francis, *LS*, 98.

43. Pope Francis, *LS*, 98.

44. Pope Francis, *LS*, 98.

45. Pope Francis, *LS*, 6.

46. Pope Francis, *LS*, 6.

47. Pope Francis, *LS*, 98 and 80.

autonomy of [God's] creature" in turn "gives rise to the rightful autonomy of earthly affairs" in continuing the "work of creation."[48]

Yet, it is precisely the human labor entailed in exercising this autonomy, in continuing the "work of creation" that "mankind" is taken to task for in Chapter 3, "The human roots of the ecological crisis."[49] Why? Because "mankind" has overreached their potential by usurping God's mastery of the universe and needs to be put in place within the order of creation. Let us review this through the prism of what constitutes "mankind's" creative prowess read as transgressions. "Mankind" has not only inherited but also magnified the first principle of creation; order from chaos—where in the "presence of something formless, completely open to manipulation," "men and women" (one of the rare occasions that "mankind" is not used generically) have "constantly intervened in nature."[50] The technological and scientific breakthroughs in a vast array of fields—from art, architecture, agriculture, biomedicine, communications, weaponry, travel to space—traverse staggering achievements on land, sea, and sky. These achievements evidence a "technique of possession, mastery and transformation"[51] over microorganisms to natural (and unnatural or nuclear) sources of energy and exceed the boundaries of earth, this "common home" to other planetary systems. Pope Francis attributes the fruits of this human labor, disparagingly, as a "technological paradigm," as the dominant order of human society and way of life that has ravaged nature.[52] The ordering from chaos is also evidenced in the creation of civilizations of, for, and by humans that are founded on institutions that include, among others, familial, educational, political, finance, legal, juridical, cultural, and religious. Pope Francis assesses these as driven by a "technocratic paradigm" that "tends to dominate economic and political life" in compelling most societies most of the time to unnecessarily privilege profits over people and the human over nature.[53]

Should this phenomenon be merely branded as a "modern anthropocentrism" where "mankind" "[prizes] technical thought over reality" in perceiving and treating nature as "an insensate order, as a cold body of facts, as a mere 'given', as an object of utility, as raw material to be hammered into useful shape?"[54] "Mankind" has faithfully followed through a biblical

---

48. Pope Francis, *LS*, 80.

49. Pope Francis, *LS*, 101–136.

50. Pope Francis, *LS*, 106.

51. Pope Francis, *LS*, 106.

52. Pope Francis, *LS*, 108.

53. Pope Francis, *LS*, 109.

54. Pope Francis, *LS*, 115.

anthropocentrism where creatures of the land, sea, and sky are created to feed the human who by virtue of being created in the likeness and image of God, in turn, invests in nature its intrinsic value in relation to its use to the human. "Modern anthropocentrism" is the execution of a biblical anthropocentrism par excellence where "mankind" has proliferated the uses of nature beyond consuming it, that is, beyond its original utility value as food for humans. In this regard, "mankind" recreates, in exercising their God-given free will and autonomy, as a collaborative partner of the Triune God, the second principle of creation, order as hierarchy. Yet, where some humans confer dignity to nature in the form of embracing its bountiful biodiversity, arguing for ecological sustainability for its own sake rather than as a means to the end of sustaining the human and championing the rights of animals, such "biocentrism" is unceremoniously labeled as a "misguided anthropocentrism."[55] Thou shalt know thy place! Biocentrism unseats anthropocentrism; the former is deemed inimical to the latter as it is framed in oppositional terms to the latter. Humankind now errs in not upholding its place in the food chain, in not recognizing and valuing their "unique capacities of knowledge, will, freedom and responsibility"—the very qualities that humankind are, in the same breath of life, admonished for in overreaching itself. In straddling "modern anthropocentrism" and its corollary "misguided" variant, humankind is damned when it does and damned when it does not, that is, recognize and value its superiority as created in the image and likeness of the Triune God, as enshrined in biblical anthropocentrism. This is to not disavow human beings "as possessing a particular dignity above other creatures." It is to not deny the "source of our nobility as human persons."[56] But when dignity and nobility of humankind are claimed, does this not leave nature as "an insensate order" or at best, imbued with less dignity and nobility?[57]

The most fallible misrecognition of its worth lies in humankind's potentiality to appropriate the third principle of creation—order as divine, that is, to extend and prevent life through animal and human experimentation, and the use of abortifacients, respectively. In breaking down the barriers of life/death, "man sets himself in place of God," rather than carry out "his role as a cooperator with God in the work of creation."[58] Respecting the "integrity of creation" through "experimentation on animals" can still be realized when it is done moderately, is done for the sake of "man," and with the recognition that "human power has limits."[59] That is the extent of what is "morally acceptable"

---

55. Pope Francis, *LS*, 118.

56. Pope Francis, *LS*, 119.

57. Pope Francis, *LS*, 115.

58. Pope Francis, *LS*, 117.

59. Pope Francis, *LS*, 130.

in terms of animal ethics that does not transgress to biocentrism: the loss of life or limb of animals is justified "within reasonable limits [and] contributes to caring for or saving human lives."[60] It is needful rather than needless suffering or death that is consonant with "human dignity" where the human person is "endowed with reason and knowledge" and the plant or animal is bereft of reason and knowledge.[61] Experimentation on humans, on "living human embryos," is therefore illicit and tantamount to "transgressing all boundaries" because "human embryos" are "endowed with reason and knowledge?" A "technology severed from ethics" blurs the lines differentiating a subject from an object of experimentation and "will not easily be able to limit its own power"[62] where the unbridled potential of (un)becoming is in fact the catalyst to human advancement.

Even more transgressive is the purposeful ending of life or potentiality of life through abortion or use of contraceptives.[63] The church's teaching is resolute and reinforced in *LS*: "Since everything is interrelated, concern for the protection of nature is also incompatible with the justification of abortion."[64] Studies drawn from the lived realities of those most affected who are the least, the last, and the lost among us show that best practices work on the intersection of "climate justice," "gender justice," and "reproductive justice" for those seeking linkages between climate change and population reduction.[65] Addressing climate change values the interrelatedness among "common but differentiated responsibilities" ("climate justice"), a feminist framework that calls not only for an "equitable share in the existing power system" but also for a deconstruction of that male-dominated system ("gender justice"), women and girls' universal access to sexual and reproductive health and rights services ("reproductive justice").[66] Hence, the silence of euphemism[67] in referring to the overpopulation of the earth as mere "demographic growth [that] is fully compatible with an integral and shared development"[68] is dangerously myopic. It is also a dishonest claim and exposes the church's lack of accountability in "refusing to face the issues"[69] of climate change and population reduction.

---

60. Pope Francis, *LS*, 130.

61. Pope Francis, *LS*, 130.

62. Pope Francis, *LS*, 136.

63. Pope Francis, *LS*, 120.

64. Pope Francis, *LS*, 120.

65. Silliman, "In Search of Climate Justice," 1–3.

66. "Definitions," 11.

67. Pittaway, "Silenced by Euphemism."

68. Pope Francis, *LS*, 50.

69. Pope Francis, *LS*, 50.

Humans have been "fruitful" and increased so exponentially that they have not only filled the earth but unsustainably subdued it (Gen 1:28). The excesses of a "throwaway culture,"[70] consumerism,[71] and social injustices[72] are justifiable laments but these, far from being disconnected from the overpopulation of the human species, are in fact its consequences in a desperate fight for a fast depleting bounty of the earth's resources. Where there is not enough to go around, and food and resources are not equitably distributed, hunger can only precede greed; one cannot have or want more if one has nothing (to eat or live on).

In sum, the Christian story as portrayed in *LS* maintains that, "There can be no ecology without an adequate anthropology."[73] Interrelatedness, which lies at the heart of an "integral ecology,"[74] must not flatten out differences among species: the harm in not seeing an "intrinsic value in lesser beings" (nonhuman) is overshadowed by the greater harm or misgiving of not seeing a "special value in human beings" as the latter is created in the image and likeness of the Triune God.[75] Upholding the "intrinsic value" in all of the creation need not be a zero-sum game where beings are locked in a dichotomous relationality of "special"/"lesser" which is, in fact, reductionist. What is the potentiality of realizing the vision of *LS*'s "integral ecology" when we can see that "the human person is considered as simply one being among others"?[76] When the human person is thus de-centered, does it necessarily mean that their "overall sense of responsibility wanes"[77] in realizing climate justice for all? There is concession in following the science, so to speak, when Pope Francis grants that "living species are part of a network which we will never fully explore and understand."[78] The grandeur of creation and the mystery of the Triune God made manifest in that creation is surely not dimmed but rather glorified with the revelation of interrelatedness that, "A good part of our genetic code is shared by many living beings." A genetic commonality for inhabitants, large and small of a "common home" from land to sea and sky[79]—where "common" is a buzzword in *LS*—enables us to contemplate the Triune God in the "beauty of the universe/

---

70. Pope Francis, *LS*, 16 and 22.

71. Pope Francis, *LS*, 34, 50, 184, 203, 210, 215, 219, and 232.

72. Pope Francis, *LS*, 36, 70, 74, 82, 142, 158, 170, and 200.

73. Pope Francis, *LS*, 118.

74. Pope Francis, *LS*, 137.

75. Pope Francis, *LS*, 118.

76. Pope Francis, *LS*, 118.

77. Pope Francis, *LS*, 118.

78. Pope Francis, *LS*, 138.

79. Pope Francis, *LS*, 1, 3, 13, 17, 53, 61, 155, 164, 232, and 243.

for all things speak of you."⁸⁰ It is fitting to now turn to other stories that start off from that premise of interrelatedness that position the human person "as simply one being among others."

Other Stories

In the second section of this essay, the stories about creation that are contextualized in Asia offer different takeaways. Where the Christian story foregrounds creation as order from chaos, order as hierarchy, and order as divine, these stories privilege creation as materiality, creation as proliferation, and creation as interrelated.

I turn first to *creation as materiality*, specifically, the materiality of the body vis-à-vis hunger—the Filipino "kumakalam na sikmura" (literally, "gnawing of the stomach")⁸¹—as a poignant reminder of the urgency of effecting climate justice, gender justice, and reproductive justice. Jeane Peracullo, an Asian-Catholic ecofeminist philosopher from the Philippines, reflects theologically from the lived realities of poor and hungry Filipino women. Hunger, as she posits:

> [/]s an embodied experience [*that*] exposes the human body as sexed and gendered; biological yet also social, political, and cultural; material yet metaphorical and symbolic; and a site of not only varied oppressions but also liberation.⁸²

Her theology from the perspective of poor and hungry women's suffering and pain stems from her awareness that women are differently and disproportionately affected by the systemic structures of domination/subjugation that cut across these multiple sites. Hunger is as such symptomatic of the pervasive oppression that these women know because they have come to own the embodied experience of hunger for food, land, and justice and yearn for liberation from dispossession and essentially a life of dignity. In this regard, "kumakalam na sikmura" refers "both to the physiological aspect of hunger as well as the state when the stomach 'communicates' its needs to the person" through demanding and insistent cries.⁸³ The body is neither inferiorized nor dichotomously positioned in contrast to the mind or rationality or knowledge as it is by western thought; the body is "material and biological—that is, 'it is flesh'."⁸⁴ We are mindful in this instance of both the Eucharist where we are nourished by the body of Christ and the incarnate Jesus who

---

80. Pope Francis, *LS*, 246.

81. Peracullo, "Kumakalam na sikmura," 26.

82. Peracullo, "Kumakalam na sikmura," 26.

83. Peracullo, "Kumakalam na sikmura," 37.

84. Peracullo, "Kumakalam na sikmura," 37.

knew hunger and satisfied it—"The Son of Man came eating and drinking."[85] The body also provides a "sense of historicity," for example, hunger for land rights, food security, and legal reform to better address gender- and sexual-based violence and discrimination faced by women. The body through indigenous spirituality also provides a "sense of continuity with nonhuman bodies," connected yet distinct.[86] "Kumakalam na sikmura" thus frames an ecofeminist praxis that is marked by "a community of care ethics" that accords epistemic privilege to the dispossessed.[87]

An ecofeminist praxis that remembers without romanticizing a body in pain recognizes that poor and hungry women's bodies—not in a monolithic sense—become sites of contestation for climate justice, gender justice, and reproductive justice, as "there can be no climate justice without reproductive justice."[88] On the question of the intersection of climate change and population reduction, the Philippines leads the way in navigating the intricacies and sensitivities of universalism (e.g., women's rights) and cultural relativism (e.g., religious conservatism among policy-makers, health providers whose rights as conscientious objectors are preserved in the RH Act). The *2012 Responsible Parenthood and Reproductive Health Act* (or RH Act) is a ground-breaking piece of legislation that provides a state-sponsored sexual and reproductive health and rights (SRHR) framework in Catholic-majority Philippines. It is aimed at tackling unplanned pregnancies, the consequences of unprotected sex, high infant and maternal mortality rates, and "the second highest population growth rate in Asia" through family planning and comprehensive sexuality education.[89] It is hailed as a "very promising first step in reducing the cycle of poverty, improving the national economy, and bettering the chances for both Filipino men and women"—essentially in tasting a life of dignity.[90] A gender-sensitive document on climate change, as opposed to a gender-neutral or, worse, a gender-blind one, is potentially transformative. It recognizes the intersectionality of poverty (and the hunger that results from that), the shift from a morally imperialistic approach in policy, and SRHR programming by developed nations imposing population control on poor communities (which includes forced sterilization) to "multifaceted, rights-respecting, environmentally sound and equitable development models"[91] that empower

---

85. Pope Francis, *LS*, 98.

86. Peracullo, "Kumakalam na sikmura," 38.

87. Peracullo, "Kumakalam na sikmura," 43.

88. Silliman, "In Search of Climate Justice," 3.

89. Nazareno, "Responsible Parenthood," 95.

90. Nazareno, "Responsible Parenthood," 122.

91. Silliman, "In Search of Climate Justice," 1.

women, in particular, to make healthy and informed decisions about their bodies.

With the materiality of bodies in creation in mind and heart, we now turn to the principle of *creation as proliferation* through a shamanic theology of sacred sustainability that flows from Malaysian Jesuit, Jojo M. Fung's long-term affinity with indigenous peoples' struggles for self-determination culminating in his initiation as a shaman in the *Murut* (indigenous from Sarawak, East Malaysia) tradition. Among his post-initiation reflections, having taken the plunge, is his contrasting the "scientific logic" or "modern logic" of "collapsing many worlds into the one world or neoliberal global capitalism"—resonant with *LS*'s much maligned "technocratic paradigm"[92]—with the "shamanic logic that the human world is but one of many worlds."[93] Where the former has the propensity to "desecrate the visible world by hollowing it of its transcendental presence," resulting in the dehumanization of the human person, an "indigenous logic" advocates that "the sacred is in all of life."[94] As such, sacredness is attributed not only to the "seen world" but also to "the unseen world" where spirits abound. In both these worlds, the sacredness of desecrated spaces and the humanity of persons are reclaimed. The human and nonhuman worlds, that is, "spirits in the unseen world," are one. Neither is "special" nor "lesser" in relation to the other. Embedded in the "indigenous logic is the experience that the indwelling presence of the divine being and shamanic spirits in our world has made sacred all things . . . that all are 'sacredly alive'."[95]

This generative spirit is further manifested in Fung's articulation of a "spirituality of sacred sustainability for the local churches of Asia" wherein spirituality is understood and profoundly experienced as the "opening of one's body space" until it becomes "increasingly borderless and porous" and when touched by the "God-who-descends unto God's people," it "transforms the web of relationships with all things, all beings and all spaces."[96] That time and space "are not independent of one another" is made tangible.[97] Through his initiation into indigenous shamanism, a religious tradition that predates Christianity in Asia, Fung's journey to "liberative engagement" in climate justice, in partnership with the *Murut* peoples, is in turn sustained by his being

---

92. Pope Francis, *LS*, 101, 109, 111–112, and 122.

93. Fung, *Shamanic Theology*, 26–27.

94. Fung, *Shamanic Theology*, 27.

95. Fung, *Shamanic Theology*, 109.

96. Fung, *Shamanic Theology*, 120.

97. Pope Francis, *LS*, 138.

a disciple of a shaman guru (elder and teacher).[98] The figure of the shaman is paradigmatic of porous borders and interlocking journeys into realms that are worldly and otherworldly, worldviews that are Christian and indigenous, and existences that are grounded in the body and spirit. His "discipling"[99] imitates the spirit of Jesus, as a Galilean shamanic figure in early Palestine tradition who wondered and wandered, where the shaman's sacred place is not restricted to "one holy place but is connected to the shaman's bodily presence and immediate communication with the divine."[100] The body becomes not only a conduit for "spirits in the unseen world" but is a spirit in connectivity with other bodies and spirits.

The third principle of *creation as interrelatedness* finds expression not only in the figures of poor and hungry women negotiating the intersectionality of poverty, climate change, and SRHR but also shamans coursing through time and space. We turn now to forest or ecology monks within the Theravada Buddhist tradition in Thailand who espouse "eco-*dhammic* ethics" as activists-ascetics in engendering "transformative environmental adult education" as well as a Buddhist environmental movement.[101] An "eco-*dhammic*" ethics is "caring for nature" (*anurak thammachāt*) in the *dhammic* sense which is understood as: "the active expression of our empathetic identification with all life forms: sentient and nonsentient, human beings and nature."[102] Beyond their well-publicized acts of ordaining trees, or standing up to loggers at risk of life and limb even to their revered Thai monarch who is sometimes ambivalent about the conservation of nature, forest monks empty themselves to achieve this "ingrained selfless, empathetic response."[103] Quite significantly, an eco-*dhammic* ethics cares "for all things in the world in their natural conditions" which translates in everyday praxis as differentiated from common (global) motivations of conserving nature for our own pleasure, physical and spiritual well-being, or even the benefit of future generations.[104] Their eco-*dhammic* praxis stems from the "realization that I do not and cannot exist independently of my total environment."[105] This interrelatedness that calls forth a selflessness borne from humility follows through a truth claim that is eschewed in *LS*, namely, that "the human person is considered as simply one

---

98. Fung, *Shamanic Theology*, 168.

99. Fung, *Shamanic Theology*, 168.

100. Fung, *Shamanic Theology*, 180.

101. Walter, "Activist Forest Monks," 336 and 343.

102. Walter, "Activist Forest Monks," 335.

103. Walter, "Activist Forest Monks," 335.

104. Walter, "Activist Forest Monks," 335.

105. Walter, "Activist Forest Monks," 336.

being among others."¹⁰⁶ It brings in unison the otherworldly (asceticism) and worldly (activism) *dhamma* of forest monks as they engender consciousness-raising among lay communities based on Buddhist principles such as: "the interdependence of society, culture and nature"; "restraint (from greed), social equity and generosity"; and "loving-kindness and respect for the community."¹⁰⁷

How does an eco-*dhammic* ethics and praxis within a Buddhist cosmology speak to an "integral ecology" as envisioned in *LS*? Where an "integral ecology" intimates a consideration of intersectionality, we, therefore, ask to what extent is the intersection of climate justice, gender justice, and reproductive justice manifest in an eco-*dhammic* ethics and praxis? A feminist analysis of the institutionalized androcentric ordering of Buddhist religious and lay communities would inform a more faithful interrogation of "the structures, processes and effects of patriarchy, the male-dominance of [green] movement leadership, [or] the gendered impacts of deforestation, and how these interact with each other."¹⁰⁸ The denial of women's access to the Sangha—the order of fully ordained male [*bhikku*s] and female [*bhikkhuni*s] monks leading to the ambivalent status of *mae chii*s (i.e., crossover between female nuns and laywomen who are at the base of the hierarchical social structure),¹⁰⁹ adds to the gender-discriminatory prohibition of women from teaching not only Buddhist scriptures to the laity but also eco-*dhammic* ethics in the "educative-activism" of Environmental Adult Education. While women are not at liberty to adopt an ascetic life indwelling the forests, burdened as they generally are by their productive and reproductive functions, a spotlight on the "gendered impacts of deforestation" would show that Thai rural and indigenous women are more greatly impacted as they are the "principal users of forest, land and other water resources."¹¹⁰ Where there is conflict over resources, often precipitated by capitalist greed (e.g., resulting in the killings and disappearances of forest monks),¹¹¹ displacement ensues which limits women's access to sexual and reproductive health (SRH) services which in extreme cases of neglect could lead to malnutrition and increase their risks of morbidity and mortality. Women's work burden increases and they are made more vulnerable to sexual harassment which is a part of the continuum of sexual- and gender-based violence during climate change extreme events, for example, walking further to fetch water or being resettled in temporary camps.¹¹²

---

106. Pope Francis, *LS*, 118.

107. Walter, "Activist Forest Monks," 336.

108. Walter, "Activist Forest Monks," 343.

109. Falk, *Fields of Merit*, 43–45.

110. Walter, "Activist Forest Monks," 342–43.

111. Walter, "Activist Forest Monks," 340.

112. Lim, "Why Prioritise SRHR," 19.

Appreciating the cogency of the third principle of creation as interrelatedness is to turn finally to the intersection of ecofeminism and Confucian cosmology. Confucianism is lauded as the bulwark of Singapore's progress and development in nation-building discourses. The late Lee Kuan Yew, former prime minister, modeled Singapore, the most affluent postcolonial nation state in Southeast Asia, home to diasporic Chinese, on the economic success of the Asian tigers of East Asia, for example, China, Hong Kong, and Japan. In looking to Eastern philosophies rather than Western Enlightenment, he became a proponent of "Asian values" that run counter to a western model of divisive, atomistic individualism in embracing (societal) cohesion, compliance, and communitarianism. Such Asian values are undergirded by Confucian-grounded virtues of "thrift, hard work, filial piety and loyalty in the extended family, and, most of all, the respect for scholarship and learning" toward self-cultivation.[113] The androcentric leanings of such self-cultivation, there and then, based on the classical model of the masculine Confucian sage shape shifts through a "redemptive imagination" (of neo-Confucianism), here and now. As such, an ethos of inclusion, regardless of one's social and biological inheritance, takes shape and form where "becoming persons" is open to all through the hard work of edification and cultural contributions to the community.[114] Becoming community through the achievement of harmony among persons finds expression in the complementary doctrines of the "rectification of names" (*zhengming*) and "ritual propriety" (*li*).[115] Problematically, through a feminist lens, these form and sustain "hierarchical power relationships—relationships between subordinating and subordinated persons,"[116] where the ruler rules over his subjects, the father over his family, and son over his (elderly and widowed) mother. The flourishing of persons within communities founded on "hierarchical harmony" is not glossed over but rather acknowledged to be susceptible to "the slippery slope" that relativizes harm and that predisposes one to "unjust chauvinistic anthropocentric views and practices."[117]

Yet hope prevails. Within the planetary model of becoming, "Qi" is a "material force" or "vital force" or "vital power."[118] A "*qi*-cosmology" eschews traditional accounts of matter as an "inherently inert substance" as well as the "bifurcation of matter and mind inherited from the European Enlightenment"[119]

---

113. Zakaria, "Culture is Destiny," 114.

114. Duncan and Brasovan, "Contemporary Ecofeminism," 233–34.

115. Duncan and Brasovan, "Contemporary Ecofeminism," 234.

116. Duncan and Brasovan, "Contemporary Ecofeminism," 234.

117. Duncan and Brasovan, "Contemporary Ecofeminism," 235.

118. Duncan and Brasovan, "Contemporary Ecofeminism," 239.

119. Duncan and Brasovan, "Contemporary Ecofeminism," 239.

which is the metaphysical equivalent of an anthropogenic climate crisis. Instead, a "*qi*-based materialism" provides "a resource for formulating a kind of naturalistic religious experience, which values persons and their environmental relata as participatory and interactive constituents of a unified filed of *qi*."[120] As an energy that fuels the "incessant transformations (becoming) of the world," *qi* is likened to "sublime vacuity (*taixu*)" where "there is neither 'matter', nor 'causes', nor 'architect'," contrary to what was taught by the first Jesuits who arrived in China around 1600. The universe is sublime "energy in incessant and invisible activity."[121] It does not require "an external cause (let alone an agency) to create the world and imbue it with a coherent order of things (*wuzhili*)" because matter is "intelligent"[122]: it is procreative. It proliferates. The "*continuity* of nature and persons" is "a continuity of energy (*yiqi*) and a continuity of pattern (*yili*),"[123] rather than order and hierarchy.

We now turn the spotlight to the "procreative harmony" of the inter-relationality of *yin* and *yang*.[124] It is easy to characterize this inter-relationality as a "dualistic metaphysics" until one realizes that "neither *yin* nor *yang* are given ontological or axiological priority."[125] Instead, they mutually imply one another as correlative and reciprocal. The traditional pictographs for *yin* and *yang* illustrate the shady side of a hill and the sunny side of a hill. These of course change places over the course of a day which render categories that define *yin* and *yang* as "[provisional] and relative to one another."[126] In terms of gender relations, LS posits that, "It is not a healthy attitude which would seek to cancel out sexual difference because it no longer knows how to confront it."[127] A *qi*-cosmology offers an alternative and fluid way of becoming masculine and feminine beyond characteristics that are contrastive and worse, hierarchized. As "day is day-becoming-night, and night is night-becoming-day," so all beings in a *qi*-cosmology are radically understood, in a departure from dichotomous couplings, as "becomings."[128] Persons in harmony with the world, become "active participants in a shared vital materiality" of a vision of what may be. This is a "vision of a trinity of the heavens, earth and persons."[129]

---

120. Duncan and Brasovan, "Contemporary Ecofeminism," 240.

121. Duncan and Brasovan, "Contemporary Ecofeminism," 240.

122. Duncan and Brasovan, "Contemporary Ecofeminism," 241.

123. Duncan and Brasovan, "Contemporary Ecofeminism," 241.

124. Duncan and Brasovan, "Contemporary Ecofeminism," 246.

125. Duncan and Brasovan, "Contemporary Ecofeminism," 247.

126. Duncan and Brasovan, "Contemporary Ecofeminism," 247.

127. Pope Francis, *LS*, 155.

128. Duncan and Brasovan, "Contemporary Ecofeminism," 248.

129. Duncan and Brasovan, "Contemporary Ecofeminism," 248.

While it is acknowledged that "persons are the most valued among the heavens, earth, and myriad things," it is incumbent on persons to value harmony, as it is but one force among others, as engendering "a prerequisite, a productive and developmental power."[130]

▌Conclusion: The Christian Story Revisited

How does the story of who the Triune God is and what this God does relate to the story of life on Earth? The Christian story that is narrated in *Laudato Si'* is a noteworthy reference, as it forms the basis of an "integral ecology" that celebrates the profound relationality of Creator and creation. The story of who the Triune God is, in that compression of time-space, has unwaveringly been: God the Father as the absolute Source of All, incarnated as the Son, and lives on through the breath of the Spirit permeating all creation. The three-person God that starts off and sustains the Christian story of creation begets a three-faceted sense of order: order from chaos, that primordial vacuity; order as hierarchy where differences in creation are not only proliferated but also hierarchized; and order as divine where the Trinitarian structure that suffuses each creature reflects the glory of the inter-relationality albeit differently ordered "three Persons."

Yet, this particular Christian story is only part of the earth's story. Catherine Keller's tehomic theology reframes that oft-told Christian story by recuperating *tehom*, the "divine womb [that] remains neither God nor not-God but the depth of 'God'."[131] A "radical interdependence" that arises "not from a prior nothing," between Creator and creature would potentially designate "creation as incarnation."[132] And *ruach*, despite two centuries of clerical misogyny, groans with creation in labor pains.[133] The Triune God, as we know it, is made fuzzy, disordered, and out of place. Creation becomes radicalized as chaotic, co-extensive (with the Creator), and immanent. The fecund wellsprings of Asian feminist ecotheologies and spiritualities, resonate with Keller's tehomic theology in offering transformative counter-narratives to the indefatigably anthropocentric but also androcentric worldview of the Christian story in *Laudato Si*. Privileging creation as materiality vis-à-vis the hungry body of the Filipino poor, creation as proliferation through the ecotheology of a Malaysian Jesuit priest-shaman and eco-*dhammic* ethics of Thai forest monks, and

---

130. Duncan and Brasovan, "Contemporary Ecofeminism," 248.

131. Keller, *Face of the Deep*, 227. Sigmund Bergmann's musings in this volume, namely on going beyond the "Anthropocene" inspired by Keller's "inter-carnation", resonates with the queer intent of this essay, in opening up possibilities of becoming and doing ecotheologies.

132. Keller, *Face of the Deep*, 218–19.

133. Keller, *Face of the Deep*, 228.

creation as interrelated through a "qi-cosmology" of Confucianism that fuels Singapore's neoliberalist pursuit of the "technocratic paradigm" serve to impregnate the Christian story of creation with differences that matter and matter that is different. And in this other queer beginning that goes beyond God the Father, Son, and Spirit lies integral hope.

■ Bibliography

Bible. New International Version. https://www.biblestudytools.com/niv/.

Definitions. *ARROW for Change* 15 (2009) 11. http://arrow.org.my/wp-content/uploads/2015/04/AFC-Vol.15-No.1-2009_Climate-Change.pdf, accessed 25 January 2021.

Duncan, Taine and Nicholas S. Brasovan. "Contemporary Ecofeminism and Confucian Cosmology." In *Feminist Encounters with Confucius*, edited by Matthew A. Foust and Sor-hoon Tan, 226–51. London and Boston: Brill, 2016.

Falk, Monica Lindberg. *Making Fields of Merit: Buddhist Female Ascetics and Gendered Orders in Thailand.* Copenhagen: NIAS Press, 2007.

Fung, Jojo M. *A Shamanic Theology of Sacred Sustainability: Church and Shamans in Dialogue for Liberative Struggle in Asia*. Quezon City: Jesuit Communications Foundation, 2014.

Keller, Catherine. *Face of the Deep: A Theology of Becoming*. London and New York: Routledge, 2003.

King, Ed. "Cardinal Hints at Main Themes in Pope's Climate Change Encyclical." *Climate Home News*, 2015. https://www.climatechangenews.com/2015/03/11/cardinal-hints-at-main-themes-in-popes-climate-change-encyclical/, accessed 25 January 2021.

Lim, Hwei Mian. "Why Prioritise SRHR in Climate Change Programming and Policymaking." *ARROW for Change* 23 (2017), 18–21.

Montini, Massimiliano and Francesca Volpe. "The Need for an 'Integral Ecology' in Connection with the UN Sustainable Development Goals." In *Care for the World: Laudato Si' and Catholic Social Thought in Era of Climate Crisis*, edited by Frank Pasquale, 56–67. Cambridge: Cambridge University Press, 2019.

Nazareno, Tala L. "The Responsible Parenthood and Reproductive Health Act of 2012: An Analysis of the Potential Effects of Family Planning and Sex Education Requirements in the Philippines." *Women's Rights Law Reporter* 35 (2013), 95–122.

Peracullo, Jeane C. "*Kumakalam na sikmura*: Hunger as Filipino Women's Awakening to Ecofeminist Consciousness." *Journal of Feminist Studies in Religion* 31 (2015), 25–44. https://doi.org/10.2979/jfemistudreli.31.2.25

Pittaway, Eileen. "Silenced by Euphemism: Sexual Torture in Conflict and Refugee Situation." *ARROW for Change* 13 (2007), 4–5.

Pope Francis. *Laudato Si': Encyclical Letter of the Holy Father Francis on Care for Our Common Home*. Vatican: Libreria Editrice Vaticana, 2015.

Silliman, Joel. "In Search of Climate Justice: Refuting Dubious Linkages, Affirming Rights." *ARROW for Change* 15 (2009), 1–3.

UN News. "COP21: UN Chief Hails New Climate Change Agreement as "Monumental Triumph." https://news.un.org/en/story/2015/12/517982-cop21-un-chief-hails-new-climate-change-agreement-monumental-triumph, accessed 25 January 2021.

United Nations. "Addis Ababa Action Agenda of the Third International Conference on Financing for Development." A/RES/69/313, Resolution adopted on 27 July 2015, 1–37. http://www.un.org/ga/search/view_doc.asp?symbol=A/RES/69/313, accessed 25 January 2021.

United Nations. "Sustainable Development Goals." http://www.un.org/sustainabledevelopment/sustainable-development-goals/, accessed 25 January 2021.

Walter, Pierre. "Activist Forest Monks, Adult Learning and the Buddhist Environmental Movement in Thailand." *International Journal of Lifelong Education* 26 (2007), 329–45. https://doi.org/10.1080/02601370701362333

Zakaria, Fareed. "Culture is Destiny: A Conversation with Lee Kuan Yew." *Foreign Affairs* 73 (1994), 109–126. https://doi.org/10.2307/20045923

On the Hope That the Christian Story May Transform the Universe Story: A South African Reformed Perspective

Ernst M. Conradie[1]

■ The Christian Story and the Universe Story

How is the Christian story of who God is and what God has done, is doing, and is expected to be doing (as reconstructed by contemporary ecotheology) related to the universe story as reconstructed by contemporary science? While this question may appear to be purely academic, in the context of the story of the emergence of what is named by some as the "Anthropocene" (and contested by others) and how its story will play itself out in this century, it becomes a crucial question. As the theme of the "Anthropocene" was

---

1. Ernst M. Conradie is a Senior Professor in the Department of Religion and Theology at the University of the Western Cape in South Africa.

How to cite: Conradie, E.M., 2021, 'On the Hope That the Christian Story May Transform the Universe Story: A South African Reformed Perspective', in E.M. Conradie & P.-C. Lai (eds.), *Taking a deep breath for the story to begin...* (An Earthed Faith: Telling the Story amid the "Anthropocene" Volume 1), pp. 95-118, AOSIS, Cape Town. https://doi.org/10.4102/aosis.2021.BK264.05

addressed in the introduction to this volume, I will focus here on addressing the question, having recognized its significance.

As is often the case, it is the "and" in the question above that intrigues. This a question that emerges in multiple other forms in theological discourse—on the relationship between God and the world, heaven and earth, church and society, church and state, religion and theology, science and theology, faith and reason, nature and grace, "ecclesiology and ethics," body and soul, general revelation and special revelation, and so forth. There may be a need to avoid sterile binaries but in each case this still has to be addressed.

In whatever way it is addressed, it is important to note that both science and theology are rooted in ordinary human experience, that is, in indigenous knowledge of the world and in the lived Christian faith of the laity. Scientific knowledge is not a destruction but a purification, expansion, and completion of ordinary knowledge.[2] Both the Christian story and the universe story are the outcome of long processes, stretching over thousands of years. How these are to be related depends upon the angle employed. A different response may be given depending on whether an order of being, an order of knowing, an order of complexity, an order of quality, an order of purpose, or an order of beauty (or wisdom or whatever else) is assumed.[3] Three preliminary observations may follow from this:

First, we humans have knowledge of the world before we can possibly have knowledge of God—both individually and in the evolutionary history of our species. An articulation of the Christian faith and theological reflection on its content and significance necessarily presupposes and employs vocabulary derived from elsewhere that are adopted and then adapted to consider the content and significance of the Christian faith. A purist position on natural theology is therefore hermeneutically impossible. Our notions of God are socially constructed, as it were "in *our* own image." While this is hermeneutically inevitable, this recognition should prompt the need for a critique of idolatry, not the theological legitimation of power relations. I will return to this aspect later.

Second, the outlines of the Christian story of God's economy were already more or less in place in the first century CE while it became possible to

---

2. These are phrases used by Herman Bavinck in his *Reformed Dogmatics 1*, 223, 226. He therefore recommends "realism" for a theory of knowledge over and against idealism or empiricism. Such realism maintains both the constraints of the human mind that keeps it from losing touch with the material world and its freedom to soar to the world of the ideal.

3. In Herman Bavinck's prolegomena, three foundations (*principia*) for theology are distinguished, namely, a *principium essendi* (God as source), a *principium cognoscendi externum* (the self-revelation of God in Jesus Christ, documented in Scripture), and a *principium cognoscendi internum* (the illumination of human beings by the Holy Spirit through faith). This yields a Trinitarian structure for his prolegomena: The Father, through the Son as Logos imparts Godself to creatures through the Spirit. See Bavinck, *Reformed Dogmatics 1*, 207–14. In my terminology, this indicates a distinction between an order of being, of knowledge, and of coming to such knowledge (faith). Such a distinction can be recognized only retrospectively so that *pro*legomena in this way comes *after* an exposition of the content and significance of the Christian faith.

reconstruct an integrated universe story on the basis of developments in astrophysics, quantum mechanics, geology, evolutionary biology, and paleoanthropology only by the late twentieth century. In terms of an order of being, the relationship remains contested. Most Christians would maintain that God as Creator was there before the universe emerged. Most secular critics would maintain that "God" is nothing but a social construction so that the world was there long before humans and their notions of God existed. In my view this is hardly a fruitful debate. Scientists remain as intrigued as theologians (and everyone else who has gazed at the stars) that the world is there in the first place—and how and why it exists. Theologians by their own admission realize that their notions of God are socially embedded and open to critique—as scientists realize that their "facts," theories, and paradigms are open to peer review and contestation. All these disciplines seek to make sense of the world that we find around us, although at different levels and from different angles, at times with profound insight, but not always so.

Third, there is no single Christian story as there is no single universe story. The integration of insights from the various sciences within an integrated history of the universe is remarkable but every aspect of that history is subject to controversy in various scientific schools of thought and any narrative version open to contestation. Likewise, the Christian tradition is a story of many conflicting stories even though they each carry a reference to the figure of Jesus the Christ.

In this contribution, I will suggest that the simplest way of understanding the relationship between the Christian story and the universe story is to maintain that versions of the Christian story redescribes, reinterprets, renarrates, and therefore translates, transfigures, and possibly transforms reconstructions of the universe story—as found in fragments among scientists but also among politicians, economists, historians, novelists, filmmakers, copywriters, glossy media presenters, gossipers, and story tellers of all stripes. Since such (mostly secular) reconstructions are always ongoing and incomplete, preliminary, contested, the task of theological redescription always remains incomplete, preliminary contested, and vulnerable as well.

In order to develop this thesis, I will first situate the origins of the Christian story in evolutionary history and then develop this position in conversation with my theological ancestors in the Reformed tradition of Swiss, Dutch, and German origin and its (often disastrous) reception in the South African context.

■ A Very Brief Account of How the Christian Story Came into Being

Sometime in human evolution, possibly around the time of the cultural awakening, humans began to raise questions that may now be described as of an ultimate nature. Such questions went beyond day-to-day mundane questions about food, shelter, safety from threats, health, social cohesion, sexual relationships, suffering, and the like. I suggest that one may identify five clusters of these questions.

First, there are questions about origins: Where do I come from? Where did my people come from? Where did the world around us come from? Why is there something rather than nothing? Second, there are questions about destiny: What will my life come to? What happens when I die? What will happen to my children, my people, my culture, my land? And later: where is history going to? What will happen to the world in the end? Third, there are questions about identity, value, purpose, and agency: Who am I and how do I relate to others around me? Why are some stronger, cleverer, more beautiful, more dexterous than me? Who are we? Why are we different from other human groups and other animals? Why are we here? What must I do, today and tomorrow, and perhaps next year? Can I make a difference? What does this all mean? Fourth, there are questions about change: What is going on around me and around us? Are there changes in the weather and the land, or do things basically remain the same? And in society? Do we need to remain here or travel further? What are children of the next generation up to? What drives these changes? What trends do we need to recognize? Can we detect a sense of direction, a sense of purpose perhaps? Fifth, there are questions about suffering, injustice, and evil: Where does evil ultimately come from? How can I/our community cope with the demands of life? Why do I experience pain and suffering and others less so? How do I deal with the aging and death of my loved ones and of myself? How should we deal with injustice, especially those forms of injustice that cannot be undone? What about oppression by other groups (a question that probably came somewhat later)? How can we overcome evil in ourselves and evil around us that overwhelm us?

A few observations on such questions may be helpful. First, these are arguably questions that most if not all humans, especially children ask. Second, these are ultimate questions that no one can give any final answer to. Answers elude us because they are not within our locus of control to fathom. Penultimate answers to ultimate questions would not suffice. That applies to science as much as it applies to philosophy, theology, and the arts. The stories we tell in response to "ultimate questions" are never all that tidy, comprehensive, or coherent. This also applies to personal identity. Even where I have to account for my own life story, my memory will be selective; there are many aspects of my life that will remain hidden to me, that are repressed at a subconscious level, that I do not and cannot grasp.[4]

---

4. Richard Niebuhr observes that the meaning of our lives typically escape us because our memories are so selective: "We do not really know what we have done and are still doing to others, not even to those closest to us, for example to our own children." He suggests that God's revelation in Jesus Christ helps Christians to disclose the deeper meaning of their past, present, and future. See Niebuhr, *The Meaning of Revelation,* 65.

Third, in order to go on living we cannot avoid provisional answers to such questions.[5] Such answers express deeply held convictions about life, the universe, and everything. Fourth, such convictions cannot be expressed as certainties but are nevertheless far from trivial; they matter. We structure our lives, our communities, whole civilizations around the answers that we give. This may well be the pathos of the human condition: we raise questions that we cannot answer but have to answer and our lives may well depend on the answers we give.[6] This prompts many anxieties, but also evokes awe and wonder. It calls for wisdom but also lead to foolishness and disaster. Finally, these answers are typically given in the form of stories that are re-enacted and reinforced through rituals. These stories have to be cosmological in scope in order to address all five the questions as sketched earlier.

As I have often argued, cosmological narratives provide us with stories of the origin and destiny of the universe and of the place of humanity within the cosmos.[7] Answers to life's ultimate questions are embedded in such a story. We tell these stories because they help us to answer such questions. They are formative because they tell us who we are, where we are, and what we must do. In the words of Thomas Berry that I have often quoted before:

> For peoples, generally, their story of the universe and the human role in the universe is their primary source of intelligibility and value. Only through this story of how the universe came to be in the beginning and how it came to be as it is does a person come to appreciate the meaning of life or to derive the psychic energy needed to deal effectively with those crisis moments that occur in the life of the individual and in the life of the society. Such a story is the basis of ritual initiation throughout the world. It communicates the most sacred of mysteries. [. . .] Our story not only interprets the past, it also guides and inspires our shaping the future.[8]

---

5. I recognize the postmodern critique of any logocentric references to an ultimate origin, destiny, center, or ground, as if it is possible to be protected from the disruption of différance. However, I am not convinced that it is possible to avoid such questions and (provisional) answers. The suspicion against totalizing answers is entirely appropriate but that also applies to any *endless* play of signifiers. In the "Anthropocene," we cannot avoid telling stories that provide such provisional answers. The *play* of signifiers is becoming ominous, especially insofar as this is born from the ennui of the consumer class.

6. Michel Serres describes the human animal as one who refuses to know what it is. See *Hominescence*, 48.

7. I am drawing here on formulations from my *Christianity and Earthkeeping*, 129-30; also *The Earth in God's Economy*, 124.

8. Berry, *The Dream of the Earth*, xi. Berry adds that "It's all a question of story. We are in trouble just now because we do not have a good story. We are in between stories. The old story, the account of how the world came to be and how we fit into it, is no longer effective. We have not yet learned the new story. Our traditional story of the universe sustained us for a long period of time. It shaped our emotional attitudes, provided us with life purposes, and energized action. It consecrated suffering and integrated knowledge. We awoke in the morning and knew where we were. We could answer the questions of our children. We could identify crime, punish transgressors. Everything was taken care of because the story was there" (123). Berry's own version of the story builds upon Teilhard de Chardin and was further developed by Brian Swimme and Mary Evelyn Tucker. This illustrates both the possibility of an integrated "story of the universe" and why any such a story will necessarily become hotly contested. See also the introductory essay on "Setting the Scene" and Heather Eaton's essay in this volume.

Cosmological narratives locate human life within a cosmic order across which the moral fabric of society is often woven. Every model of the cosmos conveys an ethos as well as a mythos. Creation stories are recalled and celebrated in worship and ritual because they tell us who we are and how we can live in a meaningful world. There seems to be an inextricable link between cosmologies and a code of moral values.[9] Cosmologies provide a sense of identity, orientation, order, meaning, and value. They offer a framework to make sense of the world around us and our place within it. They explain why things are what they are (symbolic-cognitive), what they could be (possibility and imagination), and how things should be (normative). They address the "inner depths of the human soul (emotive) and motivate people to action (conative)." Such cosmological narratives are for these same reasons also embedded in power structures and then serve to legitimize the interests of the dominant classes. They therefore invite suspicion and contestation—by telling other, competing stories. Narratives are therefore not only crucial for the formation of character but also in moral malformation and indeed moral re-formation.[10]

Sometime, who knows when, groups of humans started addressing these questions together and they did so with reference to something that is beyond themselves, perhaps a powerful force, perhaps something hidden, but certainly something that they are dependent upon. And at some point they started using words for god, gods or God to name that which is beyond themselves but nevertheless influence their lives in multiple ways. This move makes good sense if only because the five clusters of questions could be answered together in this way. God is the origin and the destiny of the world, our identity and vocation must be understood in relation to God. God is steering history toward some goal and if we suffer, this has to be addressed in relation to such a God or gods. Once this move was made, the question was no longer whether one believes in God but about the identity and character of this God or gods, or whatever other words may be used to express the referent of answers to these ultimate questions. Indeed, one cannot but put one's trust in something or someone beyond one's locus of control, including modern substitutes such as the Nation, the Party, Progress, the Market, or Lady Luck. To seek control over that which is beyond one's locus of control (the gods) is one definition of idolatry. Put differently, the focus of religious experience is not the human experience itself but what it is that is experienced (e.g., the divine presence).

Of course, any reference to God necessarily became contested as groups of people migrated and came across one another and their stories. Were there different gods or only different concretions of the same numinous, omnipresent sense of transcendence? Such contestations were often violent and mixed up

---

9. See Rasmussen, "Cosmology and Ethics," 178. See also Birch et al., *The Bible and Ethics*, 138–44.

10. See Birch et al., *The Bible and Ethics*, 144–49.

with issues of politics, economics, culture, and religion. In response to such contestations some emphasized the need to recognize all local perceptions of God as worthy of respect. Neglecting another deity was considered a more serious offense than worshipping false gods. However, with the rise of monotheism in Egypt and later of Greek philosophy there emerged a need to avoid false notions of God. Such contestation continues up to this day; even where the word god is no longer used, there is still a need to address these questions in terms of one's deepest convictions.

The Hebrew stories, at least from the figures of Abraham, Isaac, and Jacob onward, have to be understood in this light, namely, to seek clarity on the identity and character of this God with whom they were engaging. Their notions of God were contested from the very beginning, from the outside and from the inside. The Hebrew Scriptures tell the story of these contestations with multiple trajectories. Any clarity emerged only slowly and with many dead-ends. How to reconstruct such trends is also contested but I would suggest that there is a trend away from a tribal notion of God, and of the God of the affluent, landed elite, to the God of wandering Arameans, Egyptian slaves, dislocated people (Apiru), underdogs. There is also a trend away from a warrior god acting on behalf of a particular people to a God of inclusive mercy and therefore justice. The culmination of that trajectory may well be the symbol of the suffering servant in Deutero-Isaiah. Remarkably, the biblical canon juxtaposes such stories with others reflecting the ideologies of the ruling classes so that these texts and the traditions and trajectories that they elicit become a record of struggle and remain a "site of struggle."[11]

The Christian movement that emerged in the first century of our Common Era continued the quest for clarity on God's identity and character. The canonical Scriptures tell the story of the ministry, death, and resurrection of Jesus of Nazareth, proclaimed to be the Messiah. Jesus uniquely blended the symbols of the coming Messiah with the suffering servant and radicalized this by proclaiming the coming reign of God that is epitomized by the blind seeing, the lame walking, the imprisoned being free, and the poor receiving the gospel. On this basis the early Christian movement came to the conclusion not only that Jesus is the expected Messiah, but that He is "Lord" and is to be worshipped. Not only is he "truly divine" but God is actually like Jesus. In Jesus of Nazareth, odd as this may be, we gain the clearest clue of who God is and what God is like. It took three more centuries for this insight to become clarified and expressed through the selection of the canonical writings and the formulation of the Nicene Creed of 325. The latter was revised at

---

11. In the South African context, see Mosala, *Biblical Hermeneutics and Black Liberation*; West, *The Stolen Bible*; and Nürnberger, *Theology of the Biblical Witness*. The role of hermeneutics will be further explored in volume 2 of the *An Earthed Faith* series.

Constantinople in 381 to also recognize that the Holy Spirit is the Giver of Life and is to be worshipped and glorified together with the Father and the Son.

This confession captures the meaning of the story up to that point in time but it adopts an embedded timeline from creation in the first article to consummation in the third article, hinging upon the tension between death and resurrection in the second article. The confession is therefore best understood as capturing the meaning of a narrative, the Triune story of God's "economy." This story covers at least seven "chapters," namely (1) creation from the beginning onward, (2) ongoing creation, leading to (3) the emergence of humanity and human sin, (4) God's providence making room for (5) the history of salvation that leads toward (6) the formation of the church, its ministries, and missions, and (7) ultimately toward the consummation of God's work.[12] These "chapters" may be distinguished, described, and structured in different ways but few would dispute that these are among the core themes addressed in the Christian story.

This briefest of accounts of how the Christian story came into being may suffice to demonstrate five basic claims embedded in this story.

First, this was never the only version of the story; it was one among many attempts to answer the kind of questions sketched earlier. To recognize such other attempts requires categories to explain some form of similarity philosophically. This can be done through concepts such as faith, convictions, religion, worldviews, the holy, the divine, transcendence, the infinite, the absolute, the ultimate, and so forth. The retrospective need for (clarity regarding) such concepts arises inevitably but their adequacy is always relative to the point of similarity that they seek to express. None of these concepts therefore provide any foundation for understanding the Christian story. There is no generic religion, only concrete ones with often conflicting truth claims.

Second, the claim of Christians who hold this confession is that this version of the story makes better sense than any of the available cosmological narratives, especially on overcoming evil, and may therefore be proclaimed as good news to all others.

Third, the answers that they found also helped them to reformulate the questions that were raised in such a way that the questions, categories, and provisional answers that were adopted from elsewhere were always also adapted to fit in with the revised version of the story. This is exemplified by the move, mentioned above, from saying that Jesus is divine to saying that whatever is divine is defined by Jesus. It is therefore inappropriate to maintain that Christians provide particular answers to general questions as if such

---

12. As argued in *The Earth in God's Economy*.

general questions can be formulated first and independently. In an order of coming to know, the questions may have come first but theologically speaking (retrospectively) the answers helped to shape the questions.[13] The questions do not necessarily predetermine the answers; the questions are formulated with hindsight given some of the available answers. Likewise, what is regarded as common with other faith traditions is best understood as a proposal to be further discussed in conversation with others.

Fourth, Christians need not deny that they are engaged in the social construction of reality with all that this may entail, but they nevertheless typically maintain that what they confess is more receptive than creative; they understand themselves to be recipients of God's grace and ultimately ascribe the content of what they confess to God's self-disclosure in Jesus Christ (see below). Such redescription and ascription become possible only retrospectively. Perhaps this is the result of the recognition that psychological, sociological, and economic theories are inadequate because they assume that humans create God in response to some human need. They thus destroy the core aspect of the very phenomenon that they seek to explain. In response, Christians would insist that God is known only because God's wishes to be known by creatures, as is expressed in the notion of God's revelation.[14]

Finally, despite many examples to the contrary, Christians regard themselves at best as witnesses to the truth that they confess and not as the final judges of that truth. As witnesses to the Way of Jesus Christ, they may proceed in "bold humility," alongside people of other persuasions, recognizing them as fellow sojourners on an uncertain journey.

■ Reflections on God's Revelation in the Reformed Tradition, Especially in South Africa

In the Reformed tradition in which I am situated the question raised in this volume regarding the relationship between the universe story as reconstructed by contemporary science and the Christian story of God's work raises further questions on God's revelation. Although Calvin did not use such terms, Reformed discussions typically focus on the relationship between so-called general revelation and special revelation. This obviously builds upon the classic notion of the two books: the book of nature and the book of Scripture.

---

13. Barthians would concur with the second part of the sentence but in my view need to acknowledge the significance of the first part as well.

14. See Bavinck, *Reformed Dogmatics 1*, 275–76. One may say with Bavinck that revelation is the *principium externum* of the Christian faith and thus of Christian theology. As principium, it may need to be treated first. However, in the order of coming to know, one may also say that the category of revelation is introduced only retrospectively.

In the Reformed tradition, the clearest early expression of this distinction is found in Article 2 of the Belgic Confession of 1651 on "The means by which we know God":

> We know God by two means: First, by the creation, preservation, and government of the universe, since that universe is before our eyes like a beautiful book in which all creatures, great and small, are as letters to make us ponder the invisible things of God: God's eternal power and divinity, as the apostle Paul says in Romans 1:20. All these things are enough to convict humans and to leave them without excuse.
>
> Second, God makes himself known to us more clearly by his holy and divine Word, as much as we need in this life, for God's glory and for our salvation.[15]

Most Reformed churches in South Africa subscribe to the Belgic Confession. However, Article 2 has been subjected to many controversies. Without going into detail on its history of reception, let me note the following issues: First, apartheid theology typically emphasized the first part of the article given its emphasis on the orders of creation. Since racial differentiation was regarded as one of these orders, reaffirmed after Babylon (Gen 11) and its attempts to impose imperial unity, racial segregation could be portrayed as God's will. Apartheid theology was indeed a critique of British colonialism albeit in exclusivist and racialized terms! Second, the theological critique of apartheid rightly criticized such views as another form of natural theology by emphasizing the second part of the article. Such creation orders are socially constructed and cannot be made normative. Third, there is a return to the first part of the article among those (mostly evangelicals) who emphasize responsible environmental stewardship. They emphasize the beauty of God's creation and our responsibility for earthkeeping accordingly, but (awkwardly for evangelicals) this leaves the relationship between the two "books" unexplored. Fourth, there is ongoing debate on the implications of this article for the continuity/discontinuity between African traditional religion and culture and the Christian faith as mediated by missionary forms of Christianity. The question is whether indigenous African and biblical words for God refer to one and the same Triune God.[16] Evidently, some emphasize continuity (in order to critique missionary arrogance), while others emphasize discontinuity for the sake of affirming either African identity or Christian authenticity. Fifth, the gendered aspects of the relationship between the two books (Mother Nature versus the maleness of special revelation?) are left unexplored. That this remains a major concern is reflected in the paucity of significant women theologians in the Reformed tradition—and alas therefore also in the bibliography of this essay. Finally, the impact of secularization is also evident

---

15. For this English translation, see https://www.crcna.org/welcome/beliefs/confessions/belgic-confession#toc-article-2-the-means-by-which-we-know-god (accessed 19 October 2021).

16. See Conradie and Sakupapa, "Decolonising."

here: for many the two books are not authored by God but are either authored by humans (modernism) or authorless (postmodernism).

From the above it should be clear that how the universe story and the Christian story relate to each other is a loaded question in Reformed circles, especially in South Africa. I therefore need to explore the position sketched above in more detail and now with reference to Reformed debates on the relationship between special revelation and general revelation. In doing, so I need to build on some previous work in this regard:

In *Saving the Earth?* (2013) I offered a historical overview on diverging notions of re-creation in the Reformed tradition of Swiss, Dutch, and German origin. I devoted chapters to an all-male cast of John Calvin, Herman Bavinck, Karl Barth, Oepke Noordmans, Arnold van Ruler, and Jürgen Moltmann and the disastrous reception of this tradition in South Africa. This necessarily touched on the relationship between general and special revelation.

In *The Earth in God's Economy* (2015) I then offered a liturgical vision of the Triune God as the ultimate mystery of the world. I maintained that this mystery is best understood with the image of a palimpsest, a multilayered story where one text is partially effaced to make room for writing another. The most basic layer of this story[17] is indeed the presumed universe story and all subsequent layers are based on this "parchment." Reconstructions of the parchment take place through the collective efforts of the various sciences. Salvation history is not separate from human history or cosmic history. These are not disconnected histories, but one may identify more than one dimension and understanding of history. The different layers of inscription may be in conflict with each other so that an older layer is deliberately deleted (or *cross*ed out!) even though an earlier inscription may carry more significance than a later one. The Christian story of who God is and what God has done, does, and will be doing then offers an interpretation of this mystery, of the ultimate meaning of the universe story.

Since I stand by these earlier contributions there is no need here to cover the same ground. I do need to comment more explicitly on the category of revelation.

■ Six Theses on General and Special Revelation

It is crucial to recognize that the relationship between general and special revelation, like the relationship between the Christian story and the universe

---

17. In *Hope for the Earth* (2005) I suggested the notion of "cosmic inscription," that is, that the whole history of the universe is inscribed forever in the eschaton, not only in God's memory, but in all its materiality and temporality. This is then not another layer but the eschatological gathering together of all the other layers. This is not by itself an image of hope since all the evils of history are then inscribed too. But it does allow for the possibility of eschatological redemption.

story, can be approached from different perspectives—ontological, epistemological, qualitative, teleological, etc. Priorities may be assigned differently, depending on the perspective. General revelation and special revelation are often treated as two sources for knowing God but such an epistemological perspective fails to recognize that what is regarded by Christians as God's special revelation is still embedded in history. In other words: special revelation forms part of general revelation, a special part. The inverse is not true.

Following this preliminary observation, let me offer six theses on the troubled distinction between general and special revelation[18]:

- *Thesis 1: There is nothing special about the category of "revelation." It is used appropriately to acknowledge something receptive rather than constructive.*

There is no need for Christians to monopolize the category of revelation, or even to treat it in primarily religious terms. From a secular perspective there is no need to deny experiences that may be regarded as revelatory. Even from the perspective of social constructivism, "revelation" indicates the recognition that an insight is as much receptive as it is constructive. It is impossible to use the category of revelation without recognizing its experiential dimension, that is, with the recipient of such revelation. Arguably, one cannot use the category of experience without acknowledging its receptive dimension either (illustrated by Heidegger's notion of *aletheia* as uncovering). Although poets may use language innovatively to create new meaning, they are recipients of a language tradition so that language also speaks through them. Ground-breaking scientific insights are often described as "a revelation," a mystic experience, more than a "discovery," as the famous stories about Archimedes and Newton illustrate. Religious forms of experience described as preverbal "manifestations" (more than verbal proclamations) only radicalize the way in which reality shows itself as numinous.[19] The givenness of reality then may be readily interpreted as a gift, albeit both as grace and as poison. The category of revelation easily becomes poisonous when used to justify authoritarianism (claiming that my received views are "revealed"). Given issues of race and gender, claims to have received a "revelation," even the very interest in the theme of revelation (or lack thereof), therefore have to be tested, both in science and in theology. That also applies to the detective claiming that "*All* will be revealed!":

---

18. My source of inspiration here is the remarkable oeuvre of Herman Bavinck, especially his *Reformed Dogmatics* and *Philosophy of Revelation*. See also the monumental doctoral dissertation by Veenhof, *Revelatie en Inspiratie*.

19. See Tracy, *Fragments*, 224, following Mircea Eliade and Paul Ricoeur's notion of a dialectic between manifestation and proclamation.

- *Thesis 2: Christian discourse on God's revelation is rooted in such quite common if not altogether "ordinary" human experience.*

All talk about revelation "from above" comes from below. There is no need for an appeal to the miraculous; the extraordinary within the ordinary may suffice. All notions of revelation are rooted in experience. All intimations of transcendence can only be maintained from within what is immanent. This is the core insight of the modern turn to the subject, probably best articulated by Friedrich Schleiermacher. A purist, arguably Barthian position on natural theology is therefore untenable. It is historically unfounded, hermeneutically impossible, and apologetically disingenuous. In fact, one may say that all theology is in a sense natural theology.[20] If humans form part of nature, whatever they do or say is natural. In the same sense, all theology is anthropology (where Schleiermacher is correct). On this basis one may say that what Reformed Christians describe as "general revelation," even if distorted by sin, constitutes the necessary presupposition to recognize God's special revelation. Special revelation assumes general revelation.[21] The knowledge of God is only possible on the basis of God's self-revelation but this insight emerged only retrospectively.

The vehement critique of natural theology remains highly appropriate, as is best illustrated in the context of the confessing church movement in Nazi Germany and the theological critique of apartheid. However, its strategy often becomes misleading since the theological conclusions derived at after centuries of debate are used as a point of departure for critique, typically following a deductive logic. That is again entirely appropriate but only if the long, altogether human and therefore messy process of reaching such conclusions, following an inductive logic, is acknowledged. This is best illustrated by the Christian confession as expressed in the Nicene-Constantinopolitan Creed (325/381). The creeds are end-products that crystallize the meaning of a longer narrative in which those who formulated the creed are embedded.[22] For this reason the order of coming to faith is not necessarily the same as the order of coming into being. Both can only be recognized retrospectively. Only in reaching a conclusion does it become possible to say that any talk about God has been enabled by God's self-revelation from the beginning.[23] Ultimately, the knowledge of God therefore

---

20. See Conradie, "All Theology."

21. See Bavinck, *Philosophy of Revelation*, 265. Bavinck also presumes that the aim of special revelation is to maintain the original revelation of God that has been lost due to the impact of sin (191).

22. See Ritschl, *The Logic of Theology*, 48.

23. See Jüngel, *Trinity*, 15. Jüngel paraphrases a Barthian position but with sensitivity to the hermeneutical problem of how ordinary human language can express God's revelation.

cannot be reduced to a form of anthropology (which Schleiermacher underplays):[24]

- *Thesis 3: Amid considerable controversy over what it is that is being revealed, narrative theologies may favor the playful notion of a "clue," that is, a clue to the meaning of the story, to the significance of this moment in history.*

When Christians speak about revelation they assume quite different positions on what it is that is being revealed. The image of unveiling suggests that it is the identity of a person that is being revealed, in this case the identity of God as Triune. Along the same line one may speak of the character of God being revealed (and not the identity of a previously unknown God)—which emerged more slowly over lengthy encounters. Israel only gradually and grudgingly learned to understand God in terms of characteristics such as mercy and therefore justice.[25] Likewise, the New Testament confession of God as vulnerable love is easily lost if one subscribes to omnipotence, omniscience, and omnipresence.[26]

Others, focusing on individual experience suggest that it is the ultimate meaning of one's own existence that is revealed.[27] Or the place and vocation of one's community. There are some, not so many, who still maintain that propositional truths or moral commands are revealed as if from on high. Wolfhart Pannenberg maintains that history is the primary sphere within which God's revelation takes place.[28] God's self-revelation is mediated by God's actions in the world.[29] Revelation cannot be reduced to self-communication (by word), but also includes revelation by historical acts of salvation, liberation, and victory over evil. If so, theological reflection on revelation cannot merely focus on the contested cognitive status of such revelation but also has to consider the counter-experience of suffering.[30] Such actions in history cannot be reduced to salvation history either, but includes universal history. If so, revelation concerns the meaning of history, perhaps the

---

24. See the second model for relating the universe story and the Christian story as sketched in the introduction to this volume, that is, the anthropocentric attempt to base the knowledge of God on the category of religion. This highly complex debate, symbolized by the figures of Schleiermacher and Barth, cannot be resolved here. See the masterly discussion in Pannenberg, *Systematic Theology 1*, 119–87.

25. See Welker, *God the Spirit*.

26. Hendrikus Berkhof seeks to move away from these omni-characteristics by describing God's character ambiguously as "holy love," "defenseless superior power," and "changeable faithfulness." See Berkhof, *Christian Faith*, 119–54.

27. See Stroup, *The Promise of Narrative Theology*, 247.

28. See Pannenberg, *Systematic Theology 1*, 189–257.

29. Pannenberg, *Systematic Theology 1*, 243.

30. See Tracy, *Fragments*, 139.

direction or presumed outcome of history but at least the significance of this moment in history.

Narrative theologies may build on all these strands by suggesting the metaphor of a "clue." This may be found in detective stories where a master clue may help one to understand the significance of other clues. But one may also consider the art of tracking, a cross-word puzzle, a treasure hunt, finding one's way on a long journey or seeking to fathom a mystery.[31] A clue is therefore not a short-cut in the way that requesting a "sign" from God would be. The need to find and adopt clues is arguably common to all humans. Such clues need to help one to address the five ultimate questions described above. Either way, such clues are scarcely invented; they are found and then toyed with a bit. Although their significance may be far from obvious, such clues are always palpable, accessible to the human senses, and are only expressed secondarily through words (e.g., through the biblical witnesses[32]). Such clues are entirely natural; the bifurcation of the world into what is natural and supernatural (as if religion has to do with the supernatural but not the natural) should be discarded as misleading, although a multilayered notion of transcendence must be maintained.[33]

For Christians, as for other theistic traditions, the clue to the ultimate mystery can be named, always inadequately, in English with the word "God." While this does provide common ground with some others, the use of the term God does not resolve the heated debate on God's identity and character. In any case, although "God" is usually read as a proper name, it is less like a noun than a verb. Note that the common ground is found at a penultimate level, that is, in the common quest for the meaning of history but also in suggesting that this clue can be named "God." But once this clue is found, a reversal takes place at the ultimate level: God is not the clue to find the mystery of the world (which would instrumentalize God); the mystery of the world becomes a clue to find and account for God's identity and character:

- *Thesis 4: While there are many clues scattered all around, for Christians the best available clue to God's identity and character is found in what is redescribed as God's self-revelation in Jesus Christ through the Spirit. This is the master key that helps to unlock the significance of all the other clues.*

Christians would of course say that "God" is the ultimate mystery of the universe, that the world does not have its origin, life, and destiny in itself.[34] But

---

31. See Jüngel, *God as Mystery*, 376–96.

32. This accounts for a dialectic between preverbal manifestation and verbal proclamation. See Tracy, *Fragments*, 223.

33. I developed such a notion of transcendence in *The Earth in God's Economy*, 143–65. See also my essay "What is the Ecological Significance of God's Transcendence?"

34. See WCC, *Confessing the One Faith*, 35.

they would want to add that Jesus Christ is our best available clue to recognize God's identity and character. One may therefore say that, for Christians, the clue to the meaning of the story (i.e., the history of the universe) is found in the life and work of one of the historical characters in the story. This character is an unlikely candidate, one who died young, in a remote province of a mighty empire, rejected even by his own people, without children, possessions, writings, or even followers (except for his mom and a prostitute). Indeed, to suggest that God is revealed especially in the cross, that which is radically contrary to God, is to speak of the hiddenness (not the absence) of God.[35] This clue is quite palpable and indeed alive—the Logos that became flesh can be heard, seen, and touched (1 John 1:1), so that words (Scripture, kerygma) about the Word can never fully capture the meaning of this clue.[36] One may even pinpoint the clue by hoping that the palpable resurrection of the crucified Christ is the clue that proleptically unlocks the meaning of universal history. Nevertheless, the clue is not obvious, remains hidden, and may well be best kept alive in the memory of suffering and oppressed people. Indeed, in Christ, God is revealed but is also hidden the most.[37]

This clue suggests that there are indeed some similarities with other religious traditions, not least in its use of the term "God" and the role played by the Messiah, but there is something "special," that is, distinctive about this clue. This is hinted at by words such as grace, mercy, justice, and especially love to describe God's character, expressed in multiple, ongoing narratives about the Creator's often frustrated attempts to heal a broken relationship with God's own beloved creatures.[38]

This is not the only available clue—others are scattered everywhere, among others in the law and the prophets, potentially nothing is excluded. However, this is the clearest clue, the one to be excited about. Accordingly, the story therefore hinges upon one crucial episode in the life of one character, epitomized by the tension between cross and resurrection. In the Nicene Creed this clue is expressed with astonishing scope and brevity—the one who is:

> [*E*]ternally begotten of the Father [. . .] became incarnate from the virgin Mary [. . .] was crucified under Pontius Pilate [. . .] rose from the dead [. . .] ascended into heaven and is seated at the right hand of the Father [. . .] [*and*] will come again in glory to judge the living and the dead.

---

35. See the comment by David Tracy: "This God reveals God-self in hiddenness: in cross and negativity, above all in the suffering of those whom the grand narrative of modernity has set aside as non-peoples, non-events, non-memories, non-history." Tracy, *On Naming the Present*, 43.

36. See Conradie, "Is the Ear More Spiritual than the Eye?"

37. See Van Ruler, *Verzameld Werk III*, 48.

38. Herman Bavinck notes that God's self-revelation bears a historical character and unfolds its contents only gradually over the course of many centuries. See his *Reformed Dogmatics 1*, 343.

The cryptic expression to name the significance of this clue is the "economic Trinity," or even deeper, the confession that God is the mystery of history and that this God is Triune (the immanent Trinity):

- *Thesis 5: While Christians readily adopt categories from elsewhere, they also adapt such categories in the light of God's self-revelation in Jesus Christ as the best available clue. This suggests a qualitative difference between general and special revelation.*

Any categories and vocabularies derived from common human experience, language, and culture may be employed to express the content and significance of the Christian faith, no matter how crude, distorted, and ideology-infested such categories may be. There is no separate sacred language, no original, uncontaminated point of departure that can provide guarantees against such distortions. Retrospectively, one may explain the ability to use such categories with reference to God's good creation, the impact of sin, and of God's work of salvation. Put simply, the vocabulary employed in sinful words is not from the devil! Any word can become a vehicle of God's revelation; all words are embedded in the mess in which we find ourselves. In the Reformed tradition, the ability of human words to become carriers of God's revelation is also explained in terms of Calvin's notion of "accommodation": God allows Godself to be known through finite creaturely language. This is God's gracious gift of comprehensibility.[39] The finite can indeed bear traces of the infinite (because the finite depends on the infinite?), even if it is also true that the finite can never fully fathom what is infinite.

The most well-known way to explain our human ability to receive God's revelation remains (at least in the Reformed tradition) in terms of the category of general revelation. This allows Christians to see what is material, bodily, and earthly as God-given. Categories derived from elsewhere may therefore be freely adopted in theological reflection. The category of a natural *sensus divinitatis* (or Schleiermacher's feeling of absolute dependence) is not anthropologically wrong but is also not necessary as a foundation for special revelation. Any sign and symbol can become a carrier of connotations (the signified) that far transcend material signifiers. Revelation is not alien to human nature because humans were enabled to receive such revelation as God's image bearers.[40] Even if, retrospectively, Christians may maintain that although the Christian faith is not merely a particular form of the general phenomenon of religion, its emergence cannot be understood without the religious traditions that preceded Christianity. This applies especially to that of Israel, but Israel also modified earlier notions of the divine on the basis of special experiences (see above). The notion of a point of contact between

---

39. Jüngel, *Trinity*, 48.

40. See Bavinck, *Reformed Dogmatics 1*, 236.

special revelation and categories derived from general revelation to receive such special revelation became a point of dispute in the famous controversy between Karl Barth and Emil Brunner.[41] However, what may seem Christologically flawed, may be Pneumatologically necessary or would otherwise become docetic.[42] It is the Spirit who inspires ordinary human words to name the Word.

The distinction between general and special revelation does imply a qualitative difference between the available clues to God's identity and character. The clearest clues must be used to interpret the others. The clearest clues are not necessarily free from distortion, at least not to the extent that these are conveyed to us through human witnesses, but they are nevertheless clear enough to surprise, challenge, and transform our lives. This is the power of the gospel. There is no need to ensure a pure origin for the categories that we employ. What is far more important is that these categories be tested, weighed, adapted, clarified, and transformed through grappling with the clearest available clues. This is arguably also the point of the Christian liturgy. We enter into the liturgy carrying all our sins, natural theologies, idolatries and heresies with us, acting as if the world is not God's creation. Through listening to God's word and participating in the sacraments we may gradually and perhaps grudgingly begin to see the world from God's perspective, through God's eyes—as beloved, indeed as something worth dying for.[43] We are slowly allowed to see the world in the light of the Light of the World.[44] This is the meaning of revelation; it is not only about who is being revealed but also about how that illuminates the world around us.[45] We are not to look directly at the light but at what it brings to light. This changes everything, including our notions of the divine and the world around us.[46] The "liturgy after the liturgy" follows from that.

Once we have adopted and adapted (better: are adopted and adapted by) the categories we do employ to express the clues that we have found, this

---

41. See Barth and Brunner, *Natural Theology*.

42. See Van Ruler's essay (in Dutch) on "The other side of the problem of natural theology" in *Verzameld Werk* II, 239–49 (245).

43. See Hall, *The Cross in Our Context*, 24, 31.

44. This is the core argument of my *The Earth in God's Economy*.

45. The allusion here is to Niebuhr, *The Meaning of Revelation*. In his words, "Revelation means the moment in our history through which we know ourselves to be known from beginning to end, in which we are apprehended by the knower [. . .] Revelation is the moment in which we find our judging selves to be judged not by ourselves or our neighbors but by one who knows the final secrets of the heart" (80).

46. The designation of Yahweh as God and of Jesus as divine makes sense only on the basis of an extra-Christian use of the word God. Once this word is adopted it is also adapted but not to the extent that some generic notion of God is abandoned (or else Christian God-talk becomes solipsistic). See Pannenberg, *Systematic Theology 1*, 68–69. Niebuhr speaks of the radical reconstruction, the metamorphosis, the continuous conversion, the painful transformation, the revolution of our natural knowledge of what being divine may mean. See *The Meaning of Revelation*, 95.

process has to be continued. To seek to capture this in abiding formulas is to betray the need to speak anew, in the title of this volume, to take a deep breath before we continue with the story. It is sometimes suggested that this requires a process of inculturation or indigenization but this seems to assume that the Christian faith is already given and only needs to be accurately translated and transplanted into new contexts. The image that is used is that of the seed of the gospel that has to be planted in the soil of culture and language. In the Reformed tradition, this image should be regarded as misleading. The gospel is not a foreign seed (originating from Jerusalem) that has to be implanted elsewhere. There is nothing wrong with indigenous seeds! Instead, the problem is that the indigenous plants have been overtaken by invader species, by parasites, by the impact of colonization. The gospel functions more like pruning scissors that liberate the plant to be able to flourish again. Likewise, there is no need to eliminate "indigenous" notions of culture (whatever that may mean) or religion but there may well be a need to liberate and therefore transform them.[47]

There needs to be a liturgical interplay between what is indeed broad and general and what is special and of a distinctive quality. It is on this basis, again retrospectively, that Christians would want to insist that the clues they have found cannot be invented or created. They therefore use the language of God's self-disclosure to ascribe such an event. Knowledge of God is dependent upon a free and therefore contingent act of God, and cannot be reduced to a form of pantheist emanation of qualities that gradually became evident, or to human discovery or self-reflection.[48] One may praise human efforts to fathom the deepest secrets of nature, but this can only deepen a sense of mystery and the recognition of the limitations of human knowledge. Knowledge of God is the origin and the aim of knowledge of the self:

- *Thesis 6: Special revelation is not an aim in itself. It is qualitatively clearer than general revelation because of its narrow focus but its purpose is to unlock the wider meaning of history. In other words: The Christian story is there to help us to make sense of the universe story. The purpose of special revelation is to help us to recognize general revelation.*

In the branch of the Reformed tradition in which I am situated, the (deep) incarnation of God in Jesus Christ, especially the cross and resurrection, is indeed the hinge upon which history (nothing less than the universe story) turns, but this hinge does not express the direction or purpose of history. That goal is understood eschatologically as the reign of God—in every square inch of society, in every moment of history, not only in the end.

---

47. Niebuhr, *The Meaning of Revelation*, 99.

48. See Veenhof, *Revelatie en Inspiratie*, 270–71.

This is a truly remarkable insight that needs to be expressed in different aphorisms to drive the point home. One may say, for example, that salvation is not an aim in itself. Salvation is not about the Savior, or about salvation, or even about being saved, but about the being of that which is saved. Salvation is about being; having been suffocated by sin we need to be saved in order to be, in order to become what we are.[49] God's work of salvation is aimed at (restoring) God's work of creation. Christianity is not an aim in itself; it is there for the sake of the world. The church is not an aim in itself; it is an organization that is there for its non-members.[50] The well-being of society is more holy than the well-being of the church. The meal of the Holy Communion serves as a necessary preparation in order to enjoy the meal at home. One may even say that paying and spending tax is holier than tithing in the church as this is aimed at justice and equity in the reign of God. Christ came to transform culture[51] but then for the sake of allowing culture to flourish. God is not a Christian.[52] Jesus did not come to be glorified but to serve; he gave his life so that everyone could be included in the whole household of God. We are not human in order to become Christian, but we arguably do need to become Christian in order to become human.[53] Being human is not an aim in itself either; we need to become human for the sake of being, for the sake of the well-being of everything that is, including other animals, plants, and the land itself. In short, general revelation is not a contaminated starting point to understand God's revelation in Jesus Christ; instead, the goal of special revelation is to appreciate God's general revelation, God's presence in all things.[54] Special revelation (salvation) remains necessary and general revelation therefore

---

49. This is a core insight in the oeuvre of Arnold van Ruler, in contrast with Karl Barth who regards salvation as more than being, indeed the fulfillment of being. Van Ruler's theology may be regarded as a radicalization of Bavinck's emphasis on salvation as the restoration of God's good but fallen creation. It is radicalized given Van Ruler's appreciation for this earthly life, for what is material, earthly, and bodily, and his critique of any form of dualism except for the fundamental distinction between Creator and creature. See my discussion in *Saving the Earth*, 217–76.

50. This saying is attributed to William Temple.

51. Niebuhr, *Christ and Culture*.

52. Tutu, *God is not a Christian*.

53. Van Ruler, *Calvinist Trinitarianism*, 132.

54. See this formulation by Herman Bavinck in his *Philosophy of Revelation*: "Revelation, while having its center in the Person of Christ, in its periphery extends to the uttermost ends of creation. It does not stand isolated in nature and history, does not resemble an island in the ocean, nor a drop of oil upon water. With the whole of nature, with the whole of history, with the whole of humanity, with the family and society, with science and art it is intimately connected" (27).

does not replace special revelation (which can only yield a *theologia gloriae*),[55] but special revelation is not an aim in itself.

It suffices to say that Herman Bavinck's notion of a "philosophy of revelation," that is, an attempt by Christians to reflect on the significance of God's whole revelation, to relate the idea of revelation with the rest of our knowledge, remains elusive. This remains the virtue of Teilhard de Chardin's in my view an otherwise unsatisfactory attempt to offer what one may describe as a theology of evolution.

■ On the Hope that the Christian Story of God's Work Will Transform the Universe Story

How, then, is the Christian story related to the universe story? In my view these two stories (among multiple other stories) can neither be fused nor be separated from each other. To fuse them would be to legitimize reigning power relations and to undermine the prophetic voice of the Christian story. To separate them would be to misunderstand the Christian story and to undermine its plausibility as a story covering the ultimate origin and destiny of the universe. This can only lead to self-isolation. Likewise, to fuse or separate two sources for the knowledge of God in terms of general and special revelation would undermine either the possibility of such knowledge or the identity and character of God.

In my view it is best to say that the Christian story redescribes, reinterprets, renarrates, and therefore translates, transfigures, and possibly transforms not only reconstructions of the universe story but the universe story itself. Such reconstructions of the universe story are found in early myths of origin throughout the world, in various religious traditions, in schools of philosophy, in early forms of science and of course in contemporary science, popularized by gifted story tellers and film makers. One famous example may suffice, namely Stephen Hawking's *A Brief History of Time*.

In the biblical roots of Christianity the portrayals of the ultimate origin and ultimate destiny of the world are best understood as critical commentaries on rival versions of the story. Consider the priestly authors of Genesis 1 and their commentary on Babylonian creation stories to make the point that Elohim, the God of Israel, has been and remains in control of the forces of chaos, despite considerable evidence to the contrary during the Babylonian exile. Or consider Isaiah's prophetic visions of a coming peace on earth, even among animals, despite the presence of exiles in diaspora throughout the

---

55. The European Enlightenment interpreted the formulae *fides quarens intellectum* and *credo ut intelligam* accordingly. If so faith is superseded by rational knowledge. See Moltmann, *Experiences in Theology*, 71.

Mediterranean world (Isa 11:12). Or the prologue to the Gospel according to John that challenges proto-Gnostic notions of the Logos. Or the eschatological vision of a new heaven, a new earth, a new Jerusalem, in Revelations 21, despite the dominant narrative of imperial persecution. In each case, the ultimate origin and destiny of the world is redescribed and ascribed as God's beloved creation.

In telling the Christian story the hope is to transform the universe story, or at least parts thereof. This is an extremely bold claim, given the difficulties of conversion in one person's lifestyle, or in one institution, not to mention a country such as South Africa. Either way, this is not merely an attempt to defend Christian truth claims against rival versions of the story but to change the direction in which the story is currently going. That would not be possible by merely reiterating the Christian story. What is required is not merely a rival interpretation of the universe story (i.e., found among creationist versions too) but one that illuminates aspects of the universe story, more adequately than what is found in science, philosophy, or literature. Only if the universe story is taken seriously, only if the significance of this moment in its history is recognized, that is, the advent of what is named by some as the "Anthropocene," is there any hope that the direction of history can be transformed. Moreover, Christians need to remind themselves that transformation can also amount to distortion—most notably given the role of Christianity in anthropogenic climate change.[56] The direction therefore matters, as does the actual content of what is being revealed.

The claim of course cannot be that retelling the Christian story will transform the universe story; telling this story requires a vision of who God is and what this God is doing in the world. It is *Christ* that transforms culture (through the Spirit) and that is hermeneutically possible only if Christ is fully human and fully divine. It is not as if the story itself saves, or that telling the story may by itself become salvific. Telling the story has to be embedded within living the story, that is, living within the parameters of the story. Ideas coming to us noetically (through our ears) in the form of stories (or witnesses or proclamation) can indeed change the world but this is not the only source of transformation. The ministry of Jesus of Nazareth included teachings, parables, and prophetic speeches and also provocative actions, healings, traveling around and, especially, table fellowship. The incarnation of the Word cannot be reduced to words about the incarnation. God's acts in history cannot be reduced to stories about such acts (e.g., the exodus to the story about the exodus), even if such acts require narrative interpretation. Without God's acts, God's words would be empty; without God's words,

---

56. See Conradie and Koster, *The T&T Clark Handbook on Christian Theology and Climate Change*.

God's acts would be blind.[57] The task of narrative theology is only to tell this story in the hope that this will become one instrument in the work of the Spirit who is at home in all that is material, bodily, and earthly. That requires taking a deep Breath . . .

■ Bibliography

Barth, Karl and Emil Brunner. *Natural Theology.* Eugene: Wipf & Stock, 2002.

Bavinck, Herman. *Philosophy of Revelation.* London: Longmans, Green & Co., 1909.

———. *Reformed Dogmatics, Volume 1: Prolegomena.* Grand Rapids: Baker Academic, 2003.

Berkhof, Hendrikus. *Christian Faith: An Introduction to the Study of the Faith.* Grand Rapids: Eerdmans, 1986.

Berry, Thomas. *The Dream of the Earth.* San Francisco: Sierra Club, 1988.

Birch, Bruce, Jacqueline E. Lapsley, Cynthia Moe-Lobeda and Larry Rasmussen. *Bible and Ethics: A New Conversation.* Minneapolis: Fortress, 2017.

Conradie, Ernst M. "All Theology is Natural Theology: The Hermeneutic Necessity of Natural Theology?" *Nederduitse Gereformeerde Teologiese Tydskrif* 52:1&2 (2011), 58–65. https://doi.org/10.5952/52-1-6

———. *Christianity and Earthkeeping: In Search of an Inspiring Visison.* Stellenbosch: Sun Media, 2011.

———. *Hope for the Earth: Vistas on a New Century.* Eugene: Wipf & Stock, 2005.

———. "Is the Ear More Spiritual Than the Eye? Theological Reflection on the Human Senses." In *Do Emotions Shape the World? Issues in Science and Theology,* edited by Dirk Evers, et al., 177–88. Heidelberg: Springer, 2016.

———. *Saving the Earth? The Legacy of Reformed Views on "Re-creation".* Berlin: LIT, 2013.

———. *The Earth in God's Economy: Creation, Salvation and Consummation in Ecological Perspective.* Berlin: LIT, 2015.

———. "What is the Ecological Significance of God's Transcendence?" In *Nature and Beyond: Transcendence and Immanence in Science and Religion,* edited by Michael Fuller, et al., 87–99. Heidelberg: Springer, 2020.

Conradie, Ernst M. and Hilda P. Koster, eds. *The T&T Clark Handbook on Christian Theology and Climate Change.* London: T. & T. Clark, 2019.

Conradie, Ernst M. and Teddy Chalwe Sakupapa. "'Decolonising the Doctrine of the Trinity' or 'The Decolonising Doctrine of the Trinity'?" *Journal of Theology for Southern Africa* 161 (2018), 37–53.

Hall, Douglas John. *The Cross in our Context: Jesus and the Suffering World.* Minneapolis: Fortress, 2003.

Hawking, Stephen. *A Brief History of Time: From the Big Bang to Black Holes.* New York: Bantam, 1988.

Jüngel, Eberhard. *The Doctrine of the Trinity: God's Being is in Becoming.* Translated by Horton Harris. Edinburgh: Scottish Academic Press, 1976.

———. *God as the Mystery of the World.* London: Bloomsbury, 2014.

Niebuhr, H. Richard. *Christ and Culture.* New York: Harper Torch, 1951.

———. *The Meaning of Revelation.* New York: MacMillan, 1941.

Moltmann, Jürgen. *Experiences in Theology: Ways and Forms of Christian Theology.* Minneapolis: Fortress, 2000.

---

57. See Bavinck, *Reformed Dogmatics* 1, 366.

Mosala, Itumeleng J. *Biblical Hermeneutics and Black Theology in South Africa.* Grand Rapids: Eerdmans, 1989.

Niebuhr, H. Richard. *The Meaning of Revelation.* New York: MacMillan, 1941.

———. *Christ and Culture.* New York: Harper Torch, 1951.

Nürnberger, Klaus. *Theology of Biblical Witness: An Evolutionary Approach.* Hamburg: LIT, 2012.

Pannenberg, Wolfhart. *Systematic Theology Volume 1.* Grand Rapids: Eerdmans, 1991.

Rasmussen, Larry L. "Cosmology and Ethics." In *Worldviews and Ecology: Religion, Philosophy and the Environment*, edited by Mary Evelyn Tucker and John M. Grim, 173–80. Maryknoll: Orbis, 1994.

Ritschl, Dietrich. *The Logic of Theology.* Philadelphia: Fortress, 1987.

Serres, Michel. *Hominescence.* London: Bloomsbury, 2019.

Stroup, George W. *The Promise of Narrative Theology: Recovering the Gospel in the Church.* Eugene: Wipf & Stock, 1997.

Tracy, David. *Fragments: The Existential Situation of Our Time.* Chicago and London: The University of Chicago Press, 2020.

———. *On Naming the Present: God, Hermeneutics, and Church.* Maryknoll: Orbis, 1994.

Tutu, Desmond M. *God Is Not a Christian and Other Provocations.* San Francisco: HarperOne, 2011.

Van Ruler, Arnold A. *Calvinist Trinitarianism and Theocentric Politics: Essays towards a Public Theology.* Translated and edited by John Bolt. Lampeter: Edwin Mellen, 1989.

———. *Verzameld Werk Deel II: Openbaring en Heilige Schrift.* Zoetermeer: Boekencentrum, 2008.

———. *Verzameld Werk Deel III: God, Schepping, Mens, Zonde.* Zoetermeer: Boekencentrum, 2009.

Veenhof, Jan, *Revelatie en Inspiratie: De Openbarings- en Schriftbeschouwing van Herman Bavinck in Vergelijking met die der Ethische Theologie*, Amsterdam: Buijten & Schipperheijn, 1968.

Welker, Michael. *God the Spirit.* Minneapolis: Fortress, 1994.

West, Gerald O. *The Stolen Bible: From Tool of Imperialism to African Icon.* Leiden: Brill, 2016.

World Council of Churches. *Confessing the One Faith.* Faith and Order Study Document 153. Geneva: WCC, 1991.

The Trinitarian Spirit of Wisdom: A Catholic Exploration of Nature and Grace

Celia Deane-Drummond[1]

■ A Hybrid Story

I am offering in this essay what could be termed a *hybrid* storied perspective. I acknowledge that relating the Triune God to the story of life on earth arises out of my own personal situated narrative of being a Caucasian natural scientist, born in England but with an aristocratic Scottish and Welsh ancestry, specializing in plant physiology, schooled in the West, then a theologian, becoming a systematic constructive thinker who first entered the world of ecotheology in the late 1980s around the time I moved from being an Anglican

---

1. Celia Deane-Drummond is a Director of the Laudato Si' Research Institute and Senior Research Fellow in theology at Campion Hall, University of Oxford, England. She is registered as a co-researcher at the University of the Western Cape, South Africa, for the project on "An Earthed Faith: Telling the Story amid the 'Anthropocene'."

How to cite: Deane-Drummond, C., 2021, 'The Trinitarian Spirit of Wisdom: A Catholic Exploration of Nature and Grace', in E.M. Conradie & P.-C. Lai (eds.), *Taking a deep breath for the story to begin . . .* (An Earthed Faith: Telling the Story amid the "Anthropocene" Volume 1), pp. 119-139, AOSIS, Cape Town. https://doi.org/10.4102/aosis.2021.BK264.06

to a Roman Catholic. My second doctoral work focused on the pioneering theology of creation of Jürgen Moltmann.[2]

If I approach this story with my scientific and biological lens uppermost, then the Christian narrative is just one cultural expression that is part of a much bigger story of the way humanity has come, through millions of years of evolutionary change, to persist on Planet Earth and, through its own forgetfulness of its origins, treated that earth as if it were a source to be exploited rather than the very ground of our being. If I approach this story of earth as part of God's story, which is entirely possible for scientists if they are religious believers as well, then behind that grand scientific narrative there is another hidden story of God's Trinitarian action in the world, where the loving action of the Holy Spirit in that world is one of completion of a creative process informed by creaturely and divine wisdom.

If the first story of life puts more stress on "nature," the second story puts more stress on "God's story" in the creative work of grace. Both need to be considered simultaneously, even if tensions arise as along with consonance. A more detailed account of biocultural evolution and its significance for understanding humanity and our place in the natural world will not be entertained in detail. Interpreting the work of grace through its distinction from nature is typical of the Roman Catholic tradition. But half my life was spent as an Anglican. The different possible theological options[3] across distinct ecumenical traditions are first that grace has nothing to do with nature and is split off from it, which has, historically, been held to be Marcionite. An alternative position is that grace is *subsumed under* nature or evolution, which is more characteristic of animist or radical positions that tend to soften or weaken the need for salvation. Matthew Fox would be typical of this position.[4] A third possible view is that grace *replaces* nature, most characteristic of Anabaptist traditions. All is grace. A fourth position, most characteristic of Roman Catholic and Orthodox theologies is that grace *elevates* nature. A fifth position characteristic of the Reformed school is that grace *restores* nature. The differences here are clearly subtle, but the concept of replacement of nature reflects a different kind of eschatological interpretation compared with, for example, the idea of grace restoring nature, which implies a healing of what has been broken rather than an expectation of a fuller perfection in

---

2. I am also an environmental ethicist, practicing Ignatian spirituality habitually in my faith journey, while being interested throughout my career in engaging sympathetically but also critically with Eastern Orthodox sources.

3. I would like to thank Ernst Conradie for suggesting that these distinctions be clarified. See Conradie, *The Earth in God's Economy*.

4. See also Mark Wallace's essay in this volume. While authors such as Pierre Teilhard de Chardin lean towards this view, my own interpretation of Teilhard is that he offers a syncretic combination of an elevation of evolutionary narrative with a strong Christic paradigm influenced by Eastern Orthodox positions, which, ironically perhaps, pulls away from naturalism. For discussion see Deane-Drummond, *Teilhard de Chardin*.

future hope. The challenge for me as a theologian of twin ecclesial heritage is that I am also a biologist who is both convinced by evolutionary accounts, but, in common with philosophical critics, skeptical of their metaphysical adequacy. Thomas Nagel, for example, whose work I will be returning to further, generates a secular version of eschatology that finds principles for change (both positive and negative) buried within the natural order.[5] My own position, therefore, does not fit all that neatly in one of the fivefold alternatives in an ecumenical discussion of how to narrate the nature/grace relationship. It is, as my own story suggests, a hybrid one, and even if such hybridity leads to some conceptual challenges, it is closer to the theological intuition I am trying to articulate here. What will be bracketed out from the discussion is evil, sin, and salvation. Instead, I will offer a step-by-step account of fundamental theological issues appropriate to a volume on prolegomena that has, at least, a focus on the work of the Holy Spirit in creation, bringing "the deep Breath" to the fore.

My first concern is related to how to situate a nature and grace debate within the more recent historical shifts in theological hermeneutics. Can a theo-ontological approach still carry meaning within these internal debates about how theology relates to secular philosophical currents that also, at the same time, influence evolutionary biology? The answer to this question is presupposed in the alternative stories embedded in the background question for this volume, that is, whether either to incorporate a theological story *into* an evolutionary, biocultural one of life on earth, or to understand theological narrative *as* the primary framing.

Second, I will discuss a current of philosophical reflections on the natural world which open up the possibility of the transcendent and offer a different perspective on a philosophy of nature compared with standard interpretations of materialist science.

I will argue, third, that this openness to the transcendent in secular philosophical and scientific discourse complicates the traditional navigation of nature and grace in Roman Catholic thinking, including Karl Rahner's objection to neo-Thomism that he understood in terms of nature and superadded nature, created and uncreated grace.

Fourth, I will offer a critical, but appreciative, exploration of Sergius Bulgakov's constructive interpretation of the Holy Spirit as wisdom as a theo-ontology and why he fills the gap that some secular theorists are attempting to fill. My overall goal is, nonetheless, theological: how to have a meaningful discussion of the work of the Holy Spirit in the story of life of the earth.

---

5. Carl Reinhold Bråkenhielm's essay "Back to the Future" offers a helpful summary of Nagel's position which he describes as a neo-naturalistic form of evolutionary Platonism.

■ The Story as Theo-ontology or Onto-theology?[6]

As Stanley Grenz has pointed out,[7] theo-ontology is distinct from onto-theology. *Theo*-ontology takes its bearings from theology primarily rather than philosophy, so that even if that theology is influenced by philosophy, it is less self-consciously philosophical in tone. By onto-theology I mean the narrative of the Western cultural history of contemporary theological development understood through the demise of a metaphysics of Being. I am addressing here the shifts in the way theology has been constructed in ontological terms in more recent cultural history. This internal story is likely to be familiar to theologians and philosophers educated in this tradition: René Descartes' threefold substance typology of matter, mind, and God came under critical fire, initially retaining the idea of substance in either one of each of these—so substance matter was retained in Thomas Hobbes, mind in Gottfried Wilhelm Leibniz, and God in Baruch Spinoza respectively. A further attempt to renew metaphysics changed the ontological rules so that the language of substance and causality becomes replaced by that of process and creativity, therefore leading to a shift from a static to a much more dynamic ontology. The two most influential philosophers in this vein are Georg Wilhelm Friedrich Hegel and Alfred North Whitehead. Both these thinkers have been particularly influential in shaping ecotheological thought, especially in the West, across a broad spectrum of writers, especially ecofeminists. It is important to recognize how such process thinking arose so that it was both radical, but also in tune with internal shifts in theological hermeneutics. Later works of Martin Heidegger seemed to get frustrated with a process approach and ended up with a focus on the "experience of astonishment or wonder," hence opening the way for further dialogue with religions, but leaving his more explicit theological proposals somewhat vague and dissatisfying.[8] The fascination with wonder has also been an inspiration for key activists trying to energize attention toward care for the natural environment, Rachel Carson being a good example.[9]

I am not going to deal with any of the details of the works of these philosophers or activist nature writers in this essay, it is merely flagged as a reminder of background context. But the repercussions of the influence of process philosophy in particular are still being felt not just in ecotheology, but

---

6. Various parts of the sections which follow draw on a conference paper entitled Deane-Drummond, "The Spirit of Wisdom."

7. Grenz, *The Named God*, 90–130.

8. Grenz, *The Named God*, 120.

9. There are ambiguities associated with wonder alone as normative for ethics. See Deane-Drummond, "Biodiversity and Ecological Responsibility."

also in a broader discussion of the biological sciences. The point is that the unfolding cultural history of the status of being in philosophy and developments in various philosophies of particular sciences, such as the philosophy of biology, are leading to a much more complex contemporary picture than some ecotheological commentators critically engaging with modern science have often presupposed. Ecology, thought of as a "subversive" science, ironically escapes these critiques, but a bias, especially by ecotheologians, against the worth of the natural sciences on the basis of its assumed materialism, where nature is an instrumental "other" to be exploited for human benefit, lies in the background, ever since Carolyn Merchant published her influential *The Death of Nature* half a century ago.[10]

To some degree this sharp critique of the philosophy of life sciences was justified. Evolutionary science, following the Darwinian revolution, seemed to endorse a purely materialistic philosophy, so the New Synthesis evolutionary theory imagined genes as discrete units of information that were selected for in a given "external" environment. When that environment shifted, selection pressures changed, and new variants became dominant through the sieve-like process of natural selection, which filtered out all but the most suited "fittest" variants who went on to reproduce. Sexual selection added some complexity to this basic picture, again, not always appreciated by ecotheologians, but the role of the environment was perceived as "external" to a focus on selection of particular atomized genes. An alternative position that stresses a holistic ontology rather than an atomistic one,[11] portrays evolution in terms of changes in systems during development, whereby those systems are now inclusive of "external" factors, thus stressing the dynamism of change within a system as a whole in and across time. There are variants between these, such as the extended evolutionary synthesis view,[12] which, like the developmental system model, takes the ecological context much more seriously and weaves this into its explanatory account.

Heated debates between different ways of explaining the same empirical data, either according to the classic New Synthesis model, or the more recent extended evolutionary synthesis model,[13] show just how contested this area has become. It would, however, be incorrect and a serious distortion to view the extended evolutionary synthesis model as only of marginal concern among evolutionary biologists with the dominant position wedded to materialism. What is at stake, as Kevin Laland points out, is "a struggle for the very soul of

---

10. Merchant, *Death of Nature*.

11. Moss, "From Representational Preformationism"; see also Deane-Drummond, *Theological Ethics*, 6–17.

12. See Laland et al., "The Extended Evolutionary Synthesis."

13. Laland et al., "Does Evolutionary Theory Need a Rethink?"

the discipline."[14] This committed stance sounds remarkably close to an ontological claim. The philosophy of ecological science has shifted as well, though this shift has now come to be largely accepted as paradigmatic in the field, from the original dominant concept of a fairly static hierarchy to a much looser and more dynamic model which stresses flux, change, and processes through time.[15] The point is that evolutionary science, which is the backbone of how scientists describe the story of life on earth, is now, it seems, following a similar hermeneutic course to shifts in theology. Many biologically minded scientists, in my own experience, especially those trained in anthropology, are even prepared to wager that there may be other forms of knowledge that are valid in their own realms, even if, in keeping with their scientific methods, they are reluctant to stray much beyond empiricism.[16] This turn to alternative bases for knowledge, including that arising from very different worldviews, as in the traditions of indigenous communities, for example, needs to be taken seriously in crafting the story of life on earth both from the perspective of anthropology and theology. It also means that evolutionary anthropologists are now becoming rather more open to engagement with theological discourse, in so far as it opens up a different way of making meaning in the world compared with standard scientific narratives.[17]

My argument in this chapter is that while there can never be total convergence between a story of theo-ontology of the Trinity and that of a secular metaphysics of evolutionary biology and ecology, taking account of the complex changes *within* the biological sciences can inform the theological enterprise, at least to a degree.[18]

■ Philosophical Approaches to the Transcendent[19]

In a fascinating, if unconventional philosophical work, *The Incandescent*, Michel Serres has explored the philosophical significance of the way humans have evolved over fifteen billion years of embeddedness in the earth story, and why it is that humanity has become "monsters of forgetfulness," so

---

14. Laland et al., "Does Evolutionary Theory Need a Rethink?," 162.

15. Deane-Drummond, *Ethics of Nature*, 36–8.

16. Ingold, "An Anthropologist Looks at Biology."

17. Meneses and Bronkema, *On Knowing Humanity*.

18. Hence, attacking the standard philosophy embedded in the New Synthesis that arose out of classic Darwinism as either rampantly materialistic or sometimes—more extreme—as secular substitutes riffing off theism, as in Michael Hanby's work, is true only to the extent that some scientists still consistently hold to such philosophies. See Hanby, *No God, No Science*.

19. See also Deane-Drummond, "The Evolution of Wisdom."

"keeping our nature, which obeys and remains silent, on a leash."[20] Evolution confronts humanity by weakening its borderlands with the natural world, for we share a common biological basis with other life forms in an equally shared evolutionary story. While Serres decries animism that recognizes the spiritual world of soul or good and evil in that of matter, he believes that forgotten "gold veins" appear in it.[21] The gold vein he speaks of seems to refer to the ability of matter to participate in an act of knowledge, rather than simply entailing an active subject relating to a completely passive object. There is, in other words, a shared agency beyond the human subject. In this way he can claim that "The real reawakens the act of knowing that awakens it. Its faculties are joined to ours in a self-perpetuating cycle."[22]

However, and this is important for his overall narrative and intrinsic to my argument, humanity is still distinct in the story of life. It is the "white indetermination" within human cultures that Serres argues marks us out as human, for unlike other species, in humans we find a *de-specialization* toward incandescent indifference, so becoming "infinite."[23] This incandescent indifference is not the culmination of the story of life, for evolution then re-differentiates and "invents with us"—through tools and cultures a new niche is created through what he terms our "external species."[24] Other scholars have used the language of "second nature" to describe such a process. Embedded within the narrative of life is also its violence that, in Serres view, "symbolize the sides of a single power, of a same potentiality, the banks of a similar torrent, the variants of a single theme."[25] The mixture in life of both the magnificent and the terrible is such that "life springs forth with elation and streams with anguish."[26] Serres believes we cannot avoid the dark side in the story of life on earth, so "Even plants, peaceable because they only eat light, try to kill their neighbours in their little territory."[27] Such a story allows an acceptance of the parasite alongside the symbiont, the sinner and the saint, the Stalin and the St. Francis of Assisi. For Serres, technology and institutions are attempts to find deliverance from "this carnage."[28] Equally part of evolution is the ability of humanity to detach from life and its laws, but with that

---

20. Serres, *Incandescent*, 25 See also Serres, *Hominescence*.

21. Serres, *Incandescent*, 33.

22. Serres, *Incandescent*, 33.

23. Serres, *Incandescent*, 41.

24. Serres, *Incandescent*, 42.

25. Serres, *Incandescent*, 150.

26. Serres, *Incandescent*, 150.

27. Serres, *Incandescent*, 151.

28. Serres, *Incandescent*, 151.

detachment comes unpredictability and now characterizes itself as surviving by being an "Exterminator of species" through exploitation of the *élan vital* of every living thing.[29] Serres ends up with a dark sense of abandonment in light of the recognition of where hominization has taken humanity.[30] His attempt to cover up this wound by creating a universal that tries to bridge nature and culture and trying to find his way back to nature again from culture leaves more questions unresolved.[31] He remains, by his own admission, disconsolate.[32] He seems, therefore, whatever else his insights, to have become caught up in the dark shadow of his own making.

What Serres' account seems to lack is a deeper appreciation, even within the lights of naturalism, of the moral sense of the natural world that points toward the transcendent. Erazim Kohák in his classic book, *The Embers and the Stars,*[33] with *A Philosophical Inquiry into the Moral Sense of Nature* as subtitle, fares better. By "sense" of nature, he means "meaningful presence of a reality," "encountering in it its meaningful presence."[34] By "moral" he means not conformity to a set of social mores or conventions. It is also used in contradistinction to the way moral was used in the eighteenth century to denote a way of separating distinctive human freedoms from the supposedly mechanical and causal operations of the natural world.[35] But in this ancient rendering moral also signified "the ingression of the eternal sense of being of the good, the true, the beautiful into the order of time."[36] There is therefore an integrity and a presence to the natural world that goes beyond mere utility. In stark contrast with Serres, for Kohák nature in its integrity is "primordially good. The order of nature is also an order of value."[37] There is a rightness and rhythm, here, in the natural world that is not just utility and echoes the tradition of Logos. Further, "it is not alien to our human mode of being: quite the contrary, it is radically its kin."[38] If such a kinship did not exist, he argues, then humanity could not understand the natural world. A more radical step is the *re-personalization* of the inanimate world that counters the idea that the

---

29. Serres, *Incandescent,* 153.

30. Serres, *Incandescent,* 174.

31. Serres, *Incandescent,* 219–22.

32. Serres, *Incandescent,* 231.

33. Kohák, *The Embers and the Stars*.

34. Kohák, *The Embers and the Stars*, 68–9.

35. Kohák, *The Embers and the Stars*, 70.

36. Kohák, *The Embers and the Stars*, 70.

37. Kohák, *The Embers and the Stars*, 71.

38. Kohák, *The Embers and the Stars*, 74.

natural world is just "an impersonal store of raw materials from which to take but rather a personal world to which to give."[39]

Kohák's story of the life of the earth is therefore an integrated one that has profound ethical consequences for how humanity lives on the earth. If the scope of the story of life on earth is widened to include the cosmos, other prominent philosophers join the fray. Thomas Nagel, for example, in *Mind and Cosmos*, is explicit in his rejection of materialism as a satisfying philosophy of nature.[40] His bold challenge to reductionism in science, complexify even further the current public intellectual landscape of current biological science as well as philosophies of science in general.[41] Biologist Ursula Goodenough has pushed an integration of biology with religious thought further than most by combing a scientific description of biological processes while at the same time pressing for a religious naturalism, so that her feelings of deference are now attributed to nature as a whole, rather than to a Divine Being.[42] It is hard to make full sense of her attempt to keep to the storied account of nature through standard processes of natural science alongside a storied and experiential religious attachment to it, though contemporary currents within biological sciences would make it somewhat easier.[43]

■ Nature and Grace

All the above philosophical accounts offer a faint echo of theological debates on "nature," understood as the world the way God is understood in traditional theological approaches to have created it[44] and held it in being, and that of "grace." The work of grace is usually understood as shorthand for the work of God in effecting human salvation, that is, sanctifying grace. The nature/grace dialectic is not identical, however, with the creation/salvation dialectic, since creation, by being blessed, also bears the character of grace. Ignatius of Loyola and Carmelites including John of the Cross and Teresa of Avila, understood nature and grace to be in tune with one another, where nature represents grace as a dynamic sacrament in a mystical vision of unity.[45] Human

---

39. Kohák, *The Embers and the Stars*, 212. He knows that living within the world must entail compromises, but the recognition is in the acknowledgement. He argues that re-personalization of animate nature and humanity encourages respect for their integrity.

40. Nagel, *Mind and Cosmos*. See also discussion in Bråkenhielm's essay "Back to the Future."

41. Nagel, *Mind and Cosmos*.

42. Goodenough, *The Sacred Depths*.

43. It is worth noting that her book was published over twenty years ago when scientific materialism was still dominant in biological research.

44. For debate on this topic see Conradie, "What on Earth Did God Create?"

45. Fields, *Analogies*, 10–11.

creativity, the extra subjective cosmos, and their common transcendent ground were all harmonized. As Stephen Fields maintains, the Baroque cultures led to profound creativity.[46] Their God-centered culture, when fractured, opens up secularization and greater stress on a split between reason and infused supernatural habits which, then, ironically opened up a rationalist turn within theology.[47] The gap enlarged with the onset of modernism, undercut further by attention to Aristotelian philosophy in neo-Thomism, leading to a view of pure nature separate from the work of grace understood as "superadded" onto it.[48] Modernity, then, arrives at an estrangement between "the subject whose creativity can fashion the cosmos, and the graced transcendence that constitutes this creativity's source and goal."[49]

Fields' theological proposal for mending this rift between nature and grace is to find theological arguments that can help bring the two together in a way that still respects the integrity of each. Prevenient grace, that is, grace which begins its work prior to sanctifying grace assists in mending the split. In a nutshell, "prevenient grace invites human freedom to the redemption that it can reject; sanctifying grace, with the person's cooperation, renders the life of glory concretely possible."[50] Drawing on Max Seckler, Fields claims that "prevenient grace is oriented to sanctifying grace as its proper end, goal and perfection. Comingled with nature, prevenient grace embraces human freedom even as freedom embraces grace."[51] Another way a unity but distinction between nature and grace can be perceived is through a sacramental model, so that "nature gives grace a medium for its action."[52]

Fields has opened up the important question of how to relate nature and grace in a way that attempts to respect the integrity of each while healing the stand-off between them arising in modernity. He is optimistic in his belief that a Rahnerian approach is adequate for such a task. Karen Kilby and Matthew Ashley, for example, referring to the dialogue between theology and science, suggest that in Rahner's work a consideration "of the theology of grace brings us right to the edge, we would suggest, of the possibility of a useful dialogue."[53] Kilby and Ashley also draw on the classic distinction between created grace,

---

46. Fields, *Analogies*, 15.

47. Fields, *Analogies*, 16.

48. Fields, *Analogies*, 39.

49. Fields, *Analogies*, 181. Fields's idea of cooperation could have Pelagian undertones, so involvement would be preferable.

50. Fields, *Analogies*, 123.

51. Fields, *Analogies*, 321.

52. Fields, *Analogies*, 113.

53. Kilby and Ashley, "What Difference?," 209.

which elevate human nature toward salvation, and uncreated grace, which is God's presence as gift. Fields' understanding may be correct in so far as it analyses twentieth century modernity where rationality is split apart from ideas of transcendence, but as discussed in the section earlier, a secular approach to that transcendence is now both a complicating and, to some extent, a competing narrative.

Kilby and Ashley's interpretation of Rahner's engagement with nature and grace point to features that may help to understand the striving for transcendence within the secular story of human life on earth. Because Rahner locates the experience of grace at the level of transcendental experience, the anthropological search for that transcendence is also a work of grace. So:

> [/]n that region of experience where we always go beyond and transcend all particular finite objects, on that level where we always have, whether we realize it or not, an awareness of God, there grace is offered and either accepted or rejected.[54]

What Rahner is resisting is a form of neo-Thomism that separated uncreated from created grace. There are problems in his resolution, not least the fact that the kind of uncreated grace that is offered to humanity paradoxically is not on the same level as other experiences, yet at the same time emerges as "part of the general texture of our experience."[55] If this is the case, if the self-communication of God is illusive in the way he suggests, then transcendental aspirations of secular projects noted earlier could potentially be *interpreted* as in alignment with the work of God's grace. God's self-offering may not be recognized as such, for God remains incomprehensible. Yet what does the offer of grace really mean for those who do not know that they know God? Rahner's insistence on the universality of grace has some advantages in its openness but its bestowal on all human experience, whether recognized or not, makes discernment of what is or is not the work of God's grace difficult.

■ Trinitarian Spirit of Wisdom in Sergius Bulgakov: A Critical Engagement

Given what has been said so far, how, precisely, can God be conceived as being fully part of the story of life on earth, yet also its Creator and Redeemer? Trying to navigate this through the nature/grace dialectic has proved challenging. While there is some convergence between transcendent forms of biology and new theological interpretations of nature and grace, areas of dissonance remain. An alternative strategy which I will explore in this section is to start from an explicit and more dogmatic theological perspective and then work within that to consider God's activity in creation. There is no

---

54. Kilby and Ashley, "What Difference?," 217.

55. Kilby and Ashley, "What Difference?," 217.

contribution from the perspective of Orthodox theology in this volume, and while Bulgakov's work is still controversial within Orthodox theology,[56] his approach mediates between Western theology and Orthodox theology. Bulgakov's work is decidedly a *theo*-ontology, rather than an *onto*-theology, in that it takes its primary bearings from theology rather than philosophy, even though there are Platonic undertones that influence his writing. The brilliance of Bulgakov's work is that he resisted any sharp separation of the work of the Spirit in creation from uncreated grace, so avoids the problems that Rahner sought to overcome.

The first constructive issue that Bulgakov wrestles with is how to understand the Trinitarian work of creation, when traditional sources indicate that it is God the Father who is the hypostatic originator of creation. At this juncture I will flag his specific use of traditional Father, Son, and Spirit language in his description of the Trinity. Feminist scholars often object to the adoption of such language as representative of a patriarchal lineage that is important to both challenge and overturn. My own view is that Bulgakov's *sophianic* and *Trinitarian* interpretation of who God is steps away from a traditional hierarchical portrayal of God, at least to a degree. My own preference would therefore be, in general, to avoid the explicit use of Father and replace it with a more neutral term, God, or even the First hypostasis, and always use the more inclusive term "humanity" rather than "man." For him, the Second and Third hypostases participate sophianically "through their self-revelation in Sophia, who is also the self-revelation of the Father [First hypostasis] in the Holy Trinity, the divine world."[57] Importantly, it is Sophia who acts as a bridge between the world and God. Sophia is "the objective principle of divine being," by and in which God is revealed "in divine being" and through which God "creates the world."[58] Sophia reveals the two hypotheses of Word and Spirit. The revelatory work of the Son is therefore mediated through Sophia, but the first hypostasis remains "mute from all eternity," speaking in the Son, not as hypostatic Logos but as "spoken pan-logos."[59]

The Holy Spirit, in an analogous way to the Logos, is involved in the creation of the world not hypostatically but through activity, in correspondence with revelation in Sophia, action which, in the case of the Spirit, is "reality, life, beauty or glory."[60] The work of the Spirit at the very beginning of creation

---

56. Bulgakov is often treated as a religious philosopher rather than a theologian, though scholars in the West have little doubt about his Orthodox heritage.

57. Bulgakov, *The Comforter*, 191. The text in square brackets is my suggested replacement.

58. Bulgakov, *The Comforter*, 191.

59. Bulgakov, *The Comforter*, 191–92. The idea of God (the Father in Bulgakov) remaining mute is significant as it softens any sense of domination.

60. Bulgakov, *The Comforter*, 192.

allows reality to arise in the void of nothing, but it is also important to add that it is "precisely the *earth* as the ontological *place* of future creation."[61] The action of the Spirit is evidenced in the:

> [G]enerative power of the earth and water as the maternal womb, the proto-reality which has been seeded with words of the Word, the ideas of creation actualised by the life-giving force.[62]

The sexual analogies in here are, of course, troubling, but his use of the term "life-giving force" is suggestive of an embedded sense of the work of the Spirit. The Holy Spirit, "clothes creation in beauty and glory," but, importantly, this is not a static understanding of creation, for he envisages such glory as an anticipation of what is to come. So, it is "the first, preliminary manifestation on earth of the glory of the creation, the transfigured earth: this first manifestation is the planting of paradise."[63] Eden is not simply about *origins* or restoration, as about *future hope* for the earth, such that the:

> [R]ays of heavenly light that had shined over the creation in Eden have faded on earth and will not shine again until the coming of the times and seasons of its transfiguration.[64]

What precisely is Bulgakov saying about the work of the Spirit in creation? Getting this right is fundamental to a theological story of the earth's unfolding. He draws specifically on Genesis 1:2, "the earth was without form and void [*tohu vabohu*] . . . the Spirit of God moved upon the face of the waters."[65] The action of the Holy Spirit here is one of brooding, like a bird on its nest, whereby the action in the Spirit is now envisaged as *primary* to that of the Word, the "proto-reality of being, proto-matter, the earth, are produced by the action of the Spirit" which acts through "sophianic seeds" indicating, counter to common assumptions about the Spirit, an explicit relationship between the Spirit and matter.[66] Bulgakov suggests that such action points to the:

> [L]ife of matter as a reality that is to become permeated with the Holy Spirit and spiritual in this sense, that is, a reality that is to achieve its transfiguration as the "new earth" (together with the "new heaven") where the *tobu vabohu*, the chaotic formlessness and void, will be overcome.[67]

The hypothesis of the Holy Spirit shows up its maternal character in the revelation of Sophia in the creation of the world.

---

61. Bulgakov, *The Comforter*, 193.

62. Bulgakov, *The Comforter*, 193.

63. Bulgakov, *The Comforter*, 193.

64. Bulgakov, *The Comforter*, 193.

65. Bulgakov, *The Comforter*, 193.

66. Bulgakov, *The Comforter*, 194.

67. Bulgakov, *The Comforter*, 194.

The image of creaturely Sophia is shown up as reality, life, and being. But this is not so much a supramundane Pentecost, since, "the seeds of this organisation had already been implanted in the chaos itself, as its life-giving force, in conformity with the sophianic proto-image of the world." He wants to avoid such hypostatic definition of the work of the Spirit in creation in order to highlight the kenotic character of both the Logos and the Spirit, so that their hypostases are concealed in that of the Father, "without being abolished but also without being manifested," appearing like three flames behind each other.[68] What Bulgakov is keen to retain is a biblical strand that stresses revelation in the first hypostasis but mediated through the hypostases of Son and Spirit while remaining veiled in their hypostatic identity until the New Testament when the Son "is sent into the world," while withholding divine life and glory.[69] Just as there are anticipations of the Logos in theophanies prior to hypostatic incarnation, so there are sophianic revelations of the Spirit as gifts where there is hypostatic participation but non-hypostatic manifestation. The hypostasis of the Spirit is concealed *kenotically* in the hypostasis of the Father, allowing both unity but also distinction in the revelation of the Spirit. So, "all these particular and small pentecosts, which are to be united in the one hypostatic Pentecost of the Holy Spirit, cannot be conceived separately."[70]

Bulgakov's interpretation of the work of the Spirit in creation puts just as much emphasis on development and incompleteness as fullness and perfection, both resounding in the world "for all time." But his Platonic sensibilities show up in his understanding that the fullness of creation is already, in one sense, realized in the initial plan of creation, citing the sabbath rest as biblical support for such an idea. This does not diminish for him an equally strong movement of creation as a process of becoming, with an orientation toward the fullness expressed in the Logos. He ties such a movement in the Logos to "a male element of meanings and Meaning," but the being of the Logos in the creaturely Sophia is "receiving the life-force of being from the Holy Spirit reposing upon Him."[71] The aspect of accomplishment is fixed in the Divine Sophia, but the acts of becoming reside in the creaturely Sophia. The dynamics of life are within the domain of the work of the Holy Spirit as a "life-giving force" showing up a "cosmourgic" hypostasis and revealing the being of the world as a creative womb, "a proto mother" that is dependent on the Holy Spirit.[72] He therefore identifies the force of the Spirit as showing up clearly within "the earth from which all things have their being,

---

68. Bulgakov, *The Comforter*, 195.

69. Bulgakov, *The Comforter*, 196.

70. Bulgakov, *The Comforter*, 197.

71. Bulgakov, *The Comforter*, 198.

72. Bulgakov, *The Comforter*, 198–99.

the leaf of grass as well as man."⁷³ In an almost mystical passage he speaks of the Spirit as a:

> hearing and perceiving silence, in which the Word born from all eternity is born again for creation [. . .] In the creaturely Sophia this Spirit is resonance, breathing, accomplishment, life; this Spirit is *natura naturans*, which, through the word implanted in it, engenders *natura naturata* or becomes it. This Spirit is the *being* that contains all things in itself, although it does not add anything to this all from itself. This Spirit is the world in its extra-divine aseity. This Spirit is the menonic darkness of being just before dawn, the earth invisible and void, as if *prior* to the Word that will flame up in it, casting His seed in it; this Spirit is the perfect accomplishment of the transfigured world.⁷⁴

The image of the Word as male seed and the Spirit as maternal mother that he returns to at intervals implies, as I indicated above, a gender-biased stereotypical perception of creation and becoming, or at minimum a phallic symbolism. However, it would be a misreading to assume on this basis that the work of the Spirit is passive or just receptive. Rather, he goes on to add that:

> This Spirit is the natural energy of the world which can never be extinguished or interrupted in the world, but always bears within itself the principle of the growth of creative activity.⁷⁵

The full list of that energetic creative work arising out of Mother Earth includes life in all its forms, so the vegetable and animal worlds, the human race, even the "life-giving principle which pious paganism, without knowing Him, worshipped as the 'Great Pan', as the Mother of the gods, Isis and Gaia."⁷⁶

How close does he come to pantheism? He certainly edges toward this, but by putting such discussions in the context of his broader theo-ontology he names his position as panentheism.⁷⁷ Pantheism, in a modified version, should not be rejected for Bulgakov since "it is a dialectically necessary moment in the sophiological cosmology."⁷⁸ For him, recognition of a divine force in creation is part and parcel of a true understanding of the creative process. He holds to the limitation of that creative process not being identified exclusively with God without remainder, so is not exhausted by God's expression in the world of creation. Creaturely aseity shows up the world as extra-divine, even while its sophianic foundation is of divine origin. Creation can therefore neither be identified with God or separated from God, founded ontologically in the

---

73. Bulgakov, *The Comforter*, 199.

74. Bulgakov, *The Comforter*, 199.

75. Bulgakov, *The Comforter*, 199.

76. Bulgakov, *The Comforter*, 199.

77. Bulgakov, *The Comforter*, 200.

78. Bulgakov, *The Comforter*, 200.

work of the Holy Spirit as the life of creation and "the grace of creation."[79] Again, to fill out this process he relies on Platonic ideas, so speaking of "ideal seeds" coming from the Logos, actualized as forms. His position is also an aesthetic theology, thus putting emphasis on "the artistry of the Holy Spirit, Who is the Artist of the world, the Principle of form and the Form of forms."[80]

The "natural grace of creation" also overcomes the powers opposed to it, which, in this case, amounts to a "nothing" that is the "dark face of Sophia."[81] It is within this interpretation that Bulgakov can acknowledge that the life of creation is non-idyllic, and is always a struggle between life and death, so that the chaotic elements are "restrained but not tamed."[82] He insists, though, that nature is beautiful in all its forms, for even *tahu vabohu* is "clothed in the beauty of power."[83] Beauty is the exteriorized sophianicity of creation and reflects the mystical light of Divine Sophia in a way which indicates that beauty has *objective* and not just subjective content. Yet, he also describes "natural grace" as the "creative 'let there be'", in accordance with a form of the kenosis of the Spirit.[84] That natural grace "exists in the very *flesh* of the world," that is, in its matter.[85]

What is particularly important to note is that this kenotic natural grace prepares creation for receptivity to spirit through a process of sanctification. This is his, it seems to me, most important contribution to a theology of creation where the action of the Holy Spirit is exemplary of grace working within nature.[86] For:

> In sanctification we have a descent of the Holy Spirit and a communication of His force to natural and spirit-bearing creation: the creaturely Sophia is united here with the Divine Sophia, the Holy Spirit with the Spirit of God in creation.[87]

For him, it is only because of natural grace that supernatural grace, which implies both receiving and retaining the action of the Holy Spirit, is possible. He speaks, then, of the way things and matter "absorb the invisibly descending grace of the Holy Spirit the way the earth absorbs moisture."[88] The creaturely

---

79. Bulgakov, *The Comforter*, 201.

80. Bulgakov, *The Comforter*, 201.

81. Bulgakov, *The Comforter*, 201.

82. Bulgakov, *The Comforter*, 201.

83. Bulgakov, *The Comforter*, 202.

84. Bulgakov, *The Comforter*, 220.

85. Bulgakov, *The Comforter*, 220.

86. See the envisaged volumes 3 and 9 in the *An Earthed Faith* series.

87. Bulgakov, *The Comforter*, 221.

88. Bulgakov, *The Comforter*, 221.

descent of the Spirit therefore anticipates the overall *receptivity* to Spirit by matter, but that creaturely descent involves *kenosis* in that there is a limit to that spirit-bearingness, which, even in this limit, "contains the force of the being of creation."[89]

There is a unity, then, between creaturely Sophia and Divine Sophia in the work of sanctification by the Holy Spirit, such as that in sacramental acts where "matter is taken out of this world and borne into the world of grace of the future age, where God will be all in all."[90] Matter, in this case, is transfigured while ontologically remaining itself is "transparent for the Spirit" and, in communion with God, is deified. He ties such sanctification into the realization of a divine-humanity which is inclusive of the world that is being humanized, "a world that has its ontological center in man."[91] He insists, therefore, on the peak of the divine-human character of grace being manifested in self-conscious "hypostatic spirits," which in practice means human beings and angels. Sanctification applies to all matter, but creative inspiration applies to humanity. This inspiration amounts to a "manifestation of divine-humanity in creaturely divine-humanity."[92] It is a mutual permeation of the human spirit with the non-coercive Divine Spirit, while still acknowledging the human creaturely measure. Just as in sanctification matter becomes transparent for the Spirit, so in creaturely life, humanity can become transparent for the Divine Spirit. This transparency is non-hypostatic, whereas in the life of Christ the union of the divine-human Logos is a hypostatic one. The theo-anthropocentrism characteristic of Orthodox approaches is, therefore, softened through Bulgakov's inclusive sophiological account.

We find, then, in this Orthodox thinker, a constructive theological approach that demonstrates a rich and dynamic ontology of the Spirit that still carries significance within current ecotheological thought. His theology is challenging to accept or perhaps better to appreciate because it takes us into a world that seems ethereal and one that makes most sense when understood within the Orthodox traditions of liturgy and worship. While he could be read as veering toward solipsistic tendencies, that reflects, it seems to me, a cultural divergence with the West where it is harder to appreciate a Platonic understanding of reality. It is worth noting, however, that even within contemporary discussion, a pure naturalism is proving dissatisfying. Thomas Nagel has understood and to a degree adopted the philosophical lure of Platonism within his teleological version of evolutionary becoming.[93] Bulgakov helps to articulate how the

---

89. Bulgakov, *The Comforter*, 221.

90. Bulgakov, *The Comforter*, 221.

91. Bulgakov, *The Comforter*, 222.

92. Bulgakov, *The Comforter*, 222.

93. Bråkenhielm, "Back to the Future."

Spirit can work *within* creation and the story of the earth, while acknowledging the particular and distinct role of the Holy Spirit in the human story. He provides one interpretation, at least, of the role of the Holy Spirit in the work of grace and its relationship with created nature.

There are two other broad questions worth probing a little further. The first is how far his own work successfully incorporates a pantheistic dimension. His interwoven themes of the maternal work of the Holy Spirit that is creatively working within matter and his argument for a kenotic articulation of the Spirit in creation that is non-hypostatic is, it seems to me, a brilliant way to retain theological ontology without collapsing into a perspective that understands the Spirit as a form of natural emergence. Creaturely Sophia, too, has a shadowy side that permits some acknowledgment of suffering and death. While in other parts of his work there is gender stereotyping, he does not fall into the trap of associating those areas of the Spirit's work expressed in feminine symbolism just with passivity or non-activity. His own reading of evolutionary science is generally negative and somewhat naive, mistakenly believing that all evolutionary theories are simply about randomness.[94] He is correct, however, to point to a flaw in a standard scientific account of the origin of the world that generally presuppose that "out of nothing comes everything."[95] The origin of new species is not particularly well-explained by theories of natural selection, even if there may be good reasons to believe from the perspective of these theories why some species survive and others do not.

Further, a more dynamic approach to evolutionary theory, ecology, and biology in general points to a different philosophical basis, even if it does not come close to theo-ontology. Bulgakov's view of the work of the Spirit as a "life-force" resonates with other religious interpretations of creation, and even if classic biologists might resist such a view as a form of vitalism, there is a greater openness to alternative perspectives compared with half a century ago. Is his work still too anthropocentric? Certainly, contemporary ecotheologians may balk at his insistence on the place of humanity in the center of creation and the work of the Spirit as a type of humanization. However, this idea stems from his strong commitment to Christology as the meaning and purpose of the story of salvation on earth. It is in Christ that humanization takes place, and therefore it offers a strong affirmation of material being as such. The important point to note is that the story of life on earth cannot simply be collapsed into a theological story and *vice versa*, even if listening to their respective voices can be mutually illuminating. The story of life on earth has, in other words, its own intellectual integrity, as does a

---

94. Bulgakov, *The Comforter*, 207.

95. Bulgakov, *The Comforter*, 207.

theological interpretation of its meaning. At the same time, he risks saying rather too much in a cataphatic vein about the inner workings of the Trinity and not giving apophatic theological traditions sufficient weight, even though there are serious risks in so doing through resorting to mystery or even the idea of an absence of God in pure silence.[96]

■ Preliminary Conclusions

I began this essay by situating the theological story within the hermeneutical shifts in an understanding of ontology that have colored current Western approaches to theology. A largely static ontology gave way to a process model. I argued that these currents have been important not just for theology and ecotheological thinking, but also for a philosophical understanding of evolution and biology. Ecology, once thought to be a subversive science, no longer seems to be the stranger. I offered philosophies of nature that, in the case of Serres, tackles the broadest sweep of the history of life on earth, and, in Kohák, dwelled within the natural world in order to try and understand it. For Serres, humanity is always distinct, even if it has tended to forget its earth history. But this distinction comes through a de-differentiation to non-specialism that then flowered in a second nature, tools, and culture of our own making. He ended up, however, with a Hobbesian perspective on where this might lead to next, and his disconsolate vision is ultimately unappealing even if understandable in an age that recognized ecological devastation. What he failed to consider properly was the very ground of being, of earth, in which humanity is situated. Kohák acknowledged ecology in a deeper way, not just for understanding who we are, but as a shared animate partner in our becoming. He notes the rightness with the workings of ecological being that forestall materialist reductionism. Their work sits alongside other prominent philosophers such as Nagel who equally finds empiricism dissatisfying.

As I moved into the more explicitly theological discussion on nature and grace, I argued that Fields tells a related story of how God-centered cultures faded, but in its wake came a split between reason and the supernatural, pure nature, and super added nature. His solution, to argue for a form of prevenient grace seemed somewhat thin in ecological terms. Rahner still located the search for transcendence within the human spirit, even if he opened this up to include those searching for meaning. But working out how to combine this search with a work of grace was unclear and somewhat dissatisfying.

I then turned to a critical engagement with the theology of Bulgakov. Although not explicitly ecological, his focus on creation and Sophia is important in approaching how the Trinitarian story of creation might be told.

---

96. Grenz, *The Named God*, 320–3.

His approach to God's Spirit in creation as that of *natural grace* which remains sanctifying in its work, is more satisfying than Fields' *prevenient grace*. The Spirit is a brooding, maternal but active force within creation. He uses vibrant imagery to describe how the creative Spirit is the same Spirit that works to transform life and matter. By distinguishing the work of the Spirit in all creation, including humanity, as non-hypostatic, it allows for a novel kenotic approach to the life of the Spirit within the story of life on earth. He admits to the strength of pantheism without committing to pantheism without the remainder. While his attention to science is somewhat naive, his theology dictates a strong and distinct role for humanity. If he edges a little too close to being human-centered in his final theological construction, this is offset to an extent through Christological and Trinitarian reference points. The Holy Spirit is an artist within the natural world, and, if Bulgakov is taken seriously, the story of life on earth needs to be told within the story of the Holy Spirit's work of sanctification and inspiration. He gives, in other words, an important role to the person of the Spirit in the process of becoming that has a future and not just a beginning. My preference, therefore, is to situate strands of his theology within a broader philosophy of the transcendent that is currently emerging. Precisely how this might be worked out requires a more in-depth analysis of the work of the Holy Spirit in creation.

■ Bibliography

Bulgakov, Sergius. *The Comforter*. Translated by Boris Jakim. Grand Rapids: Eerdmans, 2004.

Bråkenhielm, Carl Reinhold. "Back to the Future." In *Eschatology as Imagining the End: Faith Between Hope and Despair*, edited by Sigurd Bergmann, 146–67. London: Routledge, 2018.

Conradie, Ernst M. *The Earth in God's Economy: Creation, Salvation and Consummation in Ecological Perspective*. Berlin: LIT, 2015.

———. "What on Earth Did God Create? Overtures to an Ecumenical Theology of Creation." *Ecumenical Review* 66:4 (2014), 433–53. https://doi.org/10.1111/erev.12120

Deane-Drummond, Celia. "Biodiversity and Ecological Responsibility: Wonder, Value and Paying Attention to All Creatures." *Antonianum Journal* 156 (2021), 87–113,

———. *Ethics of Nature*. Oxford: Blackwells/Wiley, 2004.

———. "The Evolution of Wisdom in a Technological World: An Exploration in Nature and Grace." In *Human Flourishing in a Technological Age*. Oxford: Oxford University Press, in press. ———. *Theological Ethics Through a Multispecies Lens: Evolution of Wisdom Volume 1*. Oxford: Oxford University Press, 2019.

———. "The Spirit of Wisdom: Sergius Bulgakov's Sophianic Trinitarian Ontology in Dialogue with Contemporary Biology." Paper delivered for a conference entitled *New Trinitarian Ontologies* in Cambridge, 14 September 2019.

Deane-Drummond, Celia, ed. *Teilhard de Chardin on People and Planet*. London: Equinox, 2006.

Fields, Stephen. *Analogies of Transcendence: An Essay on Nature, Grace and Modernity*. Washington, DC: Catholic University of America Press, 2016.

Goodenough, Ursula. *The Sacred Depths of Nature*. New York: Oxford University Press, 1998.

Grenz, Stanley J. *The Named God and the Question of Being: A Trinitarian Theo-Ontology*. Louisville: Westminster John Knox Press, 2005.

Hanby, Michael. *No God, No Science: Theology, Cosmology, Biology*. Oxford: Wiley Blackwell, 2016.

Ingold, Tim. "An Anthropologist Looks at Biology." *Man, New Series*, 25:2 (1990), 208–29. https://doi.org/10.2307/2804561

Kilby, Karen and J. Matthew Ashley. "What Difference Does Grace Make? An Exploration of the Concept of Grace in the Theological Anthropology of Karl Rahner." In *Theology and Evolutionary Anthropology: Dialogues in Wisdom, Humility and Grace,* edited by Celia Deane-Drummond and Agustín Fuentes, 209–27. London: Routledge, 2020.

Kohák, Erazim. *The Embers and the Stars: A Philosophical Inquiry into the Moral Sense of Nature*. Chicago: University of Chicago Press, 1984.

Laland, Kevin N., et al. "Does Evolutionary Theory Need a Rethink? Researchers are Divided Over What Processes Should be Considered Fundamental." *Nature* 9:514 (2014), 161–64. https://doi.org/10.1038/514161a

Laland, Kevin N., et al. "The Extended Evolutionary Synthesis: It's Structure, Assumptions and Predictions." *Proceedings of the Royal Society: Biological Sciences* 282:1813 (2015). https://doi.org/10.1098/rspb.2015.1019

Meneses, Eloise and David Bronkema. *On Knowing Humanity: Insights from Theology for Anthropology.* London: Routledge, 2017.

Merchant, Carolyn. *The Death of Nature: Women, Ecology and the Scientific Revolution*. New York: Harper Collins, 1980.

Moss, Lenny. "From Representational Preformationism to the Epigenesis of Openness to the World? Reflections on a New Vision of the Organism." *Annals New York Academy of Sciences* 981 (2002), 219–30. https://doi.org/10.1111/j.1749-6632.2002.tb04920.x

Nagel, Thomas. *Mind and Cosmos: Why the Materialist neo-Darwinian Conception of Nature is Almost Certainly False*. Oxford: Oxford University Press, 2012.

Serres, Michel. *Hominescence.* Translated by Randolph Burks. London: Bloomsbury, 2019.

———. *The Incandescent*. Translated by Randolph Burks. London: Bloomsbury, 2018.

In the Beginning . . . The Universe was Dreaming

Heather Eaton[1]

In the beginning . . . was a time of dreaming, a magical emptiness, a darkness on the face of the deep, chaos, mystery, nothingness, silence, . . . the Spirit hovered. Then creation emerged, and life came from spirit(s), breath, water, fire, clouds, Earth, mountains, mud, trees, animal spirits, eggs, eagles, turtles, and on and on. There are countless origin or creation stories that have surfaced from human symbolic consciousness for at least 200 000 years.[2] They tell us who we are, how to live, and our place within the biosphere, and within the mysteries of space and time. Most of these stories have vanished: gone extinct with their specific clans, cultures, or civilizations. Some have metamorphosed, or adapted to new circumstances, or been amalgamated with other stories. The variations are inestimable. Yet the commonalities are crucial.

---

1. Heather Eaton is Professor of Conflict Studies at Saint Paul University in Ottawa, Canada. She is registered as a co-researcher at the University of the Western Cape, South Africa, for the project on "An Earthed Faith: Telling the Story amid the 'Anthropocene'."

2. See Lewis-Williams, *The Mind in the Cave* and *A Cosmos in Stone*.

How to cite: Eaton, H., 2021, 'In the Beginning . . . The Universe was Dreaming', in E.M. Conradie & P.-C. Lai (eds.), *Taking a deep breath for the story to begin . . .* (An Earthed Faith: Telling the Story amid the "Anthropocene" Volume 1), pp. 141–162, AOSIS, Cape Town. https://doi.org/10.4102/aosis.2021.BK264.07

■ Introduction

The impetus for such stories derives from primal, interior, and collective imperatives to make sense of ourselves and of the layers of vital materiality—from cosmos to Earth to communities. It is requisite for the human species to create such reality maps, usually in the form of stories, but more on that later. Each of these stories, in one manner or another, denote human emergence from, entanglement with, embeddedness in, belonging to, and abiding within this vibrant matter.[3] The Lakota phrase, "all my relations," contains the breadth and depth of this unbreakable interconnectedness of matter, spirit, life and in this story, reverence.

Origin or creation stories use a plethora of symbols and images infused with meaning and purpose. They offer an orientation—life-navigational maps—from the farthest reaches of time and space to the inner existential forces, the latter of which is described eloquently by Ernst Conradie in his essay in this volume on a South African Reformed perspective. In addition, most origin or creation stories grapple with birth to death, suffering and joy, and everything between benevolence and malevolence. Much work has occurred on collecting, deciphering, comparing, and analyzing creation stories. They are often magical, imaginative, powerful, beautiful, and elegant stories. They have been told, sung, carved, painted, danced, and written, at times within rituals, fasting, and feasting, and with sacrifices and celebrations.

Several influences shape my approach to these topics. Growing up on Lake Huron in Canada nurtured a fascination with life forms, evolution, and the universe, coalescing into an intense desire for intelligibility and coherence, and a need to protect Earth-life. Time spent in Latin and South America, Haiti, India, and Africa strengthened concerns for social distresses and a thirst for justice. Academic theological training (predominantly Catholic) included feminist, liberation and ecological theologies, social ethics, religious experiences, and symbolic consciousness. Together these influences affirm for me that we live in a *divine milieu* (Pierre Teilhard de Chardin).

This essay is about origins stories, influenced by the questions: Is the Christian story part of the Earth's story or is the Earth's story part of God's story, from creation to consummation? How does God relate to the story of life on Earth? The essay is divided into two main sections. The first explores the function of cultural narratives, how it is that humans create such stories, and the importance of symbolic consciousness. The second explores how a contemporary universe story collaborates and collides with Christian narratives. Each has sub-sections that will assist with traversing these topics.

---

3. See Bennet, *Vibrant Matter*.

■ Stories

There are many kinds of stories. Of interest here are creation (foundational, origin, cosmological, meta/mega) stories that carry a deep mythos to orient human communities and offer guidance to navigate the exigencies of life. Religions and indigenous traditions have, par excellence, the most comprehensive and poignant creation stories, which function as worldviews or metanarratives.[4] Such cultural narratives seep into personal identities and social ethos to a degree that they are barely perceptible. My entry point is to consider their facets, structures, and functions, more so than the particular content, within two themes: cultural narratives (worldviews) and symbolic consciousness.

▮ Cultural Narratives, Worldviews, Metanarratives

The claim that humans live within stories laden with symbols has been substantiated by countless scholars from myriad cultures, and for eons. Studies on myths, stories, Weltanschauungen, worldviews or social imaginaries note the many facets and dynamics of comprehensive cultural stories. Numerous and diverse Western thinkers have focused on such narratives: for example, Michel Foucault, Clifford Geertz, Paul Ricoeur, H. Richard Niebuhr, Gaston Bachelard, Val Plumwood, Judith Butler, Cornelius Castoriadis, Sallie McFague, Ivone Gebara, Charles Taylor, Thomas Berry, and many more.

Origin stories are cultural narratives embedded in worldviews. These are diverse in emphasis and content yet share some structural and functional elements. Worldviews reveal a complex and relational tapestry of intertwining ideals, beliefs, practices, values, and influences: an amalgam of the signs, visions, ideas, ideals, and practices that interweave to produce cultural values, governance systems and social identities, and moral principles. They contain ubiquitous presuppositions or beliefs about what is truthful, real, and worthy.[5]

The most comprehensive analyses of worldviews come from the Worldviews Group[6]: a multidisciplinary European research program studying the components, explanations, and functioning of worldviews. Others, such as Robert Cummings Neville, consider worldviews to be comprehensive stories:

---

4. I am using the terms of origin or creation stories, cultural and grand narratives, worldviews, social imaginaries, world representations, and metanarratives interchangeably. See Eaton, *The Challenges of Worldview Transformation*, 121–37.

5. I have written extensively on worldviews and am drawing here on such earlier work. See, for example, Eaton, "An Ecological Imaginary," "The Challenges of Worldview Transformation."

6. See Worldviews, https://www.vub.be/CLEA/dissemination/groups-archive/vzw_worldviews/, accessed 01 March 2021.

a cultured set of signs for orienting behavior.[7] According to Rosemary Radford Ruether, worldviews combine the cultural-symbolic levels—the ideological superstructures—that reflect and sanction the social, economic, political, and religious orders.[8] David Christian comments that these large maps of time and space are full of meaning, and in the past such origin stories provided members of society with a clear idea of their place in a larger universe.[9]

Thomas Berry, a student of worldviews/cultural narratives and religious origin stories in China, India, Europe, North America, and with many indigenous groups, observed how these stories function. Each renders an account of how the world came to be and how we fit into the grand scheme of things. Berry probed how they guide and shape our personal and collective life purposes, actions and interactions, replete with ethical norms, and beliefs about origins and destinies, noting that these stories make sense only to those who live within them. Furthermore, outside of stories, human life cannot function in meaningful ways.[10] Berry was an early voice in proposing the parameters, and need for, a *universe story*.[11]

Paul Ricoeur's interest in cultural narratives, and his development of Karl Mannheim's cultural analyses on ideology and utopia, resonate deeply with the questions probed here.[12] The dialectic between ideology and utopia offers insights into worldview functioning, disintegration, and transformations. Ideologies are the governing worldviews, but operate in a hidden, inconspicuous manner, justifying and rendering meaningful social relationships, and systems of power and authority. Ideologies or worldviews are experienced as intrinsic and authentic to the self are deeply ingrained and concealed from self-awareness, and are assumed to be universal, natural, and true.[13] Utopic movements challenge, and make visible, ideologies. They challenge truth claims and power systems, and expand or alter worldviews. Social justice movements are examples of utopic efforts, confronting restrictive, unjust or corrupt social orders. They are inevitably met with resistance, and are initially refuted as false, dangerous, meaningless, or are marginalized. These are some of the reasons why ideologies/worldviews are so difficult to alter.

---

7. See Cummings Neville, "Worldviews."

8. See Ruether, "Ecofeminism."

9. See Christian, *The Immanent Frame*.

10. See Berry, *Dream of the Earth*.

11. See Eaton, *Intellectual Journey*.

12. See Ricoeur, *Lectures on Ideology and Utopia*, and "Ideology and Utopia." See also Eaton, "Ecofeminist Ethics," which offers an in depth discussion of how Ricoeur's notions of ideologies and utopia operate in cultural transformations.

13. Ricoeur, "Ideology and Utopia," 316.

It is important to recognize that when worldviews or origin stories lose their potency, there can be collective disorientation and disintegration, a loss of common ground, shared values, and collective goals, and social inaction. Émile Durkheim argued that the absence of a coherent and credible understanding of one's place in a larger universe can create a sense of disconnection, diminution, disorientation, even life-threatening despair.[14] Berry proposed that the inability to address the severity of ecological and social issues stems from dysfunctional worldviews, orienting stories, or metanarratives that make these issues, and responses, central.[15]

The aforementioned Worldviews Group also raises concerns about the ineffectiveness of many societies to address escalating social and ecological problems. They observe multiple levels of fragmentation caused by the demise of mega/meta or integrative narratives. The results are fluid, contextual, jumbled, and splintered worldviews trying to respond to cultural pluralities in information saturated, hyper-mobile, and epistemic postmodern worlds. The goals of these worldview studies are to move from "fragmentation to integration (not homogenization)"[16] of the multiplicity of worldviews to enable effective responses to current global exigencies. The tension between culturally specific worldviews and problems that require global frameworks and solutions is noteworthy.

Yet, it is not accurate to claim that human societies live according to worldviews or stories. Humans live within worldviews and stories. These are not cognitive maps or sets of beliefs: we are embedded and entangled within them. The impulse for communities to conceive of these grand narratives lies buried in the evolutionary development of hominin species. To grasp the depth of the vitality of such stories, a segue into the symbolic processes that give rise to worldviews, and their resistance to alterations, may be useful.

Symbolic Consciousness: Structures, Attributes, and Narratives

Homo sapiens and other hominins navigate existence symbolically, having evolved with capacities to live by means of a symbolic consciousness.[17] It is

---

14. See Durkheim, *Le Suicide*.

15. See Berry, *Dream of the Earth*.

16. See Eaton, "The Challenges of Worldview Transformation."

17. See Gottschall, *The Storytelling Animal*; Deacon, *Incomplete Nature*; also *The Symbolic Species*; Klein and Edgar, *The Dawn of Human Culture*; Dixon, *Images of Truth*; Van Huyssteen, *Alone in the World*, and Lewis Williams, *The Mind in the Cave*.

this mode of consciousness that allows for representations of the world to form, eventually as worldviews or social imaginaries.[18]

The evolutionary processes that led to active imagining, signs, symbols, visualizations, and world representations remain opaque. The emergence of a consciousness that could function symbolically and sustain the capacity to coordinate dreams, intuitions, images, thoughts, emotions, insights, and retention developed over millennia.[19] Experiences became layered with emotions, images, sensory feedback, memories, signs, and language. Terrence Deacon suggests that, "the thousands of symbolic units comprising the lexicon of a language (words and morphemes) effectively 'point' to one another as though comprising a complex interconnected network."[20] John Dixon asserts that remnants of ancient symbols and artifacts indicate that experiences were transmuted into systems of images to cope with, and delineate, the interior and exterior exigencies of life.[21]

I have written elsewhere that " the [D]ynamics of symbolic functioning can be dissected into aspects involving external realities of culture, context, representations and internal realities of emotions, cognition and ideation—all of which are embedded in identity formation, a sense of self, social imaginaries and bonding patterns."[22] However, this renders a superficial, even false, understanding. The division of exteriority and interiority is misleading, as are the differentiations. These processes are interrelated in ever-moving exchanges. Material interactions, contexts, events, and symbolic processes are inseparable, interwoven and enmeshed within the very "structures of human consciousness and behaviors,"[23] operating within indivisible personal and social weaves. They are shaped by, interact with, and impact material realms that strengthen reciprocities, subjectivities, and relational immanence.

This "symbolic imaginative mode of being is the modus operandi of humans."[24] A symbolic consciousness is the way humans process and navigate the world. It is not through or with symbols that we think and comprehend; it

---

18. I am drawing here on Eaton, "The Human Quest to Live in a Cosmos"; "Ecological Christianities"; "A Spirituality of the Earth"; "The Challenges of Worldview Transformation"; "An Ecological Imaginary."

19. See See Richard Klein and Blake Edgar, *The Dawn of Human Culture*. There is little agreement on when, where, how and which version of hominins began to manifest creative and symbolic thinking. See also John Noble Wilford, "When Humans Became Human," "

20. Deacon, "The Symbol Concept," 401.

21. Dixon, *Images of Truth,* 49.

22. See Eaton, "The Challenges of Worldview Transformation."

23. See Eaton, "The Challenges of Worldview Transformation."

24. See Eaton, "The Challenges of Worldview Transformation."

is *within* symbols.[25] Humans are incapable of existing outside of symbolic renderings of the world; hence Deacon's term, the "symbolic species." He argues that symbolic navigation is inextricably part of humans: symbolic consciousness is our ecological niche.

Although one can discern that hominins and other species developed forms of symbolic consciousness, it is essential to grasp that this is not a linear, or inevitable, evolutionary process. Several lineages of hominins are known to have various symbolic processes and expressions, and these developed independently, and over millennia. Research, including that of Celia Deane-Drummond and Agustín Fuentes on theological anthropology, probes multiple evolutionary trajectories that indicate that the occurrence of symbolic consciousness was neither straightforward nor inevitable.[26] Fossils of new hominins are regularly unearthed, noting distinct DNA, cranial sizes, shapes, and jaw structures, morphology, bipedalism, and habitat, updating and revising claims of human ancestry and development.

Other studies focus on tools, signs, artifacts, rituals, diagrammatic reasoning, semiotics, abstractions, memory formation as well as communal structures, parenting, social learning, and myriad symbolic expressions. Still, it is impossible to present accurate details about the emergent process of symbolic consciousness. In spite of ample evidence that symbolic consciousness emerged in hominins, it is wise to be cautious in asserting when, where, why, and how various hominins were developing, innovating, experimenting, and intensifying as symbolic species.

Attributes of Symbolic Consciousness

It is important to consider how the dynamics of symbolic consciousness amplify a sense of being. For example, the use of tools required the capacity to imagine, and indicates a nascent form of symbolic consciousness. When a rock becomes a tool, it becomes more than it is. There is a surplus of meaning. In symbolic processes, something becomes other than, or greater than, it is. In a similar vein, when humans claim, or intuit, a transcendent power or presence as Holy, Mystery or Sacred, the interpretation amplifies a sense of being.[27] These symbolized experiences become self-amplifying loops that increase the intensity and power of related experiences, which strengthens the symbol and again the experiences. This elasticity or expansion of consciousness—that we experience more than we are and can transcend our own boundaries—is a

---

25. See Dixon, *Images of Truth*.

26. See Deane-Drummond and Fuentes, *Theology and Evolutionary Anthropology*.

27. See Dixon, *Images of Truth*; Lewis-Williams, *Mind in the Cave*.

critical component of the experiential potency of religious symbols and stories.

For example, Earth symbolization is considered to be the earliest and most consistent religious symbols across time and traditions.[28] Earth activities press upon human consciousness, evoking intense affect—terror, joy, awe, inspiration, sadness, calm, love—which require representation. We are not only *responding* to these realities. These dynamics are experienced within ourselves in rapport with the dynamics of place. Experiences of caves or forests are often described "in terms of intimacy, intensity, envelopment or interiority"[29]. Gaston Bachelard's account of "the immensity of the forest" is illuminating.[30] For Bachelard, the immensity felt *in the forest* and perceived as *of the forest* is an immensity felt *within our self-consciousness*. It is an *intimate immensity*, experienced as an expansion of being, indicating a transcendent sensibility. We may describe these experiences as an encounter—mysterious, numinous, divine, sacred, or eternal—of perceiving deeper dimensions within reality. Bachelard's term the *material imagination* denotes this surplus of being and meaning within the dynamics of symbolic consciousness.

Symbols interconnect and blend into comprehensive representations of the world. It is indisputable that humans require, and live within, worldviews, social imaginaries, stories: creating a coherent and intelligible image of "the world." As mentioned before, humans are incapable of existing outside of extensive renderings of their realms and the world. The collective dimension of symbolic consciousness indicates that images, stories, and representations of the world become shared, as an organizing principle of common, social navigation. The processes that form collective symbols evade certitude. Nevertheless, each community develops a representation of an intelligible and coherent world, and believes in the veracity of the images, stories, and symbols. Furthermore, it is always formed as a narrative.

The Storytelling Animal

Humans, individually and collectively, generate and live within narratives. This is, of course, not a new idea; however, there is new evidence to support it. Jonathan Gottschall makes a compelling case that humans are "The story telling animal."[31] With verifications from evolutionary biology, psychology, and neuroscience, Gottschall shows multiple ways in which humans are always

---

28. See Dixon, *Images of Truth*; Lewis-Williams, *Mind in the Cave*; Van Huyssteen, *Alone in the World?*

29. Heather Eaton, "The Challenges of Worldview Transformation."

30. In his stellar book, *The Poetics of Space*, Bachelard describes in depth how humans interact with spaces via the imagination, symbolic consciousness, and interiority.

31. See Gottschall, *The Storytelling Animal*.

living within and reconstructing experiences in narratives. These narratives are the cognitive, communication, education, and classification modes of human experiences.

The storytelling mind seeks coherence and meaning. It is "allergic to uncertainty, randomness and coincidence. If the storytelling mind cannot find meaningful patterns in the world, it will try to impose them."[32] Such narratives are not subject to categories of fact or fiction: they are stories/worldviews. Furthermore, story is the epicenter of individual and social cohesion: "Story is the counterforce to social disorder, the tendency of things to fall apart. Story is the center without which the rest cannot hold."[33]

Furthermore, although these comprehensive stories are about everything—time, space, experiences, life/death—and are internalized as authentic, truthful, universal, and ultimate, they are contextual. The stories *live* in specific human communities, deeply internalized and embedded in myriad personal and communal processes that sustain them. They are indecipherable outside of the lived context and are not readily translatable or transferable. This is a key insight into the felt sense of veracity and certitude of something that is relative and provisional. Perhaps this explains, to some extent, why the power and meanings of religious symbols and stories are forcefully protected and yet are inscrutable without the context and the related experiences.

This also illustrates why there are countless symbols and stories. It is a language, of sorts, decipherable within the worldview. This further corroborates that there are no *a priori* reasons why symbols, religious claims, beliefs, or doctrines are truthful. The classifications of true or false are inapplicable, from a structural viewpoint. Stories and symbols are active, alive, or dynamic in individual and communal imaginative symbolic processes, or they are meaningless, dying or dead. Symbols that no longer function are abandoned or transfused with other experiences and meanings.

■ The Universe, Earth and Christian Stories in the "Anthropocene"

There is no question that the world/Earth needs new, or renewed, stories to plot a path forward that will change course, effecting different outcomes than current practices. Yet, an incredulity toward metanarratives may impede viable responses. The "end of metanarratives" has not produced all the desired liberations, although it has justifiably challenged oppressive governing stories. The postmodern shift, while giving voice to many, and requiring that knowledge claims be transparent about presuppositions and partiality, has increased

---

32. Gottschall, *The Storytelling Animal*, 103.

33. Gottschall, *The Storytelling Animal*, 138.

skepticism toward truth claims and integrative narratives. The door is wide open in some cultures to post-truth, fake news, and other variances that impede collective visions. Yet, even those previously dedicated to a diffusion of narratives, such as Arron Gaare, see the need to re-embrace some form of global vision to forge a way ahead.[34]

From another angle, new materialisms research represents a coalescing of disciplines that focus on material and energy connections at all levels of reality. The biosphere is relevant within Earth sciences and new materialisms. The language of relational immanence, reciprocity, mutuality, embodiment, and embodied subjectivities indicates the need for innovative language to denote these omnipresent entanglements and distinctiveness. Important for this discussion is a focus on planetary thinking. Intellectual work in planetary thinking is subject to, and entangled with, multiple dynamics of consciousness, cognition, affectivity, and somatic subtleties that are always in flux. Again we see different discourses articulating, with novel images, profound levels of continuity (not uniformity), interconnections, and interactions coupled with the need for global/planetary thinking and metaframeworks that protect differentiation.

To mention creation/origin, universe, or Christian, stories is to evoke the aforementioned dynamics of symbolic consciousness and the complexities of narratives. With this in mind, the following sections ponder recent knowledge of the universe and Earth processes, and how this interfaces or interferes with versions of the Christian story(ies). The context that frames this inquiry is the end of the Cenozoic era of biodiversity, unpredictable anthropogenic climate changes, and countless socio-ecological issues. Some refer to this context as the beginning of an "Anthropocene" era. Although a contentious term, my usage refers only to a basic agreement that the impacts of human communities are a geological force and are transforming the biosphere in irreversible ways. Of course, some cultures are significantly more destructive to Earth's lifeways than others.

The following discussion is divided into two sub-sections. The first considers some developments in cosmological and Earth sciences, and what they could contribute to the themes herein. The second addresses connections and conflicts between a *universe* and a *Christian* story.

Cosmology, Earth Sciences, and Planetary Thinking

There are eruptions of new knowledge from cosmology and Earth sciences to subatomic physics. Disciplinary and epistemic boundaries are becoming permeable, spawning creative ventures that bridge facts and values, and

---

34. See Gare, "Grand Narrative"; Eaton, "Global Visions and Common Ground."

knowledge and vision. This is evident in environmental humanities, new materialisms, ecological democracy/citizenship, planetary ethics, and much more. Scientists are crossing disciplinary chasms with images such as Earth's imagination, the sacred depths of nature, biophilia, the symbiotic planet, the dancing universe, the implicate order, and living cosmos to expand understanding of and appreciation for the universe and the Earth. Many are reassessing the human place, and roles, in the larger scheme of things.

These scientific discoveries have sparked interest in the fields of religion and ecology and ecotheology. Discussions and debates are ongoing, addressing the veracity of the findings, and the explanatory powers, relevance, and importance. For some, the evolutionary and cosmological evidence overturns previous stories.[35] For others it infuses new insights, and for others still it is extraneous, disputable, or contradictory.

My interest is in the relevance of cosmological and Earth sciences research, and is based on these presuppositions and claims:

- The *new* knowledge about the universe, the Earth's evolutionary processes, the biospheric dynamics, and the immeasurable continuum between human, biotic and Earth life, are crucial to notions of creation.
- Understanding more about the universe and Earth's evolutionary and biospheric dynamics expands the mind to perceive more of the breadth, depth, and dimensions of reality.
- It challenges anthropocentrism, and revises the human place in the scheme of things.
- This knowledge has religious and spiritual significance and implications, representing a breath of fresh air, of *Ruach*, of a renewing movement of the Spirit.
- It is profoundly inspiring and can be woven into cultural narratives and global visions that may help guide a way forward.
- Religious origin stories need to integrate this knowledge to be informed, relevant, and potent in an era of ecological decline and social stress.

Projects such as "Big History," "Journey of the Universe," "Epic of Evolution," "The Great Story," "The Great Turning," "Emerging Planetary Civilizations," and other variations are suggesting that this knowledge is propelling a new axial age, a new origin story, or a global shift of consciousness that can counter the so-called great acceleration.[36] While there are dissimilarities, these efforts indicate the desire for a comprehensive unifying, integrative, meta/mega framework that is scientifically informed, and can incorporate multiplicities of

---

35. See Eaton, "Revolution."

36. See "Great Acceleration", International Geosphere-Biosphere Program, http://www.igbp.net/globalchange/greatacceleration.4.1b8ae20512db692f2a680001630.htm, accessed 1 March 2021.

cultural distinctions. They see these findings—the emergent universe, Earth's evolution, hominid/hominin development—as facets of a more accurate and compelling origin story. In tandem, others are proposing socio-political initiatives such as Earth democracy, the Earth Charter, ecological civilization, or ecological and biodemocracy that see the need to find *global* charters that connect sustainability with democracy, social and ecological justice. These proposals reveal that the recent insights and information from cosmology and Earth sciences, and from concerns for inequities, democracy, and global enmeshments, necessitate new images, common ground, shared principles, and for some an integrative or meganarrative.

There are debates about which version will dominate or will erase other versions, and what the biases of each project are. These are important concerns. However, what is often missed is a study of what has, in fact, been understood about the genesis of the universe, the solar system, Earth formation, emergence and evolution of a biosphere and life, and the endless processes, entanglements, and embeddedness that are now evident. Emergent complexity theories offer details and insights into elaborate intra/inter Earth functioning which both expand differentiations and increase elaborate interconnections. These are crucial aspects of any serious reflection on "creation."

While much of the universe remains impenetrable to comprehension (dark matter, black holes, magnetar, fast radio bursts) some general conditions exist. For example, there is a time-space development sequence to the universe, that appears to be irreversible. From nothing (as far as we know) to today, 13.7 billion years of expansions, the transformations and complexifications continue in at least two trillion galaxies. The universe, where energy, matter, creation, and destruction—in gigantic proportions—is ongoing. An apt metaphor is that it is a living universe.

Earth's dynamics, of 4.5 billion years or so, are both fascinating and enigmatic. Emergent complexities and interrelatedness define evolutionary processes. Humans evolved from these immense and intricate universe and Earth dynamics. Considerable emphasis is put on human exceptionalism, which is indisputable. However, what is more foundational is human continuity with, belonging to, and being a dimension of, Earth processes. In effect, I am accentuating an overall orientation within Earth's activities that has generated a biosphere, and repeatedly regenerated immeasurable complex communities of life. Furthermore, the biosphere interconnects materiality and Earth's climate and ocean systems within myriad, indiscernible networks. Earth has flourished in different eras of life, for millennia prior to the emergence of hominids and hominins. And this storytelling animal has been generated from within, and is wholly dependent upon, Earth's processes.

Everything about Earth evolves and develops from cosmic processes.[37] All aspects of *homo sapiens* evolve and develop from Earth processes. To say that Earth formed or produced humans is inadequate language. "We emerged from and are a conscious, living part of Earth realities."[38] By extension and extrapolation, the most apt description of the universe and the Earth is as alive. In this vein, the expansion of human consciousness into an awareness of the cosmos is also the universe and Earth becoming conscious in humanity. Therefore, the human story is integral with the universe story. This is key.

Therefore, neither the cosmos nor the Earth is a backdrop to the "human drama,"[39] or a context, an unfolding, a progression, or a potential. The universe and the Earth are our source. As the universe develops, including Earth, it becomes more: more complex, interactive, entwined, vibrant, and intense. The genesis process from atoms that transform into molecules, to form stars, solar systems, planets—to this Earth with an atmosphere and biosphere, to life, "consciousness, and self-consciousness"[40]—are discernible, if not well understood. This genesis of and within the universe and the Earth are more of a becoming: not linear and determined, but creative and dynamic. In spite of extinction events and turbulent moments, Earth continues to (re)generates life.

For Pierre Teilhard de Chardin the best image is that of cosmogenesis. This implies forms of continuity and coherence between cosmogenesis, geogenesis, and biogenesis. In the same manner, evolution is a process or dynamic of the biosphere from which *homo sapiens* evolved, with a form of self-reflexive symbolic consciousness that is able to perceive that these forms of genesis are ongoing. There is, again, coherence, continuity, and integration.[41] Thus the starting point for any serious reflection on creation/origin stories has to be the universe. On this point, an integrative narrative beginning with the universe is expected, as the universe is both integral and integrated.

Is the universe a story? No, it is not. The universe is dynamic in time and space, mostly unknown. The fact that it is a time-developmental process lends itself to be framed as a narrative. Still, it is the human mind that creates a narrative structure, as one manner to deal with time: past, present, future. One could speculate if time, space, matter, and energy exist, if parallel realities occur, a uni- or multiverse, if the universe will deflate and collapse, and other

---

37. For this and the next two paragraphs, I am drawing on Eaton, "The Human Quest to Live in a Cosmos," 238.

38. See Tucker and Grim, *Living Cosmology*; Mickey et al., *Living Earth Community*.

39. Tucker and Grim, *Living Cosmology*, 219.

40. Tucker and Grim, *Living Cosmology*, 221.

41. This is not uniformity, or intelligent design where the configuration was predestined, or insinuating that Homo sapiens is the culmination. We too are enroute in these processes.

imponderables. Here, the emphasis on a universe story is not speculative. There is a keen need within humans to know our origins, purpose, and destiny. These diverse narratives are revised periodically, but are never settled. Cosmogenesis indicates that we are emergent from and integral with the universe.

Furthermore, it is good to keep in mind the vastness of the universe. Perhaps somewhere within the two trillion galaxies, and counting, life or some forms of vibrant matter have materialized. Thus, whatever story about the universe we concoct, it should be commensurate with what is known. Of course we will imagine stories where we are central or significant actors. However, in the grand schemes of things about the universe, we are not the key influence. As earthlings we have significant impact, too much for the biosphere to function well, but COVID-19 has also taught us of the potency of viruses.

Debates on a Universe Story(ies)

There are several debates that swirl around talk of a universe story. Three may be mentioned. The first is whether cultural specificities and contextual stories could be overridden by any form of charter, story, or metanarrative. Will a universe story become yet another imperialist, colonizing and dominant story? Governing ideologies can, and do, control the stories that orient human life. For example, symbols and stories of economic affluence, success, beauty, and consumerism are despotic, tyrannical narratives that have seeped into most cultures. It is disconcerting that these stories—hegemonic, oppressive, uniform, and overall causal to ecological destruction—garner fewer critiques that the concerns of incorporating the universe and Earth processes into cultural narratives. Nonetheless, the tensions among the multiplicity of narratives are indisputable. Also, there is no answer as to if or how religious creation narratives will navigate new science-infused stories. It will involve how cultures relate to the epistemologies of religion and science, their religious histories, claims and priorities, current events, and internal diversities. All religions comprise pluralities. To suggest that this universe story will erode other religious/spiritual creation stories is speculation.

A second debate is whether these cosmological and Earth sciences are factual, or are perspectival, biased, not universal, and open to multiple, even destructive interpretations. Mary Ellen Rubenstein suggests that the projects of Big History, the Epic of Evolution, and the Universe Story are implausible. She writes that "this fantasy is misguided, dangerous, and self-sabotaging. Misguided because the stories modern science tells are not universal; rather, they reflect the particular questions, assumptions, and experiments that produce them."[42]

---

42. See Rubenstein, "Cosmology and the Environment."

It is appropriate that a hermeneutics of suspicion is needed to discern imperialism, bias, and rigidity. However, there are serious flaws in Rubenstein's critiques. Clearly scientific knowledge is particular, symbolized, and the meanings are interpretations. That is the nature of all knowledge. Rubenstein's main concerns and worries are about diversity. This is the overriding interpretative framework, hermeneutic and critical lens, and, in my view, reflects a needless inflexibility. Herein lies a postmodern imbroglio about metanarratives and multiplicities. A priority on diversity obscures the import of how such comprehensive frameworks function, as well as not understanding the dynamics of symbolic consciousness from which metanarratives come. Further, the assumption that all meta- or integrative narratives are oppressive in principle is erroneous. It demonstrates a lack of awareness of the purpose of such narratives, as well as the importance of this scientific knowledge.

A third debate addresses Thomas Berry and the "Journey of the Universe"[43] project in particular. Critics chide that this is a global omniscient and omnipotent story based entirely in science, sufficiently potent to overrule other cultural narratives. They suggest that the proponents of the "new cosmology" affirm that the physical and biological sciences have revealed the unmistakable storied nature of the cosmos, from science. For example, Lisa Sideris misrepresents these projects by claiming that they are posturing a scientific account of the universe, a global myth and "transcultural truth of our having crawled from the same primal ooze, or burst from the same cosmic blast."[44] She claims that the notion of a Universe Story has an anthropocentric flavor, is linear, one-dimensional, and supports intelligent design theories. All of this is an incorrect characterization of this Universe Story. For Berry, a Universe Story is a *mega*narrative which represents the best of science, infused with meaning. It is *functional* in that it could provide common ground, and perhaps a shared appeal for ecological sustainability. This was never proposed as "one story to rule them all."

Sideris also suggests that these efforts are spiritually impoverished and are:

> [D]emonstrably lacking in what John Keats called negative capability: an ability to dwell in doubt, mystery, and ambiguity and to resist the categorization of all phenomena and experience into systematic knowledge. Proffered as narratives that inspire wonder and concern for nature, they actually chafe against uncertainty or open-ended awe.[45]

---

43. See the "Journey of the Universe" project which includes a film, book, conversations with scientists and religious scholars, university course, and a comprehensive website.

44. See Sideris, "Cosmology and the Environment"; *Consecrating Science*.

45. See Sideris, "Cosmology and the Environment."

It is difficult to consider that the work of Thomas Berry could be seen as anything other than deeply spiritual. His functional cosmology project—this new or Universe Story—is a manner of telling of cosmological and Earth's sciences findings such that anyone can see or sense the importance, and indeed magnificence and grandeur, of the realms we inhabit. His goals were to inspire, to awaken the human spirit, evoke reverence, and rouse sufficient psychic energy and ingenuity to orient human activity within the limits, rhythms, and flourishing of an Earth community. For Berry, mystery permeates the universe. It is a spiritual imperative to re-awaken a sense of the numinous, the ineffable, and the panentheistic mysteries of God. The appropriate responses of wonder, awe, reverence, and respect represent profound spiritual insights which can influence cultural narratives, actions, ethics, and ecological practices. These are the goals of Berry and the "Journey of the Universe" projects.

The Universe Story: A Meganarrative

There is new knowledge about the universe and the Earth, that tells of human origins and habitat. It is significant, and enthralling. Time, space, processes, and dynamics are relevant to the place and role of humans in the scheme of things. Story is a form, a frame, a manner of comprehension that surfaces from symbolic consciousness and the need for coherence, intelligibility, comprehension, and orientation. And, in this case, a Universe Story is a creation, origin, and mega/meta narrative: scientifically informed and instilled with meaning.

I suggest a Universe Story is a meganarrative that could function as a reference for other narratives. To reject this due to aversions to metanarratives, disagreements among scientists, or that some hold other viewpoints, is injudicious. For example, do we refute scientific knowledge about the structure of biological cells, DNA, plant/insect linkages, water contamination, evolution, and more, in the name of diversity? Or because some people are unfamiliar with these sciences?

It is crucial to discern the border zones between facts, values, intuitions, meaning, beliefs, and opinions. People may express alternative views, but there must be some assessment of veracity and presuppositions. Diverse viewpoints—merely for the sake of diversity—are not laudable goals. Some may hold ideological reasons to refute scientific findings, such as variances of biblical inerrancy, creationism, conspiracy theories, alien invasions, and more. How much time, weight and public space should be given to such views? This is an important question to answer in this era of post-truth, fake news and alternative facts.

The Christian and Universe Stories: Connections and Conflicts

What is the starting point for a reflection on Christianity and the Universe Story? What are the driving questions? What are the goals? The questions constrain the responses, and the responses differ according to what is presupposed in the questions. In answer to the first question, from my perspective, what is known now suggests that the universe is the most adequate starting point for an origin or creation story. It is not a morality tale, and does not provide knowledge about everything.[46] As Nicholas Lash states:

> The discernible oneness of the world, the interconnectedness of everything, not only makes the telling of some story of the world, some story of the whole world, a possibility; it makes it a necessity.[47]

He reminds us: "No story says everything, not even a story of everything."[48]

The quest to stretch one's mind to the farthest reaches of times and space, and render the discoveries as a Universe *Story*, represents a primordial human activity to expand awareness as far outward as possible in order to grasp the grand scheme of things and our place within. It provides parameters of time, space, process and evolution. It is mythic in its dimensions. It does not provide answers to many questions about life, love, death, social ethics, justice, sin, and more. It does shed light on, for example, the ingenuity of the biosphere, and the urgent need to protect Earth's lifeways.

Christian approaches to origin stories have often been preoccupied by *creatio ex nihilo*, and doctrines of creation, which are not threatened by the Universe Story as these can coexist peacefully. There are minority views about intelligent design or young Earth theories, which are incompatible with the Universe Story as described herein. But in fact, Christianity does not have an elaborate creation or origin story, apart from the claims of God's pre-existence, and perhaps God's omnipotence and omniscience. Genesis is an origin/creation story, with many interpretations that are contested and debated. For most this is not seen as historically or scientifically true, but it carries other truths.

It must be noted that to consider *Christianity* is a misnomer. There are variations of all kinds, as Christianity is lived in individuals and communities, and is manifested in countless historical and contemporary forms. Priorities

---

46. See Conradie, "An Ecological Moral to the Story of the Universe?"

47. Lash, *Holiness*, 28–29.

48. Lash, *Holiness*, 31.

differ greatly across and within subtraditions. Crucial topics diverge: biblical inerrancy, doctrinal conformity, institutional structures, rituals, beliefs, ethics, and theological certainties. Dissimilarities and pluralities in Christian traditions and adherents preclude any claim about *the* Christian story.

The current knowledge about the age and dynamics of the universe and of Earth is forcing a new reflection on the manner in which we can talk of God as involved with these processes. Is God creating, directing, enticing, enabling, or abiding within these processes? Views differ. What is the evidence? Theologically, there are metaphysical, ontological, doctrinal, ethical, and practical aspects.

How Does God Relate to the Story of Life on Earth?

As expected, there are countless differences on what it means to evoke God language. The internal dynamics of symbolic consciousness around this powerful symbol are inaccessible, and intense, thus I tread with caution. Those with apophatic leanings associate God with the ineffable, the numinous, the Mystery and the Unknown. Certainties are elusive. Furthermore, whatever is claimed about God is not verifiable. Those with cataphatic leanings saturate the image of God with infinite associations. The discussions of worldviews and symbols are central. Symbols perform: they shape what we see, feel, understand, commit to, and obscure what is of less value. God language is a both powerful and opaque symbol. In addition, God language resides in individual, communities and worldviews, and can never be extricated and analyzed in isolation.

If one assumes that God is elsewhere and absent or everywhere and active, or somewhere in between, then how God relates to the story of life on Earth is distinct. If the driving question is sin and redemption, then God is imaged, understood and symbolized differently than if the main question is how God is present in or to the natural world. All the pivotal theological inquiries depend on the driving questions and the worldview assumptions. For example, what does salvation mean? Is salvation an activity across time and space, such that salvation is equated more with flourishing and limiting sin? Or are we saved from the confines of the natural world, and the limits of earthly life? Are we saved from our anthropological orientations? Is salvation ongoing, a process, an event in the past, present or future, an end-time occurrence? Are we saved to, or from, some reality? What I know is that all creation, origin or religious stories have a salvific theme. The specifics, symbols, and narratives differ, but there is an impulse to want to feel complete, whole, restored, and (re)connected to the integrity of the grand scheme of things. The Universe Story provides this function, for some. It may include experiences of the surplus of meaning and being, described earlier.

The question posed in the volume, namely "Is the Christian story part of the Earth's story or is the Earth's story part of God's story, from creation to consummation?" cannot be answered with an either/or. Both are coexisting concurrently. For some Christian adherents, it is always God's universe, and cosmological and evolutionary knowledge affirms this further. However, there is no doubt that the universe and Earth, as understood through sciences, could challenge parochial visions and viewpoints. It also seems evident to me that religious stories exist in flux, relevant for varying durations in contextual and historical periods, and are transformed and reinterpreted regularly. If the Universe Story has empirical traction, it will be revised and updated, but not likely deposed. Perhaps this means that religious/Christian stories and the Universe Story are different epistemic endeavors. Or it means that the epistemic frameworks for theology need a renovation. Human cultures and stories are part of the Earth's story. The problem is when Christian stories supplant or ignore cosmology, evolution, symbolic consciousness and the plurality of religions. These should inform theological foundations.

What does consummation mean in this discussion? Is this about the reign of God taking hold on Earth? Or related to versions of the Christian doctrines of the end times? Alpha to Omega? Or is this the death of the sun in the Milky Way, and the end of the biosphere? Perhaps these symbolic renderings of the world are incompatible at this interpretive juncture.

Religious Experiences and Spiritualities

One last area related to the nexus of the universe/Earth/human awareness/God is that of religious experience. What experiences are related to the genesis and sustenance of God language within these themes? Is the Universe Story a graceful abstraction from ecological deterioration, extensive suffering, political corruption, post-truth sprawls and felt powerlessness? Perhaps for some. For others it is a restoration of awareness of the presence of God throughout time, space, the biosphere, embedded and active, omnipresent yet clandestine. In addition, it must be considered that as humans evolved, we developed a capacity for religious experiences and spiritual sensitivities because of the symbolic dynamics between the interior and exterior realms. Thus whatever we call spirituality is, in fact, Earth-derived and Earth dependent. As the outer world diminishes, so does the inner world, as these are inextricably entwined in origin, dynamics, and destiny. This is a serious, and often neglected, part of religious/theological reflections in the "Anthropocene."

Revelations and Hope

There are two Christian themes that intersect broadly and elegantly with the Universe Story as understood herein. One is that of revelation. For some, the knowledge about the universe and Earth are revelatory. Greater depth and breadth of the parameters of reality are revealed, as well as how integral humans are to the scheme of things. The aforementioned continuity shows that human intelligence, and thirst for intelligibility and coherence is bonded to an intelligibility and coherence within the universe. We belong to a vast reality out of which we developed and to which we are inextricably immersed: an intimate immensity. This is revelatory. Everything is more. For some this is a revelation that expands and deepens images of creation, of God's infinite ingenuity and gracious presence, of the desire embedded within the Earth, at least, to create and support life. The Spirit is breathing new life. That is one interpretation.

How does this mesh with the spectrum of notions of revelation(s) within Christian traditions? Again, it depends on what is included in the meaning of *Christian* revelation(s)? Answers differ depending on views of high or low Christologies, closed canons or ongoing revelation(s), biblical insights, Christian revelations as one of many or as definitive and supreme, and on what is deemed to be the content of revelations. This is an important and significant theme in this discussion, noting that across Christian traditions there is much disagreement on the meaning and scope of revelation. Furthermore, there are several ways in which themes of revelation intersect with the universe and Christian stories.[49]

A second theme is that of hope. This series considers the need for common ground, and Christian inspired narratives that offer some vision of a viable and realistic future. Shared understandings and values are critical. The tensions among diversities, subjectivities, and metanarratives are palpable, and active in many parts of the world as narratives, and peoples, collide. A question to ponder is what narratives could be more attractive, alluring and powerful than tribal, nationalist, popularist, economic, or other political narratives? These dominate public discussion as ecological considerations diminish—not in importance—but on the psychic/symbolic landscape.

Hope is a radical force. Hope is not a wish that things could be different, but that change is a genuine possibility. Hope is seeing possibilities that seem impossible, impractical, unrealistic, or overly ambitious. Hope is committing oneself to a vision, and trying to live out of that vision with as much integrity and authenticity as possible. Hope is personal and collective, giving vitality, sustenance and endurance. Hope drives resistance as much as it entices change. Hope is a central theme within Christianity as well as in the Universe Story: both told in countless ways. Here the universe and Christianity unite.

---

49. See Conradie, "On the Hope" in this volume.

■ Conclusion

There is plenty more to discuss and debate. My main preoccupations are about how to respond to the escalating ecological crises. My conviction is that we live in a *divine milieu*. The spiritual distress is acute. Climate change is an ecological and injustice multiplier. There is no one way to respond. Christians preoccupied with issues of sin, redemption, ethics, or an after-life may find a Universe Story, even if true, irrelevant. Others find it deeply inspiring and life orienting, and that it blends, perhaps not always gracefully, with Christian views and commitments. The Universe Story brings new truths that shape a vision that is meaningful and authentic. It is commensurate with other knowledge systems such as cosmological and Earth sciences, religious pluralities, new materialisms, and symbolic consciousness. In this manner, any version of Christian creation stories must reside within a universe story.

■ Bibliography

Bachelard, Gaston. *The Poetics of Space*. Translated by Maria Jolas. Boston: Beacon Press, 1964.

Bennett, Jane. *Vibrant Matter: A Political Ecology of Things*. Durham: Duke University Press, 2010.

Berry, Thomas. *The Dream of the Earth*. San Francisco: Sierra Club Books, 1988.

Christian, David. "Cosmology and the Environment." *The Immanent Frame*, September 14, 2015. http://tif.ssrc.org/2015/09/14/cosmology-and-the-environment/?source=relatedposts, accessed 1 March 2021.

Conradie, Ernst M. *An Ecological Moral to the Story of the Universe?* 2003. http://www.angelfire.com/ct3/uctrs/conradieanecologicalmoral.html, accessed 20 February 2021.

Cummings Neville, Robert. "Worldviews." *American Journal of Theology and Philosophy* 30:3 (2009), 233–43.

Deacon, Terrence. *Incomplete Nature: How Mind Emerged from Matter*. New York: W.W. Norton, 2012.

———. "The Symbol Concept." In *The Oxford Handbook of Language Evolution*, edited by Kathleen Gibson and Maggie Tallerman, 393–405. Oxford: Oxford University Press, 2012.

———. *The Symbolic Species: The Co-evolution of Language and the Brain*. New York: W. W. Norton, 1998.

Deane-Drummond, Celia and Agustín Fuentes, eds. *Theology and Evolutionary Anthropology: Dialogues in Wisdom, Humility, and Grace*. London: Routledge, 2020.

Dixon, John. *Images of Truth: Religion and the Art of Seeing*. Atlanta: Scholars Press, 1996.

Durkheim, Émile. *Le Suicide: Étude de Sociologie*. Paris: Presses universitaires de France, 1897.

Eaton, Heather. "A Spirituality of the Earth." In *The Natures of Things: Rediscovering the Spiritual in God's Creation*, edited by Norman Habel and Graham Buxton, 229–40. Eugene: Wipf and Stock, 2016.

———. "An Ecological Imaginary: Evolution and Religion in an Ecological Era." In *Ecological Awareness: Exploring Religion, Ethics and Aesthetics*, edited by Sigurd Bergmann and Heather Eaton, 7–23. Berlin: LIT, 2011.

———. "Ecofeminist Ethics: Utopic Conversations." *Ecotheology* 8 (2000), 40–57.

———. "Ecological Christianities." In *Inter-Christian Philosophies Dialogues* 4, edited by Graham Oppy and Nick Trakakis, 25–47. New York: Routledge, 2018.

———. "Global Visions and Common Ground: Biodemocracy, Postmodern Pressures and The Earth Charter." *Zygon: Journal of Religion and Science* 49:4 (2014), 917–37. https://doi.org/10.1111/zygo.12134

———. "The Challenges of Worldview Transformation: To Rethink and Refeel Our Origins and Destiny." In *Religion and Ecological Crisis: The Lynn White Thesis at Fifty,* edited by Todd LeVasseur and Anna Peterson, 121–37. New York: Routledge, 2017.

———. "The Human Quest to Live in a Cosmos." In *Encountering Earth: Thinking Theologically with a More-Than-Human World*, edited by Trevor Bechtel, et al., 227–47. Eugene: Wipf and Stock, 2018.

———. "The Revolution of Evolution," *Worldviews: Environment, Culture, Religion* 11:1 (2007), 6–31. https://doi.org/10.1163/156853507X173478Eaton, Heather, ed. *The Intellectual Journey of Thomas Berry: Imagining the Earth Community*. Lanham: Lexington, 2014.

Gare, Arran. "Grand Narrative of the Age of Re-Embodiments: Beyond Modernism and Postmodernism, Cosmos and History." *The Journal of Natural and Social Philosophy* 9:1 (2013), 327–57.

Gottschall, Jonathan. *The Storytelling Animals: How Stories Make Us Human*. New York: Houghton, Mifflin Harcourt, 2012.

International Geosphere-Biosphere Program. "The Great Acceleration" http://www.igbp.net/globalchange/greatacceleration.4.1b8ae20512db692f2a680001630.html.

Klein, Richard and Blake Edgar. *The Dawn of Human Culture: A Bold New Theory of What Sparked the "Big Bang" of Human Consciousness*. New York: John Wiley and Sons, 2002.

Lash, Nicholas. *Holiness, Speech, and Silence: Reflections on the Question of God*. Aldershot: Ashgate, 2004.

Lewis-Williams, David. *A Cosmos in Stone: Interpreting Religion and Society through Rock Art*. Walnut Creek: Altamira Press, 2002.

———. *The Mind in the Cave: Consciousness and The Origins of Art*. London: Thames & Hudson, 2002.

Mickey, Sam, Mary Evelyn Tucker and John Grim, eds. *Living Earth Community: Multiple Ways of Being and Knowing*. Cambridge: Open Book, 2020.

Radford Ruether, Rosemary. "Ecofeminism: Symbolic Connections Between the Oppression of Women and the Domination of Nature." In *Ecofeminism and the Sacred*, edited by Carol J. Adams, 13–23. New York: Continuum, 1993.

Ricoeur, Paul. "Ideology and Utopia." In *From Text to Action: Essays in Hermeneutics II*, 208–35. Translated by Kathleen Blamey and John B. Thompson. Evanston: Northwestern University Press, 1991.

———. *Lectures on Ideology and Utopia.* New York: Columbia University Press, 1986.

Rubenstein, Mary-Jane. "Cosmology and the Environment." *The Immanent Frame,* September 14, 2015. http://tif.ssrc.org/2015/09/14/cosmology-and-the-environment/?source=relatedposts, accessed 1 March 2021.

Sideris, Lisa. *Consecrating Science: Wonder, Knowledge and the Natural World*. Oakland: University of California Press, 2017.

———. "Cosmology and the Environment." *The Immanent Frame,* September 14, 2015. http://tif.ssrc.org/2015/09/14/cosmology-and-the-environment/?source=relatedposts, accessed 1 March 2021.

The Worldviews Group. http://www.vub.ac.be/CLEA/dissemination/groups-archive/vzw_worldviews/, accessed 28 February 2021.

Tucker, Mary Evelyn and John Grim. *Living Cosmology: Christian Responses to the Journey of the Universe.* Maryknoll: Orbis, 2016.

Van Huyssteen, Wentzel. *Alone in the World? Science and Theology on Human Uniqueness*. Grand Rapids: Eerdmans, 2004.

Wilford, John Noble . "When Humans Became Human," Published: *The New York Times*, February 26, 2002. https://www.nytimes.com/2002/02/26/science/when-humans-became-human.html

Taking a Deep Breath for the Story to Begin in the Public Sphere: A Chinese Christian Perspective

Pan-Chiu Lai[1]

Introduction

Taking a deep breath is necessary before articulating the Christian story of creation and salvation (including consummation) as related to the earth. It is widely acknowledged that narratives, especially totalizing grand narratives, may be used to support a particular political ideology and the related regime. However, according to Mikhail Bakhtin (1895–1975), a narrative can also be "dialogical" or "polyphonic," meaning that it can not only explicitly include episodes of dialogue or even a dialogical structure but also implicitly embody a sort of "heteroglossia," which is constituted by divergent voices representing

---

1. Pan-Chiu Lai is Professor, Department of Cultural and Religious Studies, The Chinese University of Hong Kong. He is registered as a co-researcher at the University of the Western Cape, South Africa, for the project on "An Earthed Faith: Telling the Story amid the 'Anthropocene'."

> **How to cite:** Lai, P.-C., 2021, 'Taking a Deep Breath for the Story to Begin in the Public Sphere: A Chinese Christian Perspective', in E.M. Conradie & P.-C. Lai (eds.), *Taking a deep breath for the story to begin . . .* (An Earthed Faith: Telling the Story amid the "Anthropocene" Volume 1), pp. 163–182, AOSIS, Cape Town. https://doi.org/10.4102/aosis.2021.BK264.08

conflicting ideologies or value systems.² In other words, apart from conveying and advocating a monolithic ideology, a narrative may engage in dialogue or negotiation with other narratives or discourses. As narrative is a foremost way of articulating Christian theology,³ Christian theologians have to articulate the Christian narrative(s) of the earth in the public sphere with contesting voices.⁴ This task may be quite different from articulating the Christian narrative solely for fellow Christians within the church's four walls. By taking a deep breath, Christian theologians may critically reflect once again on the prevalent Christian narrative(s) and consider how to re-articulate the Christian narrative in relation to other narratives in the same society.

This essay aims to explore the issues concerning how the Christian story may be told in response to other narratives through a case study from the Chinese-speaking world. It starts with a brief survey of ecological discourses in the Chinese-speaking "public" sphere, which is dominated mainly by three major types of narrative: the government's political propaganda, the views derived from traditional Chinese culture, and the discourses articulated by environmental scientists and/or activists.⁵ This essay will then provide a tentative suggestion concerning how Chinese Christian theology may articulate its narrative(s) in this context.

■ Ecological Discourses in Chinese Context

Before surveying Chinese Christian ecological discourses, it is important to note some of the characteristics of the Chinese context:

First, unlike many western societies, the People's Republic of China is not a liberal state where people can freely exchange their views on public issues. In mainland China, all the "public" discourses, including ecological and/or theological, will be monitored and even manipulated by the state apparatus. Books about religion or theology can be published only after political censorship, which may also apply to the objection or criticism of the state's decision on projects with tremendous impacts on the natural and cultural environments, for example, the controversial decision of building the hydroelectric Three Gorges Dam in the Yangtze River (1993–2009). In contrast, Chinese Christian theologians in Hong Kong and Taiwan enjoy greater academic freedom and can freely articulate their views. As we will see, Hong

---

2. See Holquist, *Dialogism*; Lee, *Dialogue on Monarchy*.

3. Mühling, *Post-Systematic Theology*.

4. See Deane-Drummond and Bedford-Strohm, *Religion and Ecology*.

5. See Lai, "Ecological Theology." The next two sections draw (at times verbatim) from this earlier article of the author. This previous article provides a survey of different types of ecological (secular and religious) discourse in China, which forms the foundation of the present essay.

Kong, which is a theological hub of the Chinese-speaking world, plays a very important role in the development of Chinese Christian ecological discourse.

Second, the Chinese economic system is characterized as "socialism with Chinese characteristics," which includes, to a certain extent, a free market economy with many companies owned or controlled by the government. The polarity between the poor and the rich is much more severe in China than in most of the "developed" countries. The drives for rapid economic growth at the individual, company, and governmental levels are more comparable to developing countries than to developed countries.

Third, whereas the Abrahamic monotheistic faith constitutes an important component of western culture, the most influential religious/philosophical traditions in the Chinese cultural tradition include Buddhism, Confucianism, Daoism, and Chinese popular religion. The divergence between these three Chinese traditions on environmental issues may well be more radical than that among Judaism, Christianity, and Islam.

Fourth, although the number of Christians in China increased dramatically in Mainland China for some years, Christianity in China as a whole remains as a minority group, and Christian voices are marginalized or even entirely neglected in the public sphere.

Given these characteristics of the Chinese context, it is quite understandable that the influence of the Marxist state ideology on Chinese ecological discourse is so obvious. For example, Fu Hua's book on ecological ethics, after critically surveying western discourses on ecological ethics and Chinese responses, explores the methodology for the comparative study of ecological ethics. It upholds the principle of materialistic historicism and anthropocentrism, instead of naturalism often associated with environmentalism, and further argues for integrating naturalism with historicism.[6] The book proposes four basic principles for the articulation of ecological ethics with Chinese characteristics: (1) to uphold Marxism as the guiding thought; (2) to insist on taking the Chinese people as the basis of value; (3) to inherit all of the best ecological ethics critically, no matter whether they are Chinese or western, ancient or modern; and (4) to be grounded in the great practice of the construction of modernized socialist China.[7] Considering the overall position of the book, it is quite understandable that it does not offer any serious discussion on Christian theology or traditional Chinese culture in terms of actual content. Admittedly, in many other books about ecological ethics, without any explicit reference to the Marxist ideology, the whole discussion is also oriented to the questions of survival as well as development, and focused

---

6. Fu, *Shengtai lunlixue*, 309–46.

7. Fu, *Shengtai lunlixue*, 346–54.

rather exclusively on the policy, economic, and technological issues, while the religious perspectives are entirely omitted.[8] In line with the state ideology, this approach emphasizes economic development and disregards the relevance of religion to ecological issues.

Unlike this rather "secular" approach, many Chinese publications concerning ecological ethics cover religious perspectives, but most of them tend to stereotype Christianity as an anthropocentric religion detrimental to the environment. They accept Lynn White Jr.'s thesis that the Judeo-Christian narrative of creation was part of the historical roots of the ecological crisis in the Western world. Some of these publications recognize the approach of stewardship advocated by many Christians and the relatively more environmental friendly ecotheologies articulated by some contemporary western theologians.[9] However, in most of the mentioning of ecotheology in these Chinese publications, the focus is on Western Christian theology and its significance in western societies, rather than its relevance to the Chinese context.

It is important to note that many Chinese intellectuals endeavor to retrieve, if not reconstruct, the ecological insights of the Chinese religious, spiritual, and/or philosophical traditions, especially Confucianism, Daoism, and Buddhism. In fact, the Chinese publications concerning the ecological ethics or environmental philosophy of Buddhism, Confucianism, and/or Daoism mushroomed in the last two decades or so. In addition to some general studies of the Chinese ecological ethics or views of nature,[10] there are also focused studies particular to Buddhism,[11] Confucianism,[12] and Daoism.[13] As these studies show, there are significant divergences among the Buddhist, Confucian, and Daoist positions on ecological ethics. Whereas the ecological position of Daoist philosophy appears to be naturalistic and holistic, the humanistic vision of Confucianism seems to support an anthropocentric approach to ecological ethics. In addition to its compassionate and equalitarian attitude toward all sentient beings, the Chinese Buddhist advocacy and practice of vegetarianism may give the impression of supporting animal rights. In actual practice, Ciji (Tzu Chi), a relief organization with a Buddhist background based in Taiwan, is

---

8. See, for example, Wang, *Shencun yu fazhan*.

9. See, for example, Cao, *Renxing yu ziran*, 67–78.

10. See, for example, Meng, *Ren yu ziran*; She, *Zhongguo shengtai lunli*.

11. See, for example, Liu, *Gongsheng gongrong*; Chen, *Fojiao shengtai zhexue*.

12. See, for example, Qiao, *Rujia shengtai sixiang*.

13. See, for example, Yue, *Daojiao shengtaixue*.

particularly famous for its projects and daily life practices for environmental protection.¹⁴

Many Chinese publications are conducting comparative studies of Chinese and Western environmental ethics, and some of them include a particular chapter for Christian ecotheology. For example, Wang Zhengping's book on environmental philosophy covers both Chinese and Western philosophical traditions and includes a chapter on Christian ecotheology and another chapter on ecological Marxism.¹⁵ Although the book is relatively open to a religious perspective and quite affirmative in its survey of ecotheology, especially recent developments in Western Christian theology, Wang's affirmation or appreciation is restricted to the value of ecotheology for guiding and encouraging the environmental practice of Christians.¹⁶ Without any further elaboration on the relevance of ecotheology in the Chinese context, it is reasonable to assume that Wang may have reservations on its relevance to the Chinese context, which is supposed to be very different from the western context. In fact, Wang's own position emphasizes the issue of social justice, especially the right of development of the developing countries, including China. Wang argues that although developing countries also have a moral responsibility for environmental protection, the moral demands for them can be different from those of developed countries. The developing countries should consider their concrete situations, including their culture, economic situation, stage of technological development, etc., and their resultant approaches to environmental protection can and should thus be different from those of developed countries.¹⁷

The above survey indicates that in Chinese discourses concerning ecological issues, the Christian story has been involved with or without the active participation of Christian theologians. The question for Chinese Christian theologians is not whether but how to articulate the Christian narrative about the earth in response to these contesting narratives.

■ Chinese Christian Ecological Discourses

Given the complexity of the Chinese context, Chinese Christian ecological discourses adopt various approaches in order to address various concerns:

- *An exploratory approach*: As environmental protection is primarily a modern challenge rather than a traditional theological issue, some sorts of

---

14. See Zhengyan, *Yu diqiu gong shengxi*.

15. Wang, *Huanjing zhexue*, 313–42, 343–68.

16. Wang, *Huanjing zhexue*, 342.

17. Wang, *Huanjing zhexue*, 410–15.

explorations, including creative appropriations and reinterpretations of the Christian tradition, especially the Bible, are thus required.

- *An apologetic approach*: Given the popular criticism against the so-called ecological bankruptcy of Christianity or Christianity as part of the historical roots of the ecological crisis in western societies, Chinese Christian ecological discourses should respond in various ways, including "apologetic" responses to some of the misunderstandings or unfair criticisms.
- *A reflexive approach*: Admittedly, the historical records of Christianity are not perfect, and many of the environmental criticisms against Christianity are valid. It is thus necessary for Chinese Christianity to reflect critically on the received traditions. This may involve a confessional attitude, meaning not only taking seriously the doctrinal or confessional tradition but also confessing humbly the limitations or even mistakes of the ecological heritage of Christianity.
- *A correlational approach*: Considering the dominance of the "secular" approach to ecological issues and the skepticism on the relevance of religions, especially their positive contributions to address ecological challenges, it is necessary to demonstrate why or how Christianity can be related to such challenges in a positive way. This way of arguing for the relevance of religion to ecology is reminiscent of Paul Tillich's method of correlation, which assumes either that religion is a necessary dimension of culture or that theology can provide religious answer(s) to the corresponding existential question(s).[18]
- *A practical approach*: From a practical point of view, it is necessary to spell out the ethical implications of Christian narrative(s) and to show whether or how the Christian faith can effectively invoke, generate, support, or induce concrete environmental actions or projects. As a matter of fact, some Chinese Christians are involved in environmental praxis. It is thus necessary and possible to articulate Christian ecological discourses from a practical perspective.
- *A dialogical/integrative approach*: Assuming that the Chinese cultural, philosophical, and/or religious tradition(s) may have some wisdom on ecological issues, it may be necessary and even beneficial for Christian ecotheology to engage in dialogue with Chinese Buddhism, Confucianism, and Daoism on ecological issues. It may be even better if the Chinese Christian discourses can integrate certain elements or insights from traditional Chinese culture. This may enhance the acceptability or plausibility of such Chinese Christian discourses among the Chinese people.
- *A political approach*: It is recognized that discourses on nature can be political,[19] and this is particularly obvious in China. Different from the

---

18. Lai, *Towards a Trinitarian Theology*, 66–83.

19. Scott, *Political Theology*.

western understanding of the public sphere, which is supposed to be independent of the state's domination, the so-called public sphere in China is not free from the surveillance, intervention, and even manipulation of the state. In this context, Chinese Christian ecological discourses have to deal with Marxism as the dominating political ideology as well as its propaganda concerning sustainable development in a critical way.

- *A scientific approach*: Stories about the universe are told not only by religions but also by sciences.[20] How the Christian story is to be related to modern science is an important issue for ecotheology. This is even more vital given the prevalent scientism and materialism supported by the Marxist state ideology in China.

As we will see, Chinese Christian ecological discourses exhibit most of the approaches mentioned above. An illustrative example can be found in the special issue of "Ecology and Christian Faith" published in the *CGST Journal of Theology* 26 (January 1999). This special issue consists of six essays by six authors with different academic and/or professional backgrounds, offering different approaches to ecological issues.

The first article by Carver T. Yu attempts to argue against the criticisms made by Arnold Toynbee and Lynn White Jr. that the roots of ecological crisis in the Western world can be traced back to Christian beliefs or the Bible. It counters that the source of anthropocentrism, which is behind the ecological destructive behavior in the Western world, should be traced back to the western philosophical tradition, which is associated with the culture of narcissism and a laissez-faire market economy, rather than the Bible.[21]

The second article by Stephen Lee is primarily a detailed exegesis of Genesis 1 and Psalm 8. Starting the article with reference to Lynn White Jr., it offers a critical response to White's criticism of the Judeo-Christian tradition through demonstrating that the emphasis of the two biblical texts is on God's battle against evil rather than an anthropocentric ideology.[22] Similar to the first article, the second article adopts an apologetic approach, which attempts to defend Christianity against such criticism from an ecological perspective.

The third article by Samuel Sung-Him Ho exemplifies a more reflexive and, to a certain extent, integrative approach. It reflects critically on Christian theology, advocates an aesthetic approach to nature, and draws support from both the Christian tradition and Chinese culture.[23] Although the article itself does not explicitly call for dialogue or integration with the Chinese

---

20. Matthews et al., *When Worlds Converge*.

21. Yu, "Roots of Our Ecological Crisis."

22. Lee, "*Imago Dei*."

23. Ho, "Towards an Ecological Theology."

culture on ecological issues, it does show the compatibility between the Christian and Chinese views of nature and thus the possibility of articulating Chinese Christian ecotheology through integrating Christian theology with Chinese culture.

The fourth article by Kin-Yip Louie surveys the empirical studies concerning the relationship between economic growth and environmental protection, without any theological analysis or comment.[24]

The fifth article by Wilson Lee explicates the ethical issues involved in the controversies concerning animal rights and offers a theological critique of unrestrained anthropocentrism by highlighting the common ground shared by the divergent positions advocated by Alfons Auer and Klaus M. Meyer-Abich in the affirmation of the intrinsic value of nature and by making reference to the cosmological theocentric position advocated by Jürgen Moltmann.[25]

The final article by Nancy C. M. Chen offers reflections by an environmental activist in Taiwan. It argues that although western ecotheologies might provide certain inspirations, their assistance is rather limited. It remains crucial for Chinese ecotheology to be rooted in our own cultural context. Furthermore, our ecological discourses must be informed by contemporary environmental sciences.[26]

There are also some Christians in Hong Kong attempting to integrate Chinese culture and knowledge of environmental science in their theological discourses. For example, He Jianzong (Ho Kin-chung), a well-known environmental scientist and activist in Hong Kong, in addition to his numerous scientific publications in environmental science, also published many books and articles addressing environmental issues, with some practical advice, from a Christian perspective.[27] In his book on ecotheology, which is focused on the Old Testament, he suggests that indigenous Chinese ecotheology should pay attention to the Chinese philosophical view of unity of heaven and humanity.[28] He also further attempts to compare the Christian and Confucian views on sustainable development.[29] Another example is Wang Fuyi (Wong Fook Yee), who worked as a civil servant serving the Hong Kong government's Agriculture, Fisheries and Conservation Department for about three decades, responsible particularly for the planning and management of country parks. In an article on the theological reflection of global warming,

---

24. Louie, "Economic Growth."

25. Lee, "Animal Rights."

26. Chen, "Ecology and the Church," especially 113–14.

27. For example, He and Huang, *Lüse shitu*.

28. He, *Shengtai shenxue*, 8, 15–16.

29. See He, "Duibi Rujia he Jidujiao."

he tends to adopt a stewardship approach, which is quite popular in western ecotheology.[30] However, in a more recent article, he turns to the Chinese culture and attempts to address the relationship between ecotheology and Chinese culture.[31] The examples of He and Wang indicate that the same scholar can employ different approaches in different discourses.

Reflecting on my own work, a variety of approaches are found. As a trained systematic theologian, it is natural for me to adopt an "exploratory" approach, aiming at exploring the potential significance of various western theologians, including John B. Cobb Jr.,[32] Paul Tillich,[33] and St. Thomas Aquinas,[34] for the development of ecotheology in the Chinese context.

In addition to such an "exploratory" approach, I also adopt a more "reflexive" approach that includes a critical reflection on the ecological inadequacy of the theological heritage of the Reformation as well as the Chinese Protestant churches. I argue that the traditional interpretation of the Protestant doctrine of justification by faith tends to assume an anthropocentric interpretation of salvation and rule out the participation of nonhuman beings in salvation. However, if properly reinterpreted, the doctrine may support a more environmental friendly mentality as well as lifestyle.[35] Given the ambivalence of the ecological heritage of the Reformation—with both positive and negative implications for environmental protection, the most valuable Protestant heritage lies perhaps at the Protestant spirit of continuing reformation as the slogan *semper reformanda* succinctly articulates, rather than the particular doctrines of *sola gratia*, *sola fide*, *sola scriptura*, etc.[36]

Apart from this "reflexive" approach, I also adopt a "correlational" approach. In an article for a journal of humanities and social sciences published in mainland China, based on an introduction to the ecological turn of religion commencing a few decades ago, including particularly the recent developments of ecotheology in Christianity, I attempt to argue that one of the important contributing factors behind the global ecological crisis is the economic system, which is ideologically supported by economism as well as consumerism, and existentially driven by human concupiscence. Based on this understanding of the spiritual dimension of the ecological crisis, I further suggest that religions, with their worldviews, ethics, rituals, methods of spiritual cultivation, etc., can

---

30. Wong, "Climate Change."

31. Wong, "Chinese Culture."

32. Lai, "Inter-religious Dialogue and Social Justice."

33. Lai, "Paul Tillich."

34. Lai and Wang, "Reconsidering St. Thomas's Ecological Ethics."

35. Lai, *Pluralism, Diversity and Identity*, 277-98.

36. Lai, "Ecological Heritage."

address to a certain extent the problem of concupiscence and can thus make positive and even indispensable contributions to environmental protection or discourse on sustainability.[37]

In addition to these three approaches, I also adopt a more dialogical or integrative approach. I propose that Christian ecotheology can draw from Confucianism to articulate its Christology, anthropology, etc.,[38] and further argue that Confucianism, especially neo-Confucianism, may offer a third alternative between anthropocentrism and eco-centrism.[39] I further coauthored with Lin Hongxing, a scholar of Confucianism, a book comparing the Christian and Confucian approaches to the environment.[40]

As a scholar involving in the study of inter-religious dialogue on environmental issues, I advocate a pluralistic and contextual approach to ecological ethics.[41] Furthermore, I am also aware of the importance of the economic system to the environment. However, on environmental issues, I merely touch upon the state ideology and political propaganda of the People's Republic of China on sustainable development and harmonious society,[42] without making any attempt to have a serious dialogue with Marxism.

It is rather ironic that the most significant publication in Chinese involving dialogue or integration between Christian theology and Marxism on ecological issues is a Chinese translation of a book written in English by Philip Clayton and Justin Heinzekehr, two American scholars of religion.[43] This book is rather ambitious because it advocates the compatibility and possibility of integration of not only process philosophy and Chinese thought but, more importantly, Marxism or organic Marxism to be more precise.[44] It is understandable that when one identifies unrestrained capitalism as the most important cause for the ecological crisis, one may look for socialism or Marxism as an alternative. This advocacy for Organic Marxism may seem to be better received in China than in the United States, as suggested in John B. Cobb Jr.'s foreword.[45]

Similar limitations of Chinese Christian discourses can be found in their engagement with modern science. The Chinese publications concerning

---

37. Lai, "Zongjiao yu shengtai guanhuai."

38. Lai, "Christian Ecological Theology."

39. Lai, "Beyond Anthropocentrism."

40. See Lai and Lin, *Ye Ru duihua*.

41. See Lai, "Inter-religious Dialogue on Environmental Ethics."

42. Lai, "God of Life." See also Lai, "Public Discourses."

43. Clayton and Heinzekehr, *Organic Marxism*.

44. Clayton and Heinzekehr, *Organic Marxism*, 155–75.

45. See Cobb, foreword to *Organic Marxism*, ii–iii.

ecotheology with a view to engage into dialogue with the modern scientific worldview are primarily exploratory studies of western theologies, especially Cobb's process theology,[46] without significant Chinese characteristics.

■ Analysis and Evaluation

Based on the above survey, one may notice that in order to address the discourses from (1) the Chinese cultural, philosophical, and religious traditions; (2) the Marxist state ideology; and (3) the perspectives of environmental scientists, activists, and practitioners, Chinese Christian ecological discourses employ various approaches, including reflexive, explorative, practical, apologetic, correlational, and dialogical/integrative approaches, with the political and scientific approaches relatively underdeveloped.

It is reasonable to expect that while Chinese Christian responses to the views of environmental scientists, activists, and practitioners may be quite similar to Western Christian responses, what makes Chinese Christian discourses distinctive should be their responses to the Marxist state ideology and the Chinese philosophical or religious traditions. However, at the moment, the mainstream of Chinese Christian discourses tends to disregard the state ideology and prefers to have dialogue or to integrate with the cultural, philosophical, and religious traditions of China. This contrast seems to be quite natural, given the deep-rooted Chinese theological paradigm of indigenization and the antagonistic historical relationship between Christianity and Chinese communism. This neglect of the state ideology is arguably the most glaring omission within Chinese Christian ecotheology as a whole.

It is important to note that in mainland China, Marxism is not merely a philosophical interpretation of the world associated with materialism and scientism. More importantly, it forms the ideological backbone of the dictatorship of the proletariat and gives legitimacy to the rule of the Communist Party, which has dubious ecological credentials. In terms of track record in environmental protection, the memory of massive environmental destruction under the Communist regime is still fresh. Moreover, many of the highly polluting industries in mainland China are run by state-owned enterprises or private enterprises owned by the relatives of high-ranking government officials or party leaders. Many of the environmental laws may not be enforced on these enterprises thanks to their political background. In a similar vein, voices in civil society against these environmental-unfriendly industries were largely suppressed to maintain a "harmonious society." In this light, Clayton and Heinzekehr might have mistaken their opponent by putting their fingers on capitalism and the global market economy. Particularly, their claim that most

---

46. For the Chinese studies of Cobb's ecotheology, see Cao, *Yi zhong shengtai shidai*; Huang, *Guocheng sixiang*; Wang, *Shengtai yu zhengjiu*.

democracies act in collusion with the wealthy is an oversimplification.[47] In reality, countries that have a low Gini coefficient are often more democratic. The actual Chinese experience also suggests a strong correlation between authoritarianism, economic polarization, and environmental degradation. According to the vision for a sustainable, just, and participatory society advocated by the World Council of Churches and supported by Cobb,[48] it is most likely that environmental degradation and economic polarization will keep worsening in China if the political system continues to shut itself away from people's participation. Slogans like "China is the place most likely to achieve ecological civilization" may sound encouraging,[49] but that may also display premature optimism and naivety.

Regarding the Chinese Communist Party's discourse on "ecological civilization," Bryan K. M. Mok offers a penetrating analysis with a Chinese Christian response. He argues that the Communist Party's discourse requires the underpinnings provided by the Chinese cultural traditions, which are regarded as highly ecological. However, the Chinese cultural traditions, particularly Confucianism, tend to highlight the crucial role of personal moral cultivation in the attainment of unity between humanity and Heaven, and this cultivation does not require any divine intervention or external savior. In contrast to the Confucian optimistic view of human nature, Christianity emphasizes human sinfulness and the necessity of Christ's redemption for humankind to return to the source of life and thus the establishment of ecological civilization. So, Mok suggests, from a Chinese Christian perspective, one should take a more cautious and critical "yes and no" approach to the political propaganda concerning "ecological civilization" in mainland China.[50] Mok's critical remark perceptively highlights the ideological character of discourse on "ecological civilization" and challenges its optimistic view of human nature. It leaves open the question concerning whether and how these critical points are to be incorporated into a Chinese Christian narrative of the earth.

Based on the survey, analysis, and evaluation of Chinese Christian ecological discourses, some desirable features for a Chinese Christian narrative can be outlined below:

- It affirms the initiative as well as the universality of the divine works on earth and that the divine works demonstrate and invite, without replacing, human works for the benefit of the universe.

---

47. Clayton and Heinzekehr, *Organic Marxism*, 209.

48. Birch and Cobb, *Liberation of Life*, 234.

49. This is the title of an interview with Cobb published as a journal article in Chinese. See Clayton and Heinzekehr, *Organic Marxism*, xi.

50. Mok, "Reconsidering Ecological Civilization."

- It affirms the possibility and even desirability of articulating the Christian faith with indigenous Chinese cultural resources.
- It appreciates the positive values of other religions, including their ecological wisdom and positive contributions to ecological preservation.
- It calls for a widely active human participation and cooperation between Christians and non-Christians from the grassroots, instead of relying solely on the instruction and subject to the manipulation of a totalitarian government.
- It is compatible with the modern scientific worldview and provides significant contact points for the theology–science dialogue.
- It inspires Christians to adopt a repentant attitude toward the criticisms targeted at the historical records of Christianity, rather than a "holier than thou" response to other religious narratives.

Perhaps, it is neither possible nor necessary to articulate a "grand narrative" or "meganarrative" that can combine all these features. A more realistic first step is to reconsider how to start with the resources available within the Christian tradition.

▎Reconsidering the Breath

When taking a deep breath, especially during a meditation exercise, one may concentrate on one's own breath and then begin to reflect on "breath" itself. In the Christian tradition, breath is associated with the Hebrew concept of *ruach* (Gen 2:7) and the related Greek concept of *pneuma*, which is often translated as "spirit" in English. The relevance of this concept to ecological discourses is recognized not only by Christian theologians[51] but also beyond the Christian circle.[52] One may then consider whether and how the Christian understanding of spirit is to be related to ecological issues in the Chinese context.

It is important to clarify beforehand that theological discourse about spirit should not be restricted to the doctrine concerning the being of the Holy Spirit or the third person of the doctrine of the Trinity. This is because the concept of "spirit" also applies to the whole Godhead, as the expression "God as Spirit" or "God the Spirit" suggests. Furthermore, the same concept of "spirit" applies to being human, as the expression "human spirit" seems to indicate. Finally, "spirit" is associated with life in general rather than restricted to human life, as the Nicene affirmation of the Spirit as the Giver of Life suggests. Although Pneumatology might appear to be downplayed in

---

51. For example, Hart, *Spirit of the Earth*.

52. For example, Rockefeller and Elder, *Spirit and Nature*; Hull, *Earth & Spirit*; Kearns and Keller, *Ecospirit*; Cooper and Palmer, *Spirit of the Environment*.

traditional theology, it has recently undergone a recognizable renaissance in various denominations and contexts.[53] In German Protestant theology alone, there are explorations that relate Pneumatology to various contemporary issues, including ecotheology, religion-science dialogue, and theology of religions.[54] The possible relevance of Pneumatology to Chinese Christian narratives about the earth is discussed below.

(1) In the biblical expression of God's Spirit hovering over the water (Gen 1:2), the initiative as well as universality of the work of the Holy Spirit in creation is affirmed. This affirmation of the work of the Spirit does not negate human participation. For example, in patristic theology, one of the foremost soteriological metaphors is shaping humanity with the Father's two hands, namely, the divine Word and Spirit. This kind of soteriology is associated with the doctrine of deification (*theosis*) and assumes active human participation. It further echoes the Confucian ideal of the unity of heaven and humanity in their affirmations of the cosmic role played by humanity.[55] In modern theology, Tillich's understanding of spirit as a dimension of life, which is a multidimensional unity, clearly highlights the universality of spiritual presence.[56] The significance of Tillich's Pneumatology for many other theological topics, including the doctrine of God, political theology, and theology of religions, is recognized even by Pentecostal theologians.[57] The universal presence of Spirit is also elaborated in Moltmann's Pneumatology, especially his interpretation of "Spirit of Life" with references to the Cosmic Breath of the Divine Spirit.[58] With such affirmation of the Spirit of the earth, one can affirm that the earth is not a lifeless matter subject to human exploitation. Instead, the earth is filled with Spirit, which has its own way of living and operation. This implies that nature has its own way of renewal, which has to be respected by human beings.

(2) The Christian doctrine of the Spirit affirms the legitimacy of expressing Christian faith in different languages and cultures. It is noteworthy that according to the Acts of the Apostles, at the Pentecost, the Holy Spirit made people speak in their own respective languages or dialects, instead of in just one particular language or dialect. Furthermore, the Holy Spirit further dispersed the disciples to different places and thus pluralized the Christian churches geographically, linguistically, racially, and culturally. In other words, the Christian unity preserved by the Holy Spirit (Eph 4:1–6) assumes linguistic,

---

53. Kärkkäinen, *Pneumatology*, 11–22.

54. Varkey, *Role of Holy Spirit*, especially 408–13.

55. Lai, "Shaping Humanity."

56. Tillich, *Systematic Theology 3*, 11–30.

57. Wariboko and Yong, *Paul Tillich and Pentecostal Theology*.

58. See Moltmann, *Spirt of Life*, especially 8–10.

racial, and cultural diversity, instead of homogeneity. In fact, non-Western Christian contributions to Pneumatology are well recognized.[59] For Chinese Christianity, the transmission of the Christian tradition should be primarily about the spirit of the tradition, rather than a particular text or historical form of Christianity.[60] Based on this understanding of the Holy Spirit's work, it is entirely legitimate for non-Western Christians to articulate their narratives of the earth according to their own respective cultures, spiritual traditions, and socio-political contexts.

(3) Pneumatic Christianity is arguably the most important indigenous form of Christianity in China. The Taiping rebellion (1850–1871) was led by some Hakka Chinese who had been inspired by the evangelistic leaflets disseminated by Protestant missionaries and exhibited certain "charismatic" practices, including casting out demons and spiritual healing. Their actual practices might reflect the possible influences of Chinese popular religion, especially the Hakka beliefs and practices related to "spirits." Similar charismatic phenomena can also be found in other indigenous Christian groups, including the True Jesus Church (*zhen Yesu hui*), Jesus Family (*Yesu jiating*), and the Little Flock Church (*xiaoqun jiaohui*).[61]

(4) The presence of the Holy Spirit in human religions is affirmed by various western theologians[62] and also by East Asian theologians, including particularly those who associate it with the concept of *Qi* (or *Ch'i* according to the Wade-Giles transliteration system).[63] The affinities between the concept of "spirit," especially *ruach* in Hebrew and *pneuma* in Greek, with the Chinese concept of *Qi*, which can be translated as air, spirit, vital power, material force, etcetera, have been noted by many Christian theologians, especially those from East Asia with interests in ecotheology.[64] The importance of the concept of *Qi* for the articulation of Confucian ecological cosmology has been recognized by scholars of Confucianism.[65] It is noteworthy that the concept of *Qi* is not merely a cosmological concept suggesting that the cosmos is made of *Qi*. Through affirming the unity of the myriad things of the universe, the concept of *Qi* is particularly related to the human body, as the practice of Qigong assumes. As *Qi* permeates the human body and makes it sensitive to the pain and suffering of oneself, it constitutes the possibility of further extending this

---

59. See Rogers, *After the Spirit*.

60. Lai, "Sino-Christian Theology."

61. See Yeung, "Indigenous Church."

62. A notable example is Tillich. See Lai, *Towards a Trinitarian Theology*, 114–30.

63. For example, Yun, "Pneumatological Perspectives."

64. For example, Kim, "Conception of Ecological Theology."

65. See Tucker, "Philosophy of *Ch'i*."

sensitivity to others. This is thus related to the Confucian moral cultivation, especially the cultivation of the virtue of *ren* (benevolence). This understanding of *Qi* is particularly elaborated in neo-Confucians, especially Zhang Zai (1020–1077),[66] whose cosmic spirituality exhibits certain affinities with Christian spirituality.[67]

(5) Unlike Christology, which focuses on one particular person, namely, Jesus Christ, the work of the Divine Spirit highlights the much wider participation of ordinary people. In contemporary theology, the experience of the Spirit includes the public experience of liberation, justice, and peace, rather than restricted to the subjective experience of individuals.[68] This understanding of the work of the Divine Spirit in ordinary people affirms that the divine economy is not restricted to its work through a particular divine–human person, but involves many ordinary people, including non-Christians, in the establishment of social justice and political liberation. This is reminiscent of a subtle but important shift in neo-Confucianism. In classical Confucianism, its hope is focused on the very rare appearance of an extraordinary sage (*shengren*), who can maintain the cosmic harmony perfectly with his virtue, which is exemplified in Confucius himself or a few Sage-Kings depicted in the ancient texts. Neo-Confucianism replaced this rather "messianic" hope with a more realistic or achievable ideal of noble persons (*junzi*), who are ordinary persons who sincerely and diligently cultivate their morality.[69] This shift is supported by the concepts of *Qi* as well as Spirit, which affirms the outpouring of the Spirit or the spiritual gifts to ordinary people—male and female, old and young (Joel 2:28–29). This may further affirm the role of ordinary people, instead of the elitist political leaders, in the earth's story.

(6) The importance of Pneumatology in the science-theology dialogue on divine action is recognized by theologians from various denominations or schools of thought, including particularly Pentecostal, Orthodox, and Process theology.[70] In addition to these, Tillich's understanding of spirit as a dimension of life has the potential to enrich the emerging theology–science dialogue.[71] Keith Ka-fu Chan, currently a professor of Shandong University, spells out the ecological implications of Tillich's Pneumatology in a study of Tillich's ecological Pneumatology, which includes not only Tillich's Pneumatology, ecotheology, and critical reflection on modern technology but also the

---

66. See Tu, "Pain and Humanity."

67. Pfister, "Paul Tillich and Zhang Zai."

68. Welker, *God the Spirit*.

69. De Bary, *Trouble with Confucianism*, especially 46–56.

70. See Clayton, *Adventures in the Spirit*; Smith and Yong, *Science and the Spirit*; Yong, *Spirit of Creation*; *Cosmic Breath*; Welker, *Spirit in Creation*.

71. See Kung, "Pneumatology and Emergence."

dialogue between Tillich, Orthodox theology and Confucianism on environmental ethics.[72]

(7) Christian narratives about the earth should include an element or episode of fall and repentance. The work of Spirit is associated with confession of sin and repentance (John 16:8–11; Acts 2:37–39). Proper recognition of the role of Holy Spirit in Christian narratives about the earth may support a humble and repentant attitude required in the Chinese context.

To summarize, Pneumatology can and should play a prominent role in articulating Christian narrative(s) of the earth within the Chinese context.

■ Bibliography

Birch, Charles and John B. Cobb Jr. *Liberation of Life: From the Cell to the Community*. Cambridge: Cambridge University Press, 1982.

Cao, Jing. *Yi zhong shengtai shidai de shijieguan: Mo'erteman yu Kebu shengtai shenxue bijiao yanjiu* [A Worldview for the Ecological Age: A Comparative Study of Ecological Theologies of Jürgen Moltmann and John B. Cobb Jr.]. Beijing: Social Sciences Academic, 2007.

Cao, Mengqin. *Renxing yu ziran: shengtai lunli zhexue fansi* [Humanity and Nature: Reflection on the Philosophical Foundation of Ecological Ethics]. Nanjing: Nanjing Normal University Press, 2004.

Chan, Keith Ka-fu. *Life as Spirit: A Study of Paul Tillich's Ecological Pneumatology*. Berlin: De Gruyter, 2018.

Chen, Hongbing. *Fojiao shengtai zhexue yanjiu* [Study of Buddhist Ecological Philosophy]. Beijing: Religious Culture, 2011.

Chen, Nancy C. M. "Ecology and the Church: A Retrospectus of a Taiwanese Experience." *CGST Journal of Theology* 26 (1999), 81–120 (in Chinese with abstract in English).

Clayton, Philip. *Adventures in the Spirit: God, World, Divine Action*. Minneapolis: Fortress, 2008.

Clayton, Philip and Justin Heinzekehr. *Organic Marxism: An Alternative to Capitalism and Ecological Catastrophe*. Claremont: Process Century, 2014.

Cobb, John B. Jr. Foreword to *Organic Marxism: An Alternative to Capitalism and Ecological Catastrophe*, i–iv. Claremont: Process Century, 2014.

Cooper, David E. and Joy A. Palmer, eds. *Spirit of the Environment: Religion, Value and Environmental Concern*. London: Routledge, 1998.Deane-Drummond, Celia and Heinrich Bedford-Strohm, eds. *Religion and Ecology in the Public Sphere*. London: T. & T. Clark, 2011.

De Bary, Wm. Theodore. *The Trouble with Confucianism*. Cambridge: Harvard University Press, 1991.

Fu, Hua. *Shengtai lunlixue tanjiu* [Inquiry of Ecological Ethics]. Beijing: Huaxia, 2002.

Hart, John. *The Spirit of the Earth: A Theology of the Land*. New York: Paulist, 1984.

He, Jianzong. "Duibi Rujia he Jidujiao de ke chixu fazhan shiye" [Contrasting the Confucian and Christian Perspectives of Sustainable Development]. In *Jidu zongjiao ji Rujia duitan shengming yu lunli* [Christian-Confucian Dialogue on Life and Ethics], edited by Lai Pinchao [Pan-Chiu Lai], 127–38. Hong Kong: Centre for the Study of Religion and Chinese Society, Chung Chi College, The Chinese University of Hong Kong, 2002.

———. *Shengtai shenxue chutan: jiuyue pian* [Ecological Theology: The Old Testament Perspective]. Taipei: Christian Arts, 1995.

---

72. See Chan, *Life as Spirit*.

He, Jianzong and Yiqiang Huang. *Lüse shitu: huanjing lingdao he juece* [Green Apostle: Environmental Leadership and Decision-Making]. Hong Kong: Tien Dao, 2014.

Ho, Samuel Sung-Him. "Towards an Ecological Theology: Nature and the Self." *CGST Journal of Theology* 26 (January 1999), 43–60 (in Chinese with abstract in English).

Holquist, Michael. *Dialogism: Bakhtin and His World*. 2nd ed. London: Routledge, 2002.

Huang, Ming. *Guocheng sixiang ji qi houxiandai xiaoying: Kebu shenxue sixiang yanjiu* [Process Thought and Its Postmodern Effect: A Study of John B. Cobb Jr.'s Theology]. Beijing: Religious Culture, 2008.

Hull, Fritz, ed. *Earth & Spirit: The Spiritual Dimension of the Environmental Crisis*. New York: Continuum, 1993.

Kärkkäinen, Veli-Matti. *Pneumatology: The Holy Spirit in Ecumenical, International, and Contextual Perspective*. Grand Rapids: Baker Academic, 2002.

Kearns, Laurel and Catherine Keller, eds. *Ecospirit: Religions and Philosophies for the Earth*. New York: Fordham University Press, 2007.

Kim, Kyoung-Jae. "A Conception of an Ecological Theology of Spirit and Ch'i." In *Asian Contextual Theology for the Third Millennium: Theology of Minjung in Fourth-Eye Formation*, edited by Paul S. Chung, Veli-Matti Kärkkäinen and Kim Kyoung-Jae, 285–302. Eugene: Pickwick, 2007.

Kung, Wai-han. "Pneumatology and Emergence: Paul Tillich in Dialogue with Science." PhD diss., The Chinese University of Hong Kong, 2020.

Lai, Pan-Chiu. "Beyond Anthropocentrism and Ecocentrism: Eco-Theology and Confucian-Christian Dialogue." *Ching Feng (New Series)* 2 (2001), 35–55.

———. "Christian Ecological Theology in Dialogue with Confucianism." *Ching Feng* 41 (1998), 309–44.

———. "Ecological Heritage of Protestantism in Chinese Christian Perspective." *Ching Feng (New Series)* 19 (2020), 21-47.

———. "Ecological Theology as Public Theology: A Chinese Perspective." *International Journal of Public Theology* 11:4 (2017), 477–500. https://doi.org/10.1163/15697320-12341512

———. "God of Life and Ecological Theology: A Chinese Christian Perspective." *Ecumenical Review* 65:1 (2013), 67–82. https://doi.org/10.1111/erev.12027

———. "Inter-religious Dialogue and Social Justice: Cobb's Wesleyan Process Theology in East Asian Perspective." *Asia Journal of Theology* 25 (2011), 82–102.

———. "Inter-religious Dialogue on Environmental Ethics." *Studies in Interreligious Dialogue* 21 (2011), 5–19.

———. "Paul Tillich and Ecological Theology." *The Journal of Religion* 79:2 (1999), 233–49. https://doi.org/10.1086/490399

———. *Pluralism, Diversity and Identity: Explorations of Theology and Culture*. New Taipei City: Chinese Christian Literature, 2011 (in Chinese).

———. "Public Discourses on Harmonious Society and Sustainable Development: A Sino-Christian Theological Response." *Logos & Pneuma* 40 (2014), 107–27 (in Chinese with abstract in English).

———. "Shaping Humanity with Word and Spirit: Perspectives East, West and Neither-East-Nor-West." In *Word and Spirit: Renewing Christology and Pneumatology in a Globalizing World*, edited by Anselm K. Min and Christoph Schwöbel, 131–49. Berlin: Walter de Gruyter, 2014.

———. "Sino-Christian Theology and Bible in China." In *Oxford Handbook of Bible in China*, edited by K. K. Yeo, 511–26. Oxford: Oxford University Press, forthcoming.

———. *Towards a Trinitarian Theology of Religions: A Study of Paul Tillich's Thought*. Kampen: Kok Pharos, 1994.

Lai, Pan-Chiu and Tao Wang, "Reconsidering St. Thomas's Ecological Ethics." *Universitas: Monthly Review of Philosophy and Culture* 37 (2010), 155–73 (in Chinese with abstract in English).

Lai, Pinchao [Pan-Chiu Lai]. "Zongjiao yu shengtai guanhuai" [Religion and ecological concern]. *Jianghai Academic Journal* 219 (2002), 37–42.

Lai, Pinchao [Pan-Chiu Lai] and Lin Hongxing. *Ye Ru duihua yu shengtai guanhuai* [Christian-Confucian Dialogue and Ecological Concern]. Beijing: Religious Culture Publishing House, 2006.

Lee, Albert Sui-hung. *Dialogue on Monarchy in the Gideon-Abimelech Narrative: Ideological Reading in Light of Bakhtin's Dialogism*. Biblical Interpretation Series 187. Leiden: Brill, forthcoming.

Lee, Stephen. "*Imago Dei* and *Dominium Terrae*." *CGST Journal of Theology* 26 (1999), 31–42 (in Chinese with abstract in English).

Lee, Wilson. "Animal Rights." *CGST Journal of Theology* 26 (1999), 81–99 (in Chinese with abstract in English).

Liu, Yuanchun. *Gongsheng gongrong: fojiao shengtai guan* [Living and Flouring Together: Buddhist View of Ecology]. Beijing: Religious Culture, 2002.

Louie, Kin-yip. "Economic Growth and Environmental Protection." *CGST Journal of Theology* 26 (1999), 61–79 (in Chinese with abstract in English).

Matthews, Clifford N., et al. *When Worlds Converge: What Science and Religion Tell Us about the Story of the Universe and Our Place in It*. Chicago: Open Court, 2002.

Meng, Peiyuan. *Ren yu ziran: Zhongguo zhexue shengtai guan* [Human Being and Nature: Chinese Philosophy of Ecology]. Beijing: People's Publishing, 2004.

Mok, Bryan K. M. "Reconsidering Ecological Civilization from a Chinese Christian Perspective." *Religions* 11:5 (2020), 261. https://doi.org/10.3390/rel11050261

Moltmann, Jürgen. *The Spirt of Life: A Universal Affirmation*. Translated by Margaret Kohl. London: SCM, 1992.

Mühling, Markus. *Post-Systematic Theology I: Ways of Thinking: A Theological Philosophy*. Leiden: Wilhelm Fink, 2020.

Pfister, Lauren F. "Paul Tillich and Zhang Zai: Fellow Pilgrims Seeking New Peace in Trembling Worlds." In *Paul Tillich and Asian Religions*, edited by Ka-fu Keith Chan and Yau-nang William Ng, 199–220. Berlin: Walter de Gruyter, 2017.

Qiao, Qingju. *Rujia shengtai sixiang tonglun* [Introduction to Confucian Ecological Thought]. Beijing: Peking University Press, 2013.

Rockefeller, Steven C. and John C. Elder, eds. *Spirit and Nature: Why the Environment Is a Religious Issue: An Interfaith Dialogue*. Boston: Beacon, 1992.

Rogers, Eugene R. Jr. *After the Spirit: A Constructive Pneumatology from Resources outside the Modern West*. Grand Rapids: Eerdmans, 2005.

Scott, Peter. *A Political Theology of Nature*. Cambridge: Cambridge University Press, 2003.

She, Zhengrong. *Zhongguo shengtai lunli chuantong de quanshi yu chongjian* [The Interpretation and Reconstruction of Chinese Ecological Ethical Tradition]. Beijing: People's Publishing, 2002.

Smith, James K. A. and Amos Yong, eds. *Science and the Spirit: A Pentecostal Engagement with the Sciences*. Bloomington: Indiana University Press, 2010.

Tillich, Paul. *Systematic Theology*, Volume 3. London: SCM, 1978.

Tu, Wei-ming. "Pain and Humanity in the Confucian Learning if the Heart-and-Mind." In *Pain and Its Transformations: The Interface of Biology and Culture*, edited by Sarah Coakley and Kay Kaufman Shelema, 221–41. Cambridge: Harvard University Press, 2007.

Tucker, Mary Evelyn. "The Philosophy of *Ch'i* as an Ecological Cosmology." In *Confucianism and Ecology: The Interrelation of Heaven, Earth and Humans*, edited by Mary Evelyn Tucker and John Berthrong, 187–207. London: SCM, 1992.

Varkey, Wilson. *Role of the Holy Spirit in Protestant Systematic Theology*. Carlisle: Langham Partnership, 2011.

Wang, Jun. *Shengtai yu zhengjiu: Yuehan Kebu shengtai sixiang yanjiu* [Ecology and Salvation: A Study of John B. Cobb's Ecological Thought]. Beijing: Religious Culture, 2010.

Wang, Wei. *Shencun yu fazhan: diqiu lunlixue* [Survival and Development: Earth Ethics]. Beijing: People's Publishing, 1995.

Wang, Zhengping. *Huanjing zhexue: Huanjing lunli de kua xueke yanjiu* [Environmental Philosophy: Cross-Disciplinary Study of Environmental Ethics]. Shanghai: Shanghai Renmin, 2004.

Wariboko, Nimi and Amos Yong, eds. *Paul Tillich and Pentecostal Theology: Spiritual Presence and Spiritual Power*. Bloomington: Indiana University Press, 2015.

Welker, Michael. *God the Spirit*. Translated by John F. Hoffmeyer. Minneapolis: Fortress, 1994.

Welker, Michael, ed. *The Spirit in Creation and New Creation: Science and Theology in Western and Orthodox Realms*. Grand Rapids: Eerdmans, 2012.

Wong, Fook Yee. "Chinese Culture and Ecological Theology." *CGST Journal of Theology* 53 (2012), 79–108 (in Chinese with abstract in English).

———. "Climate Change: A Theological Reflection." *CGST Journal of Theology* 51 (2011), 131–52 (in Chinese with abstract in English).

Yeung, Tin Yan. "Indigenous Church as an Offspring of Pneumatic Christianity: A Re-Examination of the Development of Christianity in Modern China." PhD diss., The Chinese University of Hong Kong, 2002 (in Chinese with abstract in English).

Yong, Amos. *The Cosmic Breath: Spirit and Nature in the Christianity-Buddhism-Science Trialogue*. Leiden: Brill, 2012.

———. *The Spirit of Creation: Modern Science and Divine Action in the Pentecostal-Charismatic Imagination*. Grand Rapids: Eerdmans, 2011.

Yu, Carver T. "The Roots of Our Ecological Crisis." *CGST Journal of Theology* 26 (1999), 9–31 (in Chinese with abstract in English).

Yue, Aiguo. *Daojiao shengtaixue* [Taoist Ecology]. Beijing: Social Sciences Academic, 2005.

Yun, Koo D. "Pneumatological Perspectives on World Religions: The Cosmic Spirit and Ch'i." In *Asian Contextual Theology for the Third Millennium: Theology of Minjung in Fourth-Eye Formation*, edited by Paul S. Chung, Veli-Matti Kärkkäinen and Kim Kyoung-Jae, 165–77. Eugene: Pickwick, 2007.

Zhengyan Fashi [Dharma Master Cheng Yen]. *Yu diqiu gong shengxi* [Symbiosis with the Planet Earth]. 2006; reprint, Shanghai: Fudan University Press, 2009.

Hearing and Telling Old and New Stories from Latin America: Challenges and Inspirations for an Earthed Faith

Marcial Maçaneiro[1] & Rudolf von Sinner[2]

■ Introduction

This essay aims at "telling the story" of divine and human actions from within and in interaction with the Latin American context. On using that word, of course, the colonial history of this context is already indicated. As is well known, "America" was branded by the German cartographer Waldseemüller inspired by the Portuguese seafarer Américo Vespucci, and "Latin" is because

---

1. Marcial Maçaneiro is Professor of Systematic Theology at the Pontifical Catholic University of Paraná in Curitiba, Brazil. He is registered as a co-researcher at the University of the Western Cape, South Africa, for the project "An Earthed Faith: Telling the Story amid the 'Anthropocene'."

2. Rudolf von Sinner is Professor of Systematic Theology at the Pontifical Catholic University of Paraná in Curitiba, Brazil. He is also a professor extraordinary at the University of Stellenbosch, South Africa.

> **How to cite:** Maçaneiro, M & Von Sinner, R., 2021, 'Hearing and Telling Old and New Stories from Latin America: Challenges and Inspirations for an Earthed Faith', in E.M. Conradie & P.-C. Lai (eds.), *Taking a deep breath for the story to begin . . .* (An Earthed Faith: Telling the Story amid the "Anthropocene" Volume 1), pp. 183-203, AOSIS, Cape Town. https://doi.org/10.4102/aosis.2021.BK264.09

of the occupation (*conquista*) by the Iberian countries, Spain and Portugal, from the fifteenth century onward, powers that also imposed their language. A telling story of non-understanding is Father Vicente Valverde's handing over a Bible to the Inca Atahualpa, upon which the Inca is told to have held it against his ear and then thrown it into the dust, saying "it doesn't speak." In an oral culture, a written book, even more so in a foreign language, does not appeal to the perceptions of those who have their own system of belief and are supposed to be welcoming to new divine messages. Beyond not literally speaking—rather than waiting to be read—the Christian story would not tell the Incas anything. The conquerors, in turn, had no real interest to seek ways to communicate the new message. Valverde readily understood Atahualpa's reaction as proof of his unbending paganism and saw the necessary justification given for the subsequent violent conquest and annihilation of the Inca Empire. The destruction that follows created its own story, the *leyenda negra* ("black legend"), and the message became a threat rather than a promise, a theft rather than a gift. Consequently, an indigenous person from Ecuador returned the Bible to Pope John Paul II during his visit in 1985 "to symbolize that he gave back the religion they had intended to teach him and asked him [the Pope] to give back the riches extracted from the West Indies."[3]

Stories told by the dominators and those told by the dominated differ. Which of them is true? And which of them tells the correct story of God's action with and within creation? A decolonial view seeking "hermeneutical fairness" has to look to the old, indigenous stories told and retold—usually orally, but occasionally registered by missionaries—and to the story of Africans brutally imported and commercialized as slaves, which developed their own religions, reinventing their story under new circumstances and surviving through dissimulation. As they emerge into visibility today, they both challenge and inspire the Christian story of God's presence in the world.

The reflections developed under the heading of "epistemologies of the South" by Portuguese sociologist Boaventura de Sousa Santos are of high importance as undergirding theory and perspective.[4] According to Santos:

> The epistemologies of the South concern the production and validation of knowledges anchored in the experiences of resistance of all those social groups that have systematically suffered injustice, oppression, and destruction caused by capitalism, colonialism, and patriarchy.[5]

Beyond the issue of justice and injustice and resistance against "epistemological colonialism," Santos criticizes the "indolence" (a term he

---

3. Dussel, "Meditações Anticartesianas," 356, n. 34.

4. Santos, *Epistemologies of the South*.

5. Santos, *The End of the Cognitive Empire*, 1.

takes from Leibniz) of a western modernity to consider perspectives and concepts that differ from its own, and the enormous "wasting" of knowledge that could enrich. Indeed, as Jens Marquardt has shown, also in the "Anthropocene" debate, voices and contributions from the Global South are highly underrepresented.[6] Among the concrete conceptual contributions, he explicitly mentions the Andean *sumak kawsay* and the Southern African *ubuntu*.[7]

Santos—himself of course a white, male, European, privileged intellectual, but one reaching out to and learning with the marginalized, for whom he has become an important advocate—calls for the need for not "vanguard," but "rear-guard" intellectuals that assist those in the concrete struggle rather than try to conform them to their own ideas. The story, he contends, has to be told by those who concretely live it. In the perspective both of the original inhabitants of the land, the indigenous peoples and those brought to the continent by coercion from Africa and enslaved to work in the mines and grand plantations, the Christian story has, to say the least, a deep ambiguity to it. While this past still has to be elucidated further and apologies and reparations are necessary, our intention here is to bring into the discussion of the story the earthed faith of those whose voices have not been heard and, therefore, important knowledge has been wasted. This knowledge is relevant in its own right, and in relation to relating to nature and the Earth in terms of the human and the divine, but also inasmuch as it contributes to reveal blind spots within the Christian faith and challenge it to a thorough rethinking of its telling the faithful story of God's presence and human role within creation.

We first discuss the project of *buen vivir,* the good life, and indigenous insight that has introduced it into the constitutions of Bolivia and Ecuador, which counts on considerable appreciation and support by Christian theologians. We then explore insights of African Brazilian traditions. Our focus is on what these old, but remolded and even "reinvented" stories tell us about the earth and its relationship with the divine, how creative transcendent forces have molded the earth and called the world into being, and what this means for the relationship between human beings to themselves, their fellow creatures, to the creator and to all that is—and how this can and, indeed, should challenge and inspire the Christian story.

---

6. Marquardt, "Worlds Apart?"; see also Conradie, *Secular Discourse on Sin*, 169. Just to note here that beyond the issue of contributions to the debate, our home country Brazil "hosts the most important biodiversity in the world, the biggest tropical forest and the major freshwater and arable soil reserves" and "is part of a small number of countries with a net positive 'credit' in ecological terms (its biocapacity exceeding its ecological footprint)"; Issberner and Léna, *Brazil in the Anthropocene*, 3.

7. Marquardt, "Worlds Apart?" 5, and passim; and also Ramose, "Globalização e *Ubuntu*."

■ Indigenous Insights: Notions of *buen vivir* in Bolivia, Ecuador, and Beyond

For the past thirty years, indigenous peoples in the Andes, together with supporting non-indigenous intellectuals and politicians, have vindicated a new paradigm of looking at the world and describing the objective of living in it: *buen vivir*, "the good living," as the term is used in Ecuador, or *vivir bien*, "living well," as is preferred in Bolivia. The Andean indigenous languages call it *sumak kawsay* or *allin kawsay* (Quechua), *suma qamaña* (Aymara). *ñande reko* (Bolivian Guaraní), and analogously *shür waras* (Ecuador/Peru) or *küme morgen* (Chilean Mapuche).[8] Since 2008, the Ecuadorian constitution has been referring to this paradigm in ninety-nine of its four hundred and forty-four articles, and in 2009, it was incorporated into the Bolivian constitution.[9] Both countries have a considerable indigenous population; in Bolivia, they are the majority. It is an emerging concept that harvests on ancient wisdom, but is also "under construction" in a specific, contemporary context, and in dialogue with "ecologists, feminists, cooperativists, Marxists and humanists."[10] Theologically, it has found grounding and created wider resonance through intercultural theologians like Swiss Catholic missionary Josef Estermann, who spent many years in Peru and Bolivia and has written extensively on Andine Philosophy and Theology.[11] One of the symbols of complementarity, correspondence, relationality, and balance is the Andine cross, called *chakana* both in Aymara and in Quechua, a "cosmic 'bridge'" or "zone of transition," in Estermann's words.[12]

The Bolivian Constitution's Eighth Article mentions that:

> [T]he state promotes the ethical and moral principles of pluralistic society: *amaqhilla, ama llulla, ama suwa* (do not be lazy, do not lie, do not steal), *suma qamaña* (*vive bien*), *ñandereko* (*vida armoniosa:* harmonious life), *teko kavi* (*vida buena*), *ivi maraei* (*tierra sin mal:* Earth without evil, also translated as 'intact environment'), and *qhapaj ñan* (*Camino o vida noble:* the path of wisdom).[13]

While the term in its English translation might evoke an idea of (individual) wellness, "feeling good," the Andean concept is far remote from such an idea. To the contrary, it has a strong social and collective component. As summarized by Unai Villalba, for Andean authors like Huanacuni, Macas, and Choquehuanca

---

8. Chuji, Rengifo, and Gudynas, "Buen Vivir," 111.

9. See, for instance, Stromquist, "In Search of the Good Life."

10. Acosta, *O bem viver*, 42.

11. Estermann, *Apu Taytayku*; *Teologia Andina*; and *Filosofia Andina*.

12. Estermann, *Apu Taytayku*, 59–76, especially 66, 75.

13. Fatheuer, *Buen Vivir*, 17–18.

(former minister of the exterior and one of the main formulators of the paradigm in Bolivia):

> Sumak is that which is full of plenitude, is sublime, excellent, magnificent, beautiful and superior, whereas Kawsay is life, to exist in a dynamic, changing and active manner. Some of them concur that the most accurate translation would be "life of fullness." Even so, other authors prefer to translate it as "good coexistence" or "harmonious life," for in their opinion the Andean world view of a life in fullness means a life of material and spiritual excellence expressed harmoniously and in relation to all beings, as well as a community's internal and external equilibrium. They also emphasise that Sumak conveys a sense of fullness that has not been reflected in Spanish, insofar as Sumak already includes "the highest possible degree" and therefore it makes no sense to speak of "living better."[14]

One of the important ingredients of *sumak kawsay* is the attribution of rights to nature as a legal entity, as occurred in Ecuador. In Bolivia, however, although there is a distinguished place for Mother Earth in the constitution, no concrete rights are attributed to her, and the industrialization of natural resources is also clearly stated—being an important backbone of Bolivia's economy, economic survival speaks louder.

Another important aspect is diversity, which made the two countries define themselves as pluri-national states. This implies wide-ranging autonomy for indigenous peoples, even in legal terms. There are important core concepts, like nature, community, and spirituality, and fundamental principles, like reciprocity, complementarity, and relationality, based on indigenous Andine, obviously non-Cartesian ontology.[15] Article 275 of the Ecuadorian constitution states:

> *Buen Vivir* requires that individuals, communities, peoples and nations are in actual possession of their rights and exercise their responsibilities in the context of interculturalism, respect for diversity and of harmonious coexistence with nature.[16]

Based on indigenous ontology—in which a western separation of the divine and the profane does not make sense, although creator and creature are not confused either—located in a concrete, pluri-national state, this paradigm seeks to translate into constitutional rite and an all-embracing, effective citizenship:

> [A]n institutionalisation needs to be constructed that materializes the horizontal exercise of power. This means to 'citizenise' [*ciudadanizar*] the State individually and collectively, creating communitarian spaces as active forms of social organization.[17]

---

14. Villalba, "Buen Vivir," 1429–30.

15. See Villalba, "Buen Vivir," 1439.

16. As translated in Fatheuer, *Buen Vivir*, 16.

17. Acosta, *O bem viver*, 34. On the notion of citizenship, see Von Sinner, *The Churches and Democracy in Brazil*.

The paradigm is discussed also in other countries, mainly in Latin America, but also beyond,[18] even though not necessarily within the political system. By retrieving this paradigm, even though not exclusively, from indigenous traditions and making it a reference for the state and society as a whole, it is explicitly seen as a step on the way of decolonization and an alternative for development, rejecting neoliberal market economy and extraction projects, not sparing the Ecuadorian and Bolivian governments themselves:

> The modern separation between humanity and nature is [. . .] challenged. *buen vivir* acknowledges extended communities made up of humans and non-humans, animals, plants, mountains, spirits, and so on, in specific territories—as with the Andean concept of *ayllu,* mixed socio-ecological communities rooted in a specific territory.[19]

Mother Earth (*Pachamama*) is a central reference within *sumak kawsay.*[20] According to the Bolivian Quechua philosopher and theologian Victor Bascopé Caero, *Pacha* expresses "the totality of time and universal space [. . .] the existential totality of life."[21] In 2010, Bolivia adopted a "Law on the Protection of the Earth," referring to the "Universal Declaration of the Rights of Mother Earth" adopted by the alternative climate summit held in Cochabamba that same year. According to *Blickpunkt Lateinamerika* of December 09, 2010, as quoted by Fatheuer:

> The law provides for the establishment of a state authority (*Defensoría de la Madre Tierra*), whose responsibilities and tasks are yet to be established. It will monitor the validity, promotion, dissemination and implementation of the rights of *Madre Tierra*. The legal text emphasizes the necessity of maintaining a balance in nature as a precondition for the regeneration of *Madre Tierra*, respect for it and the protection of its rights. The law also provides for a prohibition of the marketing of "Mother Earth" and the promotion of interculturalism. The rights of the Earth include clean air and freedom from pollution.[22]

It is about "harmony with Mother Nature," says Lúcio Flores, a Terena indigenous person from Brazil, criticizing developmentalism as it was in place at the time of the Worker's Party government.[23] *Buen vivir* also challenges

---

18. See, for instance, Valiani, "*Sumak kawsay.*"

19. Chuji, Rengifo, and Gudynas, "Buen Vivir," 112.

20. Fatheuer, *Buen Vivir*, 21, footnote 13, observes that the meaning of "Pacha" is difficult to translate, and refers to Umberto Eco (quoting L. Ramiro Beltran, in turn quoted by Iván Guzmán de Rojas, *Problemática logico-lingüística de la comunición social con el pueblo Aymara*, copied text s.d., Centro Internacional de Investigaciones para el Desarrollo de Canada), stating that there is a high flexibility in Aymara (already noted by the Jesuit Ludovico Bertonio in his Aymara grammar and dictionary written in 1603 and 1612, respectively) that enables it to translate any language into its own, but not vice-versa: *Die Suche nach einer vollkommenen Sprache*, 350–51.

21. Caero, "Terra e água," 175.

22. As translated in Fatheuer, *Buen Vivir*, 18.

23. Flores, "Bem Viver na Criação," 16.

patriarchy, even at the heart of indigenous communities themselves, and pays substantial attention to affectivity and spirituality.

Significantly and somewhat surprisingly, Alberto Acosta, the "spiritual father" of buen vivir in Ecuador and President of the Constituent Assembly for one year before he resigned because of divergences with the country's president, Rafael Correa, starts the first chapter of his book with a quote attributed to Martin Luther: "Even if the world disintegrated tomorrow, I would plant my apple tree."[24] For Acosta, *buen vivir* is, essentially, "a process originating in the communitarian matrix of peoples that live in harmony with Nature."[25] As Acosta concedes, "harmony" does not exclude conflict. Brazilian ecofeminist theologian Ivone Gebara goes even further by arguing that a Manichean separation of good and evil is not possible:

> We not only commit evil and suffer its effects, but we are also continually exposed to it from our own ontological constitution. [. . .] The destruction of peoples, forests, rivers and different groups that has been promoted in our days reveals the excesses, the imbalance in the forces of humanity and the breaking of our covenant of common life. [. . .] Our world blends order with disorder, evil with good, justice with injustice in a complex historical fabric that requires us to overcome the old dualisms and polarizations.[26]

Although quite vague and open to further questioning, the paradigm of *buen vivir* can serve as a reference and inspiration to retrieve ancient wisdom, current knowledge, and care for a live-permitting and live-enhancing future that seeks to translate into concrete legal normative and political action. Theologically, according to Dietrich Ritschl, it might inform a perception of God's counter-narrative or "alternative draft" (*Gegenentwurf*) to how human beings "manage the world" (*Weltgestaltung*), seeking the overcoming of injustice and destruction of human and nonhuman being. Rather than acting in the world, God is interpreting the world, and we are invited to adopt, based on the biblical stories, God's view on the world.[27] Such a view, built on western concepts as it is, is not incompatible, we believe, with the acknowledging, respecting, and learning from non-Western cosmovisions. Let us know see what we can learn from African Brazilian ways of telling the story.

■ African Brazilian Insights

African Brazilian religions form a rich and varied complex that emerged from African heritage in direct and constant contact with traditional, popular

---

24. Acosta, *O bem viver*, 31. Although probably apocryphal, the saying "illustrates well Luther's approach to our responsibility towards the world," as stated by Westhelle, "Working with Lutheran Forms of Christianity," 287.

25. Acosta, *O bem viver*, 32.

26. Gebara, "The Christian Story," 469–70.

27. Ritschl and Hailer, *Grundkurs Christliche Theologie*, 390–91.

Catholicism, as well as indigenous religions. Many mixtures and crossovers occurred given that families and groups of the same ethnic origin were deliberately separated as they arrived in Brazil and were sold as slaves to the landlords to work on the field and in the mines. While they were baptized in a rudimentary way on arrival or shortly thereafter, and had to observe the religious feasts, received a very modest, if any, catechesis, and their knowledge of Christianity was far from profound. Even among most immigrants from Portugal, a popular religiosity rather than a well-informed one was in place, which developed as a strong devotion to the saints, especially St. Mary, to pilgrimages and the fulfillment of vows rather than sermons and catechizing. This popular religion, mystical and magical, was widely tolerated and prone to merge with elements of African religion, while on the surface control was in place against forms of what was considered "possession" and "witchcraft," which could be severely punished and result in being sent to the Inquisition courts in Portugal. Persecution and prosecution of African Brazilian religions as "charlatanism" and "black magic" continued well into the twentieth century. This resulted in forms of dissimulation as a means of biological and cultural survival.[28] Still today, such dissimulation is called *para inglês ver* ("for the English to see"), which refers to the "clean" appearance of Portuguese slave ships as they were met by British ships combating the slave trade by their dominion of the ocean, and tried to hide their real cargo.

We have to note that these are "reinvented" religions that emerged in stronger or looser relationship with their African origins and, therefore, contain old stories retold, remolded, and mixed with locally present religiosity—as happened, of course, throughout the over one thousand years of coming into being of what we today know and read as the Bible (not to speak of all the interpretative processes implied in its translations into the world's languages), in constant reinterpretation and growing summarization along its process of confection and its *traditio* ever since.

Two main groups were brought over by the Portuguese slave ships: the so-called Sudanese, from West Africa, today's Nigeria, Benin (formerly Dahomey), and Togo, and the so-called Bantu, from Southern Africa, namely, from today's Congo, Angola, and Moçambique. Among others, a Dahomey queen, Agontimé, was enslaved by her African enemies and sold to the Portuguese who brought her to São Luís do Maranhão in Brazil. The *terreiro*, place of worship and conviviality of the *povo-de-santo* ("people of the saint," as those belonging to African Brazilian religions are commonly known) she founded, the *Casa das Minas*, is believed to have spread worship to the gods (*voduns*) of the Dahomeyan royal family.[29]

---

28. See Westhelle, *After Heresy*.

29. Da Silva, *Candomblé e Umbanda*, 28–29; and Verger, "Uma rainha Africana."

In Brazil, local expressions thus developed, more expressively in the nineteenth century, when slaves were gaining more mobility in urban settings, could own houses (some of which came to serve as religious centers, *casas* or *terreiros*) and were able to organize in groups. Such expressions are known under different names in different regions, like *Candomblé* in Bahia, *Xangô* in Pernambuco and Alagoas, *Tambor de Mina* in Maranhão and Pará, *Batuque* in Rio Grande do Sul and *Macumba* in Rio de Janeiro.[30] The most publicly visible and most African in its rites and beliefs is the Yoruba Candomblé. In the 1920s emerged *Umbanda*, mixing elements of popular Catholicism, Kardecist Spiritualism, and Indigenous religions, using the Portuguese language in its celebrations, renouncing animal sacrifices (common in Candomblé), using alcohol and smoke (uncommon in Candomblé), and seeking contact with the dead. For this very reason, being "anthropophagic," as the modernist art movement at the time called the syncretistic and miscegenating tendency they understood to be typically Brazilian, it came to be considered by many as the Brazilian religion *par excellence*.[31]

Originally ethnic and developed by the enslaved or freed descendants of Africans, especially from the 1960s onward, African Brazilian religions universalized and incorporated persons from other than African backgrounds. In the South, many members and leaders are white and of European origin. Migrating to the large urban centers in the South and Southeast, and with a middle class searching for other than traditional (Christian) forms of spiritual experiences, they started to attract intellectuals, poets, writers, and artists. But also the poor could and can be encountered in considerable numbers. Persons marginalized in society because of their sexual orientation considered deviant are welcome and frequent in African Brazilian religions. "Candomblé does not discriminate the bandit, the adulterer, the transvestite and any type of socially rejected"; while it welcomes all of these, it does not seek to transform them by morality.[32] Adaptations (often called "syncretism"), especially celebrating the divine *orixás* [orishás] on days of Catholic saints, had been a means of survival. However, more recently, some groups have insisted on their being a religion apart from Catholicism and retrieve their languages, rites, and traditions. While transmitted orally and in private, narratives from and information on African Brazilian religions are increasingly becoming available in books, first by researchers, many of whom became initiated, like French photographer and self-studied anthropologist Pierre "Fatumbi" Verger (1902-1996), French sociologist Roger Bastide (1898-1974), interestingly both a Presbyterian and a Candomblé initiate, and Brazilian anthropologist Ordep

---

30. Prandi, *Herdeiras do Axé*, 11.

31. See Prandi, *Herdeiras do Axé*, 13.

32. Prandi, *Herdeiras do Axé*, 42.

Serra, but increasingly also by their leaders. As visible in the conflict of circular versus linear time, Candomblé is also subject to the modern world, its questioning of hitherto unchallenged seniority and its rhythm imposed by the world of work and capital.[33] It continues to "reinvent" itself and retell the story in new ways.

While there is a variety of "nations" in the African Brazilian religions, the most influential is Candomblé of Yoruba origin in West Africa, namely, today's Benin and Nigeria, that can be considered the one that most preserved narrative, initiation, and ritual elements from their original lands. The main groupings are the *nagô* (Ketu, Efan, Ijexá, Egbá, and Xambá) and the *gêgê* (Fon, Ewé, Mina, Fanti, and Ashanti). The term *Candomblé* is a Brazilian creation, the dance to the sound of the drums ("atabaques"), called *candombe* by Angolans, and *ilê,* house or place, in Yoruba. Thus, *Candomblé* is the house where one dances to the sound of drums.[34] It is generally celebrated in private houses, called *terreiros*, normally owned by the religious leader, with adequate spaces for initiation periods, cooking, celebrating, planting sacred herbs, and so on.

By the process of dislocation, relating to territorially bound ancestors became impossible, even if some of them are still remembered as *egunguns*. Instead, the emphasis fell on the *orixás,* mediating divine entities related to forces of nature and aspects of the human person and society. While in Africa there are around 400 *orixás*, only twenty are worshipped in Brazil. The *orixás* are the active divine powers, while the supreme god, Olodumaré, is distant and inactive. Rather than ethical principles, it is the relationship to the *orixás* that guides the initiates' behavior. Each initiate is the "son" or "daughter" of a specific *orixá*, but usually also influenced by a second *orixá,* often of the opposite gender. This implies duties to the *orixá*, to the *terreiro* and its spiritual leader, and to others. The world is rife with spiritual forces, highly enchanted. Such conception is the opposite of a secularized world driven by science and technology, although it has learned to coexist with it. What it retrieves, and this is important for this volume, is a deep respect for all beings in their interrelatedness, and the need for, indeed duty of caring and catering for, the relations between the worldly and the divine. In health, especially visible in these times of pandemia, it calls for a complementarity of perceptions, conceptions, and healing procedures, as advocated by some precisely in view of an "ecology of knowledge."[35]

Let us now take a deep and healthy breath and have a look at some of the founding narratives of Candomblé as these relate the world to the divine.

---

33. Prandi, "O candomblé e o tempo."

34. Cunha, *Dicionário etimológico da língua Portuguesa*, 146.

35. Da Silva, Fernandez, and Sacardo, "Towards an 'Ecology of Lore and Knowledge' in Health."

■ Gods of Creation and Their Powers

The oldest narratives speak of the divine couple Olorum ("Lord of the skies") and Olocum ("Lady of the oceans"). Similar to Apsu and Tiamat in Mesopotamic mythology—and thus with connections also to the Genesis story—Olorum represents the firmament and Olocum the abyssal ocean. Both were united in the "calabash of creation" until they decided to separate, remaining the upper part for Olorum's dominion and the lower part for Olocum's dominion, like two parts of a bowl. In the upper reign were light, winds, and atmospheric forces; in the lower reign were fog, shadows, the oceans, and their dark abyss. Olorum, the lord of the firmament, was accompanied by his sons, born from Olocum: Oxalá or Obatalá and Odudua. Beyond the sons, he was assisted by Orunmilá, the oracle; Exu, the translator and messenger; Agemo, a chameleon servant; and Etun, a mythical guinea fowl (in Portuguese: *galinha-de-angola*). In this way, myth associates Olorum to the active powers of order and destiny (Orunmilá), of language and communication (Exu), of generation and action (Obatalá and Odudua), as well as of transformation (the chameleon Agemo) and expansion (Etun).[36] Olorum's and Olocum's firstborn, Obatalá, complained about the inertia and sterility of *ocum*, the topographically inferior oceanic realm. He incites his father to create something above the primordial waters, with the interest of establishing a field for his own dominion and fruition. In this moment, when Olorum thinks about the possibility of creating, he comes to be named Olodumaré—a different, but connected name, carrying the attribute of creator.

A known version of the myth briefly refers to the Olorum-Olocum couple and describes the beginning of creation:

> In a time when the world was only Olodumaré's imagination, there merely existed the infinite firmament and, below it, the immensity of the ocean. Olorum, Lord of the Skies, and Olocum, Lady of the Oceans, were of the same age and shared the secrets of what already existed and what would come to exist. Olorum and Olocum had two sons: Oxalá, their firstborn, also called Obatalá, and Odudua, the younger one. Olorum-Olodumaré commissioned Obatalá, the Lord of the White Sheet, to create the world. He gave him powers for this. Obatalá went do consult with Orunmilá, who recommended to do offerings for the success of the mission. However, Obatalá did not take seriously Orunmilá's prescriptions, as he believed only in his own powers.[37]

---

36. There are mythological variations that attribute a creating activity to the orixá Oraniã, obeying Olodumaré's command. Researchers like Pierre Verger, Juana Elbein dos Santos and Reginaldo Prandi investigated these versions, examining their African origin, provenance and the re-elaboration that occurred in Brazil. They conclude that the various versions co-exist, each with its specific emphases, as do co-exist the different "nations" of Brazilian Candomblé. These differences show the cultural wealth of the African Brazilian tradition, without compromising the legitimacy of the orixá worship of this or that "nation." In what follows, we draw freely on what was published previously on Candomblé in Maçaneiro, *Religiões e Ecologia*, 39–52.

37. Prandi, *Mitologia dos Orixás*, 503–04. Orunmilá is the orixá of the oracle; while very important in Cuba, he is virtually forgotten in Brazil (569).

Here, we can see a reservation about Obatalá's egocentric interests as he firmly believed in his own powers, thinking he deserved all the glory of creation. This is when his brother Odudua acquires a more active role in the work:

> Odudua observed everything very attentively and that day also consulted Orunmilá. Orunmilá assured Odudua that, if he offered the prescribed sacrifices, he would be the ruler of the world that was about to be created. The offering consisted in four hundred thousand chains, a fowl with five-toed feet [*Etun*], a pigeon and a chameleon [*Agemo*], beyond four hundred thousand cowrie shells. Odudua made the offerings. When the day of the world's creation had come, Obatalá went on to the border of transcendence, where Exu is the guardian. Obatalá did not make the offerings in that place, as it had been prescribed. Exu was strongly offended by this infamy and used his powers to take revenge on Oxalá. Thus, a great thirst started to plague Obatalá. Obatalá approached a palm tree and touched its trunk with his long stick. From the palm tree flowed wine abundantly and Obatalá drank the wine until he became drunk. He was totally drunk and fell asleep on the way, in the shadow of the dendê palm tree. No one dared to wake up Obatalá.[38]

Surrounded by respect, Obatalá and Odudua are revered as real entities because they are the offspring of the original gods. The same happens, later, with the figure of Iemanjá, the preferred daughter of Olocum, ladies of the oceans. The myth continues:

> Odudua had followed everything. When he made sure Oxalá was fast asleep, Odudua took the bag of creation that had been given to Obatalá by Olorum. Odudua went to Olodumaré and told him what had happened. Olodumaré saw the bag of creation in Odudua's power and entrusted him with the world's creation. From the four hundred thousand chains Odudua made a single one and descended on it to the surface of *ocum,* the ocean. Over the endless waters, he opened the bag of creation and let fall [*from it*] a small heap of soil.

> He released the five-toed fowl and it flew over the heap, and started to clean it. The fowl [*Etun*] spread the soil over the water's surface. Odudua exclaimed in his tongue: "Ilé nfé!"—which is to say "May the land expand!," a sentence which later gave name to the city of Ifé, which is located exactly where Odudua made the world. Subsequently, Odudua took the chameleon [*Agemo*] and made him walk over that surface, demonstrating, in this way, the firmness of the place. Obatalá continued asleep. Odudua left for the land to be its owner.[39]

In other versions, Oxalá is seen as the realizer of creation on command of his father Olorum-Olodumaré, without referring to his younger brother. The elements of water or abyssal ocean, of the land, and of mythical animals (guinea fowl and chameleon) are repeated in another version, with an analogous function. The narrative further describes the awakening of Oxalá-Obatalá who creates, finally, all living beings and humans:

---

38. Prandi, *Mitologia dos Orixás*, 504.

39. Prandi, *Mitologia dos Orixás*, 505.

> And so Obatalá created all living beings and created man and created woman. Obatalá modelled in clay the human beings and the breath of Olodumaré gave them life. The world was now complete. And all praised Obatalá.[40]

As one can see, there are similarities to the Genesis narrative, as well as between the Babylonian couple Apsu-Tiamat and Olorum-Olocum. It is possible that the Yoruba of the interior, moving along the rivers and commercial routes, received some influence from Semitic people that circulated between Sudan (in the North) and Abyssinia (in the South). In any case, there are a number of archetypical elements that indicate a profound connection between the land, the sky and humanity, a connection that reveals in vital elements (humus, water, breath) and in the creative ability of gods and humans (modeling, pottery, weaving, agriculture, and stock farming). The chameleon relates to the forests; the guinea fowl was a food source, domesticated in the villages' neighborhoods; the cowrie shells were gathered on the beaches during fishing activities. Without any genealogy that would explain their origin, the fowl and the chameleon are mythical entities, attributed to the mysterious divine power that operates in "time before time," before the "days and nights" of the world's creation. All this moves, in daily life as well as in the original imaginary of Candomblé, between the sky and the abyssal ocean. Both were considered infinite by mythology and defined the primordial dual order: the superior infinite, heavenly, and male (*orum*); the inferior infinite, aquatic, and female (*ocum*), each with its sovereign divinity, forming a sacred couple in a creative *coniunctio*.

Candomblé's worldview can be summarized in five specific aspects: (1) The universe is divided into two constitutive and original levels, the physical (*aiyê*) and the metaphysical (*orum*). *Orum* is an abstract concept and should not be conceived as something localized within the material world. Every being possesses a spiritual and abstract *double* in the *orum*. (2) With the separation between *orum* and *aiyê* which came about, according to some myths, by the human violation of an interdict emerged the *sanmô* (sky-atmosphere). The *ofofurú* (divine breath) separated the two levels of existence. (3) Thus, two polarities emerged: *aiyê* and *orum*, immanence and transcendence we could say, and *ilê* and *sanmô*, the earth and the sky. (4) Olodumaré irradiates the primordial energy that makes the existence of living beings possible, the *axé*. Its power is, in creation, symbolized by the "bag of creation" (that contained the clay, the fowl, and the chameleon). The irradiation of *axé* brings with it *obá*—objective, meaning, or direction that accompanies the creative energy. Both guarantee the location and movement of each being in the cosmos. (5) Candomblé does not propose a land, nor an ecology, without humanity. Free will enables the human being to intervene in the created order, for the good or for the bad. On the other hand, Candomblé is a mythical and magical rather

---

40. Prandi, *Mitologia dos Orixás*, 506.

than an ethical religion that does not operate with notions of salvation, corruption, or sin, but rather with equilibrium that, whenever broken, has to be reestablished through the appeasement of the enraged deity that creates a duty for the offender. The world with all it contains is not denied—neither the body, nor sexuality, nor food, nor the environment. Senses and intelligence are focused on the concrete interference of the supernatural in *this world* through the manipulation of sacred forces. It is this attitude and cosmovision that has been inherited and transformed by Brazilian neo-Pentecostalism that re-exports itself to Africa and the world today, even if seeing Africa as the cradle of "evil" rather than valuing this heritage—discourse and fact speak very different languages here.[41]

■ The Orixás and Nature

For the African Brazilian religions, the space between the material world (*aiyê*) and the spiritual world (*orum*) is occupied by the many *orixás*. The word refers to "sovereign" (*xá*) and to the mind or hair of humans (*ori*), by which the *orixá* takes possession of the initiate and "rides" him or her like a horse in the state of trance. Every *orixá* has his or her own personality reflected in the character of the initiate it possesses as well as in the specific worship that is due.[42] In our perception, the characteristics of the *orixás* can be summarized in three movements[43]:

> (a) *Animic:* Spiritual life is attributed to natural elements and manifestations, with "the belief that every object in the world in which we live is endowed with a spirit."[44] Clay, stones, and hills; the air or impetuous wind; the sky with the stars, the sun, and the thunders; the forest, the palm tree, and the healing leaves; the various rivers, fountains, and lakes—each one of them possesses an *animus* that gives it movement and temperament.

> (b) *Zoetic or vital*: Spiritual elements are associated to abilities and the chores necessary for life in terms of the tribe's survival and well-being. There we find sowing, cultivating, and harvesting related to earth, water, and the sun; pottery, related to earth, water, and fire; the knowledge of medicinal roots and herbs, related to the forest, palm tree, and leaves; the fabrication of metal artifacts, related to the soil, stones, and fire; the localization of sources and the success in fishing and navigation, related to water; and the hunting of animals. These practices have a functional and symbolic importance: they are useful for the survival of generations (*bios*) and express the improvement of the human spirit, capable of situating in the

---

41. See Von Sinner, "Struggling with Africa."

42. See the book by the Candomblé leader Barcellos, *Os orixás e a personalidade humana*.

43. This is our own attempt to comprehend and didactically expose the phenomenon. For other views of the orixás see Carneiro, *Candomblés da Bahia*, especially the general introduction and Chapter IV; and also Dos Santos. *Religiões de matrizes africanas*, 30–41.

44. Prandi, *Os orixás e a natureza*, 3.

world and orienting toward the future (*zoé*).⁴⁵ Thus, the *animus* acquires abilities related to its identifying element, and this gives origin to rites that celebrate or reproduce planting, hunting, the manipulation of herbs, the use of water, protection during storms, the handling of fire and metals, and the like.

(c) *Memorial*: This aspect arose when worship to the *orixás* merged with ancestor worship: the memorable ancestors (patriarchs, hunters, kings, potters, diviners, priests, messengers, blacksmiths, fishermen, and healers) became understood as *orixás* characterized by their specific actions or knowledge.⁴⁶

We can note that these dimensions do not follow upon each other in a separate or sequential mode, as it could appear, but had a complex development from the African birthplace to their configuration in Brazilian Candomblé. The identity and attributions of each *orixá* established along the centuries in a process of preservation and re-edition of ancient stories assimilated by African mythical rationality and continually rememorated in the rites and orality of teaching. As stated above, from a collective of over four hundred, about twenty-two *orixás* are worshipped in Brazil, and among them, eleven stand out: Exu, Ogum, Oxóssi, Obaluaiê, Ossaim, Oxumaré, Xangô, Oxum, Iemanjá, Iansã, and Oxalá—the king *orixá*, firstborn to Olorum—the supreme deity. Each one of them has his or her own genealogy and symbolic evolution, with central mythological nuclei and peripheral variants, where we can see many traces of the three dimensions stated above, the animic, zoetic, and memorial. Behind all of them is Olorum—deity of the skies—called Olodumaré when he is worshipped as the creator and maintainer of the vital force (*axé*), the principle of cosmic harmony:

> We live in a universe that is alive, where life is incessantly pulsing. This universe was created by Olodumaré, the unique Spirit that rules creation. Latent life in the rocks, the life that flows in the plants, life that pulses in human and other living beings, that is, in all forms of life, emanate from one unique source; therefore, all is and all are, fundamentally, one single life in Olodumaré, who commanded the *orixás* to concretize the creation which in Him, Olodumaré, already existed.
>
> If the basis that sustains all real existence were not one only, we, living beings, would have to live in a chaotic world, where diverse and contradictory forces would act separately and without direction. And if the living beings had emerged from completely different origins, and not from Olodumaré through the *orixás*, no understanding between them would be possible and they would have to live in eternal disharmony, because there would be no way to transform it by modification of the chaos in harmony. The vital force that constitutes the basis of the universe and of all of nature is one and only.⁴⁷

---

45. We use *bios* to designate biological generation, while *zoé* signifies life in its plenitude of meaning and transcendence.

46. See Prandi, *Os orixás e a natureza*, 2–5.

47. Dos Santos, *Religiões de Matrizes Africanas*, 32.

After creating the world in four days, which is the African week, Olorum-Olodumaré established an alliance with humanity, symbolized in the rainbow, and retired to the heights of the *orum,* the heavens. He entrusted, thus, the administration of the world to the *orixás* that move between the physical (*aiyé*) and the metaphysical world (*orum*). The eleven main *orixás* behave like "intelligent forces of nature"[48] and "governing spiritual entities."[49] While "intelligent forces of nature" relate to the cosmos, identifying ritually with natural elements and manifestations, "governing spiritual entities" relate to persons as archetypes of human personality.

As they are complex personalities, the *orixás* enable multiple classifications, as to their genealogy, color, gender, day of worship, and ritualistic menu. Their main identification, however, consists in the relationship of each one with nature. The *orixás* can be related to the four classical elements of nature—earth, water, fire, and air—indicating, in this way, their field of action.[50]

Among the worshipped *orixás,* Prandi emphasizes the growing value attributed to Onilé, a female *orixá* identified with Mother Earth. Nearly forgotten in popular Candomblé, Onilé's role is "slowly being retrieved" in the context of "a return to the natural world and the preoccupation with ecology."[51] Onilé, composed of *on* (lady) and *ilé* (house of the world), daughter of the creator, Olodumaré, "represents our planet as a whole; its myth can be encountered in many poems of the Ifá oracle, which is alive still today in Brazil in the memory of elders of Candomblé that were initiated many decades ago."[52] She is strong, but discrete, living in the center of the Earth, whence life flourishes with all its energy. The myth says that one day Olodumaré invited the orixás for a feast, to which they all came, luxuriously dressed: Iemanjá with pearls and corals, Oxóssi with animal skin, Ogum with golden armory, Oxalá with finest cotton, Ossaim with perfumed herbs, etc. Olodumaré then announced he would entrust the rule of the Earth to one of the orixás, this being the reason why they all were invited to the feast. But he was looking for a signal: he would entrust the Earth to the orixá that was clothed with earth itself. This was when he chose Onilé, whose presence had barely been noticed because she was clothed with earth, with earth taken from the soil, near the roots and subterranean mines. Olodumaré chose her and said that all the orixás were to honor Onilé, "because all is on Earth:

---

48. Ligiero, *Iniciação ao Candomblé,* 43.

49. Da Silva, *Candomblé e Umbanda,* 68.

50. As suggested by Ligiero in his book *Iniciação ao Candomblé,* 46–47. On the elements, see also Hobgood and Bauman, *The Bloomsbury Handbook of Religion and Nature.*

51. Prandi, *Os orixás e a natureza,* 7.

52. Prandi, *Os orixás e a natureza,* 7.

the sea and the rivers, the iron and the gold, the animals and the plants: everything."[53]

The animic vision present in the emergence of *orixá* worship endured and has consolidated, in Candomblé, the bond between religion and nature. This bond is not only notional (based on a philosophical explication of the world), but elementary (based on the identification or personification of the *orixás* with elements of nature). More than a philosophy, we have here a quite peculiar metaphysics, of African origin, orally transmitted and open to continued reinterpretations.[54]

As a whole, the *orixás* constitute a mythical version of biodiversity. In Candomblé, to keep nature alive is to keep religion alive; to keep religion alive is to keep nature alive. Thus, life is preserved. There is a current affirmation in Candomblé that says: *kosi ewé, kosi orisa*—"no leaf, no life."[55] The relationship between religion and nature shows itself in the details of the ritual: every *orixá* requires the adequate elements of nature and food to translate his or her function and place in the cosmos. For this reason, Candomblé has developed its own peculiar liturgical, alimentary, and therapeutical care: the cultivation of leaves and herbs, the treatment of cereals, the preparation of food, the preservation of forests, the hygiene in the ritual use of animals, and knowledge of natural medicine. In this way, the mythology of the *orixás* constitutes a great source of wisdom in engaging with nature symbolically and practically. On the one hand, it both preserves and dynamizes traditional religious values. On the other hand, it is a precious ecophantic record; it registers the ecological knowledge of African cultures, produces material that is useful for environmental education, and fosters sustainable practices.[56]

■ Concluding Remarks

As indicated in the introduction, we first intended to listen to the stories that have been suppressed, but are now more and more emerging. We need to listen to them, acknowledging that they are genuine and serious stories about God, the world, and humanity. Humans in the ancestral and Latin cultures of the Andes and the African Brazilian cultures affirm themselves as pilgrim and interpreter: they do not only walk, but they walk *interpreting*, as hermeneutist

---

53. Prandi, *Os orixás e a natureza*, 8.

54. See Barcellos, *Os Orixás e o segredo da vida*; and Botas, *Carne do Sagrado*. Reginaldo Prandi wrote a novel, illustrated by artist Joana Lira, that counts a creation story in the dream of a young African mother in a slave ship. As the African sets over to Brazil, symbolically the African myths become Brazilian. The myths are real narratives, while the main person of the novel is fictional: *Contos e Lendas afro-brasileiros*.

55. See Gomes and Catalão, *Kosi ewe kosi orisa*, 1857-77.

56. Verger points in this direction in *Orixás*; see also Soares, *Interfaces da Revelação*, 215-37; and Prandi, *Segredos guardados*.

of the world, of themselves and the Holy. They have ancient roots, but have adapted throughout history to dislocations, threats, and challenges of the new times. Just like Christian theology, they are constantly forced to reinterpret their foundational stories, and more and more specific hermeneutics to that are described explicitly in Afrotheology, a theology from Santo Daime, a spiritualist theology, an Umbandist theology, some of which now have state accredited bachelors courses in theology.[57] Just like the Judeo-Christian tradition, they register—orally, ritually, and sometimes also in writing—and pass on memory that guards meaning, orients the present, and opens the future. It is a dynamic memory, made *in via*, as the mystics would say, in the rhythm of the time that passes, the stations that succeed each other, births and deaths, harvests and migrations. In theological terms, this interpreting walk designs a map, an itinerary, full of *pneumatopoi*, places of the Spirit, where humans, within their culture, can find, register, and interpret creation and revelation by the divine in whose perspective they live life and find happiness.

This all is, thus, an enriching reminder that "God was present before the missionary."[58] The story of God's presence in the world, in nature, and in humanity did not begin to be told only from Columbus's and the conquerors' arrival on the continent. Indeed, it might go back up to twelve thousand years. During all these years, nomadic, agricultural, and city cultures were developed well before Europeans brought what they believed to be "civilization" and "true religion" (making sure it was not Protestant).

Such divine presence bears a character of source and fecundity (God-Father-Principle), of communication and interpretation (God-Son-Word). Even if there is no explicit Trinity, much less a Trinitarian doctrine, indigenous, and African Brazilian (and other African American) experiences and stories can be seen by Christians through a Trinitarian lens by which we can recognize the mysterious, eloquent, loving, and fruitful presence of Father, Son and Holy Spirit. While less in a mode of a prophetic discourse, there is a sapiential discourse focused on the search for the good, the beautiful, the true, and the just, in a convivial wisdom of practical and ethical consequence and theological and ecological significance.

These tendencies are, in fact, not new to the biblical and subsequent Christian tradition. However, it is in the "Christian West" that a strong distinction between humanity and the Earth most prospered and where the insertion of the human being into the universe's story was most lost. The insistence on salvation from sin still has its meaningful story to tell, but might leave us blind for the issue of good life in the midst of and within the whole of creation in its

---

57. See Silveira and Bobsin, "Afroteontologia"; and Vicentini, *A Teologia do Santo Daime*.

58. See Boff, *Christianity in a Nutshell*.

diversity and plurality. Interrelatedness rather than dualism, conviviality (*convivência,* in Portuguese)[59] rather than mere coexistence, indigenous and African Brazilian knowledge helps Christian theology to rediscover the connection of humanity to the Earth and, indeed, the universe as the place of the creator God's revelation. While the story of the divine creator and sustainer, the human steward of creation and all forces in between work as a critical mirror on human destruction of and detachment from the Earth, they also impel us to (re-)earth the faith.

■ Bibliography

Acosta, Alberto. *O bem viver: Uma oportunidade para imaginar outros mundos.* São Paulo: Autonomia Literária; Elefante, 2016.

Barcellos, Mario Cesar. *Os orixás e a personalidade humana.* 5th ed. Rio de Janeiro: Pallas, 2019.

———. *Os Orixás e o segredo da vida—lógica, mitologia e ecologia.* 4th ed. Rio de Janeiro: Pallas, 2005.

Boff, Leonardo. *Christianity in a Nutshell.* Maryknoll: Orbis, 2013.

Botas, Paulo. *Carne do sagrado—Edun ara: devaneios sobre a espiritualidade dos orixás.* Petrópolis: Vozes; Rio de Janeiro: Koinonia, 1996.

Caero, Victor Bascopé. "Terra e água: A vida no seio da *Pachamama.*" In *Nosso planeta—nossa vida: Ecologia e Teologia,* edited by Luiz Carlos Susin and Joe Marçal G. dos Santos, 175-81, São Paulo: Paulinas, 2011.

Carneiro, Edison. *Candomblés da Bahia.* Rio de Janeiro: Edições de Ouro, no date.

Chuji, Mónica, Grimaldo Rengifo and Eduardo Gudynas. "Buen Vivir." In *Pluriverse: A Post-Development Dictionary*, edited by Ashish Kotari, et al., 111-14. New Delhi: Tulika Books, 2019.

Conradie, Ernst M. *Secular Discourse on Sin in the Anthropocene: What's Wrong with the World?* Lanham: Lexington, 2020.

Cunha, Antônio Geraldo da. "Candomblé." *Dicionário etimológico da língua portuguesa*, 146, 2nd ed. Rio de Janeiro: Nova Fronteira, 1982.

Da Silva, Rafael Afonso, Juan Carlos Aneiros Fernandez and Daniele Pompei Sacardo. "Towards an 'Ecology of Lore and Knowledge' in Health: An Invitation from the Terreiros to Dialogue." *Interface* 21:63 (2017), 921-31. https://doi.org/10.1590/1807-57622016.0180

Da Silva, Vagner Gonçalves. *Candomblé e Umbanda: Caminhos da Devoção Brasileira.* 5th ed. São Paulo: Selo Negro, 2005.

Dos Santos, Edson Fabiano. *Religiões de matrizes africanas.* Rio de Janeiro: CEAP, 2007.

Dussel, Enrique. "Meditações Anticartesianas sobre a origem do antidiscurso filosófico da modernidade." In *Epistemologias do Sul*, edited by Boaventura de Sousa Santos and Maria Paula Meneses, 341-95. São Paulo: Cortez, 2010.

Eco, Umberto. *Die Suche nach einer vollkommenen Sprache.* 2nd ed. München: Beck, 1994.

Estermann, Josef. *Apu Taytayku: Religion und Theologie im andinen Kontext Lateinamerikas.* Mainz: Grünewald, 2012.

———. *Filosofia andina: Sabiduria indígena para un mundo nuevo.* La Paz: ISEAT, 2006.

———. *Teologia andina: El tejido diverso de la fe indígena.* 2 vols. La Paz: ISEAT, 2006.

Fatheuer, Thomas. *Buen Vivir. A Brief Introduction to Latin America's New Concepts for the Good Life and the Rights of Nature.* Berlin: Heinrich Böll Foundation, 2011.

---

59. See Von Sinner, "Trust and *convivência*"; and Sundermeier, "Konvivenz als Grundstruktur," especially 51-59 on the origin of the term in Latin America.

Flores, Lúcio Paiva. "Bem Viver na criação: Viver bem com o outro, com a natureza e com o Criador." In *O Bem Viver na Criação*, edited by Cledes Markus and Renate Gierus, 11–18. São Leopoldo: Oikos, 2013.

Gebara, Ivone. "The Christian Story of God's Work: A Brazilian Response." In *T&T Clark Handbook on Christian Theology and Climate Change*, edited by Ernst M. Conradie and Hilda P. Koster, 467–73. London and New York: T. & T. Clark, 2020.

Gomes, Verônica da Silva and Vera M. Lessa Catalão. "*Kosi ewe, kosi orisa*: Vivências ecológicas em um terreiro de Candomblé." *Revista AmbientalMente Sustentable* 10:2 (2015), 1857–77.

Hobgood, Laura and Whitney Bauman, eds. *The Bloomsbury Handbook of Religion and Nature: The Elements.* London, et al.: Bloomsbury Academic, 2018.

Issberner, Liz-Rejane and Philippe Léna, eds. *Brazil in the Anthropocene: Conflicts between Predatory Development and Environmental Politics*. Abingdon and New York: Routledge, 2017.

Ligiero, Zeca. *Iniciação ao Candomblé.* São Paulo: Nova Era, 1993.

Maçaneiro, Marcial. *Religiões e ecologia. Cosmovisão—valores—tarefas.* 2nd ed. São Paulo: Paulinas, 2011.

Marquardt, Jens. "Worlds Apart? The Global South and the Anthropocene." In *The Anthropocene Debate and Political Science*, edited by Thomas Hickmann and Lena Partzsch, 200–18. London: Routledge, 2018.

Prandi, Reginaldo. *Contos e Lendas afro-brasileiros: A Criação do Mundo.* São Paulo: Companhia das Letras, 2007.

———. *Herdeiras do Axé: Sociologia das religiões afro-brasileiras.* São Paulo: Hucitec, 1996.

———. *Mitologia dos Orixás*. São Paulo: Companhia das Letras, 2001.

———. "O Candomblé e o tempo: Concepções de tempo, saber e autoridade da África para as religiões afro-brasileiras." *Revista Brasileira de Ciências Sociais* 16:47 (2001), 43–58. https://doi.org/10.1590/S0102-69092001000300003

———. *Os orixás e a natureza*. http://reginaldoprandi.fflch.usp.br/sites/reginaldoprandi.fflch.usp.br/files/inline-files/Os%20orixas%20e%20a%20natureza.pdf, accessed 22 January 2021.

———. *Segredos guardados: Orixás na alma brasileira*. São Paulo: Companhia das Letras, 2005.

Ramose, Mogobe B. "Globalização e *Ubuntu*." In *Epistemologias do Sul*, edited by Boaventura de Sousa Santos and Maria Paula Meneses, 175–220. São Paulo: Cortez, 2010

Ritschl, Dietrich and Martin Hailer. *Grundkurs Christliche Theologie: Diesseits und jenseits der Worte.* 3rd ed. Neukirchen-Vluyn: Neukirchener, 2010.

Santos, Boaventura de Sousa. *Epistemologies of the South: Justice against Epistemicide.* London and New York: Routledge, 2016.

———. *The End of the Cognitive Empire*. Durham and London: Duke University Press, 2018.

Silveira, Hendrix and Oneide Bobsin. "Afroteontologia: estudo sobre Deus Segundo a cosmopercepção das tradições de matriz africana." *Estudos Teológicos* 63:3 (2020), 839–50. https://doi.org/10.22351/et.v60i3.4023

Soares, Afonso M. L. *Interfaces da Revelação*. São Paulo: Paulinas, 2003.

Stromquist, Nelly P. "In Search of the Good Life: Promises and Challenges of *Buen Vivir* for Knowledge, Education and Gender." In *Educational Alternatives in Latin America: New Modes of Counterhegemonic Learning*, edited by Robert Aman and Timothy Ireland, 39–62. London: Palgrave Macmillan, 2019.

Sundermeier, Theo. "Konvivenz als Grundstruktur ökumenischer Existenz." In *Ökumenische Existenz heute*, coauthored by Wolfgang Huber, Dietrich Ritschl and Theo Sundermeier, 49–100. München: Chr. Kaiser, 1986.

Valiani, Salimah. "*Sumak kawsay* beyond Latin America: A Proposal for Debate and Action in South Africa." *Cuadernos de Economia Crítica* 6:12 (2020), 155–65.

Verger, Pierre. *Orixás*. Salvador: Corrupio, 1981.

———. "Uma rainha africana mãe-de-santo em São Luís," *Revista USP* 6 (1990), 151–58. https://doi.org/10.11606/issn.2316-9036.v0i6p151-158

Vicentini, Amanda. *A Teologia do Santo Daime na Perspectiva de uma Teologia Pública*. Master's thesis, Pontifical Catholic University of Paraná, 2021.

Villalba, Unai. "Buen Vivir vs. Development: A Paradigm Shift in the Andes?" *Third World Quarterly* 34:8 (2013), 1427–42. https://doi.org/10.1080/01436597.2013.831594

Von Sinner, Rudolf. "'Struggling with Africa': Theology of Prosperity in and from Brazil." In *Pastures of Plenty: Tracing Religio-Scapes of Prosperity Theologies in Africa and Beyond*, edited by Andreas Heuser, 117–30. Frankfurt: Peter Lang, 2015.

———. *The Churches and Democracy in Brazil: Towards a Public Theology Focused on Citizenship*. Eugene: Wipf & Stock, 2012.

———. "Trust and *Convivência*. Contributions to a Hermeneutics of Trust in Communal Interaction." *The Ecumenical Review* 57:3 (2005), 322–41. https://doi.org/10.1111/j.1758-6623.2005.tb00554.x

Westhelle, Vítor. *After Heresy. Colonial Practices and Post-Colonial Theologies*. Eugene: Cascade, 2010.

———. "Working with Lutheran forms of Christianity." In *T&T Clark Handbook on Christian Theology and Climate Change*, edited by Ernst M. Conradie and Hilda P. Koster, 277–87. London: T. & T. Clark, 2020.

The Decolonial Imperative in African Ecotheology: A Zambian Perspective

Teddy C. Sakupapa[1]

■ Introduction

There is no denying that the contemporary ecological crisis poses a threat to various forms of life on earth and in that regard to the future of the earth. Global warming, the loss of biodiversity, climate change and rising sea levels characterize the environmental degradation of our times. In the southern African context, data on observable effects of climate change on water resources, agricultural production, ecosystems, human health, and population movement illustrate the gravity of the problem of climate change. Like many other sub-Saharan African countries, Zambia is among the most vulnerable to the impacts of climate change[2] and continues to grapple with the environmental impact of large-scale mining. The argument by South African theologian Ernst Conradie that ecotheology may

---

1. Teddy Chalwe Sakupapa is a Senior Lecturer in the Department of Religion and Theology at the University of the Western Cape in South Africa.

2. Niang et al., "Africa Climate Change," 1199.

> **How to cite:** Sakupapa, T.C., 2021, 'The Decolonial Imperative in African Ecotheology: A Zambian Perspective', in E.M. Conradie & P.-C. Lai (eds.), *Taking a deep breath for the story to begin . . .* (An Earthed Faith: Telling the Story amid the "Anthropocene" Volume 1), pp. 205–224, AOSIS, Cape Town. https://doi.org/10.4102/aosis.2021.BK264.10

"be regarded as a next wave of contextual theology"[3] rings true in many African contexts amid various readings of our time as the "Anthropocene." In this essay, I will engage with the question posed by the editors of this volume, namely, how does the story (as told by Christians) of who the Triune God is and what this God does relate to the story of life on Earth? To address this question, I will argue for a decolonial imperative in African ecotheology. As an African theologian, I am interested in the possible connections or not, that may be made between the claims and narratives of the "Anthropocene" and African discourse on ecotheology. This is crucial not least because the "Anthropocene" narrative is undoubtedly a powerful narrative of human resource exploitation, albeit one that must be subjected to decolonial critique.

The essay is structured in four main sections. The first section describes the Zambian context which is the focus of my theological analysis in this essay. This will be followed by a discussion of African ecotheological contributions with respect to Zambia. The third section will entail a discussion of the "Anthropocene" narrative and problematize the apparent collapsing of humanity into a vague "us" in narratives of the "Anthropocene." I will then argue that African theological engagement with the narratives of the "Anthropocene" needs to be a cautious one, not least because of decolonial critiques on the concept.

■ Christianity and Ecology in Zambia

The southern African nation of Zambia is a religiously pluralist country albeit predominantly Christian, partly as a legacy of nineteenth-century missionary movement and more recently of the rapid expansion of charismatic and Pentecostal Christianities. The contemporary Christian configuration in Zambia is thus best described as a mosaic of various Christian expressions. Nevertheless, the contemporary landscape of Christianity in Zambia is characterized by widespread Pentecostalization and charismatization of Christianity. These transformations of Christianity have accentuated the public nature of the Christian religion and have been a subject of scholarly attention with respect to relationships between "religion and development" and "religion and politics." However, there seems to be a lack of ecological consciousness in the increasingly charismatized and Pentecostalized forms of Christianity in Zambia, as is the case elsewhere in Africa. As Ezra Chitando observes with reference to Zimbabwean Pentecostal churches, Pentecostal churches espouse triumphalist theologies that "baptize greed and rapaciousness" and are associated with "the promise of wealth, conspicuous consumption, and the quest to be integrated into the wasteful global economy."[4] This essay calls

---

3. Conradie, "Towards an Ecological Biblical Hermeneutics," 126.

4. Chitando, "Praying for Courage," 431.

attention to the relationship between religion and ecology in Zambia with reference to the ecumenical churches and theological discourse in this regard. In recent years, there has been a substantial increase in the non-theological literature on climate change in Zambia. This is a relatively new development as much of the literature on environmental issues before the 2000s tended to focus on discourse on the environmental impact of the mining industry. Such a focus is understandable given that the mining sector is a pillar of Zambia's economy and accounts for nearly 77% of Zambia's total exports.

Research on the occupational and environmental effects of mining in Zambia indicates that mine workers, "residents in mining townships and the fauna and flora of surrounding communities," are subjected to environmental exposures of mining air-borne pollutants.[5] While the emissions of carbon dioxide from the mines have been reduced owing in part to regulatory requirements of Zambia's environmental law and the work of the Zambia Environmental Management Agency, the environmental impact of mining on local human communities, wildlife, land, and rivers remain a key issue in Zambia. This is not least because of a variety of constraints within the regulatory frameworks and institutions which have resulted in challenges to address environmental issues sustainably, despite the existence of impressive laws.[6] Other environmental problems arising from mining relates to waste rocks and the storage of mining tailings around mine locations which are hazardous for human health and the environment. In the central province town of Kabwe, a century of lead pollution from mines has earned this town a place on the list of the most polluted places in the world. Beyond the focus on mining, significant non-theological research has emerged focusing on climate change. The severe drought that Zambia experienced in 1992 can be seen as a significant turning point not only in terms of scholarly research on climate change but also in institutional changes in government—which subsequently led to policy development and the establishment of coordinating bodies. Nevertheless, the effects of climate change in Zambia such as accelerated land degradation, severe weather events in the form of floods and droughts, the drying of streams and rivers, increase in the deaths of wild animals, and increased food insecurity[7] reach further back.

---

5. Mwaanga et al., "Preliminary Review," 7.

6. Shinn, "The Environmental Impact," 46.

7. Chilufya, *Can Sustainable Agriculture*, 5–6.

■ An Ecumenical Paradigm of Advocacy

The Zambian churches' engagement with the ecological crisis has often operated within an ecumenical paradigm of advocacy in which churches seek to realize Christian responsibility by directly influencing government policy and actions on environmental issues through press statements and communiques. An example of this was a communiqué issued by the Zambia Episcopal Conference (presently known as the Zambia Conference of Catholic Bishops [ZCCB]) following its Conference on Laudato Si' in April 2016. The communiqué highlighted the "need for prudent and sustainable management of the earth's resources to reduce poverty among the people for the benefit of all and future generations" and called on the government to implement policies that protect the environment.[8] Such an approach tends to focus on ecojustice issues. More recently, Fr. Cleophas Lungu, the Secretary General of the ZCCB, called on the Zambian government "to do things that are not only politically correct but ecologically correct" by:

> [. . .] prioritizing programs that critically address impacts felt by us all, particularly the poorest amongst us, the vulnerable, the marginalized and those that live in remote communities whose cry on this earth cannot be overlooked.[9]

Similarly, within the Council of Churches in Zambia (CCZ), an ecumenical body comprising of mainly historic mission churches, programs on ecological issues have tended to focus on corporate actors. This takes the form of critiques of institutionalized practices of the state, particularly with regard to what is seen as exclusionary decision-making processes on matters that affect communities. This ecumenical political paradigm is crucial not least because of the politics of aid in the climate change agenda[10] in general and the politics of climate change adaptation in particular, of which the Zambian government's engagement with climate change is not an exception. The CCZ has thus issued several statements in which it calls for ecojustice with respect to environmental impact of mining among others. In this ecumenical paradigm, ecojustice and social justice are inseparable. As Conradie argues, environmental degradation is "not a separate concern from poverty, deprivation and economic exploitation, but often a manifestation thereof."[11] At a deeper level of analysis, the environmental and ecological challenges facing Zambian communities reveal what Werner has described as the "intersectionality of economic injustice, environmental destruction, bad governance and unlimited power

---

8. Zambia Episcopal Conference, "Communiqué on the 'Laudato Si'."

9. Association for Catholic Information in Africa.

10. Funder et al., "The Climate Change Agenda in Zambia," 23–28.

11. Conradie, *Christianity and Ecological Theology*, 24.

of external transnational corporations."[12] Undoubtedly, environmental consciousness is thus slowly becoming an economic and political issue.[13]

The above ecumenical paradigm of advocacy is but one way in which religious resources are brought to bear on ecological issues. Following Gerrie Ter Haar, I will use the phrase "religious resources" to refer to four aspects, namely, "religious ideas (beliefs); religious practices (ritual behavior); religious organizations; and religious experience."[14] The ecumenical paradigm described above may well be understood in terms of how religious organizations (networks) help facilitate religious social capital and mobilize collective social action on the basis of religious moral authority. However, a limitation of the ecumenical paradigm is that it does not seem to sufficiently engage with the unique practices of the church nor the local ecological wisdom of its members.[15] To illustrate the former, in the CCZ Training Manual on "Climate Change Adaptation, Mitigation and Resilience," there is no single reference to the Bible, spirituality, or even Christianity.[16] An attempt to tap into religious ideas (theological) and local ecological wisdom is taken up in the constructive theological reflections of a number of Zambian scholars.[17] I will return to this toward the end of the essay. Suffice it to note here that the role of religious ideas in shaping how Africans think about the world is well underscored in the broader literature on the public role of religion in Africa. In this vein, Ellis and Ter Haar argue that these religious ideas also provide Africans with a "means of becoming social and political actors."[18]

In the Zambian context, as elsewhere in Africa, an exploration of the role of African Christianity in addressing the ecological crisis also calls for scrutiny of the legacy of missionary Christianity in the shaping, deforming, and disenchantment of African religious imaginaries. This is not least because of the colonial missionary denigration of African religiosity but also the cognate issue of Christianity's entaglement with the historical dynamics that gave rise to climate change. This necessarily has to do with how the continuities and discontinuities between African traditional religion (ATR) and the Christian message are treated in contemporary ecotheology in Africa. Without

---

12. Werner, "The Challenge of Environment and Climate Justice," 54.

13. Kaoma, "Towards an African Theological Ethic," 1.

14. Ter Haar, "Religion and Development," 8.

15. There is a slight nuance within the Roman Catholic Church in Zambia given a number of theologically rich resources on ecology produced by the Jesuit Centre for Theological reflection.

16. See "Climate Change Adaptation, Mitigation and Resilience Training Manual: A Training manual prepared for the Council of Churches in Zambia."

17. See Kaoma, "Towards an African Theological Ethic"; Sakupapa, "Spirit and Ecology"; Nalwamba, "Mupasi as cosmic s (S) pirit"; and Kaunda, "Towards an African Ecogender Theology."

18. Ellis and Ter Haar, *Worlds of Power*, 2.

rehearsing the African theological debates of the twentieth century which were aimed at "clarifying the nature and meaning of African Christian identity,"[19] some contemporary voices in African theology argue that the decolonization of theology in Africa is unfinished business. In this vein, I have argued elsewhere for a view of decoloniality as methodological necessity in the contemporary African context. This would entail "delinking from hegemonic western theology and nurturing critical attitudes toward monolithic understandings of the Christian tradition" by taking seriously the "grassroots" experiences of African Christians.[20] One would therefore argue that a closer analysis of African ecotheology reveals what I would describe as a decolonial imperative, that is, a self-consciously contextual engagement with both the Christian resources and the local epistemologies. The latter finds expression in various ways but most commonly through diverse narratives that reflect African beliefs about the divine, the human–nature relationship and the place of humanity in the world. Narrative, as a basic form of human expression, is of course ubiquitous. This is succinctly illustrated by Roland Barthes as follows:

> Able to be carried by articulated language, spoken or written, fixed or moving images, gestures, and the ordered mixture of all these substances; narrative is present in myth, legend, fable, tale, novella, epic, history, tragedy, drama, comedy, mime, painting [. . .], stained glass windows, cinema, comics, news item, conversation.[21]

As I will illustrate in what follows, African ecotheologies are epistemological narratives insofar as the stories that respective theologians convey in writing are about the social worlds they research. Understood in this way, African ecotheology can be said to constitute a second-order narrative.

■ The Decolonial Imperative in African Ecotheology

The legacy of (Western) Christianity in projecting human superiority rooted in (Christian) theological anthropology has long been a subject of ecological critique as encapsulated in the well-known thesis by historian Lynn White. Describing Christianity as the "the most anthropocentric religion the world has seen," White concluded that Christianity bears a huge burden of guilt for the ecological crisis.[22] White's thesis was nevertheless overly generalized in putting the blame for ecological crisis on Christianity. As many have argued, the Christian biblical witness to the relationship between humans and nature cannot be reduced to the *dominium terrae* tradition since it does contain

---

19. Bediako, "Understanding African Theology," 15.

20. Sakupapa, "The Decolonising Content," 420.

21. Barthes, "Introduction to the Structural Analysis of Narratives," 79.

22. White, "The Historic Roots of Our Ecologic Crisis," 1205.

ecological wisdom. The issue, therefore, is about the ecological ambiguity of Christianity. As Conradie argues, it "simply cannot be denied that the technological control over nature ... by human beings was all too often explicitly or implicitly legitimised by Christian notions of dominion over the earth."[23] To address this, various theologians have sought to retrieve biblical ecological wisdom through appropriate ecological hermeneutics. In so doing, ecotheology may be understood as offering what Conradie has often described as a dual critique, namely, an ecological critique of Christianity and a Christian critique of ecological destruction.[24] In African discourse on ecotheology, the role of contemporary African Christianity in addressing the ecological crisis necessarily has to engage with debates on the continuity and discontinuity between ATR and Christianity not least because of the legacy of missionary Christianity and the continuity of coloniality long after the end of colonialism. This decolonial imperative seeks to remedy the erosion of the African concepts of interrelatedness of all being that were typical in indigenous African cultures. This African relational view of reality is also typical in other contexts such as Pacifica cultures, as Upolu Lumā Vaai demonstrates in his chapter on eco-relationality in this volume.

The legacy of missionary Christianity in alienating Africans from their culture through the denial and denigration of African religion partly explains this concern. As Congolese philosopher Valentin Mudimbe has shown, "derision of so-called primitive religions and their gods" and the "imposition of rules of orthodoxy" functioned as common approaches to conversion within missionary Christianity.[25] While conversion to Christianity did not imply mere capitulation to western domination as more nuanced analyses of the discourse on conversion to Christianity[26] and postcolonial contributions demonstrate, the missionary denigration of African culture and religion had a negative impact on African religious imaginaries, that is, how the new African converts conceived God and being, their cosmological narratives, and the ecological wisdom embedded in their traditions and "worldviews."[27] Missionary Christianity introduced western mechanistic views of the world which projected human (read: white) superiority. Operating as they did within the logic of modernity with its emphasis on progress, missionary activity in colonial Africa proceeded not only as an evangelistic mission but most overtly a civilizing mission.

---

23. Conradie, "Towards an Ecological Biblical Hermeneutics," 125.

24. Conradie, "Towards an Ecological Biblical Hermeneutics," 126.

25. Mudimbe, *The Invention of Africa*, 52.

26. See, for example, Sanneh, *Translating the Message*.

27. The term worldview is here used in a social constructivist sense. For a nuanced discussion on the use of the term "worldview" in theological discourse see Conradie, "Ways of Viewing an Evolving World."

This violent destruction of African lifeworlds came under sharp critique by the first generation of African modern theologians who reacted against the western missionary denigration of ATR by positing positive and affirmative views of African religion and its attending cosmologies. John Mbiti and Bolaji Idowu, in particular, located the African belief in a Supreme Being as a point of continuity between ATR and Christianity.[28] In his *Concepts of God in Africa*, Mbiti demonstrated that God as creator was "the commonest attribute of the works or activities of God."[29] Positing a continuity thesis, Mbiti sought to remedy western missionary assumptions in which God was portrayed as foreign to Africans. In a nuanced manner, Lammin Sanneh noted a significant implication of this valorization of African notions of God by attributing the successful implantation of Christianity in Africa to the facilitating role of ATR and the missionary appropriation of African names of God in vernacular translations of the Bible. This notwithstanding, the Eurocentric attitude of missionary translators of the Bible has not gone unnoticed. Musa Dube has notably problematized how the gender-neutral Deity of Bantu was patriarchalized in Bible translations and also pointed out the colonization of African languages through Bible translation. In the Setswana Bible, for example, Dube illustrates how the roles of *Badimo* (a Setswana word for Ancestral Spirits) are reinvented and erroneously "equated with demons and devils."[30] This raises questions on both discontinuities and continuities with the Christian tradition in African discourse on God. Such African discourse on God may be seen not only as a prolegomenon for African Christian theological discourse on God but also as an instructive for typically African ecotheology given that it describes God within the context of African relational ontology, epistemology, and cosmology. Commenting on God and nature, Mbiti observed that according to "African people, man [sic] lives in a religious universe, so that natural phenomena and objects [including human beings] are intimately associated with God." Nature is thus "not an empty impersonal object or phenomenon; it is filled with religious significance . . . God is seen in and behind these objects and phenomena."[31] Commenting on the sacrality of life in African cosmology, Magesa argues that the created order other than humanity must be "approached with care and awe not only because of its communion with God, but also because of its own vital forces and its mystical connection with the ancestors and other spirits."[32]

---

28. Sakupapa, "The Trinity in African Christian Theology," 2.

29. Mbiti, *Concepts of God*, 91.

30. Dube, "Consuming a Colonial Cultural Bomb," 41.

31. Mbiti, *African Religions*, 73.

32. Magesa, *African Religion*, 53.

African Ecotheology: African Reinterpretations of the Interconnectedness of Reality

In the last two decades, there has been considerable interest among Africans theologians and scholars of religion regarding the relationship between religion and the environment.[33] This reflects a growing recognition of the environmental crisis and more recently of climate change as typically contextual issues in contemporary times. Although scholarly work on the integrity and validity of African religion abound as discussed above, some question whether or not Christianity in Africa retains a specter of coloniality so that contemporary African Christian narratives are still far removed from grassroots experiences. In this vein, recent debates on decoloniality in African theology call attention to a deeper interrogation of coloniality. Elsewhere, I have argued that what is needed is a "decolonial imagination as a methological necessity in African theology."[34] This inevitably implies epistemological questions around how African theology constructs knowledge and which sources are deemed authentic and by whom. In similar vein, the Nigerian Roman Catholic theologian Elochukwu Uzukwu has argued that:

> [C]olonial imprints, control and language games, must be consciously and methodologically challenged in African theology in order to give priority to the local in the reframing of the Christian praxis story.[35]

In light of the decolonial imperative described above, a number of African theologians and scholars of religion, including those from Zambia, have taken up the task of reflecting on the contribution of African religious ideas to address the ecological crisis. The distinction between theological scholarship and discourse on ATR in its own right is necessary as the former stresses both continuity and discontinuity in light of the biblical witnesses, while the latter proceeds with asserting confidence in the positive role of ATR in addressing environmental challenges. Such discourse on ATR and the environment typically explore among others the role of totemism to underscore the positive environmental role of ATR. Others, however, such as the Zimbabwean scholar of religion Nisbert Taringa, question the positive assessment of ATR as being idealistic and romantic. The "ecological attitude of traditional African religion," Taringa argues, "is more based on fear or respect of ancestral spirits than on respect for nature itself."[36]

---

33. For a recent overview of these contributions, see Chitando, "Ecotheology in Africa."

34. Sakupapa, "The Decolonising Content," 418.

35. Uzukwu, "The Imperative of Location," 109.

36. Taringa, "How Environmental," 191.

Among African theologians, a common approach entails the retrieval of the ecological wisdom in traditional African culture and religion alongside a theological assessment in that regard. This has specifically focused on the retrieval of an African sense of community and a Pneumatological grounding of such communality. As Zambian theologian Kapya Kaoma points out, African Christian ecological ethics needs to draw from both the heritage of ATR and Christian theology on the basis of the similarities between the two, namely, belief in God as creator and the belief that the Spirit is present in creation among others.[37]

A Retrieval of African Communality

Zambian theologians, Chammah Kaunda, Kapya Kaoma, Kuzipa Nalwamba, and Teddy Sakupapa have highlighted the centrality of community in African contexts in their respective writings on theology and ecology. Focusing on the Simaamba Tonga of Zambia's Southern province, Kaoma illustrates how Africans exemplify the ecological injunctions of their community cultures through rituals, totems, creation myths, taboos, and customs. According to Kaoma, "African worldviews uphold the belief that all biota [are] part of the sacred web of life, with sacred links to the ancestors and the Supreme Being."[38] Kaoma highlights the ancestor cult among the *Tonga* as being crucial to the development of African ecological ethics given that it seeks to uphold the ecological balance of the ecosphere. In traditional African communities, ancestors were believed to be the guardians of the land.[39] This functional perspective on ancestors is best understood in light of African traditional cosmologies in which all are interconnected. Accordingly, Kaoma draws on the ancestor analogy to depict Jesus as the first ecological ancestor. Jesus is the "ecological ancestor to every species, and the abundant life that the Creation seeks."[40] Among the Tonga, Kaoma argues, "Jesus should become the *sikatongo*, the charismatic rain caller, who intercedes with *Leza* on behalf of God's people."[41] This is innovative not least because ancestor narratives have mostly been deployed in African theology with reference to Christology. Kaoma has also articulated the eco-social implications of *ubuntu* given the ruminations of relatedness in the concept of *ubuntu*.

---

37. Kaoma, *God's Family*, 11.

38. Kaoma, *God's Family*, 101.

39. See Ranger and Ranger, *Voices from the Rocks*; and the collection of essays in Schoffeleers, *Guardians of the Land*.

40. Kaoma, *God's Family*, 175–81

41. Kaoma, *God's Family*, 59.

Another Zambian theologian Chammah Kaunda has drawn on two nature rituals, namely, the *Chitemene* and the *Ubutwa* of the Bemba and Shila people of Zambia, respectively, to illustrate human relational bondedness with the environment. Put differently, the community to which humanity belongs extends to a cosmic community. In this vein, Kaunda intimates the sacredness of ancestral land and underscores the notions of "harmony of being" and "community of life" whose ultimate source is God.[42] Such an emphasis on community is widespread. According to Setiloane, "Belonging is the root and essence of being."[43] The Malawian theologian Harvey Sindima argues that pre-Christian African concepts emphasize "the bondedness of life" and "the interconnectedness of all living beings."[44]

A Pneumatological Understanding of African Communality

The view of community as inclusive of nonhuman nature as discussed in the foregoing is further captured by scholars who accentuate the notion of vital force as an African concept of being. As I have argued elsewhere, the notion of vital force "provides a conceptual framework in which life and relationality are emphasized."[45] A related view was earlier advanced by Gabriel Setiloane who argued that "African conceptions of being show a belief in a potency locked up in the objects and beings' or an Energy, a Force which is immanent in all things."[46] Deploying the notion of *seriti*, a *seSotho* word for vitality, Setiloane likened the human person to "a live electric wire which is forever exuding force or energy in all directions."[47] The force that is thus exuded, Setiloane argued, "is called 'seriti'."[48] Further, for Setiloane, non-phenomena such as animals, trees, hills, lakes, and mountains have *seriti*.[49] One would thus argue that the sacredness of nature is derived from nature's relationship with the creator whose vital force has animated nature. Analogically, therefore, vital force may be understood as the Spirit of God. The recovery of the African notion of vital force with its underlying idea of God's pervading presence in the whole of creation may well

---

42. Kaunda, "Towards an African Ecogender Theology," 193–95.

43. Setiloane, *African Theology*, 10.

44. Sindima, "Community of Life," 137.

45. Sakupapa, "Spirit and Ecology," 427. In that publication, I sketch the historical context behind the initial articulation of "vital force" by the Belgian Franciscan missionary Placide Tempels in his *Bantu Philosophy* (1959) and its subsequent philosophical and theological appropriation by a number of African thinkers.

46. Setiloane, *African Theology*, 24.

47. Setiloane, *African Theology*, 24.

48. Setiloane, *African Theology*, 13.

49. Setiloane, *African Theology*, 24.

be fruitful for articulating an African ecological ethos. Similarly, Nalwamba draws on various African enunciations of vitalism to articulate the notion of *Mupasi* as cosmic s(S)pirit, as a Pneumatological notion based on the African holistic view of life. The concept of Mupasi, as Nalwamba points out, "advances an antireductionist view of nature, which can be postulated as a critique of the reductionist and mechanistic approaches to nature." On this basis, she concludes that the retrieval of this notion "brings into sharp focus the power of God that gives life as a layered, coexistent way of being that transcends material-spiritual binaries."[50] This Pneumatological framing is also echoed by Kaunda in terms of "the radical awareness of the presence of the Holy Spirit in creation."[51] For Kaoma, vital force as an ecological theme in African worldviews may be understood as the spirit that holds the universe together.

The above rendition of African ecotheology as second-order narratives suggests a decolonial imperative whereby African theologians and scholars of religion deliberately and inevitably take local and indigenous epistemologies seriously to articulate meaningful African responses to the multidimensional environmental crisis of our time. By stressing the retrieval of African ecological wisdom and articulating the Pneumatological implications of African notions of interrelatedness of all being, African ecotheological discourse proceed from a decolonial perspective by resisting the perpetuation of coloniality by foregrounding the local, yet maintaining the intercultural. The Pneumatological framing of such discourse reflects an African translation of the inseparability of who the Triune God is and what this God does. How this story relates to the story of universe as told by science undeniably raises questions around the reformation of Christianity so to enable new visions and imaginations of the whole in which the human is envisaged as a part and not apart from the universe.[52] Conradie captures the constructive challenge of relating the Christian story and the universe story in terms of being able to "make use of the best available science of our day to tell the story of the universe in such a way that we can again live by this story."[53]

■ African Eco-Narratives and Narratives of the "Anthropocene"

The African ecotheological focus on interrelatedness as described above opens up avenues for intercultural theological exchange on the

---

50. Nalwamba, "Mupasi as Cosmic s(S)pirit," 7.

51. Kaunda, "Towards an African Ecogender Theology," 195.

52. Thomas Berry has raised this challenge most incisively. See Swimme and Berry, *The Universe Story*.

53. Conradie, "The Earth in God's Economy," 19.

ecological crisis. For instance, the African focus on interrelatedness resonates with what the American Lutheran theologian Ernst Simmons has described as "an entangled theology of creation."[54] Given the understanding of ecotheology as "a particular expression of contextual theology that emerges in the particular contemporary context of environmental awareness,"[55] African discourse on ecotheology may have to engage with narratives of the "Anthropocene."

Humanity as a Geological Force: Engaging Narratives of the "Anthropocene"

The notion of the "Anthropocene" has emerged as a powerful narrative to describe a new epoch in which humans have become a global geophysical force that has resulted in anthropogenic environmental changes of unprecedented scale and diversity. As Malhi observes:

> The core concept that the term is trying to capture is that human activity is having a dominating presence on multiple aspects of the natural world and the functioning of the Earth system, and that this has consequences for how we view and interact with the natural world—and perceive our place in it.[56]

The founding myth about the origins of this notion traces the term to a conference of the International Geosphere-Biosphere Programme held in Cuernavaca, Mexico in 2000 at which the atmospheric chemist Paul Crutzen suggested that humans no longer live in the Holocene but in the "Anthropocene" ("the age of humans").[57] Formally introduced to the scientific community in 2000,[58] significant debates have emerged including questions around the dating of the "Anthropocene."[59] The "Anthropocene" has since become more than a concept; it has become a set of "compelling narratives" on how the human species has evolved "from hunter-gatherers to a global geophysical force."[60] These narratives of the "Anthropocene" illumine how human activities have come to rival global geophysical processes resulting in

---

54. Simmons, "Theology in the Anthropocene," 272.

55. Deane-Drummond, *Eco-theology*, x.

56. Malhi, "The Concept of the Anthropocene," 78.

57. See Crutzen and Stoermer, "The 'Anthropocene'."

58. See Crutzen and Stoermer, "The 'Anthropocene'."

59. Among others, Crutzen suggested the eighteenth century as the start of the "Anthropocene." See Crutzen, "Geology of Mankind," 23. For a detailed discussion see Ellis et al., "Dating the Anthropocene" and Ellis, "Ecology in an Anthropogenic Biosphere."

60. Lidskog and Waterton, "Anthropocene," 395.

unprecedented anthropogenic planetary change.[61] This sense of crisis is often framed in what may well be apocalyptic terms and have inspired competing discourses most notably "eco-catastrophism," "eco-modernism," and "planetary realism."[62]

With its nomenclature of an epoch in the geologic time scale, the concept of the "Anthropocene" has stimulated research from a variety of disciplines including theology. Theological discourse on the "Anthropocene" engages with the notion through a number of theological themes such as creation, sin,[63] and eschatology. Delf Rothe analyzes how different discourses of the "Anthropocene" "rearticulate symbols, narratives and themes of Christian eschatology to mobilise competing political projects"[64] to address the threat of finitude and irreversible change. Writing on eschatology in the "Anthropocene," Michael Northcott frames the "Anthropocene" as "a Kairos moment, which requires urgent action to reduce industrial humanity's impacts on the Earth system."[65] In a recent edited volume entitled *Religion in the Anthropocene*, the contributors explore historical, philosophical, theological, ethical, and socio-political perspectives on the religious dimension of the "Anthropocene."[66] These and other variegated theological discourses on the "Anthropocene" illustrate an apparent transdisciplinarity regarding the concept of the "Anthropocene" and, as such, are suggestive of its analytical power and significance as a hermeneutical concept,[67] albeit subject to a plurality of tensions and meanings. Arguably, the ecotheological critique of traditional Christian anthropology intimated in preceding sections of this essay resonate with the underlying critique of human impacts on the Earth system in the narratives of the "Anthropocene." But whose story (stories) is (are) the narrative(s) of the "Anthropocene?"

---

61. See Simon's incisive portrayal of the "Anthropocene" as the prospect of the unprecedented. Simon, "Why the Anthropocene Has No History."

62. For a useful discussion on the key aspects of these discourses and related political projects see Rothe, "Governing the End Times?" Suffice it to note that while eco-catastrophism mirrors an apocalyptic imaginary, eco-modernists offer an oppositional approach that is optimistic of the Anthropocene and argue that one way of responding to the crisis would be through the engineering of a "good Anthropocene" through geoengineering technologies. Eco-modernist views have elicited further debates and critiques which are not within the scope of this essay. For a critique of the "good Anthropocene" thesis, see Hamilton, *Earthmasters*.

63. See, for example, Conradie, *Secular Discourse on Sin*.

64. Rothe, "Governing the End Times?" 20.

65. Northcott, "Eschatology in the Anthropocene," 105.

66. Deane-Drummond et al., *Religion in the Anthropocene*.

67. See, for instance, Clingerman, "Place and the Hermeneutics of the Anthropocene."

The Anthropos of the "Anthropocene"

That the "Anthropocene is a concept that has moral content at its core, rather than being only a scientific concept with a detachable moral significance,"[68] can hardly be dismissed. However, from an African decolonial perspective, the framing of "humans" in most narratives of the "Anthropocene" as a single, monolithic whole is deeply problematic. For example, as compelling as the narrative and evidence of the "great acceleration," a term that refers to the period of drastic increase in the impact of human activity upon the Earth's geology and ecosystems after 1945, the phenomenon has been driven by a tiny section of the human population. The focus in some narratives of the "Anthropocene" on the twentieth-century great acceleration instills "a Eurocentric, elite and technocratic narrative of human engagement with our environment."[69] Consider, for instance, the role of the Global North in perpetuating consumer and industrial capitalism or the impact of capitalist economic systems and the cognate issue of resource use. As Malm and Hornborg contend, "historical origins of anthropogenic climate change were predicated on highly inequitable global processes from the start."[70] In this vein, some argue for renaming the "Anthropocene" to be the Eurocene,[71] Capitalocene,[72] or White Supremacy Scene. Arguing from a decolonial perspective, indigenous feminist anthropologist Zoe Todd portrays the "Anthropocene" as a variation of "'white public space'—space in which indigenous ideas and experiences are appropriated, or obscured, by non-indigenous practitioners."[73]

In his influential essay "The Climate of History," Dipesh Chakrabarty makes interesting observations. He asks, "How do we relate to a universal history of life—to universal thought, that is—while retaining what is of obvious value in our postcolonial suspicion of the universal?"[74] Chakrabarty eloquently articulates the pitfalls of species thinking that is central in the dominant narrative of the "Anthropocene," albeit that he endorses the "Anthropocene" narrative as a discursive debate.[75] In a subsequent response to a critique of his

---

68. Ellis and Trachtenberg, "Which Anthropocene," 123. See also Jenkins, *The Future of Ethics*.

69. Ellis et al., "Involve Social Scientists," 192.

70. Malm and Hornborg, "The Geology of Mankind," 63.

71. See Grove, *Savage Ecology*.

72. See Moore, "The Capitalocene."

73. Todd, "Indigenizing the Anthropocene," 243.

74. Chakrabarty. "The Climate of History", 219-20.

75. In his earlier work *Provincializing Europe*, Chakrabarty was critical of universalising tendencies of western thought. Nevertheless, the critique of Enlightenment thought is this regard was not so much a denial of the achievements of Enlightenment reason as evident in the significant achievements of science in medicine or our knowledge of "global warming."

treatment of the *Anthropos* of the "Anthropocene" as highlighted above, Chakrabarty points out the social-political critique of how planetary changes often significantly affect the disadvantaged. He writes:

> [. . .] the burden of environmental risks, whether climate change-related or not, falls unevenly on different social groups, mediated by class, race, gender, and ethnicity. Fires in wealthy neighborhoods may be devastating, but are probably less devastating to households that have home insurance, have invested in fire safety measures, or own cars to flee in response to warnings.[76]

A reading of the *Anthropos* of the "Anthropocene" as an undifferentiated whole blinds attention to the realities of various forms of oppression, class struggle, and exploitation. That the consequences the ecological crisis are particularly grave for the poor and vulnerable economies demonstrates that those who have done least harm to the environment find themselves carrying the greatest burden of consequences.[77] In this regard, the effects of climate change reinforce the destructive legacy of colonialism. Taking cognizance of differential vulnerability of various human societies is therefore important to keep in mind alongside the need for recognizing differential responsibility for the change in the Earth System.

■ Conclusion

With specific reference to the Zambian context, I have argued in this essay that churches have a key role to play in developing an ecological ethos. It specifically underscored the decolonial imperative in African ecotheology with reference to second-order narratives. It was argued that ecumenical discourse on ecology has accentuated some of the ways in which religious resources may engender ecological responsibility among humans. Drawing on various African notions of communality to describe how humans are in an ontological relationship with nature given their common descent from the creator, Zambian discourse is indicative of how African concepts enrich biblical ecological wisdom and vice versa. The former is illustrated in the Pneumatological framing of Zambian ecotheological discourse which is indicative of an African translation of the inseparability of who the Triune God is and what this God does. As argued in this essay, how this story relates to the story of universe as told by science does raise critical questions about ways in which an ecological reformation Christianity may inspire new visions and imaginations of the whole. Finally, I noted the significance of narratives of the "Anthropocene" by pointing out the ways in which the dominant western conceptualizations of the "Anthropocene" narrative tend to denote

---

76. Chakrabarty, "Whose Anthropocene? A Response," 108.

77. See Chitando, "Ecotheology in Africa," 4.

a "'falsely unified' and Eurocentric story of the Earth's transformation."[78] The changes to the planetary environment pointed out in narratives of the "Anthropocene" have far-reaching consequences, especially for the poor. Therefore, one way in which African ecotheology may contribute to the interdisciplinary discourse on the crisis of our times may lie in drawing on African ecological wisdom.

■ Bibliography

Association for Catholic Information in Africa. "Engage in Actions that Are 'Ecologically Correct': Bishops in Zambia Tell Politicians." https://www.aciafrica.org/news/2045/engage-in-actions-that-are-ecologically-correct-bishops-in-zambia-tell-politicians, accessed 30 March 2021.

Barthes, Roland. "Introduction to the Structural Analysis of Narratives," In *Image-Music-Text*, 79-174. Translated by Stephen Heath. London: Fontana, 1977.

Bediako, Kwame. "Understanding African theology in the 20th century." *Themelios* 20:1 (1994), 14-20.

Chakrabarty, Dipesh. "The Climate of History: Four theses." *Critical Inquiry* 35:2 (2009), 197-222. https://doi.org/10.1086/596640

———. "Whose Anthropocene? A Response." *RCC Perspectives* 2 (2016), 101-14.

Chilufya, Gregory C. *Can Sustainable Agriculture Practices Remedy the Negative Effects of Climate Change on Food Security in Zambia?* Lusaka: Jesuit Centre for Theological Reflection, 2011.

Chitando, Ezra. "Ecotheology in Africa: An Overview and Preliminary Assessment." In *Law, Religion and the Environment in Africa*, edited by Christian Green and Muhammed Haron, 3-16. Stellenbosch: African Sun Media, 2020.

———. "Praying for Courage: African Religious Leaders and Climate Change." *The Ecumenical Review* 69:3 (2017), 425-35. https://doi.org/10.1111/erev.12304

Clingerman, Forrest. "Place and the Hermeneutics of the Anthropocene." *Worldviews: Global Religions, Culture, and Ecology* 20:3 (2016), 225-37. https://doi.org/10.1163/15685357-02003002

Conradie, Ernst M. *Christianity and Ecological Theology: Resources for Further Research*. Stellenbosch: African Sun Media, 2006.

———. *Secular Discourse on Sin in the Anthropocene: What's Wrong with the World?* Lanham: Lexington Books, 2020.

———. "The Earth in God's Economy: Reflections on the Narrative of God's Work." *Scriptura* 97:1 (2008), 13-36. https://doi.org/10.7833/97-0-711

———. "Towards an Ecological Biblical Hermeneutics: A Review Essay on the Earth Bible Project." *Scriptura* 85:1 (2004), 123-35. https://doi.org/10.7833/85-0-941

———. "Ways of Viewing an Evolving World amidst Ecological Destruction." *Scriptura* 117 (2018), 1-13. https://doi.org/10.7833/117-1-1390

Crutzen, Paul J. "Geology of Mankind." *Nature* 415 (2002), 23. https://doi.org/10.1038/415023a

Crutzen, Paul J. and Eugene F. Stoermer. "The 'Anthropocene'." *Global Change Newsletter* 41 (2000), 17-18.

Deane-Drummond, Celia. *Eco-Theology*. Winona: Saint Mary's, 2008.

Deane-Drummond, Celia, Sigurd Bergmann and Markus Vogt (eds). *Religion in the Anthropocene*. Eugene, Oregon: Cascade, 2018.

---

78. Szerszynski, "God's Anthropocene," 254.

Dube, Musa W. "Consuming a Colonial Cultural Bomb: Translating Badimo into 'Demons' in the Setswana Bible (Matthew 8.28–34; 15.22; 10.8)." *Journal for the Study of the New Testament* 21:73 (1999), 33–58. https://doi.org/10.1177/0142064X9902107303

Ellis, Erle C. "Ecology in an Anthropogenic Biosphere." *Ecological Monographs* 85:3 (2015), 287–331. https://doi.org/10.1890/14-2274.1

Ellis, Erle C., et al. "Dating the Anthropocene: Towards an Empirical Global History of Human Transformation of the Terrestrial Biosphere." *Elementa: Science of the Anthropocene* 1 (2013), 1–6. https://doi.org/10.12952/journal.elementa.000018

———. "Involve Social Scientists in Defining the Anthropocene." *Nature News* 540:7632 (2016), 192. https://doi.org/10.1038/540192a

Ellis, Michael A. and Zev Trachtenberg. "Which Anthropocene Is It to Be? Beyond Geology to a Moral and Public Discourse." *Earth's Future* 2:2 (2014), 122–25. https://doi.org/10.1002/2013EF000191

Ellis, Stephen and Gerrie Ter Haar. *Worlds of Power: Religious Thought and Political Practice in Africa*, vol. 1. Oxford: Oxford University Press on Demand, 2004.

Funder, Mikkel, Carol Emma Mweemba and Imasiku Nyambe. "The Climate Change Agenda in Zambia: National Interests and the Role of Development Cooperation." *DIIS Working Paper* 13 (2013), 1–32.

Grove, Jairus V. *Savage Ecology: War and Geopolitics at the End of the World*. Duke University Press, 2019.

Hamilton, Clive. *Earthmasters: The Dawn of the Age of Climate Engineering*. New Haven: Yale University Press, 2013.

Jenkins, Willis. *The Future of Ethics: Sustainability, Social Justice, and Religious Creativity*. Georgetown University Press, 2013.

Jesuit Centre for Theological Reflection. *Caring for our Environment*. Lusaka: JCTR, 2008.

Kaoma, Kapya J. *God's Family, God's Earth: Christian Ecological Ethics of Ubuntu*. Zomba: Kachere Series, 2014.

———. "Towards an African Theological Ethic of Earth Care: Encountering the Tonga Lwiindi of Simaamba of Zambia in the Face of the Ecological Crisis." *HTS Theological Studies* 73:3 (2017), 1–10. https://doi.org/10.4102/hts.v73i3.3834

Kaunda, Chammah J. "Towards an African Ecogender Theology: A Decolonial Theological Perspective." *Stellenbosch Theological Journal* 2:1 (2016), 177–202. https://doi.org/10.17570/stj.2016.v2n1.a09

Lidskog, Rolf and Claire Waterton. "Anthropocene—A Cautious Welcome from Environmental Sociology?" *Environmental Sociology* 2:4 (2016), 395–406. https://doi.org/10.1080/23251042.2016.1210841

Magesa, Laurenti. *African Religion: The Moral Traditions of Abundant Life*. New York: Orbis Books, 1997.

Malhi, Yadvinder. "The Concept of the Anthropocene." *Annual Review of Environment and Resources* 42 (2017), 77–104. https://doi.org/10.1146/annurev-environ-102016-060854

Malm, Andreas and Alf Hornborg. "The Geology of Mankind? A Critique of the Anthropocene Narrative." *The Anthropocene Review* 1:1 (2014), 62–69. https://doi.org/10.1177/2053019613516291

Mbiti, John S. *African Religions & Philosophy*. New York: Anchor Books, 1970.

———. *Concepts of God in Africa*. Nairobi: Acton, 2013.

Moore, Jason W. "The Capitalocene, Part I: On the Nature and Origins of Our Ecological Crisis." *The Journal of Peasant Studies* 44:3 (2017), 594–630. https://doi.org/10.1080/03066150.2016.1235036

Mudimbe, Valentin Y. *The Invention of Africa: Gnosis, Philosophy, and the Order of Knowledge*. London: James Currey, 1988.

Mwaanga, Phenny, et al. "Preliminary Review of Mine Air Pollution in Zambia." *Heliyon* 5:9 (2019), 1–10. https://doi.org/10.1016/j.heliyon.2019.e02485

Nalwamba, Kuzipa. "Mupasi as Cosmic s(S)pirit: The Universe as a Community of Life." *HTS Theological Studies* 73:3 (2017), 1-8. https://doi.org/10.4102/hts.v73i3.4624

Niang, Isabelle, et al. "Africa Climate Change 2014: Impacts, Adaptation, and Vulnerability." In *Climate Change 2014: Impacts, Adaptation and Vulnerability: Part B: Regional Aspects: Working Group II Contribution to the Fifth Assessment Report of the Intergovernmental Panel on Climate Change*, edited by Vicente R. Barros et al., 1199-266, Cambridge: Cambridge University Press, 2014.

Northcott, Michael. "Eschatology in the Anthropocene: From the Chronos of Deep Time to the Kairos of the Age of Humans." In *The Anthropocene and the Global Environmental Crisis: Rethinking Modernity in a New Epoch*, edited by Clive Hamilton et al., 100-111. London: Routledge, 2015.

Ranger, Terence O. and Terence Ranger. *Voices from the Rocks: Nature, Culture & History in the Matopos Hills of Zimbabwe*. Bloomington: Indiana University Press, 1999.

Rothe, Delf. "Governing the End Times? Planet Politics and the Secular Eschatology of the Anthropocene." *Millennium* 48:2 (2020), 143-64. https://doi.org/10.1177/0305829819889138

Sakupapa, Teddy Chalwe. "Spirit and Ecology in the Context of African Theology." *Scriptura* 111:1 (2012), 422-30. https://doi.org/10.4102/hts.v75i1.5460

———. "The Decolonising Content of African Theology and the Decolonisation of African Theology-Reflections on a Decolonial Future for African Theology." *Missionalia* 46:3 (2018), 406-24. https://doi.org/10.7832/46-3-277

———. "The Trinity in African Christian Theology: An Overview of Contemporary Approaches." *HTS Theological Studies* 75:1 (2019), 1-7. https://doi.org/10.4102/hts.v75i1.5460

Schoffeleers, Jan M. *Guardians of the Land: Essays on Central African Territorial Cults*. Gweru: Mambo, 1999.

Setiloane, Gabriel M. *African Theology: An Introduction*. Johannesburg: Skotaville, 1986.

Shinn, David H. "The Environmental Impact of China's Investment in Africa." *Cornell International Law Journal* 49:1 (2016), 25-67.

Simmons, Ernest L. "Theology in the Anthropocene." *Dialog* 53:4 (2014), 271-73. https://doi.org/10.1111/dial.12125

Simon, Zoltán Boldizsár. "Why the Anthropocene Has No History: Facing the Unprecedented." *The Anthropocene Review* 4.3 (2017), 239-45. https://doi.org/10.1177/2053019617742170

Sindima, Harvey. "Community of Life: Ecological Theology in African Perspective." In *Liberating Life: Contemporary approaches in Ecological Theology*, edited by Charles Birch, William Eakin and Jay Byrd McDaniel, 137-47. Maryknoll: Orbis Books, 1990.

Swimme, Brian and Thomas Berry. *The Universe Story. From the Primordial Flashing Forth to the Ecozoic Era—A Celebration of the Unfolding of the Cosmos*. New York: HarperCollins, 1992.

Szerszynski, Bronislaw. "Gods of the Anthropocene: Geo-spiritual Formations in the Earth's New Epoch." *Theory, Culture & Society* 34:2-3 (2017), 253-75. https://doi.org/10.1177/0263276417691102

Taringa, Nisbert. "How Environmental Is African Traditional Religion?" *Exchange* 35:2 (2006), 191-214. https://doi.org/10.1163/157254306776525672

Ter Haar, Gerrie. "Religion and Development: Introducing a New Debate." In *Religion and Development: Ways of Transforming the World*, edited by Gerrie ter Haar, 3-25. New York: Columbia University Press, 2011.

Todd, Zoe. "Indigenizing the Anthropocene." In *Art in the Anthropocene: Encounters Among Aesthetics, Politics, Environments and Epistemologies*, edited by Etienne Turpin and Heather Davis, 241-54. London: Open Humanities, 2015.

Uzukwu, Elochukwu. "The Imperative of Location: Developing Contextual Theological Method in Africa." In *The Shifting Ground of Doing Theology: Perspectives from Africa*, edited by Emmanuel Wabanhu and Marco Moerschbacher, 105-23. Nairobi: Paulines, 2017.

Werner, Dietrich. "The Challenge of Environment and Climate Justice. Imperatives of an Eco-Theological Reformation of Christianity in African Contexts." In *African Initiated Christianity and the Decolonization of Development: Sustainable Development in Pentecostal and Independent Churches*, edited by Philipp Öhlmann, Wilhelm Gräb und Marie-Luise Frost, 51–72. London: Routledge, 2020.

White, Lynn Jr. "The Historic Roots of Our Ecologic Crisis." *Science* 155 (1967), 1203–07. https://doi.org/10.1126/science.155.3767.1203

Zambia Episcopal Conference. "Communiqué on the Laudato Si' Conference," Lusaka, 25–26 April, 2016.

The Ecorelational Story of the Cosmic Aiga: A Pasifika Perspective

Upolu Lumā Vaai[1]

■ Introduction: "Born of a Cosmic Womb"

Being raised in oral communal cultures, it is a challenge to pen down a story. This is because my story is not just a personal one. Any human story is a dimension of the larger cosmic story. My story approaches ecology from a *whole of life* ecorelational perspective. I was born of a cosmic womb, not just a human womb. I am a child of the cosmos, at least from an ecorelational perspective. Therefore, I did not create relationships. I was born into relationships, and with this comes enormous responsibility, and hence a life

---

1. Upolu Lumā Vaai is the Principal of the Pacific Theological College in Suva, Fiji. He is registered as a co-researcher at the University of the Western Cape, South Africa, for the project on "An Earthed Faith: Telling the Story amid the 'Anthropocene'."

How to cite: Vaai, U.L., 2021, 'The Ecorelational Story of the Cosmic Aiga: A Pasifika Perspective', in E.M. Conradie & P.-C. Lai (eds.), *Taking a deep breath for the story to begin . . .* (An Earthed Faith: Telling the Story amid the "Anthropocene" Volume 1), pp. 225–240, AOSIS, Cape Town. https://doi.org/10.4102/aosis.2021.BK264.11

that is shaped and defined by the *deep living connections* of the Aiga (cosmic extended family).[2]

This essay raises questions and concerns from a Pasifika[3] cosmological perspective on how we often treat ecology in the dominant development and theological narratives. It tells a rather disturbing and unorthodox side of the story from the relational cosmological ways of knowing and being of Pasifika communities, tested and lived out for centuries by these communities. This story is only a story if it includes *all that is us*. It puts life into our old/new cosmic and creation-centric framework; empowers what remains to be discovered; provides the lens to interpret the experiences we have acquired and change those still to come; reframes the dominant stories we have been given, making sure ours is a liberating counter-story; and yearns to include more love for what has been unloved and has made us ashamed of the Aiga, the cosmic womb that gave us life, that gave us a story to be and to become.

■ "Stories Are Liquid Versions of Life"

"Stories are liquid versions of life," a wisdom retrieved from a conversation with Sir Edward Taihākurei Durie from Aotearoa New Zealand when he visited Fiji for the Inaugural Pacific Philosophy Conference in 2018. Sir Durie, a Maori Tikanga high court judge and indigenous elder, was at the forefront of the fight for the Whanganui River in New Zealand to be granted legal personhood. To him, because stories flow, they breathe, and therefore, the Spirit is alive in them. Mutable and passible, alterable for the sake of life, stories have the potential to both soothe and unsettle.

Tala in most parts of Pasifika refers to stories. *Talanoa* refers to the act of telling and altering these stories. Through *talanoa*, stories breathe through the telling process. Like clouds, they travel from one end of the generational horizons to another, breathing as long as communities breathe. In some Pasifika cultures, stories of the old are breathed into the mouths of the new generation through a ceremonial ritual accompanied by the words *ia faagagaina oe ele Atua fetalai* meaning "may the orator God give you a story to tell."[4] Others like the Australian Aboriginal people in the "kick the dirt" dance express the people's way of how stories travel through generations.

---

2. Aiga in the narrow sense refers to a social unit in the village comprised of immediate family members and kinship. In the broader sense this is a holistic Pasifika concept that refers to the cosmic extended family inclusive of land, ocean, peoples, ancestors, and spirits/gods that constitute wholeness of life. See Tofaeono, *Eco-Theology AIGA*, that covers the Aiga concept extensively.

3. Instead of the English term *Pacific*, I opt to use *Pasifika* to capture the common struggle of island communities under the threat of climate change and many other ecological crises. This term shifts the focus from the idea of being "peaceful" as connoted in the colonial term *Pacific* to resilience and self-determination of communities.

4. See Tui Atua, *Ia faagagaina oe ele Atua Fetalai*, iii.

People kick the dirt in order to "breathe the dust." The more the dust, the better the connection to the past stories of their ancestors who also breathe the same dust in order to create a new story.[5] Breath revitalizes stories. As long as we and stories breathe into each other, stories become vibrant and creative beyond their original time and space. Through breath, I mean deep breath, stories take new forms to shape generations. They become pathways, the "means by which we navigate the world."[6] And as stories travel from generation to generation, they become liquid stories. Fluid. Drifting. Changeable.

Pasifika is known as a liquid continent, as Epeli Hauofa reminds us that Pasifika does not refer to "islands in the sea" as explorers had assumed, but rather "our sea of islands" connected and linked by the liquid flow of the blue *moana*, our Pasifika ocean.[7] The former sees islands as small and isolated dots yet to be found and named, lost in the blue colored map of the Age of Discovery. The latter sees islands as "roomy environments that typify continental spaces,"[8] where the ocean is part of island spatiality already shared and protected by the Oceanic people for centuries. In this context, stories, therefore, are entirely shaped by liquidity, created and told from the perspective of *sea-land* spatiality and drifting cultures.

Liquidity goes against rigidity. It means, therefore, that every story has a liquid element in it for the sake of renewal. But we must not fall into the trap suggested by George Monbiot that we "cannot take away someone else's story without giving them a new one." Stories should not be a given. They should be created by communities, shaped by the dynamics of their *itulagi*, their *side of the horizon*, or else it is just another imposed colonial immutable story that normally ends up being glorified as the only story.

■ "Everything is Flesh, Bones, and Blood"

My story is an ecorelational story. I was raised in a grassroots philosophy that everything cosmic and earthy is *flesh, bones*, and *blood*. Ernst Haeckel who shifted the discussion away from the rigidity that is accompanied by the word *nature* to embracing the Earth as *ecology* argued that ecology meant the relationship of dynamic organisms of the natural environment.[9] This started an ecological revolution that dramatically changed not only how humanity understands the Earth as dynamic but

---

5. See Lin, "Dust and Dancing," paragraphs 6 and 7.

6. See Monbiot, *Out of the Wreckage*, 1.

7. See Hauofa, "Our Sea of Islands," 2–16.

8. See Havea, *RumInations*, 2.

9. Miller, "Ecology."

also its relationship with what is ecological. We begin to see that the Earth has its own ecological system that is beyond human imagination and should be respected.[10]

However, this storyline refers to ecology only as the natural environment, therefore has still not gone far enough to recognize the fluid nature of ecology where the whole Aiga is connected with ecological genes. It still treats the Earth as a separate ecological world. Worse, it treats the Earth's story outside of God's story. We still see today that most scientific theories, development frameworks, educational studies, and theological reflections are "hijacked"[11] by this narrative, fostering a perception that everything human is not ecological, but everything ecological belongs to the human. This compartmentalized narrative is reinforced by the mainstream educational system where ecology is often structured as a separate discipline from that of anthropology, economy, or theology. This approach fails to see everything as ecologically distinct yet inextricably and ecologically related.

Many ecotheologians argue that we should redeem ecology from this unhealthy narrative in order to consider it as part of the whole. However, it is not enough, as many Pasifika ecotheologians argue, to have an integrated model of ecology that pushes for the centrality of human relationship with creation until we recognize *the genealogical connection* that we hold with everything else.[12] Ecorelationality treats ecology not as an academic discipline or an interaction between religion and nature as ecotheology sometimes tends to push, but rather as a living relationship. Ecology does not come with a static body of knowledge. Rather it comes with relationship.

In the Pasifika communities, all of life is an assemblage of relationality. In the beginning was relationship. This is reflected in Patristic writings, especially the Cappadocians as I will refer to below, and in the creation stories of many indigenous communities around the world. Therefore, the cosmos is primary, a relational reality that precedes all realities, including the anthropological reality. Thus cosmic relationality is in our blood. We came into being through cosmological relationships. Ecology is always cosmological and relational. In many island creation stories, the human being is perceived as a child of a cosmic union. Therefore, human identity is defined by this cosmic genealogy. Captured in the words of Tui Atua from Samoa:

> I am not an individual; I am an integral part of the cosmos. I share divinity with my ancestors, the land, the seas and the skies [. . .] I belong to my family and my family

---

10. Vaai, "We Are therefore We Live."

11. See Vaai, "We Are therefore We Live."

12. See, for example, Boseto, "Do Not Separate Us from Our Land"; Tofaeono, *Eco-Theology*; Boseto, "God as Community"; Tuwere, *Vanua*, 35; and Bird, "Pepesa."

belongs to me. I belong to my village and my village to me [. . .] This is the essence of my sense of belonging.[13]

The same sentiment is also echoed in the words of Jean-Marie Tjibaou from Kanaki New Caledonia who was assassinated for his fight for the independence of his Kanaki people from French colonization. He said, "I am never undivided. I cannot be individual. The body is never a principle of individualization. The body is always a relationship."[14] Thus as Pasifika, we don't just understand. We understand according to the rhythms of cosmic relationships. We don't just interpret. We always interpret through the lens of holistic cosmic connectedness. We don't just live. We live according to the ecorelational values of life. It is through this *holistic gaze* that the ecorelational story was born.

This *holistic gaze* should continue to challenge theologies that centralize human existence over all other ecological lives. This is not to suggest that other cultures lack a perspective of the whole. Rather it is to suggest that a certain degree of this perspective could be achieved through integration and interconnectedness of the parts. We could easily fall into exclusivism if we lose this focus on interconnectedness. In response the Pasifika church leaders opted to script a new story of ecumenism in the region that takes the cosmos as primary. The move saw a shift from the *unity in Christ* narrative that has dominated ecumenism in the region since the early 1960s to the *Pacific household of God*.[15] The former is anthropocentric and church-centric, focusing more on the unity of churches and peoples. The latter is cosmological, taking us back to the primacy of creation, extending ecumenism to include ecology and economy. It focuses not only on the role of the churches in sustainable housekeeping but also on the eco-relationships and values of family that form the basis of its well-being. The push for a new story is not just about deconstructing and critiquing the old story but rather about creating a new one and whether the new carries the wisdom, values and needs of the Pasifika communities because these determine the sustainability of a new story.

Having this holistic perspective renavigates the direction of our faith to sail back to the Triune God, the origin of cosmological relationality. It calls for re-examining the term *relationality,* a word that did not escape the intrusion of the western colonial anthropocentric imagination, littered with simplistic non-holistic connotations where the self is always placed at the center. This is why the term anthropocentrism when still employed in a theology of hope to guide the new direction of the World Council of Churches against human greed

---

13. Tui Atua, "In Search of Meaning," 105.

14. *Cibau: Jean-Marie Tjibaou*, 28.

15. See Pacific Church Leaders Meeting, "Sowing a New Seed," 1–2. See also Havea, "A Vision of our Pacific Household," 1–10.

remains problematic.[16] This is because if relationship is a flow, then the human being should never be a center. Hence language matters in the decolonization process.

If cosmology is a relationship and not just about systems of chromosomes and sets of natural rules, then ecorelationality calls for a move beyond mere interactions and correlations to recognizing everything as family. It calls for an ecorelational theology that takes seriously cosmology as a genealogical relationship, a divided undivided whole where God is an integral part of that whole. In this divided undivided whole, when we refer to one member, we refer to the whole Aiga, where the face of the whole is manifested in the face of the one. This *holistic gaze* is something that the Cappadocian fathers have taught us in their Trinitarian theologies, especially Gregory of Nazianzus. When we speak of the one, we speak of the whole. Therefore, because one is mutually included in the whole, when one suffers, the whole suffers.[17] Ecorelationality critiques not only ecological destruction but also the systems of relationships that contribute to the collapse and destruction of this ecorelational connections. It emphasizes the shift from space to *deep living connections* within the cosmic Aiga, embracing the multidimensional relationships and its inherent values and the spirituality that constitutes space and time. It promotes a deeply fluid connectedness of an ecorelational consciousness where the cosmos is seen as a dimension of everything else.

This means therefore that creation is a network of *deep living connections* rather than a created product, where the land, ocean, and sky are considered family who continue to grow by giving and receiving from each other the gift of life. If this is the case, a dynamic "continuous creation,"[18] then the Aiga understands incarnation not just about the *Word made flesh* but also the *Word become family*. The Emmanuel who lives among us. In Africa this vision is encapsulated in the concept of *ubuntu*, the "eco-human-relational ethic" of life[19] or what John Hart calls the "creation-centric consciousness."[20] In Asia, it is found in the "cosmotheandric consciousness."[21] Incarnation, therefore, is not just a teaching about a *flesh-bearing God.* If flesh connotes relationship and family at least from the ecorelational perspective, then we can affirm therefore that all of God is realized in that which is ordinarily cosmological (not just human). Transcendence is realized in deep relationships. This realization does

---

16. Andrianos, "Ecumenical Theology of Hope," 601–02.

17. Nazianzus, *Orations* 40.41, 375.

18. Bauman, *Theology, Creation, and Environmental Ethics*, 3.

19. Kaoma, *God's Family*, 8.

20. Hart, *Sacramental Commons*, 121.

21. Panikkar, *The Cosmotheandric Experience*, 54.

not in any way compromise God's divinity. Rather, it is the very thing that affirms it. This connotes that relationality might well be considered the original and primordial form of consciousness, rooted in the very life of God. This forms the basis of the Aiga, where we realize ourselves only by recognizing the cosmic relations as *flesh, bones, and blood*. It affirms an alternative worldview where our *en-selfness* is achieved only in our *en-otherness*.

Is this not the life of the Trinity? A dynamic flow toward the other? And if God is a dynamic flow, should this not caution us not to create centers in God, as implied in the Christocentric theologies promoted by the west? Should we not learn from the decentered theology of Gregory of Nazianzus who once said:

> No sooner do I conceive of the One that I am illumined by the splendor of the Three; no sooner do I distinguish Them that I am carried back to the One [. . .] when I think of any One of the Three, I think of Him as a Whole?[22]

Does this not mean that we cannot control or centralize the dynamic flow in God? Does this not imply that whether we start with the Father, Son, or the Spirit, we would end up in the whole? Is this not why the incarnation is unique? Should it always be understood from the perspective of the whole? Should it not then caution us regarding prioritizing a redemption story that emphasizes human uniqueness and salvation of the soul? Could this not lead to to the exclusion of everything cosmic in favor of the humans as the object of divine cosmic concern?[23] The point is that the moment we create centers, either God becomes static to the point of being controlled or we humans become the center ourselves to facilitate such control of either God or salvation.

■ "We are, Therefore We Live"[24]

Because of ecorelationality that shapes many Pasifika cultures, people are more attuned to multistrand thinking rather than single-strand thinking, if I would employ the metaphor of the mat used in the everyday life of the Pasifika communities. Single-strand thinking has been used as a colonial tool to categorize and conquer. We normally teach students to prove whether God systematically fits into categories such as either priori or posteriori, objective or subjective, substance or relation, male or female, and process or solitary. In Christology, we try to prove whether Christ systematically fits into categories of either divinity or humanity, center or margin, and history or faith. What happens in this linear either/or way of thinking is that people tend to choose the more powerful categories such as divine, center, male, objective, and

---

22. Nazianzus, *Orations* 40.41, 375.

23. Northcott, "The Universe as Hypostatic Inherence," 212.

24. For more on this, especially in relation to development and climate change, see Vaai, "We Are Therefore We Live."

solitary over anything ordinary and cosmological. Pasifika theologies revolve around a lot of powerful monarchical and objective language of lordship that often fall short when it comes to resisting and transforming unjust social and religious structures.

The ecological crisis threatening Pasifika livelihoods derives from what I refer to as a pathological *narrative of onefication*[25] that, first and foremost, extracts all abundance to serve the civilization of the few digestive centers of power.[26] For colonization to function, a powerful narrative had to be created to justify the elevation of one category, one life, or one culture above others, perhaps in the light of what Laurel Schneider calls the "logic of the one" where the language and spirit of monotheism has become too powerful a foundation for a destructive colonial narrative.[27] It thrived on the ideology that all cultures have to be rescued from the depravity and backwardness of their ways and offered a more developed way—a way animated by the vision of endless growth of the powerful empires.[28] This ideology morphed into a powerful monarchical narrative that the survival of many lives is dependent upon rendering service to only one life—the human. Or one culture, namely, the neoliberal capitalist culture!

This enslavement to a onefied static system of life and understanding of reality has lost the sense of movement and dynamic motion fundamental to ecorelationality. In the spirit of the Trinitarian cosmology of the Cappadocians, creation is a dynamic motion. We are never confined to a singular system as life is a movement that also shapes the inner life of God. The Spirit is key to this dynamism.[29] Life, therefore, is a multiplicity and interplay of motion. It is a multistrand system that recognizes the flow of multidimensional ordinary relationships in the Aiga. In the spirit of relationality, it treats duality as relationally and inextricably linked. Transcendence is found in the immanence, divinity in the ordinary, cosmology in the human, light in darkness. The interconnectedness and co-inherence of these dimensions of life allows us to view life as a reality that is more than just a single entity. Those who embrace multistrand consciousness embrace complexity, multiplicity, and negotiability. Their minds are engineered to the "we are" principle where they should live

---

25. Onefication is a term that I coin to represent a system underpinned by the logic of the "singular one." This logic is often manifested in the term "oneness" which aims at glorifying one at the expense of many, centralizing and controlling benefits and resources under one culture, one economic system, or one people at the expense of many including the Earth. This is the opposite of "unity" which is about the relational plural one.

26. See Vaai, "A Dance of Relationality," 185. See also Vaai, "Relational Theologizing," 40–56.

27. Schneider, *Beyond Monotheism*, 9.

28. Empire here refers to a person, institution, government, organization or nation that sees its policies, rules, models, theologies or interpretations as the *only* universal Truth (with the capital) and as a result imposes its subjective interpretations as the objective Truth for all peoples and cultures.

29. Bergmann, "The Legacy of Trinitarian Cosmology," 6–8.

not only according to the dynamic rhythms of relationships with the land, ocean, trees, strangers, and the divine but also according to the rhythms of creative imagination not confined to the linear one truth. We are only because we live together.

In terms of complexity and multiplicity, all Pasifika Earth terms such as *eleele*, *vanua*, *whenua*, *palapala*, *aba*, or *'āina* are deeply connected with the idea that cosmology forms the human. When a Fijian says *vanua e/na tamata, tamata e/na vanua* or when a Tongan says *fonua pe tangata, tangata pe fonua* (both translated "the land is the people and the people is the land"), they speak (as "we are") of the deep connection of their identity with the Aiga. The terms for person or personhood in many Pasifika communities such as *tamata* in Fiji, *tangata* for Maori and Tonga, *taata* in Tahiti, *kanaka* in Hawaii, or *tagata* in Samoa, are all inclusive in a cosmic sense. When we speak of *tagata*, we speak not just of the self but also of the land, ocean, extended family, culture, and spirituality.

In Samoa my birthplace, the word for soil (*eleele, palapala*) is the same as the word for blood. *Ua tafe le palapala* (blood is spilled) means that the Earth loses life whenever there is bloodshed. The word for the rocks/stones (*fatu*) is the same word for the human heart. The word for the skies (*lagi*) is also used for a human head. The word for human skull (*atigisami*) is the same word for sea shell, connoting that wisdom is always connected to the ocean currents, flows, and turbulences. The word for tongue (*laulaufaiva*) connotes distribution of resources rather than digestion. When a mother tree or a hub tree is cut, the word used is *oia*, meaning "the whole forest cries in pain." This is why any cutting of hub trees should be accompanied by rituals to ask for pardon and to restore balance, as the whole forest will be affected from cutting just one tree.[30]

A woman's placenta is called *fanua*, meaning land. The land thus plays a critical role in nurturing and feeding the unborn child. During birth, it is actually the *fanua* that is severed to give life to the newborn. After birth, the mother's *fanua* (placenta) is buried in the *fanua* (land) to remind that what nurtures human life in the placenta now returns to nurture more life in the cosmic community. In most Pasifika cultures, when a child is born, the umbilical cord is buried in the land to reconnect the child to mother Earth. Through the umbilical cord, the child is disconnected from the human mother but is reconnected with mother Earth. This practice of disconnection and reconnection are central to the idea of balance, where reconnection is imperative when there is disconnection, especially when we disconnect a life from its roots. Balance and harmony are not romantic notions. They are ecorelational principles of life that inform and shape how one should relate to the other members of the Aiga and can be realized through the practice of *va*

---

30. See Vaai, "We Are therefore We Don't Have." In this section I am drawing upon formulations from this essay.

or *wa*, the respect of relational spaces in most Polynesian countries, *veiwekani* and *sautu* in Fiji, *gutpela sindaun* in Papua New Guinea, *thalapa* in Kanaki New Caledonia, or *faaaloalo* in Samoa, to name a few.

This cosmic connection demonstrates why negotiability is critical, as in the Samoan wisdom saying, "the wisdom of the wise is negotiable but the wisdom of the fool is fixed." Any wisdom that protects the Aiga is one that should have an *all-ness mindset* in order to achieve the *tofā loloto*: the wisdom of the deep. This wisdom normally goes through a lengthy and time-consuming process that involves consulting the spirits of the land, the ocean, the people, and the vision of ancestors. The process includes what is called *moe le toa* (let the *toa* sleep) where deliberation would be postponed to the next day when wisdom is not reached. The *toa* is a tree used for creating durable weapons. For the sake of durability, it needs to sleep in water for a lengthy period of time to ensure it is tough to achieve its purpose. The more it sleeps, the more it is durable. This metaphor is used for decision-making. The more time a decision is challenged with questions in consultation with the Earth and the Aiga, the more it is durable and has less costs. Cosmological well-being is achieved through ongoing questioning, consultative discernment, and critical dialogue with the whole. In other words, being ecorelational is about wrestling to understand the individual as a child of the Aiga and the Aiga as imaged in the individual.

This careful process of seeking wisdom implies that our human economies should be subject to a checks and balances system with scrutinizing mechanisms for the sake of ecology. Today, the *oikos triplets* of economy, ecology, and oikoumene is severed. While all three have their root in the Greek concept *oikos*, meaning household, the three were meant to stay connected.[31] However, like the stolen generation of Australia, each was stripped of their mutual connections and was stolen by the different empires to serve their agendas. Ecology was stolen by the scientific research empire and turned into a mere object that can be extracted, categorized, and objectively studied. Economy was stolen by the capitalist empire who stripped it of its original intention of "managing a home," and turned into a money-making institution. *Oikoumene* was stolen by the Roman Empire and later by Christianity[32] and turned into a anthropocentric system that serves the interests of the Christian Empire. Thus, for many years, *oikoumene* has been referred to as a fellowship of Christian churches who come together in

---

31. See Conradie, *The Earth in God's Economy*. See also Ayre and Conradie, *The Church in God's Household*, 8.

32. According to historian Claude Nicolet, the Greek historian Polybius wrote that "All the known parts of the oikoumene have come under the domination of Rome." See Nicolet, *Space, Geography, and Politics*, 11. Also Barbara Rossing in her work on redefining ecumenism argues that "by the first century BCE Rome laid claim on the Oikoumene". See Rossing, "(Re)claiming Oikoumene?," 76. In other words, during the Roman times, the word oikoumene was used as a synonym for the Roman empire.

unity under Christ. However, economy and ecology hardly featured in ecumenical discussions nor seen to be central to ecumenical theology. The consequence of this sharp split is that economy without ecology is aggressively capitalist, *oikoumene* without ecology is brutally anthropocentric, and economy without *oikoumene* is cruelly secular. Cosmological well-being is at risk because of this split. As a response, the Pacific Theological College and the Pacific Conference of Churches through the "Reweaving the Ecological Mat" (REM) project has offered options for mending this split by introducing to the region not only a household framework of development but also an alternative measure for health and well-being in the Pasifika communities. This is intended to complement or perhaps to challenge the notion of GDP (Gross Domestic Product) predominantly used as a tool by the capitalist system to measure growth.[33]

■ "We Don't Have the Ocean . . . We Are the Ocean"

In the dynamics of the deep living connections of the Aiga, we come to realize our own limitations and failures, especially when the *en-selfness* takes center stage at the expense of *en-otherness*. As discussed above, because the celebration of deep relationships is at the heart of life, the notion of ownership is rare. We do not own the land and the ocean. Rather, it is the land and ocean who own us. This is why the term "resource" is problematic from an ecorelational perspective because it connotes the sense that something is available to be discovered, used, and owned. Because many Pasifika cultures revolve around the "we are" cosmic way of life, the ownership idea manifested in the "we have" ideology has recently been scrutinized by Pasifika voices looking for an alternative to the current development paradigm.[34] The former is cosmological and relational. The latter is anthropocentric and capitalist. Teresia Teaiwa from the islands of Kiribati once said that "we sweat and cry salt so we know that the ocean is really in our blood."[35] This sense of deep relationship rather than ownership means, therefore, that we don't have the ocean; we are the ocean. We don't have the land; we are the land. We don't have relationships; we are relationships.[36]

Pope Francis lamented the loss of such deep living connections that:

---

33. For the household framework, see Bird et al., *Reweaving the Ecological Mat Framework*, and for the alternative measure for Pasifika health and well-being, see Siaki, *Ecological-Economic Accounts*. Both publications are available from www.pacifictheologicalcollege.com.

34. See Bhagwan et al., *From the Deep*.

35. Teaiwa, quoted by Hauofa, in *We Are the Ocean*, 41.

36. See Vaai, "We Are therefore We Don't Have," 283–84.

> [W]e have forgotten that we ourselves are dust of the earth (cf. Gn 2:7); our very bodies are made up of her elements, we breathe her air and we receive life and refreshment from her waters.[37]

When we lose remembrance, especially the memory of deep connection, we lose what it means to live within our means. The Earth has become (contra Calvin) a "theater of pain" with many suffering relatives oppressed by their own close kin. We carry every day the sin of living beyond our means. It is a sin because we no longer recognize the suffering of our own cosmological relatives by taking what belongs to them to consolidate our own.

Rooted in the word *colon*, which in both Greek and Latin means "to digest," colonization[38] has been transformed into a radically digestive capitalism that is best expressed in the Samoan saying *ole eleele le malie i vai,* meaning "a land never satisfied of excessive consumption of streams." This hegemonic racist mindset invaded every hall of economic development in the Pasifika communities and impregnated every Pasifika mind with a digestive economy. As in Tolkien's story of *The Lord of the Rings*, this economy has become, like the ring, invested with a tempting power used by the digestive centers to find them all, bring them all, bind them all, and rule them all. Consequently, it is not hard to find the correlations in the shift of emphasis from the green shire, where indigenous people live in harmony with the environment, to a Mordor type of Pasifika, where barrenness and darkness are an everyday reality. The craving to own, increase, and expand our economies has turned the Pasifika communities into a "black land" (the meaning of Mordor in Tolkien's story), unable to bring forth greenness. The islands of Nauru and Banaba in Micronesia and the mountains and forests of Melanesia are classic examples of Mordor environments, after all the extractions by these digestive economies, endorsed by local governments. Hence we have the beginning of an ecological racism, whereby one culture or one economy extracts and digests the lives and resources of all cultures and economies. This is a serious and organized crime, orchestrated against poor and marginal communities, and we often warrant it with policy and regulatory justification, allowing it to develop a system and context to cultivate. Hence, hidden in most economic systems today is the systemic sin against marginal communities that goes unnoticed every day.

The ecorelational sense of deep living connections should shape a reconstruction of a theology of stewardship for the church. The dominant push of saving the natural environment through self-limitation and all other stewardship acts cannot work unless we feel we are intimately part of what we're trying to save. How can we save something to which we are not deeply connected to? Our mindsets need to shift from the stewardship idea of caring

---

37. Pope Francis, *Laudato Si'*, 10.

38. See Vaai, "Introduction," 9.

for the Aiga that has dominated Eurocentric theology into living with the Aiga. In the ecorelational perspective, relating precedes the caring, which the latter is now been categorized as paid work in many parts of the world. "Deep solidarity"[39] with creation and empathetic stewarding means that once we (re)find that intimate genealogical spiritual connection through living with the Earth, the caring for should follow. Stewardship is about deep living connections that are always spiritual in nature. To be there and be caring for the cosmic others should start with the resolve to be with. We can only honestly love and care for the Aiga if we are deeply connected to it. Pope Francis calls this kind of deep connection "integral ecology" which allows us to see the Earth as family: "Our common home is like a sister with whom we share our life and a beautiful mother who opens her arms to embrace us."[40] In the ecorelational worldview, anything that is body-related, that communities belong to, that is part of them—they will protect and care for it with all their lives.

That is why in the ecorelational worldview, the notion of celebration is critical. In his "theology of celebration," Sione 'Amanaki Havea argued that because Pasifika is founded on such cosmological relationality, the idea of celebration of relationships underpins life and all activities.[41] Every gift is matched not initially with negation or with the doctrine of the fall, but rather with celebration. To lose this gift of celebration is to lose the realization of being gifted. Today, there is so much negation that aims at gifting ourselves by ungifting other peoples and communities. This has always been the aim of the colonial project. It creates a digestive center that facilitates this ungifting by controlling others and their wealth. This is expressed in the controlling attitude present in the wisdom saying *e tele lava le si'uvai ae sei e taele mai lava ile mata ole vai*, meaning, "the downstream is large enough to bathe but you also want to seize its source." We have even created a God and a gospel of uniformity so that we can justify this seizing project so that our cultures are perceived to be divinely gifted more than others. And in our worship, we thank this God for the abundance we have received from these ungifting practices. Today, it is hard to move back to the "we are" way of life because of the attractiveness of the "we have" narrative that shapes all political, economic, and religious developments including our everyday encounters. How can Pasifika communities contribute to changing a destructive development story that predominantly functions outside of the existing holistic wisdom "we don't have the ocean; we are the ocean"?

---

39. Rieger, *Jesus vs Caesar*, 25–26.

40. Pope Francis, *Laudato Si*, 1, 16.

41. See Havea, "Christianity in the Pacific Context," 13.

■ Conclusion: "Eat a Little and Leave a Little"

The "lies of colonization are the seeds of empire, but the resilience of its victims is the seed of liberation."[42] The nurturing ground of such resilience is the thought systems and ways of knowing of grassroots communities. For many years, the world has interpreted reality through the eyes of the "Anthropocene." This is why it is the time for Pasifika people to reright and rewrite their story. This story is only a story if it includes all that is us. In the Pasifika communities, decolonization finds its practical expression in the return to the ecorelational consciousness, the core foundational value that has been and continues to be the primary hermeneutical key for Pasifika communities to embrace cosmology.

This return has been assisted by the COVID-19 pandemic. Apart from the havoc forced upon us by this pandemic, there is no denying that it has also become a radical teacher of opportunities—especially the opportunity to redirect and redefine our economies and our perception of the cosmic Aiga and the relational dynamics involved. Our correct normal has in some ways been corrected and reconfigured by what seem to be predominantly framed as the enemy. We have witnessed during this pandemic that learning to live with and understand the Earth is the sustainable way forward. It has taught us that the dominant development narrative and all its promises cannot solve all the problems. In the Pasifika communities, it has reignited the art of relationality and collective survival as a cosmological Aiga. This is reflected in the art of rationing everything for everyone in order to survive, as in the Kiribati island wisdom, *kana teutana ao katuka teutana*, meaning "eat a little and leave a little." This ecorelational wisdom is symbolic of the importance of cosmological *en-otherness*, of always having others as part of our consciousness. It is a critique of the digestive monarchs and creators of digestive systems that promote "eat all and leave nothing."

Given the ecological crisis affecting the world, especially the poor communities, how can we contribute to addressing this global plight from our own unique contextual perspectives? To be more specific, do the Pasifika communities have the *stuff* to guide the world forward? Perhaps in the light of Marion Grau's call for a "countercyclical approach"[43] to life that while political, economic, and other institutions around the world are moving to divest from the cosmic values, isn't it time to *invest* in those values to rewrite a new story that respects all of life? As indicated in this essay, the cosmic story finds its inclusive and holistic basis in the life of the Triune God. The story of the Earth and that of God are inextricably interwoven where one might argue

---

42. See Vaai, "Introduction."

43. Grau, *Refiguring Theological Hermeneutics*, 11.

that one could only find expression and meaning in the other. From the perspective of where the cosmic story of relationality is primary, what remains a challenge is how we could rethink the Christian story to produce quality Christian earthkeepers in an era of severe ecological destruction, especially in Pasifika communities.

■ Bibliography

Adrianos, Louk A. "Ecumenical Theology of Hope for the Common Oikos and the Greed Line as Principle of Sustainability." *The Ecumenical Review* 70:4 (2018), 600–16. https://doi.org/10.1111/erev.12387

Ayre, Clive W. and Ernst M. Conradie, eds. *The Church in God's Household: Protestant Perspectives on Ecclesiology and Ecology*. Pietermaritzburg: Cluster Publications, 2016.

Bauman, Whitney. *Theology, Creation, and Environmental Ethics*. New York: Routledge, 2009.

Bergmann, Sigurd. "The Legacy of Trinitarian Cosmology in the Anthropocene." *Studia Theologica—Nordic Journal of Theology* 69:1 (2015), 32–44. https://doi.org/10.1080/0039338X.2015.1027267

Bhagwan, James, et al. *From the Deep: Pasifiki Voices for a New Story*. Suva: Pacific Theological College, 2020.

Bird, Cliff. "Pepesa—The Household of Life: A Theological Exploration of Land in the Context of Change in Solomon Islands." PhD diss., Charles Sturt University, 2008.

Bird, Cliff, Arnie Siaki and Meretui Ratunabuabua, eds. *Reweaving the Ecological Mat Framework: Towards an Ecological Framework of Development*. Suva: Pacific Theological College, 2020.

Boseto, Leslie. "Do Not Separate Us from Our Land." *Pacific Journal of Theology* 13 (1995), 69–72.

——. "God as Community—God in Melanesian Theology." *Pacific Journal of Theology* 13 (1995), 41–48.

Cibau: Jean-Marie Tjibaou. Nouvelle-Caledonie: Agence de developpement de la culture Kanak, 1998.

Conradie, Ernst M. *The Earth in God's Economy: Creation, Salvation and Consummation in Ecological Perspective*. Berlin: LIT, 2015.

Grau, Marion. *Refiguring Theological Hermeneutics: Hermes, Trickster, Fool*. New York: Palgrave Macmillan, 2014.

Gregory of Nazianzus. "Orations 40.41." In *A Select Library of Nicene and Post-Nicene Fathers of the Church*, Vol 7, 2nd series (1893), edited by Philip Scharff and Henry Wace, 375. Grand Rapids: Eerdmans, 1978.

Hart, John. *Sacramental Commons: Christian Ecological Ethics*. Lanham: Rowman and Littlefield, 2016.

Hauofa, Epeli. "Our Sea of Islands." In *A New Oceania: Rediscovering our Sea of Islands*, edited by Eric Waddell et al., 2–16. Suva: University of the South Pacific, 1993.

——. *We Are the Ocean: Selected Works*. Honolulu: University of Hawaii Press, 2008.

Havea, Jione, Margaret Aymer and Steed Vernyl Davidson, eds. *RumInations: Islands, Islanders, and the Bible*. Atlanta: SBL, 2015.

Havea, Sione 'Amanaki. "Christianity in the Pacific Context." In *South Pacific Theology*, edited by Sione 'Amanaki Havea, 11–15. Oxford: Regnum Books, 1987.

Havea, Tevita. "A Vision of our Pacific Household." In *From the Deep: Pasifiki Voices for a New Story*, edited by James Bhagwan et al., 1–10. Suva: Pacific Theological College, 2020.

Kaoma, Kapya J. *God's Family, God's Earth: Christian Ecological Ethics of Ubuntu*. Zomba: Kachere Series, 2013.

Lin, Daniel. "Dust and Dancing to Celebrate Indigenous Australians." https://blog.nationalgeographic.org/2015/07/27/dust-and-dancing-to-celebrate-indigenous-australia/, accessed 3 February 2021.

Miller, Elizabeth Carolyn. "Ecology." Cambridge Online, 30 August 2018. https://doi.org/10.1017/S1060150318000487

Monbiot, George. *Out of the Wreckage: A New Politics for an Age of Crisis*. London: Verso, 2017.

Nicolet, Claude. *Space, Geography, and Politics in the Early Roman Empire.* Ann Arbor: University of Michigan Press, 1991.

Northcott, Michael. "The Universe as Hypostatic Inherence in the Logos of God." In *Listening to Creation Groaning*, edited by Lukas Vischer, 211–29. Geneva: John Knox Series, 2004.

Pacific Church Leaders Meeting. "Sowing a New Seed of Pacific Ecumenism: Statement of Basis and Resolution." Nadi: Pacific Conference of Churches and Pacific Theological College, 2017.

Panikkar, Raimon. *The Cosmotheandric Experience: Emerging Religious Consciousness*. Maryknoll: Orbis, 1993.

Pope Francis. *Laudato Si': On the Care for Our Common Home: An Encyclical Letter on Ecology and Climate.* Strathfield: St Paul's, 2015.

Rieger, Joerg. *Jesus vs Caesar: For People Tired of Serving the Wrong God.* Nashville: Abingdon, 2018.

Rossing, Barbara. "(Re)claiming Oikoumene? Empire, Ecumenism, and the Discipleship of Equals." In *Walk in the Ways of Wisdom: Essays in Honor of Elisabeth Schüssler Fiorenza*, edited by Shelly Matthews et al., 74–87. Harrisburg: Trinity, 2003.

Schneider, Laurel. *Beyond Monotheism: A Theology of Multiplicity*. London: Routledge, 2008.

Siaki, Arnie. *Ecological-Economic Accounts: Towards Intemerate Values*. Suva: Pacific Theological College, 2020.

Tofaeono, Amaamalele. *Eco-Theology: AIGA—The Household of God: A Perspective from Living Myths and Traditions of Samoa*. Erlangen: Verlag Für Mission und Ökumene, 2000.

Tui Atua, Tupua Tamasese Efi. *Ia faagagaina oe ele Atua Fetalai*. Apia: Malua, 1989.

———. "In Search of Meaning, Nuance and Metaphor in Social Policy." In *Su'esu'e Manogi: In Search of Fragrance*, edited by Tamasailau M. Sualii-Sauni et al., 103–20. Wellington: Huia, 2018.

Tuwere, Sevati. *Vanua: Towards a Fijian Theology of Place*. Suva: University of the South Pacific, 2002.

Vaai, Upolu Lumā. "A Dance of Relationality: Vision of a Pacific Itulagi Education for Life." In *From the Deep: Pasifiki Voices for a New Story*, edited by James Bhagwan et al., 185–88. Suva: Pacific Theological College, 2020.

———. "Introduction." In *Relational Hermeneutics: Decolonizing our Mindsets and the Pacific Itulagi*, edited by Upolu Lumā Vaai and Aisake Casimira, 1–14. Suva: University of the South Pacific and the Pacific Theological College, 2017.

———. "Relational Theologizing: Why Pacific Islanders Think and Theologize Differently." *Pacific Journal of Theology* 58 (2020), 40–56. https://doi.org/10.1007/978-3-030-74365-9_17

———. "We Are therefore We Don't Have." In *The Relational Self: Decolonising Personhood in the Pacific*, edited by Upolu Lumā Vaai and Unaisi Nabobo-Baba, 283–84. Suva: University of the South Pacific and Pacific Theological College, 2017.

———. *We Are therefore We Live: Pacific Eco-Relational Spirituality and Changing the Climate Change Story*. Policy Brief No.56. Tokyo: Toda Peace Institute, 2019.

Even Rocks Are Alive: Christian Animist Disruptions of the Species Divide

Mark I. Wallace[1,2]

[*Irving*] Hallowell recounts how he once asked an old Ojibwa man whether "all the stones we see about us are alive." Though stones are grammatically animate in Ojibwa, the man (Hallowell recalls) "reflected a long while and then replied, 'No! but *some* are'."[3]

▪ Carnal Subscendence

I am drawn to the collective work of this volume, and the series in general, by the provocation in Ernst Conradie and Pan-Chiu Lai's question to us:

---

1. I am grateful to the members of the Taking a Deep Breath collective—in particular, Upolu Lumā Vaai, Pan-Chiu Lai, Sharon A. Bong, Sigurd Bergmann, and Ernst Conradie—for their generous engagement with an earlier draft of this paper and willingness to greatly improve my argument through their suggestions and critiques. "How good and pleasant it is when sisters and brothers dwell in unity" (Ps 133:1).

2. Mark I. Wallace is Professor of Religion, Environmental Studies, and Interpretation Theory at Swarthmore College near Philadelphia, USA. He is registered as a co-researcher at the University of the Western Cape, South Africa, for the project on "An Earthed Faith: Telling the Story amid the 'Anthropocene'."

3. Bird-David, "'Animism' Revisited," S81.

> **How to cite:** Wallace, M.I., 2021, 'Even Rocks Are Alive: Christian Animist Disruptions of the Species Divide', in E.M. Conradie & P.-C. Lai (eds.), *Taking a deep breath for the story to begin . . .* (An Earthed Faith: Telling the Story amid the "Anthropocene" Volume 1), pp. 241-258, AOSIS, Cape Town. https://doi.org/10.4102/aosis.2021.BK264.12

> How does the story of who the Triune God is and what this God does relate to the story of life on Earth? Is the Christian story part of the Earth's story or is the Earth's story part of God's story, from creation to consummation?[4]

If by the Christian story we mean the salvation story of God's relationship to us, and if by the Earth story, scientifically understood, we mean the account of how Earth was formed from stardust four billion years ago and evolved into its fine-tuned present state, then my answer is that the Christian story *is part of* the Earth's story—indeed, I would say that the Christian story *is subordinate to* the Earth's story. In brief compass, creation precedes redemption. Cosmology paves the way for soteriology. Common grace is the presupposition of saving grace. Ecocentrism comes before Anthropocentrism. Cosmic benefaction makes possible human salvation. A theology of nature, in other words, is prior to the foundation of and the horizon within which any formulation of *Heilsgeschichte* can and must be articulated.

To be sure, I concede that my attempt to usurp the pride of place assigned to the doctrine of redemption in Christian theology might seem off-putting at first glance. As a historical matter, I think there is no question about what I take to be the prevailing understanding of the primary role assigned to God's salvific activity in the history of Christian thought. Rank-and-file Christians and the clerical guardians of time-honored Christian belief all agree on this one central idea: the supreme teaching of the Gospel is God's love for humankind as expressed in God's infusion of justifying grace in the life of fallen human beings. Still, the three branches of the apostolic church—Orthodoxy, Catholicism, and Protestantism—have quibbled about the implications of the idea of justification in everyday piety—for example, the question of the Orthodox ideal of *theosis* in relation to a juridical notion of justification, the relation of faith and works in the process of justification, whether justification can ever be forfeited by committing grievous sins, and so forth. As well, the question whether the doctrine of justification must be correlated with the idea of Jesus's death as an atoning blood sacrifice is a hotly debated issue, in part, because the Gospel of Luke, arguably, omits any reference to the crucifixion as an exercise in substitutionary atonement.

But I digress. My point is that the concept of justification (or deification in Orthodoxy)—the full reconciliation between God and humankind through the

---

4. Even as I am drawn to this question I am slightly at odds with its formulation. In the query's second sentence the term "earth" drops into lowercase. (I am putting it into uppercase instead.) While this lowercase usage is stylistically defensible it neither makes grammatical nor theological sense to me. I capitalize Earth because it is a proper noun that names a specific place. As well, it is the particular locale of God's daily and sustaining habitation within the cosmos. Unlike lowercase earth which stands for the rich humusy *soil* within which all life is possible, uppercase Earth is the *planet* that daily rotates around the Sun, lifting its face to be warmed by its intergalactic companion and thereby vivifying all life-forms in its sunward gaze. I have changed the term to "Earth" in the second sentence of this seminal question to better speak to this difference.

offer of the free gift of God's grace to the sinner—has been the core *theoanthropocentric*[5] tenet of church teaching for two millennia. In the classical loci of dogmatic theology, *soteriology* has always preceded *cosmology* in emphasis and importance (if not chronology).[6] It is God's saving gift tendered to broken human beings, not the all-inclusive and enlivening offering of creation *per se*, that is the focal point of Christian thought and experience. In the classical model, prevenient grace, to use a familiar Wesleyan phrase, is the *a priori* condition of saving grace—both of which are exclusively defined in terms of the drama of human redemption. *Pace the classical model, I am suggesting that prevenient grace should be recast as the encircling benevolence of the gift of the cosmos as such and, thereby, the necessary precondition for the offer of saving grace in the life of the particular individual.*

This, then, is my central pushback regarding the provocation in Ernst and Pan-Chiu's question to our cohort: Is not the full range of God's grace deformed and truncated in the regnant model of human-centered salvation history because it fails to account for the limitless expanse of God's cosmic mercy and lovingkindness prior to and generative of the offer of redemption in the first place? Without the primordial gift of the life-sustaining wonder of the biosphere itself, what sense does God's proffer of forgiveness make to us, God's offspring, the ones who are entirely dependent upon a divinely ordered cosmos in which "we live and move and have our being," to paraphrase Acts 17:24?

Furthermore, if I may, could I sharpen my critique one degree more and ask, then, whether there is a place in today's theological community for a *sensus dissensus* concerning the centrality of the long-established doctrine of justification—a doctrine whose primacy has been deemed irreproachable but may now seem to be actually contributory to the viral human chauvinism that infects not only the body politic of the regnant nation states of our time but the body of Christ as well?

I make this point *in extremis* because I believe we are bearing witness at present to the death rattle of a mortally wounded civilization hopelessly addicted to the abusive extraction and burning of fossil fuels to power its economic machine. It is an understatement to say that this addiction has laid waste to the well-being of the Earth. *Sic transit mundus.* As well, I believe it is Christianity's conflicted teachings about the importance of the more-than-human-world that has handed down to people of faith today a jumbled understanding about whether creation is to be valued or denigrated in God's

---

5. This memorable phrase belongs to Karl Barth as per Santmire, *Celebrating Nature by Faith*, 15. Christian theology, as Barth puts it in his *Römerbrief*, must always operate within a single ellipse and two foci: God and humankind.

6. See the two volumes edited by Conradie, *Creation and Salvation*.

economy of salvation. *On the one hand, we recall the beauty of the lilies and the birds of the air valorized by Jesus himself but, on the other, we are taught to only do so against the backdrop of the church's teaching that human salvation, not the lilies or the birds, is the primary focus of God's act of free grace.* Christianity's muddled heritage regarding the natural world both limns with hope—and threatens to hopelessly undermine—Christians' and others' wondrous and heartfelt embrace of ecological sustainability as the great work of our time.

"There is no document of civilization," Walter Benjamin says, "that is not at the same time a document of barbarism."[7]

Christianity's alternately positive and barbaric disposition toward its home ground—the good Earth God made for the sustenance and joy of all beings—has effectively divorced human beings and their spiritual yearnings from their natural habitat—the very habitat, ironically, that renders all such yearnings possible at all. At present, the legacy of this mixed discourse saddles the church with the widely fixed bias that Christianity is an unearthly religion with little if anything constructive to say about everyday life in the natural world. The cliché is that its gaze is fixed heavenward on eternal paradise not earthbound on the vagaries of mortal existence. *Transcendence trumps subscendence*. The church's focus on an invisible and timeless heavenly reward rather than on the sensual gift of earthly existence has rendered its preachments largely irrelevant to the crucial work that is the vocation of our era: restoring Earth's Edenic promise and beauty for all beings, humankind and otherkind alike.

Instead of fashioning, then, a new but different Noah's Ark for the care and love of all species, many churches today have become insular and guarded against the labor of Earth care in our time. In the United States, prominent evangelical-friendly, so-called creation-stewardship organizations allied with Donald Trump and his ilk (e.g., the Heartland Institute and the Cornwall Alliance) have gone so far as to decry mass-movement Christian environmentalism as a "godless ideology" that seeks to undermine "law and order with mob rule."[8] Focusing on the salvation of human souls at the expense of biblically grounded Earthlust, is it any wonder that the Christian religion has lost touch with the role the verdant world of animals and plants, land and water, sun and stars plays in the well-being of all species, human, and more than human?

---

7. Benjamin, "Theses on the Philosophy of History," 256. I recently traveled to Portbou in Northern Spain to make a pilgrimage to Benjamin's final resting place. In Portbou, I saw this saying as the epitaph on his grave in a Catholic cemetery overlooking the blue expanse of the Mediterranean Sea.

8. See Jones, "A Plea to My Evangelical Friends for Biden."

And yet biblical faith, in spite of its anthropocentric drift, has long been a faith that endows all of the natural world with sacred meaning. "There are no unsacred places," says Wendell Berry, "There are only sacred places and desecrated places."⁹ Everyday, material existence—food and drink, life and death, humans and animals, earth and sky—is sacralized (or better, divinized) as the consecrated medium through which God relates to humankind and the wider community of flora and fauna. Christianity's central ritual is a group meal that remembers the saving death of Jesus by celebrating the good gifts of creation—eating bread and drinking wine. Its central symbol is a cross made out of wood—two pieces of a once-living tree now lashed together as the means and site of Jesus's crucifixion. Its central belief focuses on the body, namely, that God became flesh in Jesus and thereby becomes one of us, a mortal, breathing creature who experiences the joy and suffering of life on Earth. And Christianity's primary sacred document, the Bible, is suffused with rich, ecological imagery. This imagery follows a *green arc* that stretches from the Cosmic Potter in the *Book of Genesis* who fashions Adam from the dust of the ground and puts him in the Garden, to the River of Life in the *Book of Revelation* that flows from the throne of God, bright as crystal, vivifying the Tree of Life that yields its fruit to all of Earth's inhabitants. Christianity is a fleshly, earthly, material religion.[10]

If the essential evangelical affirmation is that "the Word became flesh and lived among us" (John 1:14)—if divinity enfleshed itself in the midst of commonplace reality—then Christianity's central teaching—in a creation-centered not a redemption-centered register—is that God is a *promiscuously carnal reality* who is generously embodied within all things, making the whole world a living sacrament of God's presence and thereby worthy of humans' affectionate concern. It may be that Christianity is still best known for its war against the flesh and dismissal of the material world as inimical to humankinds' destiny in a far-removed heaven of bodiless bliss. But as prolegomena to this proposed series, I want to propose here the idea of "Christian animism" in order to return *ad fontes* to the Johannine vision of a divinized material world. Christianimism, if I can suggest this portmanteau, answers the *status confessionis*, the "state of confessing," in our time, by enabling people of faith to live into the embodiment of God-in-the-world as a counter-testimony to Christendom's vision of Earth as a "foreign land" vis-à-vis our "true home" in heaven above.[11]

---

9. Berry, "How to Be a Poet (to Remind Myself)," 18.

10. Let me signal here my dependence on Paul Ricoeur for this reading of the Bible as bookended by a creation schema, not salvation motifs. See his little-known essay in this regard, "On the Exegesis of Genesis 1:1–2:4a." I develop this point further in my "Holy Ground."

11. Grossman, "Billy Graham's Quotes about Heaven."

And in this Christianimist vein, I also want to signal the continuity of biblical religion with the beliefs of indigenous and non-Western communities that God or Spirit enfleshes itself within everything that evolves, walks, flies, and swims in, over, and under the great gift of creation.[12] My hope is to revitalize Christian theology with a blood transfusion from within its own body of beliefs and also from native and global religious communities whose members encounter divinity in all forms of life. I suggest that this blood transfusion is a genetic match with the deep cellular structure of Christianity because it is of the same type as that structure itself—as well as being borrowed from other compatible religious traditions. As propaedeutic, my question is whether such a *ressourcement* effort is consistent with Christianity's historic Earth-based understanding of itself, even though the religion today has largely forgotten its primeval beginnings and thereby its originary vision of the world as sacred place, as holy ground, as the body of God?

■ New Materialism

To some degree, my proposal of Christian animism follows the "material turn" within contemporary continental philosophy, queer theory, critical animal studies, and quantum physics. I find especially helpful the new materialist analysis of the agential capacities of nonhuman beings, and the posthumanist disavowal of anthropocentrism, as critical insights into the formation of generative intersubjectivity across the divides that separate humankind and otherkind. A new vitalist ontology of the relational energies of the material world coupled with a new anti-speciest ethics of equal regard for all life forms provide interdisciplinary support within the church and the academy for a recovery of corporeal divinity in a Christian idiom.[13]

Nevertheless, many new materialists, such as Jane Bennett, by relying on impersonal "thinghood" language for the material world, short-circuit possible lines of conversation between new forms of Christian animism, on the one hand, and theories about vital human-nonhuman materialities, on the other hand. Over and against deep ecology and, presumably, ecotheology, Bennett rebuts a "common spirit" between "people-materialities" and "thing-

---

12. In this regard, see White, "The Historic Roots of Our Ecologic Crisis"; Quinn, "Animism—Humanity's Original Religious Worldview"; McGaa, *Mother Earth Spirituality*; Deloria, "Sacred Places and Moral Responsibility"; and Grim, "Indigenous Traditions and Deep Ecology." I develop this point further in my *When God Was a Bird*, 20–49.

13. The postcolonial recovery of animism is both consonant with, and at times at odds with, recent work in posthumanism (see Wolfe, *What Is Posthumanism?* and Koosed, "The Bible and Posthumanism") and new materialism (see Bennett, *Vibrant Matter*; Crockett and Robbins, *Religion, Politics, and the Earth*). Related to postcolonial animism are new studies in quantum physics about the co-emergence of phenomena within their entangled interactions (see Barad, *Meeting the Universe Halfway*) and about human and nonhuman agency in queer animacy and animality theory (see Chen, *Animacies*).

materialities"[14] as a hidebound expression of "discredited modes of thought" that include "animism, the Romantic quest for nature, and vitalism."[15] Prophylactically, her vibrant matter philosophy seeks to ward off becoming "infected by superstition, animism, vitalism, and other premodern attitudes."[16] By invoking the old canard of "superstition" as a put-down of indigenous worldviews, sadly, the stench of Occidentalism wafts throughout Bennett's new materialist polemic against traditional ways of knowing. Her desire to avoid the contagion of "animism [. . .] and other premodern attitudes" reflects her Enlightenment circumscription of reality according to the canons of rational empirical experience. Over and against the indigenous insight into the quality of relational personhood among all beings, Bennett posits the "dissonant connections" between "human being and thinghood"[17] played out across a "turbulent field in which materialites collide, evolve, and disintegrate."[18] Instead of the ecospiritual language of kinship or attachment—what Martin Buber calls the "drive for pan-relationship" among all beings[19]—Bennett uses mechanistic phrases such as the "assemblage of things"[20] to denote the open-ended contacts and contestations between different material formations.

Bennnett's disavowal of native people's organicist experience of the intersubjective communion enjoyed by all members of the lifeweb runs the risk of reinscribing the pernicious binary between *lifeless material objects* (e.g., landscapes or bodies of water) and *living sentient beings* (e.g., humans, animals, and plants) within her new materialist proposal. But in the language of Bolivia's *Universal Declaration of the Rights of Mother Earth* on Earth Day, 2010, we, humankind and otherkind, are best understood not as miscellaneous bits of matter within a variety of assemblages, but as members of "Mother Earth, [who are] an indivisible, living community of interrelated and interdependent beings with a common destiny."[21]

Herein lies the fault line that separates new materialism and Christian animism. Bennett's objectifying, entitative language of thinghood operates counter to the phenomenology of neo-animism expressed in the Bolivian

---

14. Bennett, *Vibrant Matter*, x–xi.

15. Bennett, *Vibrant Matter*, xviii.

16. Bennett, *Vibrant Matter*, 18.

17. Bennett, *Vibrant Matter*, 4.

18. Bennett, *Vibrant Matter*, xi.

19. Buber, *I and Thou*, 78.

20. Bennett, *Vibrant Matter*, 25.

21. See http://therightsofnature.org/wp-content/uploads/pdfs/FINAL-UNIVERSAL-DECLARATION-OF-THE-RIGHTS-OF-MOTHER-EARTH-APRIL-22-2010.pdf, accessed 21 January 2021.

declaration, and elsewhere, which assigns personhood to all beings who strive to live in harmonious relationship with one another. *In a word, persons are not things.* By distancing her project from what she calls premodern superstition and animism—namely, indigenous epistemologies of intersubjective personhood—Bennett is unable to account for the phenomenon of purposeful *being-in-relationship* experienced by human and more-than-human subjects whose yearnings for deep partnership is consistent across different orders of existence.

Apropos the intersubjectivity that defines traditional forms of knowledge, the animist ascription of personhood to all life forms locates human beings in an expansive family of kinfolk that includes "bear persons" and "rock persons" along with "tree persons" and "human persons."[22] Glossing Jesus's comment that "I tell you, if these [disciples] are quiet, then the stones will cry out" (Luke 19:40), Native American theologian George "Tink" Tinker argues that even "rocks talk and have what we must call consciousness" and then continues:

> The Western world, long rooted in the evidential objectivity of science, distinguishes at least popularly between things that are alive and things that are inert, between the animate and the inanimate. Among those things that are alive, in turn, there is a consistent distinction between plants and animals and between human consciousness and the rest of existence in the world. To the contrary, American Indian peoples understand that all life forms not only have consciousness, but also have qualities that are either poorly developed or entirely lacking in humans.[23]

Transhuman animism, therefore, flattens commonplace ontological distinctions between living/nonliving or animate/inert along a continuum of multiple subjectivities and forms of consciousness: now everything that *is*, is alive with personhood and relationality, even sentience, according to its own capacities for being-in-relationship with others. All members of the lifeweb are best understood, therefore, as relatives or kinfolk, not as things or objects. As Pagan scholar Graham Harvey says, "Animists are people who recognize that the world is full of persons, only some of whom are human, and that life is lived in relationship with others."[24]

All life forms are persons, only *some* of whom are human, because *all* beings are differentiated members of a community of relationships, only *some* of whom are recognizable as living beings by us.[25]

---

22. See "new animism" studies of human-nature intersubjectivity in Curry, "Grizzly Man and the Spiritual Life"; Stuckey, "Being Known by a Birch Tree"; and Abram, *Becoming Animal*.

23. Tinker, "The Stones Shall Cry Out," 110.

24. Harvey, Animism: Respecting the Living World, xi.

25. I develop this point further "The Stones Will Cry Out" and *When God Was a Bird*, 20–49.

■ Decolonizing Theology

Today, we have entered the fateful epoch of the "Sixth Great Extinction"—a geological time period similar to the last mass extinction event when the dinosaurs were wiped out tens of millions of years ago, the so-called Fifth Great Extinction.[26] Vertiginously, we are climbing a dangerous staircase of global warming-driven "tipping points"—catalytic chain-reaction events, such as melting permafrost, that could trigger widespread and sudden catastrophe within the heretofore self-regulating global climate system.[27] Unsustainable, mechanized (so-called) civilization has dumped billions of metric tons of carbon into the atmosphere through fossil fuels burning since the onset of coal-fired industrialization in the mid-eighteenth century. Heavy consumption of coal, oil, and natural gas, along with continued deforestation since the start of the Columbian Age, is causing global temperatures to escalate astronomically—anywhere from three to seven degrees Fahrenheit by 2050, to as high as seven to ten degrees by the century's end.

Climate change driven by carbon dependence is the direct result of the extractive worldview that came ashore in the Americas with the arrival of Columbus in 1492 CE. It is easy to think that contemporary global warming is an exceptional catastrophic event spawned by the Industrial Revolution. In fact, however, the first instance of recent global climate change occurred within a hundred years of European colonization of the New World. Set in motion by initial contact between indigenes and settlers, European diseases, armed conflicts, slavery and forced incarceration killed upward of fifty-six million indigenous people, causing large human communities to be evacuated as well as great swaths of farmland to be abandoned. Over time, these previously cleared agricultural zones filled in with new plant and forest growth. The resulting increase in trees and vegetation triggered a massive decrease of CO_2 in the atmosphere, enough to significantly cool the ambient temperature of the Earth by 1610, in what is called the Little Ice Age. Tragically, Native genocide was only the beginning of the ecocidal birth pangs that have led to the catastrophic climate sorrows of our own historical period. We are not unique. The Great Dying in the Americas five hundred years ago has now led directly to the Sixth Great Extinction of our own time.[28]

Against the monstrosity, then, of multiple climatic, genocidal, carceral, and ecological apocalypses—white colonial settlement in the Americas, the transatlantic slave trade, two global wars spawned in the soil of Christian

---

26. See this analysis in Ceballos et al., "Accelerated Modern Human-Induced Species Losses." Also see Eldredge, *Life in the Balance*.

27. See Pearce, *With Speed and Violence*.

28. I develop this point further in my "The Stones Will Cry Out"; also see Koch et al., "Earth System Impacts."

Europe, the new Jim Crow system of mass incarceration in the United States, and now the anthropogenic Great Extinction of endangered cultures, species, and habitats—it is only now that white settler societies are beginning to recognize the price that must be paid for their prized economies of extraction and degradation. As critical geologist Kathryn Yusoff writes:

> If the Anthropocene proclaims a sudden concern with the exposures of environmental harm to white liberal communities, it does so in the wake of histories in which these harms have been knowingly exported to black and brown communities under the rubric of civilization, progress, modernization, and capitalism. The Anthropocene might seem to offer a dystopic future that laments the end of the world, but imperialism and ongoing (settler) colonialisms have been ending worlds for as long as they have been in existence.[29]

The proverbial chickens have come home to roost. The apocalypse draws nigh because umpteen innumerable apocalypses have been unleashed by the colonial project for hundreds of years. As Yusoff painfully brings forth, how is it that it is only now that we are starting to realize the existential threat to planetary integrity triggered by the expansive petropolitics of our time?

As the planet becomes hotter and cascading waves of species-level extinctions are the inevitable result, our reliance on fossil fuels continues apace. This carbon addiction stems from our abusive colonial posture toward the natural world. Earth, to use Martin Heidegger's formulation, has become an extensive "standing reserve" of inexhaustible power for modern industrial development, and our exploitative disposition toward the planet belies any hope we might have of extricating ourselves from our fundamentally rapacious orientation toward the life-giving systems on which we all depend.[30] As an unfeeling standing reserve, Earth for us is no longer a "living being" or "feeling organism" with its own subjective moods and affective propensities. It cannot feel pain, or experience loss, or undergo the suffering, some claim, that only we so-called higher forms of life and other sentient beings can feel. Our techno-supply vocabulary for Earth has effectively rendered our living planet numb and silent—a dead zone of inert matter, a passive and insensible aggregation of resources, a fixed deposit of energy to fuel commercial development at all costs.

As indigenous biologist Robin Wall Kimmerer warns, "In English, we speak of the land as 'natural resources' or 'ecosystem services', as if the lives of other beings were our property."[31] As a lifeless thing, as an impersonal, mechanized repository of useful materials, Earth, in the terminology we consistently use and with which we feel most comfortable, is now, in its most basic essentiality, a "resource" of "services" to supply the needs of human society—or, perhaps

---

29. Yusoff, *A Billion Black Anthropocenes or None*, xiii.

30. Heidegger, "The Question Concerning Technology."

31. Kimmerer, *Braiding Sweetgrass*, 383.

more accurately in a market-driven economy, a "commodity" or "property" to be bought and sold in the financial marketplace, like toothpaste or pork futures or stock options.[32]

But understood from an animist perspective, all members of the lifeweb are self-organizing beings with their own moods and traits, power and agency, and corporeal vibrancy and evolutionary trajectories. In this vein, all things possess value all their own as vital contributors to diverse bionetworks and developmental complexity. It follows, therefore, that the ontological binaries we use to organize our everyday sensible experience—binaries such as *life/matter, organic/inorganic, living/nonliving,* and *sentient/non-sentient*—are really only the self-justifying oppositions we deploy to rationalize our own lofty status in the scheme of things, not actual descriptions of the way things are. In the Great Chain of Being, we arrogate to ourselves the privilege of being the first link in the sequence of life forms that run from the highest megafauna to the lowest microorganism. In effect, our typical hierarchical dualisms function as classificatory stratagems that elevate us human beings and our kind as consciously sentient, self-realizing *beings* over and against all other entities as unresponsive and unfeeling *things*.

■ Feral Rock Religion

I am suggesting that our commonplace taxonomies blind us to how the places, things, and elements around us are also living beings with relational capacities and emotional registers unto themselves.[33] Take, for example, the stone wall that runs along the level of my eye outside my study window as I write these words. Fixed and impassive, how could this squat, rocky enclosure be anything other than lifeless matter? In what sense could it be said to be a living, feeling being with agency, dispositions, and moods like the rest of us? My rock wall is made from Wissahickon schist, a beautiful, and, at one time, ubiquitous local stone, flecked with quartz and mica, that has given Philadelphia and its surrounding architecture a uniformly earth-toned and stolid appearance.

But while Wissahickon schist is aesthetically pleasing, in what sense can it be said to be affective and alive?

In response, let me suggest the following: the rocks in my wall are living beings—as are all of the rocks strewn across the stony face of the planet—precisely because they are vital structural elements in the habitat requirements and geochemical processes that support the rocks', and my family's, existence in our common Swarthmore home. *In this sense, my rock wall, the life within*

---

32. I develop this point further in my "The Stones Will Cry Out."

33. This section on "Feral Rock Religion" relies heavily on my "Elegy for a Lost World" and "The Stones Will Cry Out."

and around it, and I and my family subsist together: our mutual personhood is co-generated by the subtle and abiding interactions we enjoy within the wooded and rugged locale of Swarthmore borough. My seemingly inert and immobile rock wall is actually part of a living, swirling, buzzing ecosystem that energizes everything around it with interlocking vitality. Covered in lichen, fungi, mosses, and other microorganisms I cannot see, my stony barricade holds together the teeming community of a/biotic life forms that sustain their and my immediate niche within the larger eco-zone we co-inhabit together.

For example, the brown- and yellow-striped eastern chipmunk, in spreading much-needed seeds across the landscape of our common home, tunnels in and out of my rock wall on a daily basis. In symbiotic friendship, chipmunks aerate the wall so that water and moisture can more freely flow through its stolid presence; in turn, the wall provides cover and safety as chipmunks burrow into its solid embrace.

Here is another example of how my wall of rocks is dazzlingly alive. By controlling soil loss through sediment trapping, my stony enclosure holds steady much of the biomass that insures the well-being of the others' collective existence along with my family's household. This biomass, including my yard's surrounding thicket of trees, shrubs, and groundcover, also plays a role in Earth's carbon cycle as one of the many links in the photosynthetic food chains that make planetary life possible, in my bioregion and elsewhere. Among other critical functions, the absorption of carbon dioxide at my particular home site and the corresponding production of oxygen, now stabilized by the rock wall outside my study window, are essential to my and my family's, and all other beings', survival.[34]

Are rocks, then, not dead things, but vital members of the lifeweb necessary for our collective existence? And if this is the case, is not the rock-strewn Earth itself a vital "actant," to borrow a term from social theorist Bruno Latour,[35] with its own affective tendencies and relational capacities?

Paleontologist James Lovelock argues for the intrinsic value of *all* of Earth's living elements—including, by implication, my Wissahickon schist rock wall—in the service of the functional integrity of the biosphere writ large. Lovelock theorizes that the planet is a carefully calibrated "superorganism" in which all of its biological, physical, and chemical components are "alive" and necessary for the support and regulation of global biodiversity. Lovelock christens the living Earth "Gaia," named after the ancient Earth goddess of the Greeks, to signal the quasi-mystical powers of the worldwide biochemical interactions between animals, insects, fungi, algae, air, water, trees, soil and rocks to create

---

34. See the argument for the intrinsic value of all species, independent of their utility to meet human needs, in Primack, *A Primer of Conservation Biology*.

35. See Latour, *Science in Action*.

the ideal living conditions—including the ideal climate—for all denizens of the planet.³⁶ He calls his cosmology "the Gaia hypothesis" and frames it this way:

> The entire range of living matter on Earth, from whales to viruses, from oaks to algae, could be regarded as constituting a single living entity, capable of manipulating Earth's atmosphere to suits its overall needs and endowed with faculties and powers far beyond those of its constituent parts.³⁷

According to Lovelock, our particular human role in this well-honed biosphere is to understand how Earth's or Gaia's biophysical interactions create a steady state fit for life and then to support the capacities of this "single living entity" to maintain optimal ecosystem functionality for diverse communities of species. Lovelock writes: "The more we know, the better we shall understand . . . the consequences of abusing our present powers as a dominant species and recklessly plundering or exploiting [Earth's] most fruitful regions."³⁸ In reference to Lovelock, my corresponding point is that when we devolve into "abusing our present powers" and degrade the abilities of Gaia's interweaving elements to achieve their natural ends—in other words, when we cause any of the constituent members of diverse ecosystems to suffer needless harm—then we do injury to the vital organisms and processes that make our self-regulating planetary life system generative and sustainable. It is in this sense, therefore, that we can say that when we assail Gaia's ecosystemic balance that we are causing Earth, as an organic being, as a "single living entity," to quote Lovelock, to suffer harm, to feel pain, and to undergo trauma.³⁹

If Lovelock's Gaia cosmology is accurate, then Earth is a living, feeling being who cries out and suffers injury from the depredation brought about by human malice.⁴⁰ As Wangari Maathai says, we should be:

---

36. Lovelock, *The Ages of Gaia*.

37. Lovelock, *Gaia*.

38. Lovelock, *Gaia*, 99.

39. In addition to Lovelock, see the excellent analysis of how the work of other natural and social scientists has been used to advance spiritual understandings of nature in Johnston, *Religion and Sustainability*.

40. Is it possible to maintain that the wider, environing Earth we inhabit, as a living being, is able to feel grief and suffer trauma? Understood animistically, I am suggesting that not only is Earth system science, understood holistically in the manner of Lovelock, advancing just such a claim today, but that a searching interpretation of the Bible, now read from the perspective of Earth as a subject unto itself, will make the same argument. Consider, for example, the portrait of Earth's personal agency and emotional range in the opening pages of the book of Genesis (4:9-12) where God laments Earth's suffering in the light of Cain's murder of his brother Abel. In Genesis, Cain takes Abel to a nearby field in order to kill him, watches his lifeblood flow into the ground, and then, upon being questioned by God, purports not to know of the body's whereabouts. Here Earth is not dumb matter, an inanimate object with no capacity for feeling and sentiment, but a living and vulnerable being who experiences the terrible and catastrophic loss of Abel's death. Genesis 4's intensely accelerative and explosive descriptions of Earth's self-determining *verb-actions*—the ground *cries out* over Abel's murder; it *opens its mouth* and *swallows* Abel's vital fluid; it *curses* Cain's perfidy and *refuses to give of its strength*—depict a profoundly agential life-form with its own interior life, purposeful behavior, and affective capacities for loss, anger, despair, abjection, and revenge.

[C]oncerned about the wounds and bleeding sores on the naked body of the earth. Have we not seen the long-term effects of these bleeding sores? The famine? The poverty? The children born into hunger and disease? The destruction of forests and fertile lands? The chemical and nuclear accidents? We are strangling the earth.[41]

But why is this animist insight—the recognition of the common personhood of all life forms who suffer repeated injury—so crucial to our well-being on the planet?

It is crucial because the existential awareness that we ourselves are not the only bearers of apperceptive suffering compels us to re-situate ourselves—ontologically and ethically—in the wider personhood of Earth itself who, like us, is a living being with emotion and purpose unto itself. It is crucial because this insight into our wider belonging to a living being far greater than ourselves compels us to reimagine ourselves as integral members of a cosmic body, a supreme organism, an all-encompassing life form whose needs and requirements surpass our own, and to whom we owe our loyalty and devotion. It is crucial because this recognition of Earth's vital essence forms the basis of more-than-human sacred kinship relationships and rituals wherein all beings are now regarded as sharing a common existence together as equal co-participants in the web of life. And it is crucial because once we sense the longing of creation to be free from chronic suffering—once we sense nature's capacity to experience depredation in a manner similar to how we too experience loss and injury—then we will feel an inner drive to live our lives in harmony with all of God's creatures, all of whom, including ourselves, subside and flourish in Mother Earth's loving embrace.[42]

Or, as Lovelock puts it so succinctly, once we recognize Gaia as a "single living entity," we will then feel the "compulsive urge to belong to the commonwealth of all creatures which constitutes Gaia."[43]

---

41. Maathai, quoted in Scharper and Cunningham, *The Green Bible*, 8.

42. See the call to preserving a just and verdant Earth as sacred work in Suzuki with McConnell, *The Sacred Balance*.

43. The quotes are from Lovelock, *Gaia*, 9 and 140, respectively. Shelly Rambo writes that the task of theology in the midst of suffering is to engage in a "middle discourse" between religious triumphalism, on the one hand, and the loss of faith, on the other. To witness to trauma using middle discourse is to account for ongoing fragmentation and despair vis-à-vis the broken promise of redemption and renewal. Today, we are on a collision course with ourselves. Beyond the loss of species and habitats, rising sea levels are destroying the frontline communities of tens of millions of human beings. Wealthy countries dump heat-trapping, ice-melting gases into the atmosphere causing rising sea levels and massive flooding in low-lying nations such as the Maldives, Fiji, and Bangladesh; and in the United States, in places such as New Orleans, Houston, the Florida Keys, and coastal New Jersey and New York City, where recent hurricanes and storms have killed and displaced thousands. In its witness to this unfolding global tragedy, middle discourse theology precariously positions itself between the fractured possibility of new life and the hopelessness of despair. See Rambo, *Spirit and Trauma*.

■ Two Problems

In this essay, I began by questioning the time-tested *sensus communis* of the church that the doctrine of justification should be ascribed a unique primacy in Christian theology. I have sought to resignify Christianity's classical notion of grace away from its juridical meaning and toward a more comprehensive notion of grace as the prevenience of divinity within the whole created order. To support this move, I have expounded on the virtues of Christian animism in rapport with indigenous epistemology and in dialogue with thinkers such as Bennett, Tinker, Yusoff and Lovelock, and with special reference to the vibrantly alive Wissahickon schist wall that graces my window as I finish these thoughts.[44] But as I tie off this essay, I have two questions that challenge my thinking, one theoretical and one practical, that I would like to pose:

My first question stems from the problem of deploying a racist term such as animism to analyze the intersubjective ontology I have sketched here. This term is a difficult candidate for retrieval because it was invented as a derogatory proxy for the premodern (read: barbaric) worldviews of primordial people. At first glance, it appears that the notion of animism is hopelessly contaminated by colonial-era white supremacist assumptions about the evolutionary differences between first peoples and latter-day Europeans and Euroamericans. But today, the term is increasingly being deployed by scholars of native traditions themselves, effectively repurposing the category as a postcolonial mode of inquiry, at some remove from its racist origins, vis-à-vis the variety of relational ontologies that underlie complementary lifeworlds.[45] In this vein, animism carries a certain counterdiscursive capacity to invert the hierarchical power relations between the categories of "Christianity" and "Indigeneity" that characterize popular thinking along with the traditional academic study of religion and culture. As Darryl Wilkinson puts it:

> The new animism is therefore widely presented as a turn to an indigenous (and particularly hunter-gatherer derived) sensibility vis-à-vis the world, and a potentially corrective model for the West to follow.[46]

Could it be that the model of reality as an animate communion of sacred beings is emerging as the new paradigm, distinctly characteristic of originary people, that supersedes the necropolitics of the late capitalist West and, at times, the Western Christian imaginary as well?[47]

My second question is whether such new animism can pragmatically undergird policy decisions about how to engage in harvesting the bounty of

---

44. See further Wallace, *When God Was a Bird*, 141-72.
45. Cajete, "Philosophy of Native Science," 50.
46. Wilkinson, "Is There Such a Thing as Animism?" 84.
47. Linda Hogan, "We Call It Tradition," 21.

ecosystems that is equitable and sustainable. If, as I have noted, the core evangelical affirmation is that "the Word became flesh and lived among us" (John 1:14)—if every being is an enfleshment of divinity, in the registry of Christian animism—then how can discriminating decisions be made about bionetwork conservation and distribution of community goods? To put it bluntly, if everything is sacred, can anything be killed and consumed? In reply, my suggestion is that such allocation decisions should be made with a spiritual eye toward the well-being of the ecosystem in question. As Aldo Leopold says:

> Quit thinking about decent land-use as solely an economic problem. Examine each question in terms of what is ethically and aesthetically right, as well as what is economically expedient. A thing is right when it tends to preserve the integrity, stability, and beauty of the biotic community. It is wrong when it tends otherwise.[48]

On holy ground, whatever respectful utilizations of living beings ensure the integrity and beauty of biodiverse communities are good, and judgments that tend otherwise are not. Does this repristination of Leopold's land ethic provide the intersubjective depth and analytical clarity necessary for doing the work of responsible environmental caretaking? My suggestion is that such a panincarnational affirmation of the universal sacred, in a spirit of gratitude and joy, is the right attitudinal disposition necessary for making wise judgments about the conservation and use of natural habitats.

■ Bibliography

Abram, David. *Becoming Animal: An Earthly Cosmology*. New York: Vintage, 2010.

Barad, Karen. *Meeting the Universe Halfway: Quantum Physics and the Entanglement of Matter and Meaning*. Durham: Duke University Press, 2007.

Benjamin, Walter. "Theses on the Philosophy of History." In *Illuminations*, edited by Harry Zohn, 253–64. New York: Schocken, 1969.

Bennett, Jane. *Vibrant Matter: A Political Ecology of Things*. Durham: Duke University Press, 2010.

Berry, Wendell. "How to Be a Poet (to Remind Myself)." In *Given: New Poems*, 18. Washington, DC: Shoemaker & Hoard, 2005.

Bird-David, Nurit. "'Animism' Revisited: Personhood, Environment, and Relational Epistemology." *Current Anthropology* 40 (1999 Supplement), 67–91. https://doi.org/10.1086/200061

Buber, Martin. *I and Thou*. Translated by Walter Kaufmann. New York: Scribner's, 1970.

Cajete, George. "Philosophy of Native Science." In *American Indian Thought: Philosophical Essays*, edited by Anne Waters, 45–57. Oxford: Blackwell, 2004.

Ceballos, Gerardo, et al. "Accelerated Modern Human-Induced Species Losses: Entering the Sixth Mass Extinction." http://advances.sciencemag.org/content/1/5/e1400253.full, accessed 13 February 2021.

Chen, Mel Y. *Animacies: Biopolitics, Racial Mattering, and Queer Affect*. Durham: Duke University Press, 2012.

Conradie, Ernst M., ed. *Creation and Salvation, Volume 1: A Mosaic of Selected Classic Christian Theologies*. Münster: LIT, 2011.

---

48. Aldo Leopold, *A Sand County Almanac*, 262.

———. *Creation and Salvation, Volume 2: A Companion on Recent Theological Movements*. Münster: LIT, 2012.

Crockett, Clayton and Jeffrey W. Robbins. *Religion, Politics, and the Earth: The New Materialism*. New York: Palgrave Macmillan, 2012.

Curry, Patrick. "Grizzly Man and the Spiritual Life." *Journal for the Study of Religion, Nature and Culture* 4 (2010), 206-19. https://doi.org/10.1558/jsrnc.v4i3.206

DeJonge, Michael P. "Bonhoeffer, Status Confessionis, and the Lutheran Tradition." *Stellenbosch Theological Journal* 3 (2017), 41-60. https://doi.org/10.17570/stj.2017.v3n2.a02

Deloria, Vine Jr. "Sacred Places and Moral Responsibility." *Worldviews, Religion, and the Environment: A Global Anthology*, edited by Richard C. Foltz, 83-91. New York: Wadsworth, 2002.

Eldredge, Niles. *Life in the Balance: Humanity and the Biodiversity Crisis*. Princeton: Princeton University Press, 1998.

Grim, John A. "Indigenous Traditions and Deep Ecology." In *Deep Ecology and World Religions: New Essays on Sacred Ground*, edited by David Landis Barnhill and Roger S. Gottlieb, 35-57. New York: SUNY, 2001.

Grossman, Cathy Lynn. "Billy Graham's Quotes about Heaven: 'I'm Just Passing Through this World'." *USA Today*, February 21, 2018. https://www.usatoday.com/story/news/nation/2018/02/21/billy-grahams-most-notable-quotes/858852001, accessed 11 February 2021.

Harvey, Graham. *Animism: Respecting the Living World*. New York: Columbia University Press, 1976.

Heidegger, Martin. "The Question Concerning Technology." In *The Question Concerning Technology and Other Essays*, 3-35. Edited and translated by William Lovitt. New York: Harper Perennial, 1977.

Hogan, Linda. "We Call It Tradition." In *The Handbook of Contemporary Animism*, edited by Graham Harvey, 17-26. London: Routledge, 2014.

Johnston, Lucas F. *Religion and Sustainability: Social Movements and the Politics of the Environment*. Sheffield: Equinox, 2014.

Jones, Peter. "A Plea to My Evangelical Friends for Biden." *The Cornwall Alliance for the Stewardship of Creation*. October 23, 2002, https://cornwallalliance.org/2020/10/a-plea-to-my-evangelical-friends-for-biden, accessed 12 February 2021.

Kimmerer, Robin Wall. *Braiding Sweetgrass: Indigenous Wisdom, Scientific Knowledge, and the Teaching of Plants*. Minneapolis: Milkweed Editions, 2013.

Koch, Alexander, et al. "Earth System Impacts of the European Arrival and Great Dying in the Americas after 1492." *Quaternary Science Reviews* 207 (2019), 13-36. https://doi.org/10.1016/j.quascirev.2018.12.004

Koosed, Jennifer L., ed. "The Bible and Posthumanism." *Semeia* 74 (2014), 1-12.

Latour, Bruno. *Science in Action: How to Follow Scientists and Engineers Through Society*. Milton Keynes: Open University Press, 1987.

Leopold, Aldo. *A Sand County Almanac: With Essays on Conservation from Round River*. Oxford: Oxford University Press, 1966.

Lovelock, James. *Gaia: A New Look at Life on Earth*. Oxford: Oxford University Press, 1979, 2000.

———. *The Ages of Gaia*. New York: Norton, 1988.

McGaa, Ed (Eagle Man). *Mother Earth Spirituality: Native American Paths to Healing Ourselves and Our World*. New York: Harper and Row, 1990.

Pearce, Fred. *With Speed and Violence: Why Scientists Fear Tipping Points in Climate Change*. Boston: Beacon, 2008.

Primack, Richard B. *A Primer of Conservation Biology*, 2nd ed. Sunderland: Sinauer.

Quinn, Daniel. "Animism—Humanity's Original Religious Worldview." In *The Encyclopedia of Religion and Nature*, edited by Bron R. Taylor, et al., Volume 1, 81–83. New York: Continuum, 2005.

Rambo, Shelly. *Spirit and Trauma: A Theology of Remaining*. Louisville: Westminster John Knox, 2010.

Ricoeur, Paul. "On the Exegesis of Genesis 1:1–2:4a." In *Figuring the Sacred: Religion, Narrative, Imagination*, edited by Mark I. Wallace, 129–43. Translated by David Pellauer Minneapolis: Fortress, 1995.

Santmire, H. Paul. *Celebrating Nature by Faith: Studies in Reformation Theology in an Era of Global Emergency.* Eugene: Wipf & Stock, 2020.

Scharper, Stephen Bede and Hilary Cunningham. *The Green Bible*. New York: Lantern, 2002.

Stuckey, Priscilla. "Being Known by a Birch Tree: Animist Refigurations of Western Epistemology." *Journal for the Study of Religion, Nature and Culture* 4 (2010), 182–205. https://doi.org/10.1558/jsrnc.v4i3.182

Suzuki, David and Amanda McConnell. *The Sacred Balance: Rediscovering Our Place in Nature*. Vancouver: Greystone Books, 1997.

Tinker, George "Tink." "The Stones Shall Cry Out: Consciousness, Rocks, Indians." *Wicazo Sa Review* 19 (2004), 105–25. https://doi.org/10.1353/wic.2004.0027

Wallace, Mark I. "Elegy for a Lost World." In *Post-Traumatic Public Theology*, edited by Stephanie N. Arel and Shelly Rambo, 135–54. New York: Palgrave Macmillan, 2016.

———. "Holy Ground: Protestant Ecotheology, Catholic Social Teaching and a New Vision of Creation as the Landed Sacred." *Journal of Catholic Social Thought* 4 (2007), 271–92. https://doi.org/10.5840/jcathsoc20074214

———. "The Stones Will Cry Out." *Kosmos Journal* (Summer 2019), https://www.kosmosjournal.org/kj_article/the-stones-will-cry-out/, accessed 31 January 2021.

———. *When God Was a Bird: Christianity, Animism, and the Re-Enchantment of the World*. New York: Fordham University Press, 2019.

White, Lynn Jr. "The Historic Roots of Our Ecologic Crisis." *Science* 155 (1967), 1203–07. https://doi.org/10.1126/science.155.3767.1203

Wilkinson, Darryl. "Is There Such a Thing as Animism?" *Journal of the American Academy of Religion* 85 (2017), 289–311.

Wolfe, Carey. *What Is Posthumanism?* Minneapolis: University of Minnesota Press, 2010.

Yusoff, Kathryn. *A Billion Black Anthropocenes or None*. Minneapolis: University of Minnesota Press, 2018.

Index

A

aesthetics, 55, 57-59, 68-70, 161, 223
Africa, 1-4, 13-15, 28, 43, 49, 55, 70, 73, 95, 103-105, 116-119, 141-142, 163, 183, 185, 190, 192, 196, 202-203, 205-206, 208-213, 220-223, 225, 230, 241
    African Communality, 214-215
    African ecotheology, 205-206, 208, 210, 212-214, 216, 218, 220-222, 224
    African theology, 210, 213-215, 221, 223
African Brazilian religions, 189-192, 196
African Traditional Religion, 104, 209, 223
Aiga, 225-226, 228, 230-238, 240
ancestor(s), 2, 49, 97, 192, 197, 212, 214, 226-228, 234
animism, 125, 241, 245-248, 255-257
Anthropocene, 1-4, 8-19, 21, 30, 33-35, 38, 43-46, 49-52, 55, 60-71, 73-75, 77, 91, 95, 99, 116, 119, 141, 149-150, 159, 163, 183, 185, 201-202, 205-206, 216-223, 225, 238-239, 241, 250
    good Anthropocene, 3, 16, 18, 218
anthropocentrism, 80-81, 151, 165, 169-170, 172, 180, 229, 242, 246
apartheid theology, 35, 104
apocalypse, 64, 69-70, 250
Asian values, 89
atmosphere, 16, 52-53, 55-60, 62, 153, 195, 249, 253-254

B

Bachelard, Gaston, 143, 148, 161
Barbour, Ian, 39, 41, 43
Bavinck, Herman, 34, 41-43, 96, 103, 105-107, 110-111, 114-115, 117-118
Bergmann, Sigurd, 2, 14, 49-53, 55-63, 65-69, 71, 91, 138, 161, 221, 232, 239, 241
Berry, Thomas, 27, 38, 40, 43, 46, 65, 68, 99, 117, 143-145, 155-156, 161-162, 216, 223, 245, 256
biodiversity, 81, 122, 138, 150, 185, 199, 205, 252, 257
Bong, Sharon, 66, 73, 75, 77, 79, 81, 83, 85, 87, 89, 91, 93, 241
Buddhism, 165-166, 168, 182
Bulgakov, Sergius, 121, 129-138

C

Candomblé, 190-193, 195-199, 201-202
Cappadocians, 228, 232

China, 63, 89-90, 144, 164-165, 167-169, 171-174, 177, 180, 182, 223
    Chinese Christianity, 168, 177
    Chinese culture, 164-165, 168-171, 182
Christian Faith and the Earth, 1-3, 12, 14
Christian story, 7, 17, 21, 24, 30-31, 33-35, 37, 39-42, 44, 49, 67, 73-77, 83-84, 91-92, 95-98, 100, 102-106, 108, 110, 112-116, 118, 142, 150, 158-159, 163-164, 167, 169, 184-185, 189, 202, 216, 239, 242
Christianimism, 245
Christology, 136, 172, 178, 180, 214, 231
climate (see also weather), 3, 7, 12, 14, 16, 18, 20, 33, 44-45, 52-53, 56, 59, 61-64, 68-71, 74, 82-88, 90, 92, 116-117, 150, 152, 161, 171, 182, 188, 202-203, 205, 207-209, 213, 219-224, 226, 231, 240, 249, 253, 257
    climate change, 3, 7, 12, 14, 33, 52-53, 62-64, 68-70, 74, 82, 85, 87-88, 92, 116-117, 161, 171, 182, 202-203, 205, 207-209, 213, 219-223, 226, 231, 240, 249, 257
    climate justice, 14, 74, 82-86, 88, 92, 209, 224
clues (metaphor), 109, 112-113
colonialism (see also decoloniality), 2, 25, 36, 104, 184, 211, 220
    colonization, 113, 212, 229, 232, 238, 249
    epistemological colonialism, 184
compassion, 10, 42, 49, 51, 54, 59, 63
Confucius, 92, 178
    Confucian cosmology, 74, 89, 92
    Confucianism, 89, 92, 165-166, 168, 172, 174, 177-181
Conradie, Ernst M., 1-7, 9, 11, 13-15, 17, 19, 21, 23, 25, 27-29, 31, 33-37, 39, 41-45, 47, 49, 53, 69, 73, 95, 97, 99, 101, 103-105, 107, 109-111, 113, 115-117, 119-120, 127, 138, 141-142, 157, 160-161, 163, 183, 185, 201-203, 205-206, 208, 211, 216, 218, 221, 225, 234, 239, 241, 243, 256
consummation, 6-7, 14, 22, 34, 37, 40, 44, 73, 102, 117, 138, 142, 159, 163, 239, 242
cosmology, 29, 38, 46, 49-51, 61, 66, 68, 74, 88-90, 92, 100, 118, 133, 139, 150, 152-156, 159, 161-162, 177, 181, 212, 230, 232-233, 238-239, 242-243, 253, 256
cosmogenesis, 26, 153-154
creation, 1-3, 6-9, 11, 13-14, 22, 34, 37-38, 40, 44, 46, 50-51, 54-55, 59-60, 64-65, 67-68, 70, 73-81, 83-84, 86-87, 89,

91-92, 100, 102, 104-105, 111-112, 114-117, 120-121, 127, 129-138, 141-143, 150-154, 156-161, 163, 166, 176, 178, 182, 184-185, 192-195, 197, 199-201, 214-218, 226, 228-230, 232, 237, 239-240, 242-246, 254, 256-257
   creation and salvation, 2, 14, 44, 163, 243, 256-257
   creation theology, 51

D
Daoism, 165-166, 168
Deacon, Terrence, 145-147, 161
Deane-Drummond, Celia, 2, 14, 28, 44, 50, 62, 69, 119-125, 127, 129, 131, 133, 135, 137-139, 147, 161, 164, 179, 217-218, 221
decoloniality, 210, 213
cecolonization, 188, 210, 224, 230, 238
Durkheim, Émile, 145, 161

E
Earth, 1-5, 7, 9, 12-14, 16-17, 19-21, 27-28, 37-38, 40, 42-45, 50-55, 59-70, 73, 76-78, 80, 82-83, 90-91, 96, 99, 102, 105, 109, 112, 114-117, 119-121, 124-125, 127, 129, 131-134, 136-138, 141-142, 144-146, 148-154, 156-164, 167, 174-182, 185-188, 195-196, 198, 200-201, 205-206, 208, 211, 216-223, 227-228, 232-234, 236-239, 242-247, 249-254, 257
   Earth system, 3, 16-17, 63, 69, 217-218, 220, 249, 253, 257
   Earth system science, 253
Eaton, Heather, 4, 13, 27, 99, 141, 143-151, 153, 155, 157, 159, 161
eco-dhammic ethics, 87-88, 91
Ecocene, 49-50, 52, 54, 56, 58, 60-62, 64-70
ecofeminism, 74, 89-92, 144, 162
ecology, 2-3, 13-14, 21, 44-46, 50-51, 53, 66, 68, 70, 74-75, 83, 87-88, 91-92, 118, 123-124, 136-137, 139, 151, 161, 164, 168-170, 179, 181-182, 192, 195, 198, 201, 206-207, 209, 214-215, 217, 219-223, 225-229, 234-235, 237, 239-240, 246, 256-257
   ecological discourse, 165
   ecology of knowledge, 192
   ecorelational, 225-230, 232-238, 240
ecumenism, 229, 234, 240
   ecumenical theology, 4, 14, 138, 230, 235, 239
Edwards, Denis, 2, 13-14
evolution, 8, 27, 40, 52, 61, 64, 97, 115, 120, 123-125, 137-138, 142, 151-154, 156-157, 159, 161-162, 197
   biological evolution, 27
   Epic of Evolution, 151, 154

F
Fields, Stephen, 80, 88, 92, 127-129, 137-138, 151
forest monks, 87-88, 91, 93
fragments, 6, 24, 26, 31-32, 38, 43-44, 46, 97, 106, 108-109, 118
Francis, Pope (see also *Laudato Si'*), 44, 66, 73-86, 88, 90, 92, 125, 235-237, 240

G
Gaia, 21, 45, 133, 252-254, 257
gender justice, 74, 82, 84-85, 88
God (see also Trinity), 1-15, 21-26, 28-37, 39-47, 49-51, 53-55, 58, 60-61, 65, 67, 70, 73, 76-81, 83, 86, 91-92, 95-120, 122, 124, 127-131, 133-135, 137-139, 142, 156-162, 169, 172, 175-176, 178-180, 182, 184-185, 189, 192, 199-202, 206, 211-212, 214-216, 220-222, 226, 228-232, 234, 237-240, 242-246, 248, 253-255
   continuity thesis, 212
Gottschall, 145, 148-149, 162
grace, 4, 7, 9, 12, 14, 36, 55, 96, 103, 106, 110, 119-122, 124, 126-130, 132, 134-139, 161, 242-244, 255
   common grace, 9, 55, 242
great acceleration, 17, 19, 34, 61, 63, 151, 162, 219

H
Haught, John, 27, 38, 44
Holy Spirit, 56, 67, 79, 96, 102, 120-121, 130-132, 134-136, 138, 175-177, 179-181, 200, 216
Hong Kong, 15, 89, 163-164, 170, 179-180, 182
hope, 6, 10-11, 13-15, 26, 28, 31, 34, 43-44, 55, 67-69, 89, 92, 95-96, 98, 100, 102, 104-106, 108, 110, 112, 114-118, 121, 131, 138, 159-160, 178, 229-230, 239, 244, 246, 250
household (metaphor), 2, 9, 13, 114, 229, 234-235, 239-240, 252
   household of God, 114, 229, 240
hunger, 74, 83-85, 92, 254
   kumakalam na sikmura, 74, 84-85, 92

I
Indigeneity, 255
   indigenous p)eoples, 86, 185-187
integral ecology, 66, 74-75, 83, 88, 91-92, 237
integrity of creation, 75, 81
itulagi, 227, 240

J
Journey of the Universe, 27, 46, 151, 155-156, 162
Jüngel, Eberhard, 22, 26, 32, 45, 107, 109, 111, 117

justice (see also climate justice), 10-11, 14, 22, 35, 42, 49, 51, 54, 74, 82-86, 88, 92, 101, 108, 110, 114, 142, 144, 152, 157, 167, 171, 178, 180, 184, 189, 202, 208-209, 222, 224
justification, 9, 24, 82, 171, 184, 236, 242-243, 255

K

Keller, Catherine, 27, 60, 63, 66, 70, 91-92, 175, 180
kenosis, 134-135
Kohák, Erazim, 126-127, 137, 139

L

Lai, Pan-Chiu, 1, 15, 17, 19-21, 23, 25, 27, 29, 31, 33, 35, 37, 39, 41, 43, 45, 47, 49, 73, 95, 119, 141, 163-165, 167-169, 171-173, 175-177, 179-181, 183, 205, 225, 241
Lash, Nicholas, 20, 23, 31, 45, 157, 162
Latin America, 183-184, 186, 188, 190, 192, 194, 196, 198, 200-202
Latour, Bruno, 21, 45, 252, 257
Laudato Si' (see also Francis), 66, 73-75, 91-92, 119, 208, 224, 236-237, 240
Logos, 5, 34, 76, 78, 96, 110, 116, 126, 130, 132, 134-135, 180, 240
Lyotard, Jean-François, 16-17, 45

M

Maçaneiro, Marcial, 183, 185, 187, 189, 191, 193, 195, 197, 199, 201-203
Marx, Karl, 17, 42
    Marxism, 165, 167, 169, 172-174, 179
McFague, Sallie, 13, 24, 45, 143
meteorology, 52, 55-57, 68
Metz, Johann Baptist, 25-26, 45
Moltmann, Jürgen, 4, 14, 22, 26, 34, 45, 67-68, 105, 115, 117, 120, 170, 176, 179, 181
mystery, 10-12, 22, 26, 32, 45, 60, 78, 83, 105, 109, 111, 113, 117, 137, 141, 147, 155-156, 158

N

narrative, 5-9, 12, 15, 18-30, 32-33, 35-40, 42, 44-46, 62-68, 70-71, 97, 102, 107-110, 116-122, 125, 129, 148, 150, 153, 156, 162-164, 166-168, 174-175, 179, 181, 189, 192, 194-195, 206, 210, 217-222, 228-229, 232, 237-238
    cultural narratives, 142-144, 151, 154-156
    grand narratives, 6, 15-19, 29, 64, 143, 145, 163
    meganarratives, 15, 17, 20, 29
    metanarratives, 15-16, 20, 25, 29, 143, 145, 149, 155-156, 160
    narrative theology, 5-7, 21, 23-26, 28-30, 32-33, 35, 39, 44-46, 108, 117-118

nature, 3, 7-8, 10, 13-14, 18, 23, 32, 34, 37-39, 41-42, 44-45, 50, 53-54, 56, 58-61, 63, 65-66, 68-71, 73, 76-82, 87-88, 90, 96-97, 103-104, 107, 111, 113-114, 117, 119-130, 132, 134, 136-139, 145, 151, 155, 161-162, 166, 168-170, 174-176, 179-182, 185, 187-189, 192, 196-202, 206, 210-213, 215-216, 220-223, 227-228, 237, 242-243, 247-248, 253-254, 257
    natural theology, 8, 37, 96, 104, 107, 112, 117
    nature and grace, 7, 96, 119-122, 124, 126-130, 132, 134, 136-138
    theology of nature, 8, 37, 181, 242
neo-Thomism, 121, 128-129
new materialism, 60, 246-247, 257
Niebuhr, H. Richard, 23, 25, 31-32, 39, 41-42, 45, 98, 112-114, 117-118, 143

O

Oduyoye, Mercy Amba, 1-2, 14, 27
oikos (metaphor), 5, 202, 234, 239
oikoumene, 234-235, 240
onefication, 232
onto-theology, 122, 130
orixá(s), 191-199, 201-202

P

Pacific, 68, 225-226, 229, 235, 237, 239-240
    Pasifika, 225-240
panentheism, 133
Pannenberg, Wolfhart, 22-23, 29, 31, 46, 108, 112, 118
pantheism, 133, 138
peace, 3, 14, 35, 49-50, 68, 115, 178, 181, 240
pneumatology, 2, 14, 56, 175-181
postcolonial, 16, 39, 74, 89, 211, 219, 246, 255
posthumanism, 246, 257
process theology, 173, 178, 180
providence, 6, 9, 34, 102

Q

Qi (ch'i), 89-90, 92, 177-178, 180
    Qi-cosmology, 89-90, 92

R

Rahner, Karl, 121, 128-130, 137, 139
Rasmussen, Larry, 29, 46, 100, 117-118
reconciliation, 6, 9, 22, 28, 34-35, 43, 47, 242
Redeeming sin? (project), 2, 14
relationality, 49, 78, 83, 90-91, 186-187, 215, 228-229, 231-232, 237-240, 248
    ecorelational, 225-230, 232-238, 240
religious experience, 34-35, 90, 100, 159, 209

Index

revelation, 7–8, 23, 25, 27, 31–32, 36–37, 41–43, 45–46, 83, 96, 98, 103–115, 117–118, 130–132, 159–160, 200–201, 245
    general revelation, 7, 96, 103, 105–107, 111–114
    special revelation, 7, 96, 103–107, 111–115
Ricoeur, Paul, 24, 30, 46, 106, 143–144, 162, 245
rocks, 197, 207, 214, 223, 233, 241–242, 244, 246, 248, 250–252, 254, 256
Rolston, Holmes, 27, 46

S

salvation, 1–2, 6, 8–10, 14, 22, 25–26, 34, 36, 44, 51, 102, 104–105, 108, 111, 114, 117, 120–121, 127, 129, 136, 138, 158, 163, 171, 182, 196, 200, 231, 239, 242–245, 256–257
Samoa, 228, 233–234, 240
Scripture, 7, 24, 35–36, 45, 96, 103, 110
Serres, Michel, 13–14, 17–18, 46, 99, 118, 124–126, 137, 139
shamanic theology, 74, 86–87, 92
Sideris, Lisa, 155, 162
South Africa, 1, 3, 13, 15, 49, 73, 95, 103–105, 116, 118–119, 141, 163, 183, 202, 205, 225, 241
space, 9, 13, 21, 51, 58, 60, 64–68, 71, 76, 80, 86–87, 91, 141–142, 144, 148–149, 152–153, 156–159, 161, 188, 196, 219, 227, 230, 234, 240
spirituality, 12, 35, 76, 85–86, 120, 146, 159, 161, 178, 187, 189, 209, 230, 233, 240, 246, 257
state ideology, 165–166, 169, 172–173
status confessionis, 245, 257
strange(r), 51, 59, 68, 137
subscendence, 241, 244
Swimme, Brian, 27, 38, 46, 99, 216, 223
symbol, 11, 16, 24–25, 31, 68, 92, 101, 111, 146–147, 158, 161, 245
    symbolic consciousness, 141–143, 145–148, 150, 153, 155–156, 158–159, 161
synergy, 51–52, 56–57, 59, 68

T

Taiwan, 164, 166, 170
talanoa, 226
tehomic theology, 91
Teilhard de Chardin, Pierre, 26, 46, 99, 115, 120, 138, 142, 153
theo-ontology, 50, 122, 124, 130, 133, 136, 138
Theopolitics of the Earth, 61–62
Tracy, David, 13–15, 24–25, 31–32, 35, 38, 43–44, 46, 106, 108–110, 118

transformation, 42, 45, 61–62, 64, 66–67, 70–71, 80, 112, 116, 143, 145–146, 148, 162, 193, 221–222
Trinity, 6, 11–12, 22, 36, 39, 45, 50, 76, 79, 90, 107, 111, 117, 124, 130, 137, 175, 200, 212, 223, 231, 240
    Trinitarian Cosmology, 49–51, 61, 66, 68, 232, 239
    Triune God, 6–7, 12, 21–22, 29, 36–37, 39, 43, 45, 49–50, 73, 76, 78–79, 81, 83, 91, 104–105, 119, 206, 216, 220, 229, 238, 242
two books (metaphor), 103–105

U

universe story, 27, 39–43, 46, 95–98, 100, 102–106, 108, 110, 112–116, 118, 142, 144, 153–161, 216, 223

V

Vaai, Upolu Lumā, 66, 211, 225, 227–229, 231–233, 235–241
Van Huyssteen, Wentzel, 145, 148, 162
Van Ruler, Arnold, 105, 110, 112, 114, 118
vital force, 89, 197, 215–216
Von Sinner, Rudolf, 183, 185, 187, 189, 191, 193, 195–197, 199, 201, 203

W

Wallace, Mark I., 51, 60, 66, 120, 241, 243, 245, 247, 249, 251, 253, 255, 257
weather (see also climate), 49–64, 66, 68–71, 98, 207
White, Lynn Jr, 17, 47, 166, 169, 210, 224, 246, 258
Whitehead, Alfred North, 27, 122
wisdom, 6, 22, 27, 49, 51–52, 55–56, 60, 63, 96, 99, 119–122, 124, 126, 128–130, 132, 134, 136, 138–139, 161, 168, 175, 186, 189, 199–200, 209, 211, 214, 216, 220–221, 226, 229, 233–234, 237–238, 240, 257
    ecological wisdom, 27, 175, 209, 211, 214, 216, 220–221
worldviews, 14, 35, 37, 42, 44, 46, 64, 87, 102, 118, 124, 143–146, 148–149, 158, 161–162, 171, 211, 214, 216, 221, 247, 255, 257

Y

yin and *yang*, 90

Z

Zambia, 205–209, 213–215, 221–222, 224

www.ingramcontent.com/pod-product-compliance
Lightning Source LLC
Chambersburg PA
CBHW081145230426

43664CB00018B/2814